# THE POLITICS OF BLACK AMERICA

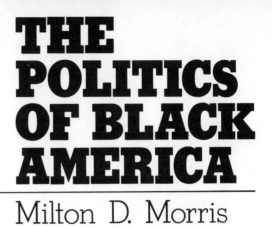

# THE POLITICS OF BLACK AMERICA

Milton D. Morris

Southern Illinois University at Carbondale

HARPER & ROW, PUBLISHERS
New York   Evanston   San Francisco   London

Sponsoring Editor: Ronald K. Taylor
Project Editor: Richard T. Viggiano
Designer: Howard S. Leiderman
Production Supervisor: Bernice Krawczyk

THE POLITICS OF BLACK AMERICA

Library of Congress Cataloging in Publication Data
Morris, Milton D
    The politics of Black America.

    Includes bibliographies and index.
    1. Negroes—Politics and suffrage.    2. Black
nationalism—United States.    I. Title.
E185.615.M63    323.1'19'6073    74-34342
ISBN 0-06-044619-6

To Marcia Diane, Marlene Denise,
and all the other little black children whose
brighter tomorrow makes today's struggles worthwhile

# CONTENTS

# PREFACE

There is a deceptive calm on the racial front in the United States today. The "creative tensions" that Martin Luther King, Jr., sought to create as an inducement to change in race relations are no longer readily observable. The widespread racial violence that a few years ago enveloped the nation has now disappeared; the Black Panthers who once advocated liberation by any means necessary have now put aside their guns for new forms of community involvement and political action. On college campuses the once dramatic, even strident, demands by blacks for full inclusion and recognition in all phases of higher education are rapidly yielding to more traditional pursuits of academic achievement—grades, diplomas, and jobs.

The meaning of this calm is not entirely clear because blacks have not yet overcome. Most of the frustrations that precipitated the upheavals of the last decade still exist. One likely explanation is that the gains of the past two decades must now be consolidated, and new approaches must be developed to meet changing circumstances. Nowhere is this consolidation and reorientation more apparent than in the present pattern of political activity among blacks. Evidence exists of a strong and growing conviction that in this society, at this time, vigorous wide-ranging political activity by blacks is the most effective approach to the pursuit of fundamental change in race relations. This new development makes it especially important that we examine the black political experience over time, and identify the problems and challenges that confront blacks in the political arena.

THE POLITICS OF BLACK AMERICA attempts to describe the political experience of blacks in broad terms. Although I have endeavored to concentrate on the more salient aspects of this experience and to evaluate them in a dispassionate and nonpolemical manner, the undertaking presents a variety of problems. First, there may be substantial disagreement about what are in fact salient aspects of the black experience, and even greater disagreement about their interpretation. Second, black political life is more complex and contradictory than might initially seem apparent. Several aspects are still inadequately studied, making attempts at a comprehensive and organized overview both difficult and sometimes faulty. Finally, THE POLITICS OF BLACK AMERICA is permeated by a certain mood that may not be universally shared, and in my view is not conceded frequently enough even by those who do. It is a sense of profound pride and admiration for the strength, resiliency, and creativity of black America, which is reflected in their epic political struggle for survival and for the dignity to which all human beings are entitled. It is my hope that in the classroom and elsewhere this text will provide new insights into the political world of black America, and will help to stimulate both pride in the achievements of the past and a measure of confidence for the future.

In preparing this book I have incurred debts to a number of conscientious individuals who cannot all be thanked individually. I must, however, acknowledge my gratitude to the many scholars on whose works I have been able to draw in preparing this study; to my colleagues at Southern Illinois University—Steve Wasby, Jack Van Der Slik, and John S. Jackson III; to graduate students who contributed at various points along the way—Carolyn Cobe, Jim Romano, and Annette Ryan; and to the students in my government courses who provided the stimulation for the project. Finally, my greatest debt is to my wife Merrillie, for her incredible patience and diligence in typing the entire manuscript several times and in providing vital criticisms from time to time.

Milton D. Morris
Washington, D.C.

# Looking at
# the Problem of Race
# and Politics

# 1

# Introduction

The black presence in America is an old one. It began in 1619 when the first 20 black people disembarked at Jamestown. During most of the time since then blacks have existed either in complete bondage as bondsmen and slaves or in a peculiar state of semifreedom. The legitimacy of bondage was undermined by the Civil War, but the black presence remained, and blacks continued to be victims of the ruthless oppression and exploitation of white society. Over all these years American society has grappled with the dilemma of the black presence, while blacks have worked, fought, and died to end their oppression and claim a status equal to that of whites in the society.

Until recently, this long, tortuous, and complex struggle was ignored or touched upon only in brief and fragmentary fashion by all except a relatively small group of scholars. Political scientists were particularly inattentive to this issue and thus almost completely ignored what is clearly one of the most vital aspects of the American political experience. Not long ago Donald Matthews noted that although "the Negro problem" long has been one of the most important domestic problems confronting the nation, only six articles containing the word *Negro* in the title appeared in the *American Political Science Review* between 1906 and 1963. Three others dealt with "civil rights," while over 2600 articles were published in the political science disciplines' leading journal during this time.[1] The dramatic social upheavals of the 1960s compelled greater attention to the dilemma of black Americans and to its implications for the political system, yet since then scholarship on the subject has been fragmentary and deficient in several respects.

A deceptively large number of titles obscure the paucity of extensive scholarly examination of the distinct political experience of black Americans. Even more serious is the failure of political scientists to relate this experience in any significant way to interpretations or evaluations of the larger American political experience or to the performance of the American political system.

[1] Donald R. Matthews, "Political Science Research on Race Relations," in Irwin Katz and Patricia Gurin, eds., *Race and the Social Sciences* (New York: Basic Books, 1969), p. 113.

This neglect is not entirely the result of a conspiracy of silence motivated by racism; at least three other major factors have contributed to it.

First, American political scientists have been deeply committed to certain flattering conceptions of the American political system and have been inclined to ignore, or treat as incidental aberrations, evidence that seems to disrupt or contradict these conceptions. The popular image of a democratic polity committed to the principles of justice and equality for all could not tolerate the reality of inequality and systematic oppression that has been the experience of blacks.

Even though this stubborn insistence on preserving the myth of harmonious, democratic politics has now yielded to the demand for greater realism and honesty, a second obstacle to consideration of the black experience in studies of American politics has been the emergence of models of the political process that do not facilitate thorough consideration of the peculiar status of black America. The pluralist model, which emphasizes the diffusion of power among widely scattered groups in the political system, suggests that public policy is a result of short-term conflict and cooperation among these groups.[2] This view of the political process has considerable merit, except that it usually overlooks the fact that the black segment of the society is rarely a part of this process of shifting alliances. The pluralist model assumes that the major issues in the political arena around which these alliances form are supported by large sectors of the society, or at least do not consistently evoke the strong hostility of the overwhelming majority. This support has not existed for the issues most important to blacks, so that even when they are free to participate fully the pluralist process fails to operate on their behalf.

Similarly, the elitist model of the political system which emphasizes a hierarchical distribution of power in which a relatively small group of influentials holds a preponderance of power leaves blacks outside the structure of power.[3] As Edward Greenberg rather forcefully suggests, both pluralist and elitist models present an image of government that is disadvantageous to blacks and suggest the futility of traditional political involvement by them.[4] The pervasive impact of the systems approach to political science further clouds the picture by suggesting an almost idyllic view of a stable, demand-response mechanism as basic to democratic politics. Public policy is seen as a function of demands made on the political system, but little if any attention is given to what happens when demands from some sectors of the society constantly fail to evoke desired responses. While these models facilitate

[2] The classic example of this approach is Robert A. Dahl, *Who Governs* (New Haven: Yale University Press, 1967) and *Pluralist Democracy in the United States, Conflict and Consent* (New Haven: Yale University Press, 1967).

[3] See for example C. Wright Mills, *The Power Elite* (New York: Oxford University Press, 1956); Peter Bachrach, *The Theory of Democratic Elitism* (Boston: Little, Brown, 1967).

[4] Edward Greenberg, Neal Milner, and David Olson, eds., *Black Politics* (New York: Holt, Rinehart & Winston, 1971), pp. 14–15. See also Duane Lockard, *The Perverted Priorities of American Politics* (New York: Macmillan, 1971), pp. 13–20.

interesting political science investigation, they inevitably result in disregard for the distinct and complex problems blacks face within the political system unless deliberate care is exercised.[5]

Third, the behavioral revolution in the social sciences discouraged serious attention to problems such as those raised by racial conflict as political scientists shied away from normative or policy-oriented issues in their zeal to create a "pure science of politics." One analysis concludes in this connection that behavioralists became preoccupied with "technique rather than substance, contemplative theory rather than policy relevant theory, and neutral academic conservatism rather than progressive social transformation."[6] It is this aloofness from these real problems that helps to explain why the upheavals of the 1960s caught social scientists by surprise.

This book undertakes an examination of the political experience of black Americans. It does not provide a new or distinct interpretation of this experience, nor does it attempt to offer specific solutions to the complex, many-faceted problems that continue to face blacks in the political arena. Instead, the objective is the more modest one of attempting to describe and analyze some salient aspects of the political attitudes and behavior of blacks throughout their troubled existence in the United States. This undertaking relies primarily on a review and synthesis of the growing but still fragmented body of research relating to black political life. Hopefully it will provide a clearer picture of the political experience of blacks, and a greater understanding of the problems and challenges that blacks continue to face in the political arena.

Several important considerations justify this concern with the black political experience. Many of these considerations have been expressed frequently in connection with the overall importance of making the black experience an integral part of the educational curriculum. Without repeating these, I will identify three vital considerations that lend relevance and even urgency to the effort. First, and perhaps most obvious, is the turbulence of the times. Centuries of patient and mostly restrained efforts by black Americans to improve their status in American society through participation in political life have yielded to more vigorous thrusts into the political arena. The "revolution" of the 1960s is eloquent testimony to the total commitment of blacks to realize for the first time the full promise of the democratic creed. Almost in unison concerned blacks express the view that political activity holds the key to further progress, and with increased determination they are attempting to penetrate every sector of the political system. This clear determination by blacks no longer to be pawns in the political game, but actors sharing political power, has far-reaching implications for the political process and the future of the society.

[5] For one suggested adaptation of the systems model to the study of black political life, see Matthews, *op. cit.*

[6] James A. Bill and Robert Hardgrave, *Comparative Politics, The Quest for Theory* (Columbus, Ohio: Merrill, 1973), p. 17.

A second cause for concern with the black political experience is the inherent importance of the subject in any attempt at a genuine understanding of the total American experience. No matter how we view American political life to date and its prospects for the future, the black presence emerges as a central and often tormenting issue. Conflicts surrounding blacks have been at the core of almost all of the major national crises and have motivated some of the most profound developments in the Constitution. The character of the founders of the nation, the depth of the nation's commitment to its formally espoused values, and the quality of the political system's performance are all touched by the presence of blacks. Thus, while blacks have not always been active or influential participants in the political system, they have profoundly and consistently affected it. Because they are so inextricably intertwined in the national experience, no account of this experience is plausible without serious attention to blacks.

Black America has often been viewed as "a problem," "a dilemma" with which the political system has had to cope by completely ignoring it, suppressing it, or pacifying it. Such an emphasis completely obscures the fact that the black man's epic struggle for survival and for inclusion into the political system has been immensely functional for the system. The search for a solution to the twin problems of powerlessness and oppression has been pursued with remarkable imagination and has been a source of innovation for the political system. Not only have blacks pioneered in utilizing the legal process as a positive instrument for change but, as Greenberg observes, they have "moved beyond a reliance on orderly politics and have drastically expanded the political arena to include lunch counters, bus terminals, and the streets themselves."[7]

Third, the present political world of black America with its distinct orientations toward politics and patterns of political behavior is not entirely understandable when viewed outside the totality of the black experience. For example, findings that blacks are less politically efficacious, trusting, or participant-oriented than whites indicate present conditions that cannot be entirely explained by reference to a standard set of socioeconomic variables as is often attempted. They are explainable by reference to the distinct historical experiences of the black population vis-à-vis the American political system. For both blacks and whites, therefore, a study of this kind is an important aid to understanding a complex reality. It is vital both to the assessment of progress toward a humane and harmonious society and to realistic appraisals of the prospects for the future.

The black political experience in America is a subject that lends itself readily to impassioned polemics and provides innumerable issues on which a study of this kind could plausibly focus. This is clearly evidenced by the variety of the existing literature on the subject, and by the fact that after

---

[7] Greenberg, Milner, and Olson, *op. cit.*, p. v.

almost a decade of research and organization of courses loosely called "black politics" there is still considerable uncertainty among scholars about the character and thrust of black politics. The purpose here is not merely to add to this body of literature, but to identify and explore in a systematic way those issues and problems that seem central to an understanding of the political world of black America. Toward this end, three specific concerns give direction to the book.

The first concern is to examine the impact of race and racial conflict on the political structures and processes of multiracial societies. It is hardly contested that race has a distinct and profound impact on political life in virtually all multiracial societies. In many cases it seems to be the central issue, yet very little effort has been made to explore and specify the nature and extent of its impact. While this exploratory effort cannot be thoroughly and conclusively undertaken here, we will attempt to identify some pertinent findings and to look at the experience of other multiracial societies when they contribute to our understanding of the issue.

As with several other areas of social life, comparative perspectives can substantially improve our understanding of racial conflict within the United States through the new conceptual models that they encourage and the new insights that comparisons provide. Toward this end, Chapter 2 explores the utility of comparison. The purposes of this particular effort are limited, however, and should therefore be clearly indicated. First, these comparisons appear to be the most convenient way of broadly examining certain political implications of racism and racial conflict, although no attempt is made to develop a clear-cut conceptual framework to be consistently applied throughout the study. However, the conceptualization of black-white relations as a form of subordinate-superordinate relationship (which is the underlying source of racial conflict) is developed in Chapter 2 and utilized throughout the study. Second, the chapter helps to indicate the global character of racial conflict, and focuses attention on South Africa as one case of a rigidly maintained subordinate-superordinate system in which efforts similar to those utilized in the United States have been made, but with very different results.

A second concern of the study is to describe and evaluate the methods by which blacks have sought to induce change in their status. Blacks have occupied a distinctly subordinate status in American society, and the thrust of their political activity has been to alter this unfavorable position. In emphasizing the centrality of this struggle for change, one scholar observes that "black politics is based upon the growing consensus among Negro Americans that their lot in life is unacceptable and that their politics is to change that situation."[8] The overriding importance of the struggle for fundamental change gives to black politics its special dynamism and helps to

---

[8] T. M. Tomlinson, "Contributing Factors to Black Politics," *Psychiatry* 33, 2 (May 1970), 141.

distinguish it from the status-quo-oriented politics of the white society. The fact that this struggle has been waged with some success in spite of the severe constraints imposed by a subordinate status in the society adds another unique dimension to black politics.

A third concern of the book is to explore the internal dynamics of black political life. In his study of black politics in urban areas, James Q. Wilson demonstrated that black political life is shaped both by powerful external forces like geographic concentration, racism, and weak economic position, and also by internal forces such as an absence of consensus on goals and the failure of some crucial community institutions.[9] A broad-gauged examination of the black political experience over time indicates that the subordinate status of blacks and their consequent powerlessness in the society have had profound consequences for the internal politics of the black community. These conditions tend to breed frustration, demoralization, and disunity—conditions that are even now painfully obvious features of black political life.

Inevitably a study of this kind poses organizational problems, especially since it employs no single well-developed conceptual or organizational framework. A measure of arbitrariness therefore must be conceded in deciding what aspects of the black political experience are examined and how these are organized. The contents reflect my judgment about what is most important from a political science viewpoint in providing a background against which to evaluate future strategies for political action. Quite possibly important omissions exist; hopefully they are not so grave as to distort the total picture. In the organization of the material I have been motivated primarily by the desire to bring to the study an essential order and clarity that does not now seem to exist, and to do so in a way that will facilitate integration of the black experience into the mainstream of the political science curriculum.

[9] James Q. Wilson, *Negro Politics, The Search for Leadership* (New York: Free Press, 1960), pp. 23–27.

# 2

# Approaches
# to the Study
# of Black Politics

In spite or perhaps because of the rapid growth in the literature on black politics there has been little attention to the theoretical or conceptual frameworks that guide investigations. Mack Jones of Atlanta University has complained that in the rapidly growing subfield of black politics "much of what is done proceeds in an atheoretical manner, and when a theoretical network is evident, it is likely to be one with limited relevance for the black experience."[1] The apparent inattentiveness by political scientists to the need for developing theoretical or conceptual frameworks suitable for the study of race and politics in the United States continues to be one of the major obstacles to understanding the black political experience in American life. It is particularly noteworthy at a time when social scientists have become extremely attentive to such frameworks and their consequences for understanding.

Two sets of circumstances have contributed heavily to the absence of effective approaches to the study of black political life. One is the piecemeal and haphazard way that research in this area has been conducted. There have been few attempts at comprehensive studies of the black political experience. On the contrary, political scientists have been preoccupied with a few specific areas of concern. One such area is black political leadership. Problems of leadership selection, leadership styles, and occasionally the quality or effectiveness of leadership have all been subjects of inquiry. Rarely have these studies provided considerable insight into the many other facets of black political life. Black political participation has been a second prominent concern as scholars have attempted to describe and explain its levels and patterns. More recently, attention has been directed at describing and explaining political attitudes of black Americans. Invariably these researches involve

[1] Mack H. Jones, "A Frame of Reference for Black Politics" in Lenneal J. Henderson, Jr., ed., *Black Political Life in the United States* (San Francisco: Chandler, 1972), p. 7.

comparisons with the white society. While these efforts are important, they are highly limited in the light they shed on the political world of black America.

The second major hindrance to development of frameworks for the study of black politics has been the tendency to view black America as just one more ethnic group that is becoming an indistinguishable part of a pluralist society. The basic question of whether one treats the black experience as part of the ethnic group experience in the United States or as a unique experience distinct from that of other ethnic groups is still a topic on which scholarly opinion is sharply divided. Although profound differences between the black experience and that of other ethnic groups have been noted, there remains the uncertainty about whether race constitutes a dimension that necessitates distinct approaches to analysis. A result of this uncertainty is that several scholars still attempt, directly or indirectly, to force the black political experience into the mold of ethnic group politics rather than to search for distinctive approaches.

These conditions notwithstanding, it is possible to identify some broad propositions about race relations that have been influential in shaping perceptions in this area. Although they cannot all be regarded as clearly developed theoretical or conceptual approaches, they do provide some directions for inquiry, suggest explanations for existing patterns of race relations, and offer clues to the conditions under which change in existing patterns of race relations may be expected to occur. It seems entirely appropriate that we begin our study by reviewing and evaluating briefly a few of these propositions, because in some cases they have had considerable influence on the existing studies in this area and altogether represent distinct perspectives that can considerably enhance our understanding of the impact of race on political life. An awareness of such approaches is of value to the student, because the conceptual framework one adopts or the assumptions one brings to the investigation of any segment of reality determine how investigations are undertaken, the kinds of questions raised for analysis, and the conclusions reached.

The recent race-relations literature reflects four fairly distinct conceptual approaches. For convenience we will identify them as (a) the moral-dilemma approach, (b) the power-relations approach, (c) the modernization approach, and (d) the colonized-people approach. All of these approaches differ in scope, precise focus and in the solutions they suggest for the racial conflict that characterizes American life. To varying degrees they all have been subject to substantial scrutiny.

## The Moral-Dilemma Approach

The publication in 1944 of a monumental study of American race relations by the Swedish sociologist Gunnar Myrdal marked a new departure in the history of American race relations and in scholarship on the subject. The study was significant in two crucial respects. It was the first comprehensive scholarly examination of the reality of black oppression in America and thus tore away the mantle of ignorance behind which the society comfortably hid. Equally important, it generated a wealth of new insights into the study of race relations that have sustained decades of further research and continue even now to have a significant impact on the study of race relations.

The central thesis on which Myrdal's study rested was the alleged contradiction within American society between a strong commitment to democratic values on the one hand and the presence of racial oppression on the other. Myrdal saw this contradiction as a profound moral dilemma for white America and the root of our race-relations problems. Noting that the "Negro problem" was a problem at the heart of the white American, Myrdal asserted that

> ... at bottom our problem is the moral dilemma of the American—the conflict between his moral valuations on various levels of consciousness and generality. The American Dilemma ... is the ever-raging conflict between, on the one hand, the valuations preserved on the general plane which we shall call the "American Creed," where the American thinks, talks and acts under the influence of high national and Christian precepts, and on the other hand, the valuations on specific planes of individual and group living, where personal and local interest, economic, social and sexual jealousies; considerations of community prestige and conformity; group prejudice against particular persons or types of people and all sorts of miscellaneous wants, impulses and habits dominate his outlook.[2]

Myrdal's entire approach to race relations revolved around this alleged conflict between general valuations and beliefs that he called the "democratic creed" and particular attitudes and behavior. It prompted his conclusion that solution to the problem of race relations rested in a gradual process of reconciling particular attitudes and conduct with general beliefs. Thus, in Myrdal's view, the enormous compendium of injustice he presented and the years of virulent racism could be eradicated by simply practicing stated beliefs or removing the discrepancies between white America's general commitment to democratic beliefs and its discriminatory attitudes toward blacks.

Myrdal's thesis has been immensely influential. With a few exceptions, two decades of scholarship utilized it as the starting point for further investigations. The conviction expressed did not owe its existence to Myrdal. Individuals, both black and white, had long appealed to lofty democratic and Christian principles in seeking to alleviate the suffering of blacks. Indeed, an important segment of black political activity rested upon a firm belief in the

[2] Gunnar Myrdal, *An American Dilemma* (New York: Harper & Row, 1948), p. lxxi.

"basic goodness" of the white American and the prospect of closing the gap between belief and practice. Myrdal's forceful and articulate assertion of this conviction, however, considerably increased its plausibility as an approach to solving racial problems.

The moral-dilemma approach is significant not only for its diagnosis of the root of America's racial conflict, but also for the implication that change in the pattern of race relations is to be sought through changing the attitudes of white Americans. It does not altogether ignore economic and political factors that contribute to racial oppression, but treats them as secondary to the problem of attitudes. Taking this cue, several scholars have approached the issue of race relations through the application of psychological theories of attitude formation and attitude change. One such prominent example is the use of theories of cognitive dissonance advanced by Leon Festinger.[3] Festinger postulates an inclination or desire by the individual to reduce inconsistencies concerning his values, his environment, and his behavior. For example, an individual acquires stereotypes of blacks as lazy, untrustworthy, unpatriotic, and so on. Exposure to blacks at some time may confront the individual with evidence contradicting his stereotypes. This contradictory evidence is said to be dissonance-producing. The individual, uncomfortable with this dissonance, attempts to achieve cognitive consistency by modifying his attitudes or perception of blacks.

During the last decade, Myrdal's moral-dilemma approach to race relations in the United States has been subjected to extensive scrutiny both empirically and conceptually. Donald Prothro and Charles Grigg tested empirically the assertion that there is a discrepancy between support for basic democratic principles and the specific attitudes and beliefs of individuals. They report that between 94 and 98 percent of their sample supported broad democratic principles, while on questions involving specific application of these principles the sample was much closer to total discord than to perfect consensus.[4] More recently Frank Westie tested Myrdal's moral-dilemma hypothesis and found clear confirmation for the assertion that there is substantial discrepancy between support for the "democratic creed" and the specific valuations of white Americans. He also found that although a few of his respondents recognized no contradiction and thus felt no dilemma, most did—and these attempted to remove the dilemma by adjusting their specific valuations to conform to their general support for the democratic creed. Westie thus concluded that "this suggests that Myrdal's optimism is not unjustified and lends little support to the fear that people might react to the dilemma by renouncing their allegiance to the democratic tenets of the American creed."[5]

[3] Leon Festinger, *A Theory of Cognitive Dissonance* (New York: Harper & Row, 1957).

[4] Donald Prothro and Charles Grigg, "Fundamental Principles of Democracy: Bases of Agreement and Disagreement," *Journal of Politics* 12 (May 1960), 276–294.

[5] Frank Westie, "The American Dilemma: An Empirical Test," *American Sociological Review* (August 1965), 527–538.

On the other hand, Nahum Madalia has been critical of Myrdal's basic assumption "that social change in complex societies takes the form of increasing the consistency of 'particular' with 'general' values." He has suggested that existing evidence indicates that the very opposite is more likely to be true. The process of social change which produces modern complex societies often increases the number of incompatible values held by individuals and decreases rather than increases "the tendency for individuals to behave in a way consistent with their own core values."[6] These observations are supported, Madalia believes, by the tendency in complex societies toward (a) role differentiation and (b) a physical separation of contexts of action that are governed by particularistic norms from those governed by universalistic norms. This is evidenced by the tendency to accept matter-of-factly "integrated" work and business environments while rejecting "integration" in one's neighborhoods, social organizations, and so on. Furthermore, Ira Katznelson suggests that Myrdal's "ethical moral approach begs the question: What are the social, economic and political origins of relationships of racial inequality, and what social, economic and political factors sustain such relationships?"[7]

An earlier and even more vehement rejection of Myrdal's moral-dilemma approach is that by Oliver Cromwell Cox, who criticized Myrdal for ignoring the problem of power while "seeking to regenerate the individual through moral preachments." Cox finds the implications of Myrdal's hypothesis even more serious than the limitations imposed by emphasis on the American creed as a value premise. He contends that Myrdal's hypothesis supports the illusion that emphasis on moral means is all that is necessary to bring about change, and in doing so the hypothesis is merely contributing to the maintenance of the status quo.[8] Indeed, if Myrdal's hypothesis is fully accepted, it would appear to discount vigorous direct struggle for change in preference for a strategy of gentle persuasion.

Even more persuasive than the arguments adduced by these scholars are the clear, cold lessons of history. As Joseph Roucek points out, many organizations have expended large sums of money and energies in efforts to effect change in racial attitudes, and the continued existence of these organizations only testifies to their failures.[9] In short, Myrdal's vision of changed race relations resulting from changes in white attitudes—elimination of the gap between generalized values and specific ones—has not worked. Charles Silberman's chilling but perceptive observation summarizes the problem with Myrdal's approach:

[6] Nahum Z. Madalia, "Myrdal's Assumptions on Race Relations: A Conceptual Commentary," *Social Forces* 40, 3 (March 1962), 226.

[7] Ira Katznelson, "Power in the Reformulation of Race Research," in Peter Orleans and William R. Ellis, Jr., eds., *Race, Change and Urban Society* (Beverley Hills, Calif.: Sage, 1971), p. 62.

[8] Oliver Cromwell Cox, in *Caste, Class and Race: A Study in Social Dynamics* (Garden City, N.Y.: Doubleday, 1948), p. 538.

[9] Joseph S. Roucek, "Minority-Majority Relations in Their Power Aspects," *Phylon* 17 (1956), 26.

The tragedy of race relations in the United States is that there is no American Dilemma. White Americans are not torn and tortured by the conflict between their devotion to the American creed and their actual behavior. They are upset by the current state of race relations, to be sure, but what troubles them is not that justice is being denied but that their peace is being shattered and their business interrupted.[10]

## The Power-Relations Approach

Discounting emphasis on the moral basis of racial problems and the need to change the attitudes of individuals, some scholars now urge that we view race relations within the context of power relations. Roucek, for example, argues that majority-minority relations in American society are simply another aspect of the universal power struggle that characterizes political life. He regards the claims made by majority and minority groups primarily as weapons in the struggle for power. Because self-interest dominates the activities of both groups, Roucek suggests that gains by the minority group will come as a result of the power that that group exercises in the political system.[11]

In an effort to develop a general theory of minority-group relations, Hubert Blalock also argues that discrimination is based ultimately on power relationships between dominant and subordinate groups, and that race relations can be analyzed in terms of "power contests" between racial groups. From this perspective, Blalock urges an approach to race relations that emphasizes the utilization of power to achieve desired goals. Roucek defines power on the group level as "the sum total of all those capacities, relationships, and processes by which compliance of others is secured." Blalock views it as "the actual overcoming of resistance in a standard period of time," and suggests that this power is a multiplicative function of two variables—"total resources and the degree to which these resources are mobilized in the services of those persons or groups exercising power."[12]

From a perspective similar to that of Roucek and Blalock, James Coleman undertakes a study of change in race relations by posing the problem of "how a distinct subgroup in society, with little power and without direct resources for gaining more power, can nevertheless come to gain those resources."[13] Coleman observes that the cluster of high political power, economic well-being, education, and effective opportunity is found principally among whites, whereas blacks have little political power and are handicapped by poverty, poor education, and lack of effective opportunity. The central task as he sees it is to find means of improving the power at the

---

[10] Charles Silberman, *Crisis in Black and White* (New York: Vintage, 1964), p. 10.

[11] Roucek, *op. cit.*, p. 30.

[12] Hubert M. Blalock, Jr., *Toward a Theory of Minority-Group Relations* (New York: Wiley, 1967), p. 110.

[13] James S. Coleman, *Resources for Social Change* (New York: Wiley, 1971), p. 1.

command of the black population. Toward this end, Coleman undertakes an accounting of the actual resources available to blacks, examines methods by which potential resources can be converted, and then suggests how these may be brought to bear on the struggle for social change.

The power-relations approach urged by Roucek, Blalock, and Coleman is in many respects identical to the concept of black power that gained popularity after 1965 and has been clearly spelled out by Stokely Carmichael and Charles Hamilton.[14] There is a common assumption that the racial discrimination experienced by blacks is a function of their lack of power in the political system. Coleman advocates mobilization of individual and community resources by blacks in order to maximize their influence. Similarly, Carmichael and Hamilton urge the development of group solidarity in order to bargain from a position of strength in a pluralist society. They emphasize that "before a group can enter into the open society, it must first close ranks."[15]

By discounting the expectation of fundamental change in deep-seated racial attitudes and emphasizing the power of the group as the key to inducing change, the power-relations approach fits smoothly into the pluralist framework, where the allocation of values is seen as a function of group competition. Furthermore, the power-relations approach stresses the need for internal organization of black political life. There are, however, some short-comings of the approach that should be noted.

The assumption that discriminatory treatment is entirely a function of a power disadvantage resulting from minority status considerably oversimplifies the racial problem. The relative powerlessness of blacks in the political system is itself a result of deliberate discriminatory policies that are not overcome as readily as Coleman and others suggest. For example, Coleman considers numbers (the size of the black population) a crucial resource, but the effectiveness of numbers even in a democratic polity is dependent on unimpeded opportunity to participate fully in the political system. Until recently black Americans were denied such opportunity and black South Africans, in spite of their large numbers, continue to be totally excluded from the political system.

Because black political powerlessness is an integral part of the overall assignment of inferior status in society, steps to alter this condition invariably induce hostility by the dominant white society. The widespread uneasiness exhibited by whites about the black-power slogan is illustrative of this. In the only major empirical test of attitudes toward the black-power slogan, Joel Aberbach and Jack Walker found its meaning unclear to many, but at the same time "the overwhelming majority of whites are frightened and bewildered by the words black power. . . . The slogan represents an unmistakable

---

[14] Stokely Carmichael and Charles V. Hamilton, *Black Power: The Politics of Liberation in America* (New York: Vintage, 1967), pp. 34–57.
[15] *Ibid.*, p. 44.

challenge to the country's prevailing racial customs and social norms. . . ." [16]
It seems, therefore, that the power-relations approach cannot entirely escape
the impact of racial attitudes. Jones' suggestion that the power-relations
approach contain the specification that "the ideological justification for the
superordination of whites is the institutionalized belief in the inherent superiority of that race"[17] is thus clearly vital to any serious consideration of the
concept.

Finally, it should be observed that the effectiveness of a group in a
pluralist political system is directly related to the kinds of goals that the
group seeks and the degree to which other elements in the political system
feel constrained to oppose these goals. Blacks may therefore mobilize their
resources thoroughly only to remain a permanent and isolated minority
unable to influence public policy in areas of greatest concern to them. Thus
the power-relations approach has merit to the extent that it describes one
approach blacks will find helpful under certain limited conditions, but it falls
far short of an adequate explanation of race relations or as a solution to the
unfavorable status of black Americans.

## The Modernization Approach

Some scholars have attempted to view the problem of race relations from a
developmental perspective. Here racial discrimination and racial conflict in
multiracial societies are seen as related to specific levels of socioeconomic
development and are considered to change as the society develops. Although
much is still unclear about the dynamics of the development process or the
specific consequences of development, existing knowledge of this process
seems to provide evidence that its impact may be worthy of consideration.

There is a widely shared consensus among social scientists that socioeconomic development or modernization profoundly alters traditional attitudes and values in a society and creates conditions conducive to the development of new attitudes and values. Particularly significant among these
changes are the transformation from agrarian to industrial societies and the
consequent emergence of new forms of social organization, evaluation of
individuals on the basis of achievement rather than ascriptive criteria, and the
mobilization of individuals for new and more active roles in political life.
There is, however, very little evidence concerning whether or to what extent
modernization alters established patterns of race relations.

Pierre van den Berghe's distinction between "paternalistic" and "competitive" types of race relations is suggestive of one way in which level of

---

[16] Joel Aberbach and Jack Walker, "The Meanings of Black Power; A Comparison
of White and Black Interpretations of a Slogan," *American Political Science Review* **44**,
2 (June 1970), 373.

[17] Jones, *op. cit.*, p. 9.

development may be relevant for race relations.[18] The paternalistic type of race relations—characterized by a master-servant pattern of relationship, roles and statuses sharply defined along racial lines, rigidly ascriptive division of labor, and the maintenance of social distance through an elaborate set of rituals that emphasize subservience and dominance—is found primarily in "pre-industrial societies, in which agriculture and handicraft production constitute bases of the economy." The preabolition societies of northeastern Brazil, the western Cape Province of South Africa, the West Indies, the southern United States and most colonial societies reflect this pattern of race relations. Van den Berghe notes that although there is conflict in these societies, race relations are based on the acquiescence of the subordinate group and are sustained by an elaborate ideology of racism.

Competitive race relations, on the other hand, are characteristic of industrialized, urbanized societies. Race functions as a basis for distinctions and affects the division of labor, but there are also important class distinctions. In these societies the franchise is often restricted, formally or informally, to members of the dominant group. Traditional mechanisms for maintaining subservience and social distance break down and are replaced by intense competition between subordinates and the working class of the dominant group. Under these conditions physical segregation is introduced, and the society becomes compartmentalized into racially homogeneous communities with duplication of basic social institutions like churches, schools, and recreational facilities. The United States, South Africa, and the United Kingdom are examples of this type of society.

Van den Berghe is not primarily concerned with describing the impact of modernization on race relations, but his typology clearly suggests that the level of development has a profound impact on the pattern of race relations. This impact could be even more carefully observed if instead of two ideal types one conceives of a continuum bounded on one end by the paternalistic type of race relations in a traditional society and on the other by the competitive type in a modernized society. Observe, however, that in van den Berghe's conception of the two types differences occur in the *form* in which subordination is maintained, but not in the fact of subordination.

In his study of blacks in Southern politics, Harry Holloway employed the developmental approach. His study is based on two closely related hypotheses: (1) "The South may be regarded as a traditional society that has been modernizing for several decades," and (2) "the Southern Negro may be viewed as an ethnic group comparable to ethnic groups in the North."[19] From examination of several Southern communities considered to be repre-

---

[18] Pierre L. van den Berghe, *Race and Ethnicity: Essays in Comparative Sociology* (New York: Basic Books, 1970), pp. 34–36.
[19] Harry Holloway, *The Politics of the Southern Negro* (New York: Random House, 1969), pp. 3–4.

sentative of various stages of development, Holloway attempts to demonstrate that the level of black political participation and the style of this participation vary directly with the apparent level of development of the community.

In the rural South, blacks are discouraged or otherwise prevented from voting, as widespread enfranchisement is perceived by whites as a threat to the status quo. On the other hand, blacks are deeply apathetic, considering politics as the business of white folks and feeling they lack the basic skills for effective participation. In sharp contrast to these rural characteristics, Holloway finds Atlanta illustrative of the impact of modernization. He notes that

> basic to the process (of development) are population growth accompanied by urbanization and industrialization. With these advances there is improved transportation and communications, so the city increasingly forms ties that transcend local and regional relationships. The city becomes receptive to national and international influences that reduce insularity and regionalism. Politically the changes include an expanding electorate, with new Negro voters added to the general increase.[20]

On a much larger scale, the British Institute of Race Relations, under the auspices of UNESCO, explored the impact of one crucial aspect of the development process—industrialization—on patterns of race relations. The study draws upon the experience of several widely separated multiracial societies—Brazil, the southern United States, the Caribbean, Malaya, and others.[21] Surveying findings from these societies, Herbert Blumer concedes that certain traditional expectations of industrialization make it seem a particularly crucial force in altering race relations. Among the more widespread expectations he identifies are (1) it induces commitment to a rational, secular outlook, (2) it replaces status relations with contractual relations, (3) it brings into being impersonal market situations, and (4) it facilitates physical and social mobility. These developments are all expected to undermine an established social order and to create new patterns of social relations.[22]

Blumer concludes that existing evidence indicates that in spite of these wide-ranging expectations, industrialization is not necessarily a strong force for change in race relations. Although industrialization has far-reaching impact on various aspects of social life, it does not necessarily facilitate change in well-developed patterns of race relations. He suggests that the "intrinsic structural requirements of industrialization need not, contrary to much a priori theorizing, force a rearrangement in the relations set by the racial

---

[20] *Ibid.*, p. 324.

[21] Guy Hunter, ed., *Industrialization and Race Relations* (London: Oxford University Press), 1965.

[22] Herbert Blumer, "Industrialization and Race Relations," in Guy Hunter, *op. cit.*, pp. 220–253.

system." Generally, the structures and relations arising from industrialization conform to the pattern of race relations and, as one study of South Africa indicates, may reinforce the existing structures.[23] The experience of blacks in the South, according to Blumer, supports this view. There industrialization fits into a racial mold fashioned by slavery, the Civil War, and Reconstruction. As industrialization altered the traditionally agricultural South, blacks "moved from the bottom of the social ladder in agriculture into the corresponding position in the industrial structure." They were consistently relegated to menial, unskilled, low-paying jobs in industry.

Change in well-established patterns of race relations, Blumer contends, occurs primarily as a result of forces outside of industry. Ultimately, while industrialization creates conditions for change, the direction of change is a function of political activity. Thus although the process of modernization, particularly industrialization, has implications for race relations, the evidence suggests that its role is at best indirect. It creates some conditions that are conducive to securing change in race relations, but it does not independently alter highly developed patterns of race relations.

## The Colonized-People Approach

The three approaches we have discussed thus far focus on two basic concerns. They attempt (1) to account for the persistence of racial discrimination against black Americans, and (2) to identify the forces or conditions that precipitate change in well established patterns of race relations. All three help to clarify aspects of race relations and the processes of change, but they exhibit substantial limitations. They direct attention to forces that are potentially capable of affecting the pattern of race relations, but fall far short of a clearly satisfactory framework for the analysis of race and politics in the United States. Most notably they make no attempt to define clearly the status of blacks in the society or to assess the full nature and impact of racism.

Recently some scholars have attempted an approach to race and politics in America that begins with a delineation of the status of blacks in the society and proceeds to an explication of the conditions essential to the achievement of change in their status. The essence of this approach is a conviction that black America constitutes a distinct national entity existing in a colonial type of relationship to white America. This perception of the status of blacks provides the framework for wideranging analyses of the black experience and the nature of the forces against which blacks must work.

One of the first attempts to apply the colonial analogy to the condition of blacks is that of Harold Cruse in his essay entitled "Revolutionary

[23] Heribert Adam, *Modernizing Racial Domination: South Africa's Political Dynamics* (Berkeley: University of California Press, 1971).

Nationalism and the Afro-American." Cruse observed then that, like the peoples of underdeveloped countries, black Americans are victims of hunger, illiteracy, cultural starvation, and the psychological reactions to being ruled by others not of their kind.

> From the beginning, the American Negro has existed as a colonial being. His enslavement coincided with the colonial expansion of European powers and was nothing more or less than a condition of domestic colonialism. Instead of the United States establishing a colonial empire in Africa, it brought the colonial system home and installed it in the Southern states. When the Civil War broke up the slave system and the Negro was emancipated, he gained only partial freedom. Emancipation elevated him only to the position of a semi-dependent man, not to that of an equal or independent being.[24]

Focusing on the "dark ghetto" of Harlem, Kenneth Clark came to a somewhat similar conclusion. He observed that "the ghettos are social, political, educational and above all economic colonies. Their inhabitants are subject peoples, victims of the greed, cruelty, sensitivity, guilt and fear of their masters."[25] Elaboration and application of the colonial thesis as an effective analytical framework was first undertaken by Stokely Carmichael and Charles V. Hamilton in *Black Power.* They suggested then that although blacks enjoy legal citizenship, they exist in a colonial condition fashioned and maintained by institutional racism. This colonized condition, Carmichael and Hamilton suggest, is reflected in the political powerlessness of the black population, in its economic dependence and ineffectiveness, and in its social isolation.

More recently Robert Blauner provided a thoughtful analysis of the colonial approach to the black experience.[26] Blauner notes that it suffers from a measure of imprecision, and he attempts to specify the areas in which the experience of black Americans parallels that of victims of conventional colonial rule. He suggests, first, that conventional colonialism and American racism "developed out of the same historical situation and reflected a common world or economic and power stratification." Both the slave and the colonial victim provided vital resources for Western industrialization. Second, in both the internal version of colonialism and the conventional one, the colonizing power undertook a deliberate program of transforming or destroying indigenous values, orientations, and ways of life. Third, Blauner points out that racism is common to both forms of colonialism. Racism as a principle that sustained colonial domination is reflected in the fact that

---

[24] Harold Cruse, "Revolutionary Nationalism and the Afro-American," *Studies on the Left* **2**, 3 (1962), 13.

[25] Kenneth Clark, *Dark Ghetto: Dilemmas of Social Power* (New York: Harper & Row, 1965), p. 11.

[26] Robert Blauner, "Internal Colonialism and Ghetto Revolt," *Social Problems* **16**, 4, 393–408.

except for the limited case of Japanese imperialism, the major examples of colonialism involve subjugation of nonwhites by white Europeans.

Blauner identifies three objective conditions that characterize both the black colony in America and the conventional colony. The first is political powerlessness. The black ghettos are without power; decisions affecting the destinies of their population are made within the white power structure, far removed from black hands. The second is economic dependence. In the same way that the ghetto is governed from outside, its economic institutions are owned and controlled by persons far removed from the ghetto. As a rule, black communities are not self-supporting; they produce no resources that are applied to the development of the community. Finally, like the conventional colony, black America has been systematically stripped of social roots and led to inculcate the values and attitudes of the colonial power.

Similarities observed between the political attitudes of black Americans and those of victims of conventional colonialism tend to strengthen further the colonial analogy. A. W. Singham finds that like colonials, black Americans have been deliberately directed away from extensive political participation. Through various techniques the dominant group attempted a depoliticization of these marginal groups. He finds, too, a similarity in the subject orientation to government characteristic of colonial peoples and black Americans, suggesting that both groups tend to perceive government as benefactor and oppressor; they are most often in contact with the welfare and law enforcement agencies of government. He suggests that psychological legacies of marginal status, which are still evident in many former colonies and among black Americans, continue to constitute serious constraints on political life.[27]

The colonized-people approach makes some vital contributions to study of the black experience. Unlike other approaches, it proposes a definition of the status of blacks in the society and a specific type of relationship to the political system, steps that are crucial starting points for an orderly study of black political life. Second, the colonized-people approach provides a plausible basis for linking the experience of black Americans and the other victims of European oppression throughout the Third World. The common interests and aspirations of these widely separated peoples have been alluded to by several commentators, but a stronger and clearer basis for these common interests and aspirations emerges when viewed in this way.

From this perspective, the distinction between black Americans and other ethnic groups becomes unmistakably clear. The various other ethnic groups voluntarily joined the society. They chose to live in cohesive communities and in most cases did so for only a short time. During this time, they managed to acquire substantial economic and political power.[28] For them, a

[27] A. W. Singham, "The Political Socialization of Marginal Groups," *International Journal of Comparative Sociology* 8, 2 (September 1967), 190.
[28] *Report of the National Advisory Commission on Civil Disorders* (New York: Bantam, 1968), pp. 279–281.

colonial experience sustained by racism has not really existed. This colonized condition is thus unique to the black population and is considered by proponents of the colonized-people approach to be the only plausible basis for analysis of the black political experience and for assessing approaches to the struggle for change in black life.

The other approaches seem to imply waiting for the effects of evolutionary processes ultimately to produce some unspecified form of improvement in race relations, or relying on outputs from a political system in which blacks are at a permanent disadvantage in influencing the allocation of values. On the contrary, the colonized-people approach suggests the immediacy of the demand for change, suggests the orientation of such change as the acquisition of a substantial measure of autonomy, and—for some elements of the black community—the eventual emergence of a separate political community.

In spite of the distinct contributions it makes as an approach to black politics, the colonized-people approach exhibits substantial weaknesses and has been vigorously criticized. Critics have tended to view this approach as a form of intellectual radicalism or as a deliberate attempt to dramatize the black plight by use of a concept with overwhelmingly negative connotations. For example, van den Berghe comments that "to call Afro-Americans an internal colony may be emotionally cathartic but contributes nothing to the analysis either of colonialism as an international system or of the United States as a racial caste society."[29] Van den Berghe further suggests that by designating black America a colony, the meaning of the term "colonial" is merely being reduced to "oppressed," and colonialism is merely one specialized form of oppression.

Conflicting interpretations of racial violence also reflect disagreements about the colonial argument. While Blauner and others see the violence as akin to colonial revolts, Robert Fogelson[30] argues vehemently against this view. He insists that there are fundamental differences between race riots in the United States and colonial revolts, and he suggests that these differences merely reflect basic differences between the racial problem and the colonial situation. Fogelson suggests at least three respects in which the two situations are different: (1) In the United States blacks have greater opportunities than colonial peoples to enter the middle class and exert political power; (2) white Americans and their leaders have a more ambivalent attitude toward blacks than European colonialists had toward the people they colonized; and (3) the ghetto is a colony only if by *colony* is meant a dependent neighborhood, which would apply to portions of the modern metropolis. The ghetto is

---

[29] Van den Berghe, *American Political Science Review* 65, 3 (September 1971), 855.

[30] Robert M. Fogelson, *Violence as Protest: A Study of Riots and Ghettos* (Garden City, N.Y.: Doubleday, 1971), pp. 10–11.

exploited, he suggests, not by the white society as a whole but a fragment of it, and it is done to avoid rather than oppress the occupants of ghettos.

Finally, it should be observed that proponents of the colonized-people approach focus almost exclusively on the "ghetto as colony" without specific reference to the black majority living outside the ghetto. Cruse saw the colonial situation taking shape in the South. Kenneth Clark, however, saw the teeming ghettos of New York City with its "invisible walls" as the colonial enclaves. Similarly, Carmichael and Hamilton as well as Blauner describe ghetto situations as analogous to colonialism. It remains unclear whether the approach seeks to be inclusive of the black population nationally or only that portion caught in urban slums.

## Summary and Conclusion

A review of the literature on race relations clearly indicates that the recent increase in scholarly attention to problems of race and politics in the United States has not been matched by efforts to develop broad-range frameworks for analysis. There is even some uncertainty about the extent to which social scientists can fruitfully maintain a distinct focus on race. Leo Kuper recently observed that race cannot appropriately be elevated to the level of a basic determinant of human affairs as Marxists have done with economics.[31] Van den Berghe also has concluded that, at least from the perspective of sociology, race has no claim to a special place in a general theory of society even though it may command substantial interest and attention.[32] These observations notwithstanding, it is apparent that race is an important and sometimes central element in the politics of several societies and thus requires careful and extensive analysis. An indispensable aid to such analysis is development of analytical or conceptual approaches that permit clear understanding of the impact of race on political life and the methods by which change occurs in established patterns of race relations.

In various ways the four approaches we have examined contribute to our understanding of the issue of race relations and suggest approaches to change. However, their contributions are limited in some important respects. They derive from interpretations of American political and social life that are not in all instances supported by firm evidence, and they are easily contradicted when applied to multiracial societies outside the United States. For example, it is important to consider individual attitudes and community values in studying race relations, but Myrdal's formulation seems applicable only in a society embracing the democratic values he associates with the "American creed" and where there is, in fact, an apparent desire to implement those values fully. Similarly, the power-relations approach is limited in

[31] Leo Kuper, "Theories of Revolution and Race Relations," *Comparative Studies in Society and History* **B**, 1 (1971), 87–107.
[32] Van den Berghe, *Race and Ethnicity, op. cit.,* p. 9.

that it assumes smooth operation of a pluralist system of politics in which various competing groups may influence decision making. Not only is there substantial controversy about whether this form of pluralism is in fact characteristic of the American political system; it is clearly not descriptive of most other multiracial societies. Furthermore, even if this competitive pluralist approach is applicable in conflicts for specific, limited goals among equally situated groups, it is unlikely that it would be applicable where there is deep irreconcilable conflict over a subordinate group's status.

# 3

# Comparative Approaches to Race and Politics

One of the primary obstacles to development of more effective conceptual frameworks for the study of race and politics generally or black politics in the United States is the provincialism that has characterized most investigations to date. Racial conflict is virtually a global phenomenon, affecting widely separated societies at all levels of political and economic development. Although it seems most frequent and most intense in black-white relations, racial conflict occurs wherever peoples of different races or colors must share a common homeland. In this regard, it is noteworthy that "the week of the Los Angeles riots was also the week when Malaysia broke apart because brown men could not control their dark suspicions of yellow men, and when black and brown men resumed their efforts to slug it out in Southern Sudan."[1]

There is considerable evidence, too, that the attitudes and values that trigger racial conflict are global. The effort to establish the inherent superiority of one race over all others is an old and pervasive one. It provided the impetus for, and justification of, centuries of subordination of nonwhite peoples by whites through the institutions of slavery and later of colonialism. It has been a prominent force in the international behavior of states[2] and is reflected in the domestic politics of virtually all societies in which the population is divided by race or color.

In spite of this global scope of racial conflict, research has been largely particularistic in that it has been descriptive of specific situations and almost entirely confined to the United States. Both Pierre van den Berghe[3] and R. A.

[1] Quoted in "Preface to the Issue 'Color and Race,' " *Daedalus* (Spring 1967), iii.
[2] Robert K. Gardiner, "Race and Color in International Relations," *Daedalus* (Spring 1967), 296–311. See also George Shepherd and Tilden LeMelle, *Race Among Nations: A Conceptual Approach* (Lexington, Mass.: Heath, 1970).
[3] Pierre L. van den Berghe, *Race and Racism* (New York: Wiley, 1967), p. 5.

25

Schermerhorn[4] affirm this domestic focus with their finding that about 90 percent of all research on race relations is confined to the United States. In part, at least, this preoccupation with the United States is explained by these considerations: (1) The prevalence, persistence, and high visibility of racial conflict in the United States tends to encourage preoccupation with the domestic problem; (2) traditionally, political scientists have tended to view racial conflict outside the United States as incidental to colonial rule and hence unworthy of special attention; and (3) the unavailability of conceptual frameworks that facilitate cross-national investigation. Whatever the reason, however, this limited focus on racial conflict has the disadvantages of over-emphasizing specific features of the American experience in race relations and encouraging overreliance on culture-bound concepts in studies of the problem.

In this chapter we explore the utility of a comparative approach to the study of race and politics in the hope that comparison can clarify some ways in which race affects political life both generally and particularly within the United States. The effort should also serve to direct attention to the experiences and aspirations of other nonwhite peoples in multiracial societies. This second objective is especially appropriate at this time when black Americans are exhibiting heightened interest in and concern for the black peoples of other lands, especially those of Africa. The comparison focuses primarily on the United States and South Africa as prominent cases, although comparison need not be confined to these two countries.

## Problems of the Comparative Approach

The comparative approach to investigating racial conflict is one fruitful approach to understanding. Not only can it substantially increase awareness of the scope and complexity of race relations and racial conflict, but by elevating the level at which these issues are examined it can considerably enhance our understanding of the impact of race on politics. In this connection, one study suggests that "the use of several cultures and social contexts from which to generate new hypotheses not only provides a wider variety of data but also contributes to the establishment of theoretical models on a more general and universal level."[5]

Comparative studies of race and politics pose some formidable problems, however, that may have impeded efforts in this direction. The first and perhaps most basic problem is associated with the wide differences among societies with respect to how race is defined and how racial distinctions are made. In spite or perhaps because of its wide usage and important social and

---

[4] R. A. Schermerhorn, *Comparative Ethnic Relations: A Framework for Theory and Research* (New York: Random House, 1970), p. 7.

[5] Norman Yetman and C. Hoy Steele, eds., *Majority and Minority* (Boston: Allyn & Bacon, 1971), p. 84.

political impact, there is no clear, universally accepted definition of race. Van den Berghe identifies four very distinct connotations of the concept: (1) *Race* has been loosely used as a synonym for *species,* as in *human race;* (2) *race* is frequently used to identify a group of individuals who share certain cultural characteristics, as in the Jewish race or French race; (3) physical anthropologists have called races the various subspecies of *Homo sapiens* characterized by certain phenotypical and genotypical traits such as "mongoloid," "negroid," and so on; (4) social scientists use *race* to mean a human group that identifies itself, or is identified by others, as distinct from other groups by virtue of innate or immutable physical characteristics that are in turn believed to be intrinsically related to nonphysical attributes.[6] Even though the fourth use of *race* is the one most frequently utilized, there are wide differences in the criteria used to classify individuals into racial groups.

In a comparative study of slavery and race relations in Brazil and the United States, Carl Degler points out important differences in how racial classifications are made in the two countries. In the United States one is either black or white, with no legally or socially significant intermediary position, while in Brazil the existence of a large number of terms descriptive of various gradations in color reflects a socially significant continuum of colors from black to white.[7] In his study of race and color in Central America, Julian Pitt-Rivers reports other significant peculiarities. He finds that segregation, American style, is nonexistent in Central America, because language and economic and social considerations are all associated with color in making racial distinctions.[8] Orlanda Patterson reports similar findings indicating that in South and Central America, "money whitens."[9] This apparent lack of consistency considerably complicates efforts at comparison, and suggests that in such efforts one may more usefully focus on groups that are identified as racially distinct rather than on any objective criteria for racial classification.

A second important obstacle to comparative studies of race and politics is the almost complete absence of effective conceptual or theoretical frameworks essential to the development of reliable and valid generalizations about race relations. As the existing literature amply demonstrates, the area of race relations is extremely complex, and this complexity increases when one attempts cross-national comparisons of its political aspects. One factor contributing to this complexity is the fact that class and/or economic status is often inextricably associated with race in shaping patterns of social and political organization, making precise determination of the impact of race

[6] Van den Berghe, *op. cit.,* p. 9.
    [7] Carl M. Degler, *Neither Black Nor White* (New York: Macmillan, 1971), pp. 213–239.
    [8] Julian Pitt-Rivers, "Race, Color and Class in Central America and the Andes," *Daedalus* (Spring 1967), 542–559.
    [9] Orlanda Patterson, "On the Fate of Blacks in the Americas," *Public Policy* 27 (Spring 1972), 30–32.

extremely difficult. The point here is that invariably class lines coincide with perceived racial lines, so that it is difficult to determine whether class condition or race is the primary determinant of behavior.[10]

In spite of the obstacles noted here, some scholars have undertaken highly informative comparative studies of specific aspects of race relations. One such undertaking is that by Philip Mason, who highlights what he terms a "revolt against Western values" by focusing on three widely separated "cult-movements" among nonwhites—the Ras Tafaris of Jamaica, the Cargo Cultists of the South Pacific, and the Black Muslims of the United States.[11] Although the movements differ in important respects, the differences are overshadowed by what Mason suggests that they have in common.

The movements reflect conflict between whites and nonwhites with respect to culture—the traditions, values, and attitudes that distinguish one community of people from another. The cultural dimension of conflict between whites and nonwhites appeared as an integral part of the anticolonial struggle and is poignantly expressed by Frantz Fanon in his now classic observation that "the unconditional affirmation of African culture has succeeded the unconditional affirmation of European culture."[12] Rejection of a vaunted Western system of values also found colorful expression in forms such as the concept of negritude advanced by Leopold Seghnor, Aimé Cessaire, and others. In his study, Mason demonstrates that the trend is not confined to the victims of traditional colonialism. Subordinate groups that at one time strove mightily to become a part of a common Western culture have now turned their backs on this culture.

In the United States, the black Muslims exemplify the rejection of Western (white) values and the Western stereotype of "Negroes." They claim commitment to a system of values rooted in a new and positive perception of the black past, its present capabilities, and its future prospects. Mason suggests that black intellectuals share with the Muslims resentment at oppression, ostracism, and indifference, and the search for identity or "cultural pedigree." He sees in the less widely known and more primitive cult movement, the Ras Tafaris, forces similar to those reflected in Muslim beliefs. Members of the Ras Tafaris claim to be descendants of the Ethiopians, vehemently reject white institutions and values, and seek to return to the land of their ancestors, Ethiopia. In their own way, the Cargo cults also resemble the Muslims and Ras Tafaris in that they too maintain a system of beliefs based on rejection of Western values even while desiring Western goods.

A second imaginative approach to comparison is demonstrated by A. W. Singham's study entitled "The Political Socialization of Marginal Groups."[13]

---

[10] For a discussion of this problem see Leo Kuper, "Theories of Revolution and Race Relations," *Comparative Studies in Society and History,* B, 1 (1971), 87–107.

[11] Philip Mason, "The Revolt Against Western Values," *Daedalus* (Spring 1967), 328–352.

[12] Frantz Fanon, quoted in Mason, *op. cit.*

[13] A. W. Singham, "The Political Socialization of Marginal Groups," *International Journal of Comparative Sociology,* 8, 1 (September 1967), 182–198.

The principal focus of the study is a comparison of the problems of blacks in the United States and Great Britain in becoming an integral part of their respective political communities and the attitudes they have developed as a result of their marginal status. The study reaches much farther afield, however, probing aspects of political life in several multiracial societies and particularly in colonial and former colonial territories. Singham finds that, while Britain and the United States have permitted integration of various immigrant groups into the political life of the dominant group, blacks have never been fully accepted. They have remained "marginal groups" on the fringes of the political system.

Singham suggests that this marginal existence, shared by black Americans and colonial peoples alike, has important consequences for their political attitudes. They share strong negative attitudes toward government. Their orientation toward the government is primarily that of "subject" rather than "participant," and they exhibit low levels of political efficacy. Singham concludes that studies of the position of blacks in these societies should proceed from the recognition that they are a culturally plural group—that is, a group with which other groups in the society do not share common values.

Although highly insightful and suggestive of the utility of such comparison, these efforts focus on very limited aspects of political life. The approaches utilized do not facilitate broad-range comparison of the entire political process in multiracial societies. In attempting to find bases for such comparisons it is essential first to examine some basic ways in which race affects political life, and then to focus on those forces that seem common and central to the politics of multiracial societies.

## The Impact of Race on Politics

Race and skin color possess no inherent political significance. Edward Shils notes that they are not like religion, which involves membership in a community of believers, or like kinship, a tangible structure to which individuals belong.[14] Yet race is one of the most potent forces in political life. In spite of its obvious significance, it is still unclear precisely how and under what conditions race becomes salient for a political system. It is apparent that the impact of race on political life varies from one multiracial society to the next, and that although racial conflict is widespread, there are differences in the goals toward which conflict is directed.

In their most basic form, racial differences constitute a basis for what has been termed "ascriptive" or "trait" cleavage.[15] This is distinguished from "attitudinal" or "behavioral" cleavage by its high visibility, permanence, and intensity. Many social scientists deal with ascriptive cleavages in the context

---

[14] Edward Shils, "Color, The Universal Intellectual Community, and the Afro-Asian Intellectual," *Daedalus* (Spring 1967), 279.

[15] Douglas Rae and Michael Taylor, *The Analysis of Political Cleavages* (London: Yale University Press, 1970), p. 1.

of pluralism, since these cleavages become institutionalized, producing distinct patterns of political, social, and cultural organization. Leo Kuper and M. G. Smith define pluralism as "a social structure characterized by fundamental discontinuities and cleavages and a cultural complex based on systematic institutional diversity."[16] Van den Berghe suggests that plural societies are characterized by

1. Relative absence of value consensus
2. Relative presence of cultural heterogeneity
3. Relative presence of conflict between the significant corporate groups
4. Relative autonomy between parts of the social system
5. Relative importance of coercion and economic interdependence as bases of social integration.[17]

Pluralism suggests that fundamental divisions characterize multiracial or multiethnic societies, but it does not specify the form of relationship between the distinct racial groups. A typology based on different patterns of stratification provides such a specification, suggesting how the various groups are related to one another. Donald Horowitz suggests that racial or ethnic differentiation may be viewed in terms of horizontal or vertical patterns of stratification.[18] A vertically stratified society is usually associated with race relations founded on slavery, as in the United States and Brazil, or on total conquest, as in South Africa and colonial areas. *Vertical stratification* here refers to a structure of inequality manifested by differences in prestige, power, and economic status, and by rituals or modes of behavior that reflect a pattern of subordinate-superordinate relations.

On the other hand, "parallel ethnic structures" exist in horizontally stratified societies, each structure with its own criteria of stratification and no formal presumption of subordination or superordination. Max Weber characterized horizontally stratified societies as forms of "ethnic coexistence."[19] This designation implies that two or more distinct racial or ethnic groups coexist when there is no subordinate-superordinate relationship, when no racial group formally claims or seeks to institutionalize superiority over others.

Race or ethnicity may provide the basis for either vertical or horizontal patterns of stratification. To this extent race functions like any other ethnic trait. The crucial difference with stratification systems based on race is that unlike other forms of ethnic stratification, they are virtually immutable. Van

    [16] Leo Kuper and M. G. Smith, *Pluralism in Africa* (Berkeley: University of California Press, 1969), p. 27.
    [17] Van den Berghe, *op. cit.,* p. 35.
    [18] Donald L. Horowitz, "Three Dimensions of Ethnic Politics," *World Politics* 23, 2 (1971), 232–244.
    [19] H. H. Gerth and C. Wright Mills, eds., *From Max Weber: Essays in Sociology* (New York: Harcourt, Brace, Jovanovich, 1958), cited in Horowitz, *op. cit.,* p. 233.

den Berghe notes that "racial stratification results in nearly impermeable caste systems more easily than other ethnic traits."[20] The cleavage lines are highly visible and permanently drawn, and will therefore be much more resistant to change than in cases where other ethnic characteristics give rise to such systems.

The pattern of racial stratification in existence in a society affects political life in several crucial respects and is the basic determinant of the pattern of race relations and the manner in which race affects political life. In one comparative study, Barbara and Victor Ferkiss examine the impact on politics of two racially ordered cases of horizontal stratification—Trinidad and Guyana. Both societies exhibit political systems dominated by racial cleavages between blacks (creoles) and Indians. During the preindependence period, extensive biracial cooperation existed as both groups coalesced within a single party. However, in spite of efforts to maintain the semblance of a nonracial approach to politics, the political parties have become organized almost entirely along racial lines since independence and when competition becomes intense at election time, a "racially-based 'them or us' is prominent on the hustings, especially at the local level."[21] These two societies may be considered horizontally stratified because although they are divided along racial lines, the members of neither racial group have been observed to assert, and/or seek to establish, superiority over the other.

The two racial groups possess some separate but parallel social and political organizations and equivalent access to the political system. Their political activities stress competition for patronage, general economic interests, cultural interests, the desirability of a positive self-image, and the need for physical and psychic security.[22] Conflict is not excluded from horizontally stratified societies but is limited as groups compete for specified goods, and the goal of domination is absent or far removed from serious contemplation by most members of the societies. Furthermore, as Donald Rothchild observes, there is the likelihood that mechanisms for ethnic or racial balancing may develop in these societies. These may include a federal pattern of political organization, proportional representation in the principal political institutions, and conceivably coalition government, designed in each case to ensure to each group a level of involvement consistent with its size in the society.

This competitive style of politics in horizontally stratified societies is in sharp contrast to the characteristics of vertically stratified societies. Vertical stratification is common though not exclusive to societies with black-white populations. In almost all instances the white population is dominant regardless of the proportional size of the black population. To varying degrees the

[20] Van den Berghe, *op. cit.,* p. 27.
[21] Barbara and Victor Ferkiss, "Race and Politics in Trinidad and Guyana," *World Affairs* **134,** 1 (Summer 1971), 5.
[22] *Ibid.,* p. 7.

vertical character of a stratification system reflects white claims to racial superiority; whites monopolize positions and resources of the political system and limit or altogether exclude blacks. Such a political system has as its primary task preservation of the superordinate-subordinate pattern of relations. Thus while in horizontally stratified societies the major social groups compete for specific values, the focus of political activity in vertically stratified societies is the pattern of social organization. Members of the subordinate racial group(s) have change in their subordinate status as their primary political objective.

Thus far we have attempted to distinguish between two basic types of multiracial societies. In one, political institutions reflect racial cleavages and racial groups compete for limited objectives, but there is no attempt at dominance by one group. In the other, there is a relationship characterized by dominance by one group over others, and political life is marked by protracted conflict over the structure of society. This classification of societies as horizontally and vertically stratified is not altogether satisfactory, because it does not accommodate all of the many significant differences observable between these societies. However, it provides a starting point for a broad comparison of the politics of these societies. Furthermore, it facilitates observation of some fundamental ways in which race affects the character of political life.

Although both types of systems are of interest to us, we will here focus on the *vertically stratified* society. Horowitz expects that vertically stratified societies will be less stable than horizontally stratified ones unless stability is maintained by application of increasing levels of coercive power by a government controlled by the superordinate group. Conflict, perceived and/or active, between the subordinate and superordinate groups is the essence of politics in these societies. In other words, in societies that are vertically stratified on the basis of race, politics is primarily concerned with the struggle for fundamental social change and resistance to such change. A comparative study of race and politics may therefore fruitfully focus on this conflict.

The conflict flowing from vertically stratified forms of social organization is protracted and many-faceted, but it is possible to proceed by focusing on the most visible forms of conflict—for example, violent racial conflict. The focus on conflict is appropriate not only because of its centrality for political life, but because it facilitates consideration of those structures, processes, and strategies that are most consequential for resisting or inducing change in race relations.

## Violence and the Struggle for Change in the United States and South Africa

The United States and the Republic of South Africa are both vertically stratified societies in which basic cleavage lines are based on race. In both countries the black population occupies a subordinate status, and the white population is superordinate. This is the case in the United States, where the black population is a numerical minority (no more than 11 percent of the population) and in South Africa where it constitutes a large majority (approximately 65 percent). The two societies differ in several very important ways, one of which is with respect to the rigidity of the cleavage lines.

In the United States, the cleavage lines initially drawn by the institution of slavery have persisted but in considerably modified form, having yielded to the steady attacks of the subordinate group, often with the government's assistance. As a consequence, the more visible rituals and symbols of black subordination have been removed gradually, resulting in a loose stratification system. In South Africa the cleavage between the two groups has steadily deepened as government, by a complex array of laws and regulations, has vigorously intensified the subordination of the nonwhite population. This formal and elaborate system of black subordination reflected in total segregation, economic exploitation, and almost total exclusion of blacks from the political system in South Africa is known as *apartheid*. The pattern of structured inequality manifested in sharp differences with respect to prestige or social status, political influence, and economic status is thus apparent in both societies, but to substantially different degrees.

In both societies a central issue in political life is the effort of the subordinate group to achieve far-reaching changes in the social structure. The principal objective of the subordinate groups in the two societies is similar—achievement of what black South Africans call a "nonracial society" and what black Americans term "racial equality" or "first-class citizenship." In neither society is this goal shared by all members of the subordinate group. Aspirations toward some form of racial separation have been voiced in both societies by small but rapidly growing sectors of the subordinate groups.[23]

Violence has been a prominent part of the struggle for change in both societies, particularly since the first decade of this century, when determined, organized efforts for change became prominent aspects of domestic life. Several observers within and outside the country have written about the harshness of black subordination in South Africa and have speculated about the likelihood of violent upheavals within the near future. This speculation has been heightened by the many episodes of violence experienced in the United States during the last decade, by the rapid achievement of independence by African states and especially by the impressive achievements of the liberation armies fighting to end Portuguese occupation in Angola and Mozambique. Van den Berghe suggests, for example, that "once the colonial territories north of South Africa have achieved their independence, the

---

[23] In South Africa the Pan Africanist Congress has apparently rejected the idea of coexistence with whites and advocates instead establishment of a black republic. In the United States, such disparate groups as the Congress of Racial Equality, The Nation of Islam, and the Republic of New Africa are exponents of separatism.

collapse of white domination in that country (South Africa) will be imminent."[24] Although there is a scarcity of information on racial violence and on the attitudes of the subordinate group toward violence in South Africa, it is possible to identify some broad parallels between the United States and South Africa with respect to the genesis, character, and effectiveness of racial violence in the two societies.

### The Genesis of Racial Violence

In spite of its widespread occurrence, racial violence has not been extensively studied outside the United States. Even after a decade of frenzied investigations from a variety of perspectives, the phenomenon within the United States is not thoroughly or comprehensively explained. Although social scientists now generally agree that racial violence is not merely the irresponsible behavior of social misfits, we are still without satisfactory answers to such basic questions as "what conditions precipitate racial violence?" In part, at least, this lack of understanding results from the tendency of investigators to examine specific demographic, political, or ecological characteristics of communities in which racial violence occurs. These studies have not only been inconclusive, but have encouraged a tendency to view racial violence as a peculiarly American phenomenon growing out of specific conditions of life in urban America. As a consequence, the explanatory hypotheses generated from these studies may not be applicable to essentially the same phenomena occurring in a different social setting.

In view of the prevalence and pervasiveness of racial violence, the theoretical models derived from broader studies of civil violence may provide a basis for a comparative analysis of racial violence. Ted Gurr has developed one theoretical model of political violence that can be helpful in explaining racial violence. The essence of the model is that relative deprivation, defined as the actors' perceptions of discrepancy between their value expectations (the goods and conditions of life to which they believe they are justifiably entitled) and their value capabilities (the amount of these goods and capabilities they are able to get and keep), induce frustration and, consistent with the causal relationship postulated by the frustration-aggression hypothesis, results in aggressive behavior.[25]

Gurr's model appears applicable primarily to violence at the individual level. That is, to individuals frustrated for any reason may be expected under certain circumstances to respond violently. Gurr notes, however, that it is possible "to identify events and patterns of conditions that are likely to be viewed as unjust deprivation by groups or some classes in society." He

[24] Van den Berghe, *South Africa: A Study in Conflict* (Middletown, Conn.: Wesleyan University Press, 1965), p. 262.

[25] Ted Gurr, "A Causal Model of Civil Strife: A Comparative Analysis Using New Indices," *American Political Science Review* 42, 4 (1968), 1104.

suggests that whether research ought to focus on "conditions collectively defined as frustrating, or directly on perceived deprivation is an operational question whose answer depends on the researcher's interest and resources."[26] Given our concern here with a collectivity—in this case a subordinate racial group—we might utilize the same model by viewing members of a subordinate racial group as aggregate victims of what one group of scholars term "systemic frustration." They identify three components of systemic frustration: (1) frustration interfering with the attainment and maintenance of social goals, aspirations, and values; (2) frustration simultaneously experienced by members of social aggregates and hence also complex social systems; and (3) frustration that is produced within the structure and processes of social systems.[27]

Gurr's model does not specify a deprivation-producing agent. The Feierabends and Nesvold propose that systemic frustration may stem from "specific characteristics of social change." I propose that racial violence is precipitated by systemic frustration, which is in turn a consequence of subordination in a vertically stratified society. A racially based vertical stratification system is the frustration-inducing agent. A subordinate status in such a society, assigned on the basis of race, renders unachievable the goals perceived as legitimate by the subordinate group, creating conditions to which racial violence is a response.

Although broad societal characteristics have not frequently been adduced in exploring the geneses of racial violence, a few social scientists have pointed to their potential significance as explanatory factors. One early study of race and minority riots concluded that

> Violence is more likely to occur when the minority group is not content to accept the assignment of low rank from the so-called majority group and when it attempts a redefinition of the situation which will bring about assimilation or at least equal status without assimilation.[28]

Similarly, Allen Grimshaw observes that "in societies where the boundaries of ethnic membership are coterminous with those of socially enforced patterns of subordination and dominance, the intensity of social violence is likely to be greater."[29]

[26] Ted Gurr, "Psychological Factors in Civil Violence," in Ivo K. and Rosalind Feierabend and Ted Gurr, eds., *Anger, Violence and Politics* (Englewood Cliffs, N.J.: Prentice-Hall, 1972), p. 38.

[27] Ivo K. Feierabend, Rosalind Feierabend, and Betty Nesvold, "Social Change and Political Violence: Cross-National Patterns," in Robert Graham and Ted Gurr, eds., *The History of Violence in America* (New York: Bantam, 1970), pp. 635–636.

[28] H. O. Dahlke, "Race and Minority Riots—A Study in the Typology of Violence," *Social Forces* 30 (1952), 420.

[29] Allen Grimshaw, "Three Views of Urban Violence: Civil Disturbance, Racial Revolt, Class Assault," *American Behavioral Scientist* 11, 4 (1968), 2.

Focus on the general structure of society as a source of common group experiences associated with violent racial conflict is particularly useful for comparative purposes because (1) it encompasses, but is not limited to, the specific manifestations of subordinate status in a single society; (2) it is unaffected by the size of the subordinate groups so that whether the subordinate group is a numerical majority or minority is of little relevance to the model; and (3) it shifts our focus from the highly changeable symptoms of a malady to the malady itself.

### The Pattern of Racial Violence in the United States and South Africa

By racial violence I mean all destructive or disruptive group activities by members of one racial group against the person and/or property of another racial group, or against the agents and property of a government perceived as representing the interests or will of one of the groups.[30] Violence is therefore racial when participants are distinguishable primarily on the basis of race and are motivated by forces or circumstances perceived as associated with race. This includes not only "private" group acts of violence but also those by agents of the state, because the performance of police, soldiers, and other agents of the state appears to be inextricably linked with racial violence wherever it occurs.

Although both the United States and South Africa exhibit traditions of sporadic racial violence, the level of violence as measured by the number of reported incidents has been much higher in the United States than in South Africa. This is especially true of the years since 1963. A reliable count of these incidents is obviously extremely difficult to obtain but one study reports a total of 76 reported episodes of racial violence of the kind described above within the United States between 1913 and 1963,[31] while there were only about 35 such episodes in South Africa between 1910 and 1961. Another study reports a total of 239 instances of racial violence in the United States between 1963 and 1968,[32] while in South Africa there were only five such incidents during the same period. It should be noted, however, that between 1961 and 1963 a sharp increase in "conspiratorial-type" race violence occurred in South Africa.[33] More than 200 such incidents, almost all very small and inconsequential, were reported by the government.

[30] We are primarily concerned with collective or group violence; nevertheless, we are aware that this excludes from consideration the countless individual, daily acts of violence, such as abuse by the police, lynchings, and murders, that are directly and indirectly related to race. For a thorough survey of this type of violence in South Africa, see A. Sachs, *South Africa: The Violence of Apartheid* (London: International Defense and Aid Fund, 1969).
[31] Stanley Lieberson and Arnold Silverman, "The Precipitants and Underlying Conditions of Race Riots," *American Sociological Review* 30 (1965), 888–889.
[32] Bryan T. Downs, "Social and Political Characteristics of Riot Cities: A Comparative Study," in James Geschwender, *The Black Revolt* (Englewood Cliffs, N.J.: Prentice-Hall, 1971), p. 336.
[33] Government records introduced in the South African Supreme Court detailed 193 such acts between October 1961 and June 1963. See Edward Feit, *Urban Revolt in*

We may compare patterns of racial violence in the United States and South Africa by utilizing a classification suggested by Morris Janowitz in a study of racial violence in the United States.[34] Janowitz identifies three broad types of racial violence—communal riots, commodity riots, and political riots. He describes communal riots as ecologically based racial clashes at the boundaries of expanding black neighborhoods. They result in large part from the desire of the superordinate group to protect its status from real or imagined assaults by the subordinate group. Movement of blacks into the urban job market and into hitherto all-white residential neighborhoods was a particularly prominent inducement to communal riots in the United States, especially in the years immediately after World War I.

This form of racial violence has been almost nonexistent in South Africa because government, from which the subordinate group has been effectively excluded, reinforced and defended the lines separating subordinate and superordinate groups. Since the massive labor conflict (the Rand Revolt) of 1922, stimulated in part by white fears of losing jobs to blacks, the government has excluded blacks by legislation from portions of the labor market in which they would represent a source of competition for white workers. Similarly, with legislation like the Native Trust and Land Act of 1936 and subsequent amendments and, in urban areas, the Group Areas Act of 1957, government has removed the possibility of black intrusion into white residential communities as permanent residents. Thus, while communal riots served to keep the subordinate group "in its place" in the United States, government undertook that task in South Africa. The Durban riots of January 13–16, 1949, in which Africans rioted against Indians, resulting in the death of 137 Africans and Indians, represent the only major episode of communal rioting during the period under review.

Commodity riots are instances of racial violence in which hostility is directed by the subordinate group at the agents and symbols of the superordinate group. This type of riot dominated the post-World War II scene in the United States, reaching its peak in the massive urban upheavals between 1964 and 1967. Almost all major episodes of racial violence in South Africa have resembled the commodity riots, and such riots reached their peak in South Africa between 1959–1961. Commodity riots in both countries have been primarily ghetto riots, generally far removed from white communities. Invariably they have been spontaneous upheavals precipitated by specific governmental action or by action of the police. These characteristics with respect to urban violence in the United States have been well documented. In South Africa, the Cato Manor riot is representative.

The Cato Manor riot began on June 18, 1959, when about 200 African women armed with sticks attacked the Cato Manor Beer Hall, chasing out

---

*South Africa, 1960–1964* (Evanston, Ill.: Northwestern University Press, 1971), pp. 325–345.

[34] Morris Janowitz, "Patterns of Collective Racial Violence," in Graham and Gurr, *op. cit.*, pp. 412–444.

male African patrons and destroying Beer Hall facilities after a police raid on "illegal" liquor stills operated by the women. Two days of violence ensued in which large-scale arson and looting of municipal buildings, beer halls, and buses occurred, and in which 4 persons died and 24 were wounded. Peace was restored in the Cato Manor area only after extensive police action and the arrest of several hundred riot participants.[35]

In South Africa, riots of the commodity type also took place outside the major urban areas as Africans in rural, tribal communities occasionally responded violently to policies implemented by the government. For example, as news of the Cato Manor riot spread to some rural areas of Natal Province, violent outbursts occurred in several of these areas, resulting in considerable destruction of property. By August 21 an estimated 10,000 persons, mostly women, had participated in the riots, and about 624 had been sentenced to prison terms for their role in the incidents.[36] Reviewing the pattern of racial violence in South Africa, Leo Kuper notes

> Characteristically, race riots in South Africa involve the police and Africans, since the police are the main agents of racial aggression, to which African reaction is likely to be the destruction of government and municipal property in the locations (the segregated, often fenced-off areas of living to which urban Africans are confined) and sometimes of schools and churches.[37]

As spontaneous, unplanned episodes triggered by specific experiences associated with the subordinate status of the participants, commodity riots are often not explicitly political events with clearly defined objectives. Most participants in commodity riots do not immediately perceive their actions or demands in clearly political terms. Those Africans who emerged as spokesmen during the Cato Manor riot, for example, confined their stated grievances to the conduct of the police and to the government's liquor policies. Official assessments later reflected the view that the underlying cause of the riots was poor wages. In the United States, too, only a relatively small percentage of the participants in the riots regarded them from the outset as political events.

Although in the two societies there are clear differences in the specific circumstances surrounding the occurrence of this form of racial violence and the characteristics of the communities in which it occurred, participants in racial violence in both societies have in common an apparent sense of frustration with their subordinate status. Assessing one outbreak of commodity rioting in Natal in 1960, an African spokesman noted of the riot: "It is the voice of oppressed people who have no other means of voicing their grievances before the government of the land. . . . I lay the blame at the door of the multiplicity of laws and their regulations, which are harshly adminis-

---

[35] See Leo Kuper, "Rights and Riots in Natal," *Africa South* 1, 2 (1965), 20–26.

[36] M. A. Jaspar, "South Africa, 1960–1961: The Transition from Passive Resistance to Rebellion," *Science and Society* 25, 2 (1961), 102–106.

[37] Leo Kuper, *An African Bourgeoisie* (New Haven, Conn.: Yale University Press, 1965), p. 13.

tered by men who show no sympathy. Men and women of urban areas and rural areas suffer and feel the same."[38] T. M. Tomlinson comes to a somewhat similar assessment of recent racial violence in the United States:

> What produces riots is the shared agreement by most Negro Americans that their lot in life is unacceptable, coupled with the view by a significant minority that riots are a legitimate and productive mode of protest. What is unacceptable about Negro life does not vary much from city to city and the differences in Negro life from city to city are irrelevant. The unifying feature is the consensus that Negroes have been misused by whites. . . .[39]

Although lacking in clearly defined political objectives, commodity riots have important political implications. As a type of political violence, these incidents are reflective of the frustration felt by the involved group and require response from government, which must either remove the source of frustration or intensify subordination by application of increased coercive power. As one scholar suggests, in the face of this kind of violence "the prevailing consensus of interest and power groups must choose between social-economic-political adjustments and the unpromising course of infinite escalation and counter-escalation."[40]

Not all racial violence is spontaneous and unplanned. Under certain conditions violence may come to be perceived as an efficacious instrument for bringing about desired change. This has been the case in both the United States and South Africa. In the two societies, direct commitment to violence as an instrument of change came after extensive application of other, non-violent techniques. Janowitz observes that in the United States racial violence began to take on an explicitly political character after 1967, when it became more premeditated and instrumental. In South Africa the shift to this form of violence came in mid-1961, after the government had banned all protest organizations and prohibited virtually all forms of action designed to induce change. This planned, explicitly political violence in which a very limited number of participants undertake such acts as political assassinations, small-scale terrorism, and sabotage or guerrilla activities is not entirely separable from the spontaneous outbursts of violence we have just described. It is clearly different, however, coming as a last resort after other kinds of attempts to induce change have failed or proved inadequate.

### Nonviolent Forms of Conflict—Prelude to Violence

In both societies violence, especially conspiratorial forms, may be viewed as the culmination of a process of steadily intensifying struggle for

---

[38] Quoted in Kuper, *op. cit.,* p. 19.

[39] T. M. Tomlinson, "The Development of a Riot Ideology Among Urban Negroes," *American Behavioral Scientist* 2, 4 (1968), 29.

[40] H. L. Nieburg, "Violence, Law, and the Social Process," *American Behavioral Scientist* 2, 4 (1968), 17.

change. In the United States the evolution of this struggle, from the discreet litigative efforts of the National Association for the Advancement of Colored People (NAACP) to the strident advocacy of liberation by any means necessary, has been widely known and is further examined below. In South Africa an almost identical pattern of gradual movement toward the deliberate, instrumental use of violence can be observed by tracing briefly a few high points in the struggle.

As is the case for black Americans, three distinct phases, each marked by a reliance on a particular strategy for securing change in the status of Africans, are discernible in South Africa. The first phase began in 1912 with the organization of the African National Congress (ANC), originally called the South African Native National Congress (SANNC), only three years after a similar organization, the NAACP, came into being in the United States. Both organizations pursued efforts for change through reliance on the techniques of persuasion and negotiation or bargaining. Like the NAACP, the ANC operated on the premise that the political system could be induced by these methods to initiate change voluntarily. Unlike the NAACP, which focused its activities with substantial success on an autonomous judiciary, the ANC was compelled to rely on periodic petitions to the South African and British governments. Failing in these efforts, it finally concentrated on participation in the Natives' Representative Council, a powerless advisory body established in 1936 when the few blacks possessing the franchise in Cape Town were removed from the regular voters role. These efforts by the ANC failed to secure any improvement in the status of Africans. Reviewing the activities of the Natives' Representative Council, which was finally abolished in 1951, one observer concludes that "it is difficult to recall a single important reform introduced as a result of the good advice annually tendered by this 'advisory' body."[41]

By 1949 several crucial developments compelled the ANC to discard its strategy of persuasion of, and cooperation with, the South African government and move toward a more vigorous program of action. The organization never managed to achieve a large or unified following, and its record of total failure to achieve its objectives created severe internal strains, prompting major reevaluation of strategy. Furthermore, World War II unleashed waves of new aspirations among the oppressed peoples of the world, and black South Africans found new bases for aspiring to change in their subordinate status. Of greatest significance for Africans was the change of government in 1948 when the Afrikaner-dominated Nationalist Party gained power. Afrikaners moved swiftly to solidify their power, to eliminate blacks from any form of access to the political system, and to intensify greatly the subordination of nonwhites.

[41] Julius Lewin, *Politics and Law in South Africa* (London: 1963), p. 36; quoted in Feit, *op. cit.,* p. 13.

In the face of these powerful new forces, the ANC launched a program of nonviolent direct action against, or resistance to, further subordination. Through the use of civil disobedience—boycotts and strikes—it attempted to force change in the policies of government. The Defiance Campaign of 1952 represents one of the highlights of this effort. Along with other nonwhites, large numbers of Africans attempted to force repeal of the Pass Laws, the Group Areas Act, and the Suppression of Communism Act by deliberately disobeying these laws. When the campaign ended, approximately 8,500 persons had been arrested and imprisoned in the effort. The Alexandria bus boycott of 1957 and the potato boycott of 1959 are other instances of nonwhite efforts to induce change. These efforts reached their peak with the tragic massacre of 69 Africans at Sharpeville on March 21, 1960, after which the African National Congress and its offshoot of the previous year, the Pan Africanist Congress (PAC), were banned. The final act in this phase of the struggle came in May 1961 when the government responded to a proposed "stay-at-home" strike by Africans by calling out the army to crush it.

These efforts by blacks in South Africa paralleled the nonviolent protest activities of black Americans spearheaded by the Southern Christian Leadership Conference and the Student Nonviolent Coordinating Committee between 1957–1964. Unlike the case in the United States, however, the South African effort ended in complete failure about a decade after it began. Edward Feit, one of the leading authorities on the ANC, states that "when all ANC campaigns up to 1960 are accounted for, the debit side of the balance sheet far exceeds the credit side. In no case had the ANC been able to induce the government to change its course by one iota."[42] It is against this background of failure and the ruthless intervention of government that the ANC and PAC committed themselves to planned political violence. At the Revonia trial in 1963, Nelson Mandela, one of the leaders of the ANC arrested by the South African government, summarized the situation thus:

> We of the ANC always stood for a nonracial democracy, and we shrank from any action which might drive the races further apart than they already were. But the hard facts were that fifty years of nonviolence had brought the African people nothing but more and more repressive legislation, and fewer and fewer rights. It may not be easy for this Court to understand, but it is a fact that for a long time the people had been talking of violence—of the day when they would fight the white man and win back their country—and we, the leaders of the ANC, had nevertheless always prevailed upon them to avoid violence and to pursue peaceful methods. When some of us discussed this in May and June of 1961, it could not be denied that our policy to achieve a nonracial state by nonviolence had achieved nothing.[43]

[42] Feit, *op. cit.*, p. 25.
[43] Nelson Mandela, *No Easy Walk to Freedom* (New York: Basic Books, 1965), p. 168.

With the suppression of existing organizations and the decimation of their leadership through mass arrests by the South African government, new organizations emerged among Africans to pursue a campaign of conspiratorial violence. On December 16, 1961, Umkonto we Sizwe (Spear of the Nation), an outgrowth of the ANC, announced its existence with several widely separated acts of sabotage. Somewhat earlier, POQO (Pure), allegedly affiliated with the PAC, launched its own campaign of sabotage and terror. For almost two years, between 1961 and 1963, the two organizations remained daring if somewhat naive instruments of opposition, symbols of resistance to subordination, and for many a small source of hope.[44]

When the organizations were finally crushed by South African authorities, with mass arrests, executions, and imprisonment of leaders and members of the organizations, it had made little significant impact on the government and clearly no progress in effecting change. Rather, its efforts resulted in further refinements of the formidable instrument of subordination and oppression referred to as *apartheid* in South Africa. Planned political violence among black Americans, such as that associated with the Black Panthers, fared no better because of both the gross ineptness of the effort despite far more favorable conditions than in South Africa, and the inability of its proponents to secure the support of more than a minute portion of the black population.

## Some Bases of Differences in the Two Societies

This exploratory comparative effort is not aimed primarily at providing a conceptual framework for the examination of race and politics in the United States which follows, but it is instructive in some important respects. First, by identifying and clarifying the pattern of subordinate-superordinate relations which characterizes black-white relations in the society and the basic thrust of black political activities in relationship to this status-ordering, it suggests an underlying consistency and sense of direction to black political activities. Second, although it recognizes and emphasizes important differences between the present conditions of life for black Americans and Africans in South Africa, the study attempts to emphasize the fundamental similarity in status of the nonwhite populations in these societies as well as virtually all other societies of similar racial composition. Third, brief comparison of the struggle in both societies to achieve fundamental change in the pattern of race relations permits us to identify some of those characteristics of the societies that facilitate or obstruct change.

[44] One of the most extensive and perceptive studies of these organizations and their activities is that by Feit, *op. cit.* See also Fatima Meer, "African Nationalism—Some Inhibiting Factors," in Heribert Adam, *South Africa: Sociological Perspectives* (London: Oxford University Press, 1971), pp. 148–151. See also a review of the background and goals of these activities in Mandela, *op. cit.,* pp. 162–189.

In both societies the political life of the black population is shaped by its subordinate status and by the desire to alter that status in spite of the severe constraints under which it operates. Black Americans have managed to secure elimination of most of the symbols and rituals of subordination and achieve almost full access to the political system even though decades of varying degrees of exclusion from political life continues to adversely affect their style of politics. In sharp contrast black South Africans remain victims of total and ruthless subordination and continue to experience complete exclusion from political life—this in spite of the remarkably similar approaches that the two groups have taken in their efforts to induce change.

The vast differences in responses to the struggle for change in the two societies are important for our study. They require us to identify the forces that facilitate change in one society and obstruct it in the other, and they help us to identify those conditions or circumstances that made change possible in the United States even in the face of a still widespread racism. In accounting for these different responses, we need to examine differences within the subordinate and superordinate groups as well as differences in the political systems of the two countries.

First, difference in the relative size of the two racial groups in each society contributes to different outcomes of the struggle. White Americans have been able to make concessions to black demands because such concessions do not appear to threaten their superordinate status. As less than 12 percent of the total population, black Americans are not likely to alter the structure of society fundamentally even when they are given full opportunities to participate in the political system. On the contrary, white South Africans, as a minority in that society, perceive virtually any concession to demands by blacks as a threat to the highly valued status quo and indeed as a threat to their survival. The significance of population size for race relations has been demonstrated in some parts of the United States. Donald Matthews and James Prothro found in their study of Southern politics that where the black population in a community was small, obstacles to political participation were not formidable, but they became so as population size increased.[45]

Second, in the United States change has been facilitated by deep divisions within the superordinate group. The North-South cleavage that culminated in the Civil War and continued through reconstruction was responsible for first bringing large numbers of blacks into the political arena as black voters were needed to strengthen the position of one group against the other. In spite of linguistic and cultural differences between Afrikaners and other Europeans, there have been no such conflicts among white South Africans. In fact, aside from minor differences regarding specific aspects of the apartheid policy, there is considerable cohesiveness regarding the vertical structure of the society. There has therefore been no need to bring portions

[45] Donald Matthews and James Prothro, *Negroes and the New Southern Politics* (New York: Harcourt Brace Jovanovich, 1966), pp. 115–120.

of the subordinate group into the political arena for the tactical advantage of one segment.

On the other hand, the subordinate group has been deeply divided in both societies and especially so in South Africa. Differences between Northern, urban blacks and more rural, Southern blacks—differences growing out of conflicting conceptions of the desirable goals and the techniques by which they ought to be pursued—have been formidable impediments to effective political action by black Americans. The divisions are much more complex and profound among black South Africans and seem to affect more directly their capacity for effective action to change their position in society. The many tribal divisions, the cleavage between urban and rural populations, and the formal, artificial divisions created by South Africa's apartheid policies have all contributed to the pathetic ineffectiveness of the group.

There are sharp differences in political attitudes and values that may be considered a third factor contributing to different outcomes in the two societies. Heribert Adam observes that protest and symbolic political violence have not been successful in South Africa because in that society there are no values considered applicable to blacks and whites alike and no functional public opinion to which appeals can be fruitfully directed.[46] The situation is substantially different in the United States, where the values reflected in the democratic creed have been universalized over time to include blacks. On the basis of these values, blacks have been able to appeal to an effective public opinion to which government, on various levels, has been forced to respond.

A final source of the different experiences of the two subordinate groups is the different type of political system in the two societies. A highly centralized parliamentary system in South Africa has proven less susceptible to pressures for change in race relations than the more decentralized one in the United States, where the executive, legislative, and judicial structures are autonomous and sometimes capable of responding separately to demands by blacks. The different international positions occupied by the two countries are also related to the kinds of responses they make to efforts for change. The prominent role of the United States in the international system, especially its assumed role as a custodian and exponent of democratic values, has rendered it highly vulnerable to external pressures for change. South Africa's limited role in the international system, on the other hand, permits it to be virtually impervious to external pressures.

[46] Heribert Adam, *Modernizing Racial Domination: South Africa's Political Dynamics* (Berkeley: University of California Press, 1971), p. 111.

## SELECTED BIBLIOGRAPHY

Berreman, Gerald D. "Caste in India and the United States." *American Journal of Sociology* 66 (September 1960), 120–127.

Beteille, André. "Race, Caste and Ethnic Identity." *International Social Science Journal* 23, 4 (1971), 519–535.

Blalock, H. M., Jr. "A Power Analysis of Racial Discrimination." *Social Forces* 39 (October 1960), 53–59.

Bowker, Gordon. "Interaction, Intergroup Conflict and Tension in the Context of Education." *International Social Science Journal* 23, 4 (1971), 536–547.

Coleman, James S. "Race Relations and Social Change." In Irwin Katz and Patricia Gurin, eds., *Race and the Social Sciences.* New York: Basic Books, 1969.

Coleman, Lee. "Race Relations and Developmental Change." *Social Forces* 46, 1 (September 1967), 1–8.

Gist, Noel, and Anthony Dworkin,. *The Blending of Races.* New York: Wiley, 1972.

Gluckman, Max. "New Dimensions of Change, Conflict and Settlement." *International Social Science Journal* 23, 4 (1971), 548–563.

Halperin, Manfred. *Applying a New Theory of Human Relations to the Comparative Study of Racism.* Denver: University of Colorado, 1969.

Henderson, Donald. "Minority Response and the Conflict Model." *Phylon* 25, 1 (Spring 1964), 18–26.

Kuper, Leo. "Political Change in Plural Societies: Problems in Racial Pluralism." *International Social Science Journal* 23, 4 (1971), 594–607.

Larsen, Knud, S. Schwendiman, and David Stimson. "Change in Attitude Toward Negroes Resulting from Exposure to Congruent and Noncongruent Attitudinal Objects." *Journal of Peace Research* 2 (1969), 157–161.

Lévi-Strauss, Claude. "Race and Culture." *International Social Science Journal* 23, 4 (1971), 608–625.

Lieberson, Stanley. "A Societal Theory of Race and Ethnic Relations." *American Sociological Review* 28 (December 1961), 902–909.

Morgan, William, and Terry Nichols Clark. "The Causes of Racial Disorders: A Grievance-Level Explanation." *American Sociological Review* 38, 5 (October 1973), 611–624.

Newman, William. *American Pluralism: A Study of Minority Groups and Social Theory.* New York: Harper & Row, 1973.

Osborne, Richard H. *The Biological and Social Meaning of Race.* San Francisco: Freeman, 1971.

Pavlak, Thomas J. "Social Class, Ethnicity, and Racial Prejudice." *The Public Opinion Quarterly* 37 (Summer 1973), 225–231.

Rex, John. *Race, Colonialism and the City.* London: Routledge & Kegan Paul, 1973.

Rinder, Irwin. "Minority Orientations: An Approach to Intergroup Relations Theory Through Social Psychology." *Phylon* 26, 1 (Spring 1965), 5–17.

Singer, L. "Ethnogenesis and Negro-Americans Today." *Social Research* **29**, 4 (Winter 1962), 419–432.
Van der Zanden, James W. "Sociological Studies of American Blacks." *The Sociological Quarterly* **14** (Winter 1973), 32–52.
Wilson, William. *Power, Racism and Privilege.* New York: Macmillan, 1972.
Witton, Ron. "Australia and Apartheid: The Ties That Bind." *Australian Quarterly* **45** (June 1973), 18–31.

# Blacks and the Political System: The Problem of Subordination in a Democratic Polity

"Away back in the days of bondage they thought to see in one divine event the end of all doubt and disappointment; few men ever worshipped Freedom with half such unquestioning faith as did the American Negro for two centuries. To him, so far as he thought and dreamed, slavery was indeed the sum of all villainies, the cause of all sorrow, the root of all prejudice; Emancipation was the key to a promised land of sweeter beauty than ever stretched before the eyes of wearied Israelites. In song and exhortation swelled one refrain—Liberty; in his tears and curses the God he implored had Freedom in his right hand. At last it came—suddenly, fearfully, like a dream. With one wild carnival of blood and passion came the message in his own plaintive cadences:

> Shout, O children!
> Shout, you're free!
> For God has bought your liberty!

Years have passed away since then . . . and yet the swarthy spectre sits in its accustomed seat at the Nation's feast. In vain do we cry to this our vastest social problem:

> Take any shape but that, and my firm nerves
> Shall never tremble!

The Nation has not yet found peace from its sins; the freedman has not yet found in freedom his promised land. Whatever of good may have come in these years of change, the shadow of a deep disappointment rests upon the Negro people—a disappointment all the more bitter because the unattained ideal was unbounded save by the simple ignorance of a lowly people."

W. E. B. Du Bois
*The Souls of Black Folks*
(New York: Fawcett Publications, 1969), p. 18.

# Democratic Politics
# and Black Subordination

When Americans celebrate the Fourth of July they commemorate much more than the birth of another sovereign state. Firmly rooted in the lore of America is the conviction that they celebrate the birth of "modern democratic government." Precisely what democracy meant in this context was not entirely clear to the founders of the nation and even now remains somewhat murky. Motivated by the views of European political philosophers like John Locke, these early Americans attempted to fashion a system of government based upon two fundamental tenets: (1) The equality of individuals in the society as far as rights and obligations were concerned; and (2) the limited character of governmental power with respect to the individual. To a considerable extent these themes—equality and liberty—inspired and justified rebellion from Britain and have remained the central elements of the American political culture.

If, as Donald Devine suggests, political culture "is a historical system of widespread, fundamental, behavioral, political values actually held by system members,"[1] it is one of the profound ironies of history that a society deeply committed to these "democratic values" created and maintained the subordinate-superordinate structure we described in the preceding chapter. Such a pattern of social organization is obviously in sharp conflict with these democratic values, or what Gunnar Myrdal labelled the "democratic creed." Examination of the black political experience requires that we consider this peculiarity in American culture and try to determine what factors contributed to the development and persistence of this pattern of subordinate-superordinate relations between blacks and whites in the society.

This inquiry inevitably begins with the observation that "racism" also has been an important part of the American political culture. In this context, racism is not being used merely as another odious epithet, but as a concept

[1] Donald Devine, *The Political Culture of the United States* (Boston: Little, Brown, 1972), p. 17.

49

denoting a set of attitudes and beliefs that affect virtually all aspects of social relations. Pierre van den Berghe defines it as

> . . . any set of beliefs that organic, genetically transmitted differences (whether real or imagined) between human groups are intrinsically associated with the presence or absence of certain socially relevant abilities or characteristics, hence that such differences are a legitimate basis for invidious distinctions between groups socially defined as races.[2]

This racism is a pervasive and deep-rooted attitude that is at least as old as the first meetings of blacks and whites on the continent. To an extent it goes beyond the purely black-white encounter in America and can be viewed as part of a larger "disease" of cultural chauvinism which the colonists brought with them from Europe. Contempt by the colonists for the native Americans, and their early desire to Christianize them, and failing in that to exterminate them, reflects this larger cultural chauvinism. Racism can be viewed as the most visible and persistent manifestation of white America's cultural chauvinism. The extent to which it permeates American society is suggested by Joel Kovel's observation that "racism, far from being the simple delusion of a bigoted and ignorant minority, is a set of beliefs whose structure arises from the deepest levels of our lives—from the fabric of assumptions we make about the world, ourselves and others and from patterns of our fundamental social actions."[3]

Racism prompted creation and maintenance of the subordinate-superordinate structure of the society. It has had important and continuing consequences for the place accorded blacks in the political system, the distribution of goods and services by the system and, in some respects, the very structure of the political system itself. The extent of this impact is reflected throughout this survey of the black political experience but the distinction suggested by Carmichael and Hamilton between "individual" and "institutional" racism helps to clarify its total impact.[4] One involves overt acts of hostility by individual whites against blacks and their property, while the other involves the operation of established and respected institutions in society. Knowles and Prewitt further illustrates the two types by observing that

> The murder by Ku Klux Klan members and law enforcement officials of three civil rights workers in Mississippi was an act of individual racism. That the sovereign state of Mississippi refused to indict the killers was institutional racism. The individual act by racist

[2] Pierre L. van den Berghe, *Race and Racism* (New York: Wiley, 1967), p. 5.
[3] Joel Kovel, *White Racism: A Psychohistory* (New York: Pantheon, 1970), p. 3.
[4] Stokely Carmichael and Charles Hamilton, *Black Power: The Politics of Liberation in America* (New York: Random House, 1967), pp. 4–5.

bigots went unpunished in Mississippi because of policies, precedents, and practices that are an integral part of that state's legal institutions.[5]

Instances of institutional racism, of course, are not confined to a few states or to legal institutions but embrace virtually every level and area of political life in the society.

## The Origins of Black Subordination

The Kerner Commission reported in 1968 that American society was "rapidly moving toward two societies—one black, one white, separate and unequal."[6] This characterization of American society was appropriate then except for one important flaw. America is not in the process of *becoming* two societies; it has always been two separate and unequal societies. The structure of black subordination took shape with the gradual emergence of the institution of slavery within a relatively short time after the first European settlers appeared. Students of American slavery have identified several factors that encouraged its growth, the most prominent of them being economics. In addition to its economic aspect, slavery clearly served as an effective instrument of social control, providing a permanent, highly visible, legally supported mechanism for black subordination.

Not all blacks in America were slaves. In 1790 there were about 60,000 blacks in the country who were not slaves, and by 1860 this number had grown to over 485,000.[7] All blacks, however, both slaves and nonslaves, became victims of the status ordering provided by slavery. Nonslaves shared the subordinate status of the slave, thus these people, often called "free Negroes," were never really free but were trapped by their color in an offensive and humiliating form of subordination. This fact about American slavery was emphasized by John Woolman, an early Quaker opponent of the institution, who pointed out that the system of racial slavery was unique and particularly sinister because slavery had come to be associated with black color and liberty with white.[8]

Black subordination through the institution of slavery was legitimized by a complex array of laws and customs designed to ensure the dehumanization of all blacks or at least establish their inferiority to whites. The laws of the land defined slaves as "chattel" rather than "persons" and imposed severe

[5] Louis Knowles and Kenneth Prewitt, *Institutional Racism in America* (Englewood Cliffs, N.J.: Prentice-Hall, 1969), p. 4.

[6] *Report of the National Advisory Commission on Civil Disorders* (New York: Bantam, 1968), p. 1.

[7] Karl Taeuber and Alma Taeuber, "The Negro Population in the United States," in John P. Davis, ed., *The American Negro Reference Book* (Englewood Cliffs, N.J.: Prentice-Hall, 1966), pp. 98–100.

[8] Winthrop Jordan, *White over Black, American Attitudes Toward the Negro 1550–1812* (Baltimore, Md.: Penguin, 1968), p. 274.

constraints on every area of the lives of all blacks, notably marriage and family relations, movement and assembly, education, religious practice and interpersonal relations within and across racial lines. This form of institutionalized subordination persisted unimpeded until 1863, when the exigencies of civil strife forced its termination.

Societal attitudes and values are persistent. They are not swept away by hasty and half-hearted decrees; thus while the Civil War destroyed the formal institution of slavery, it left largely untouched the basic status-ordering of the society. Slavery was an efficient means of maintaining black subordination but it was not indispensable to the preservation of this condition. In fact, in the Northern states where slavery hardly existed, blacks remained thoroughly and effectively subordinated by law and custom as both slaveholders and nonslaveholders shared a common perception of them. Abraham Lincoln, later the president whose executive order freed the slaves and who often has been lauded as the liberator of black people, apparently reflected the general consensus with his commitment to preservation of the subordinate status of blacks as this assertion in 1858 suggests:

> I will say, then, that I am not, nor ever have been, in favor of bringing about in any way the social and political equality of the white and black races . . . and while they [blacks and whites] do remain together there must be the position of superior and inferior, and I as much as any other man am in favor of having the superior position assigned to the white race.[9]

Much has been written about the continuing consequences of slavery, such as its destruction of the social and cultural values of the black population and the deep psychological scars it has left on them,[10] but its most far-reaching impact on black political life may be the permanent relegation of blacks to a lower status than whites. So profound was its impact that many blacks for a long time perceived themselves as inferiors, and white Americans accepted as natural and desirable this subordinate status for blacks.

After the total abolition of slavery by the Thirteenth Amendment in 1865, new devices were utilized to maintain the subordinate status of blacks. The "Black Codes," a harsh series of laws passed immediately after the Civil War, virtually reimposed total slavery and were employed to maintain full control over the black population. Partly as a result of these laws, Congress intervened to restrain white Southerners in these excesses and to alleviate the hardship on blacks. Later terroristic activities by whites, a series of laws and constitutional changes, and the economic vulnerability of blacks combined to ensure their continued subordination. Over the years since the Civil War

[9] Quoted in Richard Hofstadter, *The American Political Tradition* (New York: Knopf, 1951), p. 116.
[10] Stanley Elkins, *Slavery* (Chicago: University of Chicago Press, 1968), pp. 81–139.

substantial changes have occurred in the techniques by which black subordination is maintained. Although the more visibly offensive aspects of this subordination have been gradually removed, the basic subordinate-superordinate structure remains.

The perception of blacks as belonging to a lower status than whites is so deeply a part of the cultural heritage of Americans that it continues to operate even though many whites appear to have intellectually rejected the old thesis of "Negro inferiority." A 1963 opinion survey by William Brink and Louis Harris revealed the deep continuing prejudice toward blacks among white Americans. Sixty-six percent of them still thought blacks were less ambitious than whites, 60 percent thought they smelled different, 55 percent thought they had looser morals, and 41 percent thought they wanted to live by handouts.[11] A more recent empirical study by Angus Campbell further documents this pattern of white attitudes and clarifies for us the character of these attitudes. He reports that

> White Americans are racist in degree. Some would like to keep the black man in his place, send him back to Africa if necessary. Most would not go that far but many would oppose legislation that would bring Negroes closer, especially into their neighborhoods. Some white people give verbal approval to equalitarian principles as they apply to race but they are disturbed by the pace of change in race relations which they see going on around them. Finally, there is a minority of the white population who seem to have no apparent racist orientation, who are sympathetic to the various aspects of the black protest, and in some cases contribute support to it.[12]

Black subordination in American society long has been viewed as inconsistent with the ringing assertion of the Declaration of Independence that "we hold these truths to be self-evident, that all men are created equal, that they are endowed by their Creator with certain unalienable Rights, that among these are Life, Liberty, and the Pursuit of Happiness." Well before the doctrines of liberty and equality fueled the sparks of rebellion among the American colonists, opponents of slavery like the Quakers emphasized the contradiction between the institution of slavery and the Christian beliefs of the European settlers.[13] By the time of the break with Britain in 1776, a group of philosophers, the environmentalists, went beyond the religious and moral arguments of the Quakers to stress the flagrant discrepancy between the stated commitment of Americans to liberty and equality and the realities of human bondage in the form of slavery.[14] With even greater passion, the

---

[11] William Brink and Louis Harris, *Negro Revolution in America* (New York: Simon & Schuster, 1963), pp. 140–141.

[12] Angus Campbell, *White Attitudes Toward Black People* (Ann Arbor, Mich.: Institute for Social Research, 1971), p. 156.

[13] Jordan, *op. cit.*, pp. 290–292.

[14] *Ibid.*, pp. 294–296.

"black abolitionists" utilized all of these arguments against the subordination of the race and urged not only an end to slavery but the granting of the full rights of free people to blacks. Frederick Douglass' celebrated Fourth of July oration succinctly expressed the abolitionist feeling:

> Americans! your republican politics, not less than your republican religion, are flagrantly inconsistent. You boast of your love of liberty, your superior civilization and your pure christianity, while the whole political power of the nation as embodied in the two great political parties, is solemnly pledged to support and perpetuate the enslavement of three million of your countrymen.[15]

These are essentially the same themes that have dominated the twentieth-century struggle for change in the subordinate status of black Americans. They were invoked by revolutionaries like Monroe Trotter at the turn of the century;[16] they were articulately formulated by Myrdal in 1945 in his description of white America's "moral dilemma." These themes were again echoed by Martin Luther King and the hosts of activists in the civil rights movement of the 1950s–1960s. The discrepancy between the bold commitments to liberty and equality and the subordination of blacks has been central to the black political experience, and has been a persistent theme in the struggle for change. This anomaly has been described more often than it has been explained. While we cannot here attempt to unravel the complex array of factors that have contributed to the persistence of black subordination in American society despite apparently conflicting beliefs, it is necessary and appropriate that we examine some of these factors. Among those that are of particular significance are (1) the peculiar circumstances surrounding the birth of the nation, (2) emergence of an ideology of racism, (3) the impact of democratic ideology and the democratization process, (4) the consequences of a federal system.

## The Birth of the Nation and Black Subordination

### The American Revolution and the Status of Blacks

The American revolution which resulted in the birth of an American nation is now one of the most celebrated revolutionary episodes of all time. The event is so thoroughly shrouded in myth and sentiment that it is rarely critically evaluated, and then hardly ever in terms of its implications for black people. However, some of the more careful students of the event provide important insights into why it left untouched the elaborate institution of

[15] Frederick Douglass, "Fourth of July Oration," in Herbert J. Storing, ed., *What Country Have I? Political Writings by Black Americans* (New York: St. Martin, 1970), p. 35.

[16] In this regard see John Brisbane, *The Black Vanguard* (Valley Forge, Pa.: Judson Press, 1970), pp. 35–44.

black subordination, slavery. They suggest that (1) in contrast to the gigantic social upheavals accompanying other revolutions, the American revolution was an extremely superficial one that did not fundamentally alter the society, and (2) the revolution was not guided by a potent and far-reaching set of new values but by limited economic self-interest. In a brief but insightful analysis, Pierre van den Berghe suggests that the break with Britain and the establishment of a republic were not the bold revolutionary steps most historians suggest. On the contrary, the much romanticized revolution "was in fact a movement of political emancipation by a section of the white settlers against England."[17]  The eminent American historian Daniel Boorstin also concludes that the American revolution was hardly a revolution, "it was one of the few conservative colonial rebellions of modern time."[18]

These analyses do not ignore the existence of genuinely revolutionary sentiment among the colonists; rather they suggest that those revolutionary sentiments did not give primary impetus to the revolution. This impetus came from the economic interests of a group of wealthy settlers. The revolutionaries such as Sam Adams and Tom Paine were vital instruments but were never the decisive influences on the revolution. The implications of these observations are significant. Because of the conservative and superficial character of the revolution, there was no major social upheaval that substantially altered the patterns of thought and practice that developed during the colonial era. In fact, the revolution left most Americans untouched and even indifferent to the event and their values and institutions remained intact.

One basic reason for the conservative character of the revolution and the superficiality of its impact is that the American colonies were not oppressed, "colonial societies." In sharp contrast to the experience of the nonwhite peoples of Asia, Africa and the Caribbean, they were not subjected to systematic exploitation by a "foreign power." The government holding final authority was distant, but not alien and was generally protective and benevolent rather than oppressive. The principal sources of discontent in the colonies were a few radical intellectuals and the Eastern merchants and traders. The genuinely oppressed, the slaves, were only peripheral to the revolt.

Instead of introducing a genuinely new equalitarian set of values, the much celebrated Declaration of Independence presented primarily a rationale for rebellion. Boorstin notes the sharp contrast between the United States Declaration of Independence and the French Declaration of the Rights of Man and the Citizen. The American document, he suggests, was "situation-specific" and drew heavily upon the Whig theory of the British revolution of 1688, in sharp contrast to the broad sweep of the French document and its

[17] Van den Berghe, *op. cit.,* p. 77.
[18] Daniel J. Boorstin, "The American Revolution: Revolution Without Dogma," in Edward Keynes and David Adamany, *The Borzoi Reader in American Politics* (New York: Knopf, 1971), p. 40.

exposition of new and fundamental principles.[19] It is not surprising, there-fore, that such a revolution left a culture of religious bigotry and racism intact, and that its principal instrument served as a document to which people referred vaguely, without a need to fully implement its principles. Whatever freedom or liberty was achieved by the American revolution was confined to whites only. In one of the many ironies of black political life in America, a black man, Crispus Attucks, was the first casualty in the struggle for indepen-dence—for freedom that excluded black people. Minor outcroppings of rage notwithstanding, slaves retained their shackles and other blacks continued in their awkward state of limbo, neither slave nor free.

## Constitution Making and the Status of Blacks

In what became a pattern in the development of the American political system, the birth of the nation involved a compromise perpetuating slavery. Thomas Jefferson's first draft of a Declaration of Independence contained a strong indictment of slavery as an immoral institution inflicted on Americans because of Britain's greed. Some other delegates also shared Jefferson's discomfort with slavery, but before the document could be approved, denun-ciation of slavery had to be deleted. So fervent was the commitment to the enslavement of blacks in some colonies that the issue threatened to obstruct agreement on a declaration of independence. As Jefferson wrote later, "Southern states wanted to continue slavery," and "[our] Northern brethren, though their people had very few slaves themselves, yet they had been pretty considerable carriers of them themselves."[20] With this compromise the ground was laid for the strange coexistence between a dedication to freedom and equality on the one hand and a commitment to racial oppression and subordination on the other.

The founders of the Federal Republic in 1789 gave further strength to this contradiction. In drafting what often has been hailed as a great charter of modern democratic government, they took care specifically to protect the institution of slavery. Although they refused to sully the document with use of the word "slave," their deliberations included the issue of slavery. The learned men, perhaps the most august gathering of Americans up to that time, debated the nature of the slave—whether he is a "person" or "property." None other than James Madison concluded of the slave that "they partake of both these qualities, being considered by our laws, in some respects as persons, and in other respects as property. . . . The Federal Constitution, therefore, decides with great propriety on the case of our slaves, when it views them in the mixed character of persons and of property."[21] By tacit

[19] *Ibid.,* pp. 44–45.
[20] Quoted in Eli Ginzberg and Alfred Eichner, *The Troublesome Presence, Amer-ican Democracy and the Negro* (New York: Mentor, 1964), p. 50.
[21] In Alexander Hamilton, *The Federalist* (New York: Putnam, 1923), pp. 340–341.

agreement they refused to examine the implications of slavery for the principles they so fervently embraced. Instead the slave, dealt with in the context of representation and taxation for the Southern states, became the subject of one of the great compromises of the Constitutional Convention.

Because slaves were considered "property" and not "persons," the Northern states refused to have them included in the "population" of the South when computing representation among the states. On the other hand they insisted that they all be counted in computing the taxes for these states. The South took the opposite position whereupon both sides agreed, after a long stalemate, that five slaves would be counted as three persons for both representation and taxation. This agreement, known as the "Three-fifths Compromise," resolved one of the major controversies of the Constitutional Convention and at the same time represented an endorsement of "a less than human" status of blacks.

Treatment of the issue of slavery by the Constitutional Convention further illustrates the limited extent to which concepts such as liberty and equality influenced creation of the political system. Aside from the Three-fifths Compromise, the Constitution went on to explicitly protect the slave trade for at least twenty years, protected the traders from import taxes of more than $10, and by requiring a two-thirds majority in the Senate to ratify treaties, protected slavery from the President's treaty-making powers. The constitution, van den Berghe points out, was essentially a compact between a Northern bourgeoisie and a Southern slave-owning aristocracy, and more than anything else it was designed to protect the interests of these two groups.[22] This interpretation is consistent with Charles Beard's classic economic interpretation of the Constitution. Beard concludes that the Founding Fathers were motivated more by their own economic interests and a desire to ensure economic prosperity than by a desire to protect democratic and humanitarian values.[23] Richard Hofstadter's analysis goes even further, pointing out that while the Founding Fathers were advocates of liberty, they were not committed to the modern conception of democracy, but to property.[24] Thus their principal objective was to protect property rights rather than extend liberty to those most in need of it. Furthermore, since any change in the status of blacks threatened the economic well-being of the wealthy, political values were formulated and articulated in such a manner as to ensure continued black subordination.

## The Ideology of Racism as a Source of Black Subordination

We have suggested that black subordination which began prior to the Declaration of Independence continued undisturbed afterward because of the super-

[22] Van den Berghe, *op. cit.*
[23] Charles Beard, *An Economic Interpretation of the Constitution* (New York: Macmillan, 1913), pp. 152–188.
[24] Hofstadter, *op. cit.*, pp. 10–12.

ficiality of the revolution and the essentially limited economic aims of the national leaders. Even among those who perceived an uncomfortable inconsistency between the values espoused by the Declaration of Independence and the new Constitution, an array of circumstances compelled a rationalization of the inconsistency and eventually a repudiation of some of those values. Eventually black subordination ceased to be something which white Americans apologetically supported. It became a positive good justified by an ideology of racism. The forces contributing to this shift are several, but three were particularly prominent: (1) economic necessity, (2) fear, and (3) the imperialist impulse.

For a long time the economic benefits of slavery were modest. In fact it even appeared unprofitable in some slave states and declining in value. Eli Whitney's invention of the cotton gin in 1794 dramatically altered this by sharply increasing the demand for cotton and in turn the need for slave labor on cotton plantations throughout the South. This major industrial innovation suddenly made any thought of changing the status of blacks grossly inconsistent with the economic interests of the society. Slavery became so inextricably related to the new economic prosperity that to an increasing number of people the abolitionist arguments became almost irresponsible. Once-timid apologists of slavery quickly began to find arguments asserting its necessity, desirability, and even its righteousness.

The link between slavery and "unopposed capitalism" has been frequently emphasized, perhaps most effectively so by Stanley Elkins, who argues persuasively that the institution of slavery and its uniquely brutal and totally dehumanizing practice in the United States were direct consequences of unbridled capitalism.[25] Looking back at this period, W. E. B. Du Bois asserts that "once slavery began to be the source of vast income for men and nations, there followed a frantic search for moral and racial justifications. Such excuses were found and men did not inquire too carefully into either their logic or truth."[26]

A second and equally potent factor in seeking new rationalizations for the oppression and enslavement of blacks was fear. White Americans had always been fearful of the seething black slave population and the prospect that it might one day rise up and destroy its oppressor. This fear lay behind many of the stringent rules affecting the slave as well as the black nonslave populations of many states. By the early 1800s there was new cause for even more widespread fear among whites. Throughout the Caribbean and in the several slave states, slaves resorted to violence to liberate themselves. The first and most dramatic fruit of these revolts was the birth of the Republic of Haiti. In 1804 the black slave population of that French colony, led by Pierre Dominique Toussaint L'Ouverture, erupted in revolutionary violence

[25] Elkins, *op. cit.*, pp. 37–52.
[26] Quoted in Carey McWilliams, *Brothers Under the Skin* (Boston: Little, Brown, 1964), p. 252.

to overthrow French rule and establish a black Republic. Gruesome accounts of this and several less dramatic but equally significant uprisings throughout the Caribbean were widely reported in the American press.

These events had an enormous impact on white Americans. As Winthrop Jordan observes, "To trace the spread of Negro rebellion in the New World and to examine American responses to what they saw as a mounting tide of danger is to watch the drastic erosion of the ideology of the American Revolution."[27] Several states responded by attempting to isolate their slave population from the infectious urge for liberty and the revolutionary impulse it produced. They enacted severe restrictions on the importation of "Negroes" and prohibited entry to "West Indian Negroes" over 15 years of age. Most significantly, they came increasingly to view the association of liberty with the black population as dangerous. White society would be safer if there were no "careless talk" about the rights of black people.

The recognition that the desire for liberty was contagious, and among the black population represented a threat to the domestic tranquility, became a crucial issue in white attitudes toward blacks. It was heightened by relatively small outbreaks within the United States. The uprisings led by Gabriel Prosser in 1800, by Denmark Vesey in 1822, and by Nat Turner in 1831, seemed to confirm these fears and to prolong them. It did not really matter that the revolts were relatively minor or that the Haitian situation had no parallel in the United States. The fear that blacks would seek their liberty at all costs became a major justification for maintaining their bondage. Although slaves were perceived as the principal threats, all black people, including freedmen, came to constitute a danger. They were increasingly subjected to rigid controls, and denied freedom of movement and freedom to participate in political life.

White fear of blacks is not confined to these early years; over time it has been a strong force in shaping white attitudes toward blacks, and in influencing the style and content of white politics. Even now it constitutes one of the principal bases of white hostility to black efforts at changing their lot in society. It played a large part in the development of one-party politics in the South and was almost the only issue in Southern politics for generations. Its impact is equally pervasive outside the South, as indicated by the pattern of responses to the varied expressions of black discontent during the 1960s—such as the burning of decayed ghettos—or the black power concept and demands for economic and social changes. Only an overpowering or what Holden terms "pathological" fear explains such bizarre twists in American politics as the enormous popularity achieved by George Wallace as a candidate for President in 1972 and which he retains even at this writing. Although a relatively successful governor in his state, Wallace's national popularity rests primarily on a flagrant defiance of the law in his effort to prevent a black

[27] Jordan, *op. cit.*, p. 375.

student from registering at the University of Alabama and his skill in capitalizing on white fears by resurrecting racism as a "respectable" theme in American national politics. These contemporary manifestations of fear by whites make it easy to grasp the nineteenth-century passion to suppress and control the black population both slave and free.

Important changes were also occurring at that time in national attitudes toward the entire question of slavery when it emerged as a major national controversy in 1819 with debate over the Missouri territory. Northerners, for practical and political reasons, resisted further expansion of slavery into new territory while the South championed such expansion. The Missouri Compromise temporarily resolved this national crisis but it further contributed to a militant, proslavery attitude among Southerners and hastened widespread indulgence in the elaborate ideology of racism that developed to justify not only slavery but the subordination of all black people. Slavery was justified as humane and consistent with the "inferiority of the Negro race." Biblical arguments were adduced showing that the black race was cursed or was ordained to serve whites. Pseudoscientific arguments sprung up to buttress the claim of "Negro inferiority" by providing evidence of their lower intelligence and suitability only for supervised manual labor. Before long what had been felt and institutionalized in somewhat guilty fashion had a plausible argument in its favor. "Negro inferiority" quickly became an almost universally accepted belief.

The rise of a racist ideology in America coincided with a similar trend in Western Europe. A dramatic outpouring of racist literature set the stage for a century of intensely racist thought and actions by Europeans. According to van den Berghe, this development became very prominent by the 1830s.[28] Michael Banton argues that it reached its peak between 1850 and 1854 as the most influential racist publications clustered around this period.[29] Robert Know, *The Races of Men: A Fragment;* J. A. De Gobineau, *Essai sur l'inégalité des races humaines* (trans. as *The Inequality of the Human Races*), and J. C. Nott and G. R. Glidden, *Types of Mankind,* are representative of this genre. The scholarship of this era concentrated on finding "scientific explanations" of racial differences and at the same time establishing unequivocally the superiority of the white Anglo-Saxon races over the nonwhite races. Several prominent American scholars contributed significantly to the effort. Their findings, not surprisingly, coincided with the domestic need to rationalize or explain away the treatment of the black population.

Formulation of this ideology of racism was enormously aided by the appearance of Charles Darwin's *On the Origin of Species by Means of Natural Selection* in 1859. The work was not concerned with the origins of races, but its findings were soon applied to the area of race relations. Darwin suggested

[28] Van den Berghe, *op. cit.,* p. 16.
[29] Michael Banton, *Race Relations* (New York: Basic Books, 1967), pp. 28–33.

that existence was a competitive process in which the strong survived and the weak perished. Social Darwinists soon equated the principle of the survival of the fittest with right of this element to rule. With this reasoning it became possible to justify subordination of black people within the United States and colonization and exploitation of other "inferior," i.e., nonwhite peoples.

This rise of racist thinking coincided with the renewed efforts in Europe and later in the United States to colonize and plunder the non-Western world. Colonialism seemed somewhat more tolerable, less grating on the conscience of a "civilized people" when they could point to their unquestioned superiority over the oppressed "native." Oppression itself came to be justified as a benevolent and humane effort by "superior peoples" to civilize and Christianize the heathen savages who occupied colonial areas and who Rudyard Kipling matter-of-factly referred to as "lesser breeds without the law." The convergence of the imperialist impulse and racist doctrines is clearly demonstrated in the expansionist activities of the United States during the nineteenth century and in the domestic debate on this activity. Expansionism on the American continent and later in the Pacific was supported in primarily racist terms, and domestic racial attitudes were quickly transferred to these areas. For example, in commenting on the Supreme Court's decision in a Mississippi case permitting disfranchisement of blacks, the *Nation* observed that it is "an interesting coincidence that this important decision is rendered at a time when we are considering the idea of taking in a varied assortment of inferior races in different parts of the world which of course could not be allowed to vote."[30] Some prominent academicians concluded approvingly that in the process of colonizing millions of Asiatics the Republican Party had changed its views on race relations and accepted those of the South.[31] The colonialist argument was that colonized people were inferior and incapable of self-government and thus needed the protection and guidance that the benevolent white race was willing and eager to bestow. Essentially the same view of blacks in the South prevailed.

## Democracy and the Black Experience

We observed earlier that the drafters of the Constitution had a very limited conception of democracy, one more oriented to the protection of their property interests than recognition of the equality of individuals in the political arena. But early in the nineteenth century the then Western world experienced a dramatic upsurge in the mass impulse to participate in the political process. This process of democratization, or as Lucian Pye and others characterize it, "the crisis of participation" in America opened the

[30] Quoted in C. Vann Woodward, *The Strange Career of Jim Crow* (New York: Oxford University Press, 1955), p. 54.
[31] *Ibid.*

"Nixon is recalling all the school busses—
they're politically unsafe."

political arena to the masses introducing what we now know as popular democracy. The many virtues attributed to this essentially modern form of democracy ordinarily would lead one to expect that with it came considerable improvement in the position of blacks in the society. Indications are, however, that the process of democratization in America brought with it no immediate benefits for blacks. In some important respects it served as a formidable obstacle to change in their status, and even intensified their subordinate status.

In the United States, as in South Africa, Rhodesia, and the United Kingdom, black subordination has persisted alongside commitment to "mass participation" in politics. Noting that in societies of this kind democratic procedures or principles usually are applicable to the superordinate group only, van den Berghe characterizes them as "*Herrenvolk democracies.*"[32] Carl Degler observes that in the United States blacks were not only excluded from participation but in at least two basic ways this form of democracy operated

[32] Van den Berghe, *op. cit.*

to their disadvantage. He points out that in societies like Brazil where there was no commitment to democratic values blacks, during and after slavery, fared better than they did in the United States. In this country assertion of the equality of individuals imposed on whites the need to justify black subordination by destroying his humanity, by stressing in every way possible that he was less than human.[33] This need contributed to the harshness of black life and to the seemingly ridiculous extent to which white Americans often went in affirming black inferiority.

Degler's second observation about the impact of democracy on blacks relates to its overt use as an instrument for maintaining black subordination. He observes that periods of rapid democratization and extension of the franchise to large segments of the masses coincided with vigorous new efforts to reinforce black subordination. In the minds of lower-class or poor whites, blacks—slave or free—were competitors, and these whites fought against every move that seemed to threaten their own status and economic well-being. As these masses entered the political arena as voters under the banner of Jacksonian democracy, Degler concludes, "new cognizance was given in both society and politics to the wishes and prejudices of the common man."[34] Thus as the removal of property qualification to suffrage brought the poor into the electorate, the condition of blacks deteriorated. In those states where nonslave blacks held the right to vote such as the New England states, New York, Pennsylvania, New Jersey, North Carolina, Tennessee and Maryland, this right was quickly withdrawn or severely circumscribed. In several other states the upsurge of this mass democracy was accompanied by the imposition of stringent new controls on the black population. In the same vein C. Vann Woodward concluded that in the post-Civil War South, "political democracy for the white man and racial discrimination for the black were often products of the same dynamics." As black and white workers were thrown together in the new industrial towns and had to compete for work, poor whites became more insistent on discriminatory laws. He concluded that "the barriers of racial discrimination mounted in direct ratio with the tide of political democracy among whites."[35]

With uncanny insightfulness, Alexis de Tocqueville recognized and commented on the sinister consequences of American democracy for the black population:

> I do not believe that the white and black races will live in any country on an equal footing. But I believe the difficulty to be still greater in the United States than elsewhere. An isolated individual may surmount the prejudices of religion, of his country, or of his race; and if

[33] Carl Degler, *Neither Black Nor White* (New York: Macmillan, 1971), pp. 356–357.

[34] *Ibid.*, pp. 358–360.

[35] Woodward, *op. cit.*

> this individual is a king, he may effect surprising changes in society; but a whole people cannot rise, as it were, above itself. A despot who should subject Americans and their former slaves to the same yoke might perhaps succeed in commingling the races; but as long as the American democracy remains at the head of affairs, no one will undertake so difficult a task; and it may be foreseen that the freer [that is, more democratic] the white population of the United States becomes, the more isolated it will remain.[36]

The vote in the hands of the masses has continually provided the impetus for discriminatory laws and practices and has served to restrain political leaders from pursuing policies likely to be. beneficial to blacks. The presidential elections of 1972 provided new evidence of the power of the democratic process in matters of race relations. Traditional champions of equal opportunities for blacks were forced to retreat by embracing the convenient bogey of opposition to "quotas" as a new threat to America. Long-standing supporters of school integration clung to the straw man of "forced busing" in beating a quick retreat before the aroused masses of voters who insist on largely segregated school systems.

The role of democracy as a device for perpetuating black subordination is considerably enhanced by the peculiarly political character of virtually every facet of public life. Not only are traditionally "political" roles filled by popular election, but law-enforcement, judicial, and some administrative or bureaucratic roles as well. This means that few significant roles are free from the direct pressures of the popular vote. Popular racial attitudes thus influence virtually every area of public life.

These observations are not intended to blame the entire ordeal of black Americans on the democratic process or to suggest that democracy is itself sinister. They emphasize that democratic values held by Americans have not been a significant hindrance to the institutionalization of racism. Rather these values have been easily adapted to the task of maintaining black subordination. To protect everyone in the society, the democratic process as it exists in America requires the existence of an overarching set of values that includes everyone on equal terms. "Popular democracy" has been the handmaiden of racism in the United States because of the absence of such values.

## Federalism and the Black Experience

Federalism may be more readily viewed as a structural characteristic of the American polity rather than a cultural or attitudinal one. It is considered here, however, because values and attitudes basic to the cultural tradition of America are reflected in federalism and because these values along with the

---

[36] Alexis de Tocqueville, *Democracy in America* (New York: Knopf, 1945), pp. 373–374.

federal structure have been crucial in perpetuating black subordination. Racism and attitudes toward federalism have been so intimately linked that it is hardly possible to study one without reference to the other. Even a cursory review of the federal relationship quickly reveals that the black presence was one important factor in its adoption, and that this black presence and the many problems of race relations have been continuing and highly potent forces in shaping the existing pattern of federalism.

Federalism was one of the genuine innovations introduced by the American constitution in 1789. Several factors contributed to the adoption of this form of political organization. These included (1) the practical problems resulting from development of thirteen distinct colonial societies each with its separate interests and over a decade of experience with virtually complete independence within the fatally flawed Confederacy; (2) some of the more thoughtful members of the Constitutional Convention saw federalism as a device for ensuring free and limited government by decentralizing power. It is clear, however, that different interests and customs which the separate units wanted to preserve weighed heavily in favor of the adoption of federalism, and that the black presence constituted the most notable of these different interests and customs. In fact, James Madison conceded that the basic division among the states represented at the Constitutional Convention was not between large and small states, as is often suggested, but between those states that permitted slavery and those that did not.[37]

Those colonies in which slavery was a valued institution felt threatened by antislavery sentiments elsewhere and federalism, along with other specific constitutional guarantees, afforded protection for the institution. On the other hand, federalism provided an escape for the national government from direct responsibility for slavery. As Mark De Wolfe Howe suggests, "the decision of the framers of the Constitution that the domestic destiny of slavery was to be in the hands of the states and not in those of the Nation meant, of course, that Congress should not by positive law sustain slavery or by negative law end it."[38] With abolition of slavery federalism became even more important in ensuring the continued subordination of blacks. Their status remained largely within state jurisdiction, and the states—especially the Southern states—spared no effort in legislating black subordination. During the decade immediately following the Civil War the national government intervened briefly and halfheartedly in efforts to define the status of blacks and to protect them from the atrocities of Southern state governments, but the effort soon ended and blacks again became helpless victims of the state governments under whose jurisdiction they found themselves.

[37] Farrand, *op. cit.,* 110.
[38] Mark De Wolfe Howe, "Federalism and Civil Rights," in Archibald Cox, Mark De Wolfe Howe, and J. R. Wiggins, eds., *Civil Rights, The Constitution and the Courts* (Cambridge, Mass.: Harvard University Press, 1967), p. 38.

In evaluating American federalism, William Riker concludes that it is difficult to find any evidence that federalism has in fact operated to protect individual freedom. On the contrary he suggests, "it is impossible to interpret federalism as other than a device for minority tyranny."[39] The history of black America's efforts to alter their subordinate status has, in fact, been largely that of overcoming the roadblocks imposed by federalism. Duane Lockard asserts in this regard that "in retrospect it is clear that the independence of the Southern states helped greatly to assure their complete discretion in handling not only the institution of slavery but also the social and economic condition of the "freedmen."[40] Burke Marshall points to the use of federalism in obstructing efforts for significant change, noting that in the South "state police power and Criminal processes have been used in retaliation against efforts to encourage Negroes to exercise their right to the vote and to protect the caste system. They have also been used to defy federal court orders."[41]

Throughout the nation's history the national government has been more sympathetic than the Southern states to the plight of blacks. On those occasions when the national government attempted to respond to vital needs of blacks either by legislative or judicial action, the rights and prerogatives of the states have been invoked to obstruct national effort. The first major Civil Rights Act passed by the national government in 1873 was invalidated by the Supreme Court on the basis of a distinction between federal and state jurisdictions. Ever since that time, arguments based on "states' rights" principles have been utilized in efforts to prevent implementation of national norms in the area of race relations. It is one of the chilling facts of American history that decades of efforts to enact a federal antilynching law were frustrated by arguments about possible usurpation of state authority by the national government. The shrill appeals to states' rights reached their peak after the Supreme Court's decision in *Brown vs. Board of Education* in 1954. Alabama, followed shortly afterward by Georgia, Mississippi, South Carolina and Virginia, all adopted resolutions of "nullification," declaring the Court's decision null and void in their states. The nullification acts proved to be mere symbols of defiance, since their major premise—the claim that states possess final authority to decide what is constitutional—was discredited long before that time. It is significant, however, that when Governor George Wallace of Alabama made his infamous stand "in the schoolhouse door" to prevent black students from entering the University of Alabama in 1962, he was defending a long-standing symbol of black subordination by invoking "the sovereign right of states" against the federal system.

[39] William H. Riker, *Federalism: Origin, Operation and Significance* (Boston: Little, Brown, 1964), p. 142.
[40] Duane Lockard, *The Perverted Priorities of American Politics* (New York: Macmillan, 1971), p. 90.
[41] Burke Marshall, *Federalism and Civil Rights* (New York: Columbia University Press, 1964), p. 9.

Against this background the following assessment of American Federalism by Riker appears beyond serious challenge.

> The main beneficiary (of federalism) throughout American history has been Southern whites, who have been given the freedom to oppress Negroes, first as slaves and later as a depressed caste. Other minorities have from time to time also managed to obtain some of these benefits; e.g., special business interests have been allowed to regulate themselves, especially in the era from about 1890 to 1936, by means of the judicial doctrine of dual federalism, which eliminated both state and national regulation of such matters as wage rates and hours of labor. But the significance of federal benefits to economic interests pales beside the significance of benefits to the Southern segregationist whites. The judgment to be passed on federalism in the United States is therefore a judgment on the values of segregation and racial oppression.[42]

One weakness of Riker's analysis is that it makes the Southern states the sole villains in utilizing federalism as a means of perpetuating black subordination. This is clearly not the case, for federalism served the rest of the nation as a convenient excuse for not really trying to bring about significant change. Federalism as an obstacle to change in the condition of blacks was thus all the more formidable because it shielded whites outside the South from blame for some of the excesses of the South, and by contrast made forms of racial subordination outside the South seem insignificant.

The role of federalism in perpetuating black subordination is not confined to the formal constitutional protection it provides to the "legally" established symbols and rituals of subordination. Even where the states'-rights argument has given way to the imposition of national norms, federalism continues to facilitate delays in the full implementation of these national norms. The federal structure, Lockard notes, provides "a special set of weapons for resistance" in the form of countless legal, constitutional and administrative devices that can long delay and sometimes defeat a detested national decision."[43] Nowhere have these special weapons been more widely displayed than in the areas of voting rights, school desegregation and the administration of justice.

American federalism has changed drastically in recent years as the role of the national government increased substantially vis-à-vis state government. Several powerful forces have contributed to this change, among them an increasing trend toward urbanization and technological development, and increase in the financial power of the national government (and hence its larger role in education, medical care, welfare and other social services for the society). One of the most potent forces for change, however, has been the efforts of blacks to alter their position in the society. Federalism has been

[42] Riker, *op. cit.,* pp. 152–153.
[43] Lockard, *op. cit.,* p. 91.

affected by the black struggle in at least three ways: (1) The national government has been forced to play a larger role in protecting citizens in the exercise of constitutionally guaranteed rights as a result of the civil rights struggle and the consequent atrocities by local law enforcement officials. (2) A series of Supreme Court decisions highlighted by *Brown vs. Board of Education* (1954) considerably reduced the freedom of states to enact discriminatory laws and required compliance with nationally stated policies of nondiscrimination. (3) Legislative responses to black demands, particularly the 1964 Civil Rights Act and the Voting Rights Act of 1965 have extended the powers of the federal government into areas once reserved almost exclusively to the states. Under the pressures of black political activism, the Fourteenth Amendment and other portions of the Constitution like the Commerce Clause have been extensively developed and broadened to enhance national governmental powers vis-à-vis the states.

## Summary

The persistence of black subordination in a society which from the outset claimed a strong commitment to democratic values and belief in the equality of individuals is not, upon examination, a paradox as is often suggested. We have observed that the subordinate-superordinate pattern of relationship emerged with the beginning of American colonial societies and persisted unchanged after independence because of the very limited and superficial character of the American revolution. Thereafter a variety of factors contributed to the development of an ideology of racism—a set of rationalizations for black subordination—which relied upon self-serving interpretations of the Bible, pseudoscientific jargon, and the distortion of genuine scientific research. This racist ideology was not a product of Americans alone but was a Western European undertaking and functioned to justify pursuit of imperialist policies in which virtually all nonwhite peoples were victims.

Democracy has been often invested with virtues it does not merit. It has not been an obstacle to racism or to black subordination. On the contrary, this chapter suggests that it served as an instrument for black subordination. In the United States democracy had a limited meaning, one that protected the interests of wealthy upper classes rather than those of the entire society and even when the concept was extended to embrace mass participation in politics, subordinate groups were excluded from the democratic process. Of even greater consequence for the black experience, however, is the extent to which it became a weapon utilized by the masses to ensure and reinforce the subordinate status of blacks. This in spite of the fact that for almost 200 years black spokesmen pursued their struggle for change by appealing to the democratic and humanitarian values of America. In recent years further development of conceptions of democracy, the many external pressures on the United States as a "champion of democratic values" and the highly competitive character of politics has increased the extent to which the democratic process has contributed to black advancement. Finally, the federal structure of the political system took shape primarily under the impetus of the black presence, and over time has had its most significant impact on the society by preserving black subordination.

# Black Americans
# and the Problem
# of Citizenship

One of the most perplexing and persistent issues with which thoughtful blacks have been concerned is the nature of their relationship to the United States. Addressing the American Anti-Slavery Society in 1847 Frederick Douglass raised the issue with the poignant question, "What country have I?"[1] Looking out at the millions of his enslaved brothers and his own very tenuous status as a black man, Douglass conceded that he had no love for America and that, in fact, he had no country. Almost 120 years later Malcolm X raised the same troubling question, concluding that while the various European immigrant groups quickly became Americans in fact; for blacks, not even their birth in America has made them Americans. Of himself he asserted:

> No I'm not an American. I'm one of the twenty-two million black people who are the victims of Americanism. One of the twenty-two million black people who are the victims of democracy, nothing but disguised hypocrisy. So I'm not standing here speaking to you as an American, or a patriot, or a flag saluter, or a flag-waver—no, not I. I'm speaking as a victim of this American system. And I see America through the eyes of the victim. I don't see any American dream; I see an American nightmare.[2]

Reflecting similar sentiments, some blacks have found in the Nation of Islam, the Republic of New Africa and similar groups a new focus for their loyalties. The Reverend Jesse Jackson's recent efforts to encourage acquisition of Liberian citizenship by blacks, in addition to their American citizenship, is another example of the concern. This does not mean that most blacks have gone so far as to deny being Americans. In fact, several extensive studies

[1] Philip Foner, ed., *The Life and Writings of Frederick Douglass, Vol. 1* (New York: International Publishers, 1950), p. 236.
[2] *Malcolm X Speaks* (New York: Merit Publishers, 1965). Reprinted in Herbert J. Storing, *What Country Have I* (New York: St. Martin, 1970), p. 149.

indicate that blacks perceive themselves as Americans and have been at least as patriotic as other Americans. To varying degrees, however, the question of "identity" is pertinent for all black Americans. The special problem it poses is part of the legacy of white racism and the status ordering built upon it.

## The Significance of Citizenship

Although we cannot fully deal with this perplexing issue here, the problem of citizenship for blacks provides a convenient focus for examining this dimension of black America's political experience. The present chapter reviews the process by which blacks have moved toward full American citizenship in order to demonstrate the uniqueness of their experience in this regard and the still tenuous character of their status. We will begin by specifying in brief and general terms what is implied by the concept of citizenship. Frequently citizenship is used in a very broad sense to indicate a status that provides one with certain basic rights and responsibilities in an organized society. One major study suggests that it implies fundamental equality of rights as part of a societal community including the right to participate in the life and activity of that community.[3] Definitions of this kind emphasize two important components of citizenship—the social and the legal/political.

The social component of citizenship suggests that one is a member of a specific community. Citizenship is therefore a crucial aspect of an individual's identity. It helps to answer the question "Who am I?" by establishing a clearly fixed social affiliation. This social component of citizenship contributes to the satisfaction of what Peter Merkl describes as man's existential need to identify with an image of himself involving his place in history, geography and society.[4] This question of identity with which citizenship is related is crucial for everyone, but especially for groups like blacks whose complete and involuntary detachment from their homeland heightened their identity crisis.

The second important aspect of citizenship concerns certain specific legal and political rights and responsibilities that accrue to all members of a society. The precise nature and extent of these rights and privileges vary from one society to another and from one period of the society's development to another. Usually each society defines these rights and responsibilities in terms of its own system of values and beliefs. No attempt has been made to specify formally all of the rights and privileges of American citizens, but tradition, legislation, and court decisions over the years provide a fairly clear idea of what is involved. As early as 1824 Justice Bushrod Washington in the case of *Corfield vs. Coryell* identified some of the rights of citizenship as

---

[3] See for example H. Mark Roelofs, *The Tension of Citizenship* (New York: Holt, Rinehart & Winston, 1957), pp. 1–31, 155–156; Dennis F. Thompson, *The Democratic Citizen* (New York: Cambridge University Press, 1970), pp. 26–29.

[4] Peter Merkl, *Modern Comparative Politics* (New York: Holt, Rinehart & Winston, 1970), p. 163.

> ... protection by the government; enjoyment of life and liberty; the right to acquire and possess property; the right of a citizen of one state to pass through or reside in other states for purposes of trade or profession; protection by the writ of habeas corpus; the right to institute and maintain court actions; exemption from higher taxes than are paid by other citizens of the state; and the elective franchise, as regulated by the laws of the particular state in which it is exercised.[5]

These are still considered to be among the basic elements of citizenship.

Members of a society do not usually "actively struggle" for citizenship. It is a routine part of one's inheritance as a member of an organized society. There may be conflicts about the character and extent of the benefits and obligations attached to citizenship, but rarely controversies over the fact of citizenship. All sovereign states establish rules that determine who are citizens or how one becomes a citizen. Two of the oldest and most widely used criteria are (a) *jus soli*—one's place of birth, and (b) *jus sanguinis*—the nationality of one's parents. Additionally, states provide procedures (naturalization) for inducting members of another society into their own as citizens. All these applied in the United States, but not for blacks even though they were among the earliest inhabitants of the American colonies. For generations they were generally denied the status of citizen, and even though a series of major upheavals finally resulted in formal allocation of citizenship status, they are still seeking to secure its full application.

The question of citizenship and the allocation of rights consequent to citizenship have been crucial issues in the development of many nation-states. In his study of the development of Western European society, Reinhard Bendix reports that a core element of nation building was the codification of the rights and duties of citizens. A crucial issue here concerned how inclusively citizenship was defined. Bendix suggests that in most Western European states there was a gradual process of broadening the scope of citizenship to include the lower classes as part of the process of nation building.[6] Focusing on the British experience, T. H. Marshall utilizes a three-dimensional conception of citizenship rights in explaining the gradual process by which citizenship was conferred on the entire population. The first step involved the allocation of legal or civil rights such as the right to equal justice before the law, liberty of person, freedom of speech, and the right to own property and negotiate contracts. The second step involved allocation of political rights such as the franchise and access to public office. The third step concerned social rights, the right to basic welfare or economic security, and sharing the social heritage of the community.[7]

[5] *Corfield vs. Coryell* 6 Fed. Cas. 3230, 546, 552 (1823).
[6] Reinhard Bendix, *Nationbuilding and Citizenship* (New York: Wiley, 1964), pp. 74–101.
[7] T. H. Marshall, *Class, Citizenship and Social Development* (London: Cambridge University Press, 1950), pp. 10–27.

In the United States citizenship was not quite as problematic as it was for Europeans. Very early in the national experience a relatively articulate belief system stressing equalitarian principles emerged that helped to clarify to some extent the character of American citizenship. Nevertheless, the question of citizenship and the full rights and responsibilities it conferred remained important issues in the United States as practice fell far behind the bold equalitarian principles the society espoused. The poor, the unschooled, and females were only gradually accorded what may be considered full rights and responsibilities of citizenship. In fact, despite professed hostility to class distinctions, American politics quickly developed and maintained a highly visible class character. White men of substantial wealth and education were for a long time the legitimate participants in political life and the only "full citizens." As the participatory sentiment became more widespread, access to the political arena was gradually extended to the poor, to females, and in most cases to individuals with little if any formal education.

For blacks the issue has been much more complex. They were not members of a class of people whose lack of wealth or education temporarily excluded them from the full rights and responsibilities of citizenship. Their race and the status it conferred on them were the basic obstacles, and this fact distinguishes them from almost all other distinct groups in the society. Each step toward the acquisition of citizenship—legal, political, and social— has been slow and tedious, much more so than for the many immigrant groups that have become part of the American political community.

Up to 1863 the issue of citizenship was irrelevant for all blacks except the approximately 485,000 who were not slaves. These "free Negroes" around whom the question of black citizenship rights prior to the Civil War revolved, varied widely in economic status. A few were visibly wealthy, a small but substantial number was active in public life, but the overwhelming majority were poor. While small numbers of them secured some citizenship rights, they were never viewed by the society as entitled to citizenship. After 1863 they were joined by approximately four million of their brothers who were no longer slaves but still not members of the political community.

An evaluation of black America's exclusion from citizenship rights and the efforts for their inclusion, suggests that in addition to the fact of direct racism at least three important factors contributed to their difficulty in achieving full citizenship rights. First was the casualness of the national government on the question of citizenship as a result of which criteria for citizenship became primarily a state, rather than national, responsibility. Second, citizenship conferred political power, and acquisition of political power by blacks threatened the ability of whites to control and exploit them. Third, citizenship symbolized equality and directly threatened the carefully maintained subordinate-superordinate relationship.

## Blacks and Citizenship—The Early Pattern of Exclusion

The question of citizenship for Americans was not a significant source of controversy until after 1850. During the colonial era it was assumed that the colonists were British subjects, and although practice varied widely among the colonies some blacks were also regarded as British subjects. The Articles of Confederation, adopted in 1776 as the first constitutional document binding the thirteen colonies, provided the first formal statement of citizenship, asserting that

> ... the free inhabitants of each of these states, paupers, vaga-
> bonds and fugitives from justice excepted, shall be entitled to all the
> privileges and immunities of free citizens in the several states and the
> people of each state shall have free regress to and from any other state.

That blacks were included in this statement is evidenced by the fact that the delegate from South Carolina unsuccessfully attempted to amend the statement to read "free white inhabitants."[8]

The Constitutional Convention in 1787 made no change in this arrangement; in fact although introducing the phrase "citizens of the United States" it conspicuously omitted any further definition of national citizenship, leaving the problem to the states. As the repositories of citizenship, states varied widely in the citizenship rights conferred on blacks, but in no state were the rights conferred equal to those guaranteed to whites, and in some cases these rights were completely denied. As a rule, the Northeastern states in which slavery had been abolished provided limited citizenship rights; the slave-holding states provided very little or none. Not only were blacks generally denied such basic rights as the franchise in most states, they were severely limited in other respects. Some states enacted special legislation requiring registration of all blacks who entered the state, limited the time they could spend there, and in a few cases completely prohibited their entrance for more than a few days. In Tennessee, for example, blacks who entered the state were required to register with county courts providing detailed description of themselves. By 1807 they were required to secure registration certificates when changing counties and to carry a copy at all times. In 1831 blacks were prohibited altogether from entering the state to reside for more than 20 days.[9]

Thus as far as blacks were concerned, a confused state of affairs existed as the various states arbitrarily fixed rules compromising or altogether eliminating their status as citizens. In the South, free blacks represented a threat to the institution of slavery and were thus considered undesirable. In some Northern states, in spite of their small numbers, blacks were considered

---

[8] Peter Bergman and Jean McCarroll, eds., *The Negro in the Continental Congress* (New York: Bergman Publishers, 1969), p. 31.

[9] For a survey of similar restrictions in other states see Winthrop Jordan, *White over Black* (Baltimore, Md.: Penguin, 1968), pp. 406–414.

consequential to the outcome of elections and thus were excluded from participation or faced formidable obstacles to their participation.[10]

The National government made no effort formally to follow a clear and consistent policy regarding black citizenship but it established a pattern of practice affirming the exclusion of blacks from citizenship status. This was reflected in both laws passed by Congress and in administrative decisions by the national government. In 1790 Congress limited naturalization to white immigrants only, implying thereby that nonwhites were not eligible for citizenship. Two years later it limited service in the militia to "white male citizens" and later prohibited blacks from performing such tasks as handling the mail and serving as captain of vessels plying United States waters. More significantly the Department of State refused to grant passports to blacks, as this would constitute a concession of citizenship. Instead it issued "traveling letters" to those permitted to travel abroad. In 1821 Attorney General William West declared that free Negroes were not citizens under the Constitution; thus while the government was willing to grant letters certifying that they were free and born in the United States, it could not regard them as entitled to the full rights of citizens when traveling abroad.[11]

This denial of citizenship reflected a determination by white society to maintain the distinctly subordinate status of blacks. It corresponded with the widespread feeling of the time that while blacks were physically present in the society they were not and could not really be part of it. This feeling existed even among many of those who vigorously opposed slavery. They hardly contemplated acceptance of blacks as equals in society as full citizenship would imply, believing instead that they could either be returned to Africa or made to adjust to permanent subordination. "Free blacks" were not by any means content with the denial of citizenship. They were fully aware of its implications, especially the political rights involved, and worked vigorously to secure the most basic rights of citizenship, particularly the right to vote.[12] Their efforts were mostly limited to petitions to the state and national legislatures and to efforts to mobilize white popular support.

The issue of citizenship for blacks created little national controversy until the very eve of the Civil War. Suddenly and dramatically the Supreme Court's decision in *Dred Scott vs. Sandford* thrust the issue before the nation to further inflame the rapidly escalating conflict between North and South on the issue of slavery. Dred Scott, a slave, had been taken by his master to live

[10] Charles Wesley, "Negro Suffrage in the Period of Constitution-Making," *Journal of Negro History 1787–1865* 32, 2 (April 1927), 154–167. For a detailed study of the situation in New York see John L. Stanley, "Majority Tyranny in Tocqueville's America: The Failure of Negro Suffrage in 1846," *Political Science Quarterly* 84, 3 (September 1969), 412–435.

[11] Leon Litwack, "The Federal Government and the Free Negro 1790–1860," *The Journal of Negro History* 43 (October 1958), 269–275.

[12] Leon Litwack, "The Emancipation of the Negro Abolitionist," in Eric Foner, ed., *America's Black Past* (New York: Harper & Row, 1970), pp. 168–170.

in Illinois, a nonslave state, and later in the Louisiana territory north of 36°30' in which slavery had been prohibited by the Missouri Compromise of 1820. On his return to Missouri, Dred Scott sued in Federal Court to obtain his freedom on the ground that he had resided in "free territory" and was thus entitled to freedom. When the case reached the Supreme Court, the majority denied the petition on the ground that Dred Scott was not a citizen and lacked "legal standing" before the courts. Going far beyond the specific issue raised by Scott's plea, the Court with an air of finality sought to clarify the status of "the Negro" in the United States. Chief Justice Taney, on behalf of the majority, dealt with the issue thus:

> The question before us is whether the class of persons described in the plea (Negroes) in abatement compose a portion of this people, and are constituent members of this sovereignty? We think they are not, and they are not included, and were not intended to be included under the word "citizen" in the Constitution and can therefore claim none of the rights and privileges which that instrument provides for and secures to citizens of the United States.[13]

The drama of *Dred Scott vs. Sandford* was not that the Court broke new ground or that it departed from widely held views about the status of blacks. It was rather that years of informal practice had been endowed with constitutional sanctity through affirmation by the Supreme Court at a time when the rapidly intensifying conflict between the North and South could not stand such a forthright and unequivocal statement.

In reaching its decision that Dred Scott was not a citizen because Negroes were not regarded as "a part of the body politic," the Court relied on existing practice and on what it considered to be widespread public sentiment on the question. Specifically it pointed to (a) the absence of any clear intention by the drafters of the Constitution to confer citizenship on Negroes; (b) the several laws enacted in the states that indicated a desire to withhold full citizenship from Negroes; (c) the actions of the national government that clearly reflected an intention to withhold citizenship from Negroes.

Reliance on the pattern of practice cited by the Court and even its interpretation of these practices were vigorously criticized, and most effectively so in a strong dissenting opinion by Justice Curtis. Nevertheless the Court clearly had on its side strong evidence from common attitudes and public policy to support its decision. Chief Justice Taney and his colleagues were not solitary champions of white racism—merely uncritical reflectors of the society's racism. Thus while Frederick Douglass fumed that "the national conscience would not accept such an open, glaring tissue of lies as that decision is and has been over the years shown to be,"[14] Robert Purvis was

---

[13] *Dred Scott vs. Sandford* 19 How. 393 (1857).
[14] Frederick Douglass, "Speech on the Dred Scott Decision," in Howard Brotz, ed., *Negro Social and Political Thought 1850–1920* (New York: Basic Books, 1966), p. 250.

more nearly correct in urging blacks not to "comfort themselves with thoughts of the decision's unconstitutionality because it was in perfect keeping with the treatment of the colored people by the American govern- ment from the beginning to this day."[15] The Court's failure in the Dred Scott decision was not a misinterpretation of past attitudes but, according to Eugene Rostow, it was a failure of intuition. In attempting to restore a rule that corresponded to earlier public feelings the Court failed to question the social or moral basis of this rule.[16]

Large sectors of the society expressed outrage at the Dred Scott decision, yet not entirely—or even primarily—because of its pronouncement on black citizenship. In an unprecedented lack of judicial restraint the Court unraveled the precarious balance that had been struck between the slave interests and opponents of the expansion of slavery. It declared unconstitu- tional the Congressional action underlying the Missouri Compromise and thus provided a decisive victory for proponents of the further expansion of slavery. For blacks, the decision was far-reaching. Its immediate impact was devastating because it formally and unequivocally excluded them from the political system and from any hope of equality of rights in the society. Viewed in a larger time frame, however, the Dred Scott may have been beneficial for blacks. It placed forthrightly before the nation the question of the black man's status in society and heightened the urgency of a solution, especially after abolition dramatically increased the number of people exist- ing outside of the political community.

## Black Inclusion: The First Steps

Talcott Parsons conceptualizes movement from a position outside the polit- ical community to one within it as "a process of inclusion."[17] This inclusion process, he suggests, involves the gradual acquisition of the full rights and duties of citizenship by the excluded group. For the black population of the United States this process of formal inclusion began soon after the Civil War and has continued, not as a steady process of movement toward full citizen- ship but as a frustrating process of advances and retreats that tend to leave suspect the gains achieved even today. Perhaps one of the most significant features of the inclusion process for blacks is that it occurred in the absence of any clear national commitment to the process. The absence of such commitment—in fact a widespread hostility to black inclusion throughout the society—has given the effort its unique character.

After the Civil War the one-half million "free blacks" to whom citizen-

---

[15] *The Liberator*, April 10, 1857, quoted in Litwack, "The Federal Government and the Free Negro," *op. cit.*, p. 278.

[16] Eugene Rostow, "The Negro in Our Law," *Utah Law Review* 9 (1965), 844.

[17] Talcott Parsons, "Full Citizenship for the Negro American? A Sociological Problem," in Talcott Parsons and Kenneth Clark, eds., *The Negro American* (Boston: Houghton Mifflin, 1965), p. 715.

ship rights had been denied were joined by almost four million former slaves, all of whom enjoyed almost none of the legal, political, or social rights of citizens. The first step toward a resolution of this dilemma was taken on April 13, 1866, with passage by Congress of a bill entitled "An Act to Protect All Persons in the United States in their Civil Rights and Furnish the Means of Their Vindication." The bill embodied the first formal definition of national citizenship, providing that "all persons born in the United States and not subject to any foreign power, excluding Indians not taxed, are hereby declared to be citizens of the United States."[18] Further, it guaranteed to all citizens the basic legal rights traditionally enjoyed only by whites. This was an extremely limited step designed to confer on blacks legal rights only and not "political rights" according to Lyman Trumbull, then Chairman of the Senate Judiciary Committee.[19] Even this limited step evoked considerable opposition, however, and finally was vetoed by President Andrew Johnson. In his veto message, President Johnson complained that it was unwise to grant citizenship to newly freed slaves who were unfamiliar with the nation's laws and institutions, and that the bill aimed at "a perfect equality of the white and colored race" and would make it impossible for states to exercise any discrimination between the different races. . . ."[20]

The President's opposition to the Congressional effort to confer basic legal rights on blacks brought to a climax a major disagreement between the Executive and Legislative branches of government about the nature and extent of the problems of the Southern Negro and the proper approach to reconstruction. Not only did the Congress override Johnson's veto, but as the conflict intensified and Southern atrocities against blacks mounted, that lawmaking body resorted to increasingly strong measures against the South. With passage of a series of "reconstruction acts" in 1867, Congress undertook fully the task of directing the reconstruction effort.[21] The Republican majority at this time was more concerned with the desire to maintain its control of the Congress than it was in the fate of the Southern blacks. Prior to the Civil War, Southern representation in the House of Representatives was affected by the Three-Fifths Compromise whereby every five slaves counted as three persons in the apportionment of representation in the House of Representatives. With the slaves free, the Southern population would be dramatically increased and with it Southern representation. The enfranchisement of blacks appeared to many of these legislators a reliable device to assure continued Northern Republican control in Congress.[22] This concern, coupled with the obvious vulnerability of Southern blacks, motivated pro-

---

[18] In Bernard Schwartz, *Statutory History of the United States, Civil Rights 1* (New York: Chelsea House, 1970), p. 101.

[19] *Ibid.*, p. 113.

[20] *Ibid.*, pp. 150–155.

[21] See John Hope Franklin, *Reconstruction After the Civil War* (Chicago: University of Chicago Press, 1961), pp. 69–84.

[22] There is substantial disagreement among scholars about the motivation for adoption of the Fourteenth Amendment. See for example LaWanda and John Cox,

posal of the Fourteenth Amendment, ratified on July 9, 1868. This Amendment incorporated and expanded on the provisions of the 1866 Act, providing the first constitutional definition of citizenship done in such a way as to clearly include the black population. It states:

> All persons born or naturalized in the United States, and subject to the jurisdiction thereof, are citizens of the United States and the State wherein they reside. No State shall make or enforce any law which shall abridge the privileges or immunities of citizens of the United States; nor shall any State deprive any person of life, liberty, or property, without due process of law; nor deny to any person within its jurisdiction the equal protection of the laws.

This Amendment is easily the most significant addition to the Constitution aside from the Bill of Rights. Not only did it promptly alter the formal legal status of blacks within the United States, but by prohibiting states from impinging upon the privileges and immunities associated with citizenship, and especially by affirming the right to "the equal protection of the laws," it sought to protect them from the hostility of state government.[23] Over time the Amendment has become the most vital single source of constitutional protection for the rights of individuals especially vis-à-vis state government. Precisely what was included in these privileges and immunities became major legal controversies, since they were not specified or otherwise distinguished from state citizenship.

One decade after the Dred Scott decision the Fourteenth Amendment unequivocally brought blacks into the political community, but it took another amendment, the Fifteenth, adopted two years later (March 30, 1870) to ensure basic political rights. Section one of that Amendment states: "The right of citizens of the United States to vote shall not be abridged by the United States or by any State on account of race, color, or previous condition of servitude." This political right of citizens was easily the most important single issue to most blacks, and for good reasons. Myrdal, in his analysis of American society, identified the most important of these reasons. He stressed the peculiar vulnerability of the politically excluded by noting that the United States has not had a tradition of independent, law-abiding administration of local or national affairs. On the contrary, there has been a persistent movement toward increasing the direct control of the electorate over public affairs. The individual's well-being is assured not so much by the virtue of the office holder as by the individual's power to replace the office holder.[24] In

---

"Negro Suffrage and Republican Politics: The Problem of Motivation in Reconstruction Historiography," *Journal of Southern History* 33, 3 (August 1967), 303–330; Linden Glenn, "A Note on Negro Suffrage and Republican Politics," *Journal of Southern History* 36, 3 (August 1970), 411–420.

[23] For extensive studies of the Fourteenth Amendment see Bernard Schwartz, ed., *The Fourteenth Amendment* (New York: New York University Press, 1970).

[24] Gunnar Myrdal, *An American Dilemma* (New York: Harper & Row, 1944), pp. 523–526.

short, the well-being of the individual is dependent upon his political power. It is not surprising therefore that the question of citizenship quickly became synonymous with the right to vote. For both blacks and whites, citizenship meant political rights and privileges, and to a great extent these rights and privileges appeared to be the great equalizer.

Concern with the consequences of the acquisition of political power by blacks was one basis for white opposition to their inclusion as citizens, but there was also the fear that it symbolized full social equality, thus altering the subordinate-superordinate status ordering. This attitude is most clearly expressed in remarks by Thomas Hendricks, Democratic Senator from Indiana, during Senate debate on the proposed Fourteenth Amendment.

> We have been justly proud of the rank and title of our citizenship, for we understand it to belong to the inhabitants of the United States who were descended from the great races of people who inhabit the countries of Europe and such immigrants from those counties who have been admitted under our laws. The rank and title conferred honor at home and secured kindness, respect and safety everywhere abroad; but if this amendment be adopted we will then carry the title and enjoy its advantages in common with the Negroes, the coolies and the Indians.[25]

Although a measure of black inclusion was accomplished by the Fourteenth and Fifteenth Amendments, special circumstances surrounded the undertaking that must be borne in mind. First, it was done in the face of strenuous objections from the President, who exerted all his energies to prevent it. Second, the Southern states, where this inclusion was most significant, vigorously opposed it and its success became entirely dependent upon the military occupation of the South under the Congressional plan of reconstruction. Third, in promoting black inclusion, Congress was not guided by strong national sentiment for black inclusion, the merits of the issue, or even by any deep convictions about the justice of their actions. Instead, their actions were motivated by the political advantages which would accrue to the Republican Party from a large bloc of eternally grateful black voters in the South. There were, it must be conceded, a few legislators like Charles Sumner of Massachusetts who long considered full enfranchisement the only honorable course of action, but such legislators were indeed few in number.

It should also be observed that black inclusion was handled as a Southern problem when in fact it was a national one. Successful inclusion required a high level of national commitment which in fact never existed. Even while the issue was being vigorously debated, several Northern states were withholding from blacks important rights and responsibilities of citizenship. As late as 1865 Connecticut, Wisconsin, and Minnesota rejected proposed constitutional Amendments designed to enfranchise blacks. Ohio rejected a similar proposal in 1867, a year after the Reconstruction Act

---

[25] In Schwartz, *op. cit.*, p. 270.

enfranchising Southern blacks was passed. For these reasons, the citizenship rights acquired by blacks at this time proved extremely tenuous.

The tenuous status of the black citizen resulted not only from the above-mentioned factors but also from the untenability of political power without social preparation or economic power in a hostile society. Blacks throughout the South were largely a landless, poverty-stricken mass who depended on whites for virtually everything—land, tools, and the food they needed for survival from one crop to the next. Documenting this desperate condition, C. Vann Woodward reports that in Georgia and portions of Mississippi not more than one in every 100 black farmers owned land, and the situation was not appreciably different in the other Southern states.[26] The nation simply ignored this economic plight of the former slaves. Thus even as some blacks hailed passage of the Fourteenth and Fifteenth Amendments and the new rights and privileges they conferred, others were troubled. Some blacks were concerned about the unpreparedness of the black population for exercising the franchise. Slavery, after all, was not conducive to citizenship training and thus most of the four million blacks were not equipped for the responsibilities thrust upon them. Many assumed the responsibility optimistically like Beverly Nash, a former slave elected to the South Carolina Constitutional Convention, who said:

> I believe, my friends and fellow-citizens, we are not prepared for this suffrage. But we can learn. Give a man tools and let him commence to use them, and in time he will learn the trade. So it is with voting. We may not understand it at the start, but in time we shall learn to do our duty.[27]

Others, like Martin Delaney, Dr. R. I. Cromwell, and James Lynch, offered to train their black brothers in the "duties and responsibilities of citizenship."

The obvious political expedience involved in the efforts at inclusion was another source of concern to blacks, who argued that what they needed most was "security of life, liberty, and property rather than voting rights." The Colored National Labor Convention went to the heart of the problem in pointing out that political equality was meaningless without corresponding economic independence. It concluded that "the government in giving the Negro his freedom has given him the freedom to starve, and in giving him the ballot box has given him a coffin."[28] It was not long before the accuracy of this assessment became apparent. Within a decade after these first steps toward the inclusion of blacks major reverses set in, erasing for most the tentative steps toward full citizenship.

[26] C. Vann Woodward, *Origins of the New South* (Baton Rouge: Louisiana State University Press, 1951), p. 205.

[27] Quoted in John Hope Franklin, *op. cit.,* p. 87.

[28] Quoted in Elsie M. Lewis, "The Political Mind of the Negro, 1865–1900," *Journal of Southern History* **21**, 2 (May 1955).

Serious attention had never really been given to the social dimension of citizenship for blacks. In the South the Freedmen's Bureau met certain basic needs of the former slave, but continuing educational and economic programs were virtually nonexistent. The most visible gains were in the political arena as the Republican party helped to mobilize large numbers of black voters through organizations like the Liberty League of America. For a brief period their voting power transformed Southern politics as substantial numbers of blacks won seats to several state legislatures and others held high administrative posts. In South Carolina, for example, blacks constituted a majority of the lower house of the legislature until 1874, and a black man, Francis L. Cordozo, served as State Treasurer.[29]

Slowly, inexorably several forces combined to reverse the limited gains experienced by blacks immediately after the Civil War. Because the most visible gains were in  the political field, the most dramatic reverses occurred here, but ground was actually lost in all areas of citizenship rights. The four most potent forces contributing to the reversal were (1) the fragility and inefficiency of the new Southern state governments, (2) widespread use of violence as a political tool by Southern whites, (3) rapid change in the attitudes of Northern whites to the issue of race relations in the South, and (4) a process of gradual judicial emasculation of the Fourteenth Amendment as it applied to blacks.

The governments of the Southern states in the immediate post-Civil War years were seriously flawed in several respects, but the most frequently emphasized flaw was widespread corruption and inefficiency. In part those conditions grew out of the unique postwar conditions of the South in which many inexperienced individuals were elected to office and became victims of unscrupulous politicians, many of them Republicans who had recently migrated to the South. In a larger context, corruption in Southern politics seemed to have been part of a national trend of the times, which saw corruption in virtually all levels of government. Corruption and mismanagement were, however, tied to black participation in politics and helped justify a vigorous campaign by Southern whites to drive blacks from the political arena.

Widespread political violence employed by Southern whites against blacks and against organizations like the Freedmen's Bureau and the Union League, which helped to maintain black influence, was very effective in reducing black involvement in politics. Clandestine organizations like The Knights of the White Camelia, The White Brotherhood, The Council of Safety, or the most widely known Ku Klux Klan sprang up and wreaked terror on the black population with nighttime atrocities—whippings, murders in a variety of grotesque forms, and destruction of property—or merely

[29] For extensive discussion of the extent of black participation in the postreconstruction South see Franklin, *op. cit.*, pp. 85–126.

threats. The terror tactics which deprived blacks of the most rudimentary of all citizen rights—protection of life and property—were widely supported by white Southerners, especially leaders of the rapidly growing Southern Democratic party. State governments were incapable, and in many instances unwilling, to protect blacks. The Congress intervened through legislation like the Ku Klux Klan Act, which gave the President power to declare martial law and suspend habeas corpus in states where black citizens were not protected. Even such seemingly drastic steps failed to halt antiblack violence as Presidents lacked both the will and the manpower to implement the laws.

The lack of national commitment to black citizenship and the expediency that characterized the first attempts at inclusion were clearly reflected in national attitudes toward white atrocities in the South. Whites outside the South quickly lost interest in the cause of Republicanism in the South and with the entire program of Reconstruction which was responsible for black gains. Rising sensitivity to the economic disadvantages of continued racial turmoil and the bright prospects for rapid economic gains in a peaceful South were combined with new concern for the rights of states by Northerners; the latter now urged that the responsibility for Southern blacks be left in the hands of their former slave owners who were now regaining power throughout the South. According to Eli Ginzburg and Alfred Eichner, this attitude was clearly reflected in the pages of the *Nation,* then one of the most prestigious national periodicals. In advocating an end to national efforts on behalf of "the Negro," the periodical's editorial in 1879 suggested that "there is no political machinery to protect ignorance and inexperience completely against skill, vigor and unscrupulousness, and Southern whites boast the possession of all three."[30] It further urged that the wisest procedure was to leave every Southern state to its own people, and where Negroes were treated too badly they would leave. This new attitude was also widely shared in the United States Senate, where by 1872 a large faction of the Republican party began urging "immediate and absolute removal of all disabilities imposed on account of the rebellion." The faction claimed instead that local self-government with impartial suffrage would be greater protection than centralized power.

What is referred to as the Compromise of 1877, by which Rutherford Hayes gained the Presidency over Charles Tilden in a Presidential election decided by the House of Representatives, was only the final act in a slowly unfolding drama—the exclusion of blacks from the political system. Details of the alleged compromise vary; the essentials are as follows: Tilden, the Democratic Presidential candidate received over 270,000 popular votes more than Hayes, the Republican candidate, but Republican-controlled "returning boards" in the South certified the Republican slate of electors over the

---

[30] Quoted in Eli Ginzberg and Alfred Eichner, *The Troublesome Presence* (New York: Mentor, 1964), p. 166.

winning Democratic slate, thus creating a controversy to be resolved by the Congress. As Robert Brisbane tells it, "Sometime during the last two or three days of February, 1877, representatives of the two parties meeting in the Wormley Hotel in Washington, D.C., agreed that Hayes would be President in return for the prompt removal of federal troops from South Carolina and Louisiana by the new administration."[31] For their part, Southern Democrats promised to safeguard the rights of blacks. Hayes, who prior to the election vigorously defended efforts to protect the rights of blacks, promptly withdrew federal forces and left the black population to the care and keeping of white Southerners.

It was not long before the results of violence and terror were sanctified by the Courts. In one step after another, the Supreme Court proceeded to reestablish the power of the states and reduce those of the national government with respect to the rights of citizenship. The process began in 1873 with the Supreme Court's decision in the *Slaughter House Cases.* The issue had nothing to do with race relations, but dealt with a challenge to a Louisiana statute enacted in 1869 which granted to one corporation a slaughterhouse monopoly in Louisiana for 25 years. Independent butchers, claiming that it deprived them of their privileges and immunities as United States citizens, sought to have the law nullified. In a 5–4 decision the Court ruled that the Fourteenth Amendment contemplated no radical change in the relations of state governments with the national government or the relations of either of these governments to the people. The Court further suggested that the Congress considered the privileges and immunities of the United States citizenship primarily as those owing their existence to the federal government, or that arise out of the nature and character of the national government.[32]

The decision, a conservative interpretation of the Fourteenth Amendment, was in keeping with the shift toward a new emphasis on states rights. This was particularly pleasing to Southerners, since the ruling implied that the Fourteenth Amendment gave the federal government no new powers in the area of civil rights. The states were therefore free to protect the privileges and immunities of citizenship in their own way. A decade later the Supreme Court returned to the Fourteenth Amendment, this time in response to a challenge growing out of the Civil Rights Act passed by Congress in 1875. The relevant portion of the act provided

> That all persons within the jurisdiction of the United States shall be entitled to the full and equal enjoyment of the accommodations, advantages, facilities and privileges of inns, public conveyances on land or water, theaters and other places of public amusement; subject only to the conditions and limitations established by law and applicable alike

[31] Robert Brisbane, *The Black Vanguard* (Valley Forge, Pa.: Judson Press, 1970), p. 20.

[32] *Slaughter House Cases,* 16 Wall 36 (1873).

to citizens of every race and color, regardless of any previous condition of servitude.[33]

The Supreme Court invalidated the Civil Rights Act in what became known as the Civil Rights Cases on the ground that the Fourteenth Amendment gave Congress no positive powers over civil rights, merely the power to nullify state laws which violate the Fourteenth Amendment. It further held that the Fourteenth Amendment guaranteed protection only against violations by the state and not those of private individuals or institutions. The decision virtually stripped from the national government any power to protect the rights and interests of blacks under the Fourteenth Amendment. Ironically the same amendment, while ineffective in protecting the rights of blacks, became a major source of protection and privilege for big business corporations that were treated as "juristic persons."

In 1896 the Supreme Court took the final step in establishing the second-class status of blacks in American society. At issue was a Louisiana statute enacted in 1890 which required passenger trains to provide "equal but separate accommodations for the white and colored races." In June 1892 Homer Plessy, a black man, boarded an East Louisiana train in New Orleans and took a seat in a coach reserved for whites. He refused to move to a coach reserved for "coloreds" and was arrested. In the case, *Plessy vs. Ferguson* (1896) the Supreme Court ruled that laws providing separate public facilities for blacks and whites were constitutional so long as the facilities provided were equal. Speaking for the majority of the Court, Justice Brown asserted that "we consider the underlying fallacy of the plaintiff's argument to consist in the assumption that the enforced separation of the races stamps the colored race with a badge of inferiority." The Court took the position that inferiority was involved only if Negroes chose to interpret the rule that way. The lone dissent from the ruling was by John Marshall Harlan, who declared that "[our] Constitution is color-blind and neither knows nor tolerates classes among citizens. . . ." Nevertheless, the "separate-but-equal" doctrine became the principal constitutional pillar of second-class citizenship for blacks because it gave constitutional protection to a vast assortment of rituals and symbols associated with their subordinate status. It provided the constitutional foundation for separation and for invidious distinctions between the races in virtually every area of life.

The Court's decision in *Plessy vs. Ferguson* provided the constitutional basis for a system of apartheid or "Jim Crow" in American parlance. Segregation was common practice in several areas of life throughout many parts of the country, but it was sporadic. After 1896 "a wall of separation" between the races quickly developed and at least in the South it was totally inclusive, affecting everyone, everywhere in virtually every area of life. Woodward observes that

[33] In Schwartz, *op. cit.,* pp. 661–662.

Jim Crow laws applied to *all* Negroes—not merely to the rowdy, or drunken, or surly or ignorant ones. The new laws did not countenance the old conservative tendency to distinguish between classes of the race, to encourage the "better" element, and to draw it into a white alliance. Those laws backed up the Alabamian who told the disfranchising convention of his state that no Negro in the world was the equal of "the least, poorest, lowest-down white man I ever know. . . ." The Jim Crow laws put the authority of the state or city in the voice of the street-car conductor, the railway brakeman, the bus driver, the theater usher, and also into the voice of the hoodlum of the public parks and playgounds. They gave free rein and the majesty of the law to mass aggressions that might otherwise have been curbed, blunted or deflected.[34]

The structure of American apartheid remained intact throughout the South and, with the assistance of Woodrow Wilson, in the nation's capital until the end of World War I, when the first hesitant steps were taken in retreat from a full-fledged American version of apartheid.

In comparing the United States and South Africa we identified several of those factors that have operated to encourage retreat from the system of apartheid in the United States. One additional factor is the mass migration of blacks from the rural, agricultural South to Northern urban areas. This created severe strains including widespread violence that prompted demands among some "liberal" whites for improved race relations; it made the structure of apartheid in its complete and rigid Southern form virtually impossible to maintain, and it created a new set of political dynamics in which urban political organizations found it necessary to win and retain black political support. Thus gains were slowly realized in the struggle for full citizenship for blacks.

## Full Citizenship as a Contemporary Problem

Much has changed in the pattern of American race relations over the years, but blacks still cannot be said to have become full members of the political community. With a substantial degree of accuracy they can still be called "second-class citizens." One survey of black leaders in 1964 revealed that although these leaders perceived profound changes in the conditions of black life in the society, they were unanimous in the belief that full citizenship is not yet a reality.[35]  In fact, full inclusion into the political community has been a principal goal of black political activism over the years, and even today it retains its prominent place.

In a fundamental sense, acquisition of full citizenship implies destruction of the subordinate-superordinate pattern of race relations. In assessing

---

[34] Woodward, *op. cit.*
[35] Daniel Thompson, "Civil Rights Leadership: An Opinion Study," *Journal of Negro Education* 32, 4 (Fall 1963), 426–436.

progress toward this goal we may examine black inclusion by reference to Marshall's three stages of citizenship rights. The historical pattern reviewed here indicates that progress toward full American citizenship for blacks has followed the pattern suggested by Marshall to a certain extent. The first steps toward citizenship were limited to acquisition of "legal rights." In conceding this, white Americans did not run the risk of altering the subordinate status of blacks; they merely sought to provide the minimum right attached to citizenship. As a practical matter, formal concession of full legal rights has not really meant equality before the law in fact. The evidence is overwhelming that equality before the law is far from reality. To be black and poor is often to be subject to a range of disabilities not experienced by others. Thus the suggestion that this aspect of citizenship has been realized speaks to a formal state of affairs only. The second stage—political rights—came next, and although it was formally conferred by 1870 it is becoming reality only after almost a hundred years of persistent effort.

The social component has been the most elusive aspect of citizenship. Although today blacks suffer relatively few impediments to full exercise of their legal and political rights, an enormous gulf continues to separate them from the rest of the society in the social sphere. Some reported changes in white attitudes notwithstanding, there is still considerable evidence of a widespread perception of blacks as social inferiors among whites. The rituals and symbols of social distance have become considerably more subtle and thus less obvious, but in many areas they persist intact. Equally significant is the fact that on almost any set of social indicators blacks emerge substantially lower than their white counterparts. The Kerner Commission report in 1968 clearly documented the great disparities between blacks and whites with respect to levels of employment, occupation, income, and education. Several studies since that time confirm the continued existence, and in some cases still widening gap between the two races especially with respect to earning capacity. Full acceptance by the society and unimpeded access to the social benefits of citizenship thus remain outside the grasp of the black population.

Incompleteness of the inclusion process is only a small part of the problem that faces blacks. The potentially more consequential part of the problem is the tenuousness of the advances achieved. Black inclusion thus far

**TABLE 5.1**   *Ratio of Negro Income to White Income*

| | Median Family Income | | |
|---|---|---|---|
| Year | White | Negro | Ratio: Negro to White |
| 1971 | $10,622 | $6,440 | 60.6 |
| 1970 | 10,216 | 6,278 | 61.5 |
| 1969 | 9,794 | 5,999 | 61 |
| 1968 | 8,937 | 5,360 | 60 |
| 1967 | 8,274 | 4,919 | 59 |
| 1966 | 7,792 | 4,506 | 58 |
| 1965 | 7,251 | 3,886 | 54 |

*Source:* U.S. Bureau of the Census. *Current Population Reports,* Series P–23, No. 39 and Series P–60, No. 85; and *Civil Rights, Progress Report 1970* (Washington, D.C.: Congressional Quarterly), 46.

has been a result either of conflicts among whites from which blacks have been incidental beneficiaries, or the accumulation of piecemeal concessions primarily designed to diffuse crises. Conspicuously missing has been significant evidence of a basic commitment to the notion that blacks are or ought to be full members of the political community. It is significant that no President before John F. Kennedy ventured to propose such a commitment as national policy.

The tentativeness of black advancement toward complete inclusion is reflected in the laws that now protect their status. Other Americans enjoy legal, political, and social rights on the basis of a broad consensus within the society that they belong to that society and are entitled to the benefits of belonging. The studies by Bendix and Marshall suggest the gradual inclusion of the European lower classes in full citizenship on the basis of a consensus

**TABLE 5.2**   *Income and Educational Attainment, 1971*

| | | Median Income, 1971 | | |
|---|---|---|---|---|
| | | Black | White | Negro Income as a Percent of White |
| Elementary: | Total | $ 5,170 | $ 7,036 | 73.5 |
| | Less than 8 years | 4,956 | 6,256 | 79.2 |
| | 8 years | 5,951 | 7,831 | 76.0 |
| High School: | Total | 7,456 | 11,042 | 67.5 |
| | 1 to 3 years | 6,628 | 10,028 | 66.1 |
| | 4 years | 8,165 | 11,466 | 71.2 |
| College: | 1 or more years | 12,249 | 14,742 | 83.1 |

*Source:* U.S. Bureau of the Census, *Current Population Reports,* Series P–23, No. 39 and Series P–60, No. 85.

within the society. In sharp contrast, black Americans are protected by specific statutes that depend for their enforcement on the whim of the President or the particular composition of the Supreme Court. In some instances, as with the political rights of Southern blacks, they exist by legislation for a fixed period of time—five years in the case of the 1965 Voting Rights Act, and the continuation of those rights remains a major political controversy whose outcome cannot be confidently predicted. The concern among many blacks is clearly not unfounded that today's gains may be quickly erased, as in the postreconstruction era. The grim reality is that black Americans exist without benefit of a broad consensus that they belong to the society in which they live.

# 6

---

# Response to Subordination:
# The Pattern of Black
# Nationalist Thought

The ordeal of a subordinate status evoked from blacks a wide range of responses. Many stretched to its limits the meager resources at their disposal in working for change, and as this study shows, the effort has continued in a variety of ways. In addition to these kinds of efforts, blacks pondered their dilemma and advocated several approaches to the problem of improving their situation. The body of thought generally referred to as black nationalism reflects these efforts, provides invaluable insights into the depth and variety of black responses to their condition, and serves as a useful backdrop against which contemporary black political thought and behavior may be studied. In this chapter we will therefore examine black nationalist thought in terms of its meaning, its primary emphases, and its functions for the black political subculture.

On the afternoon of Friday, March 10, 1972, I stood just outside the main auditorium of the Gary, Indiana high school where the First National Black Political Convention was underway. For a while virtually everything seemed overshadowed by the presence of members of several black nationalist organizations competing for the attention and support of the bustling black crowd. Black Muslims impeccably dressed in traditional business suits tirelessly distributed copies of *Muhammad Speaks,* the Muslim newspaper. Representatives of the Republic of New Africa strutted about conspicuously in full military attire, and Imamu Baraka and his retinue of Pan-African nationalists, clad in black pajama-style dress, added a peculiar kind of color and drama to the assembly. More important, these organizations demonstrated the resurgence of black nationalism in a bewildering variety of forms as part of the contemporary world of black America. These three groups are only a small part of the several organizations which now claim the nationalist label and identify their activities and objectives in nationalist terms.

90

## The Meaning of Black Nationalism

Despite its renewed prominence and the fact that it has been extensively discussed by both scholars and polemicists for a long time, the meaning of black nationalism remains somewhat unclear. On the one hand the concept has been rather narrowly interpreted as a "separatist ideology" or a form of radicalism associated with the Black Muslims (Nation of Islam). Thus two of the major studies of black nationalism focus exclusively on the Muslims[1] and a third one attempts to ascertain the level of support among blacks for black nationalism by measuring the level of support for the Black Muslims.[2] On the other hand, some scholars have viewed it much more broadly as the body of thought and expressions of black consciousness and solidarity within the United States and throughout the diaspora. This view is suggested by August Meier, Elliott Rudwick, and John Bracey in their observation that

> The term "black nationalism" has been used in American history to describe a body of social thought, attitudes, and actions ranging from the simplest expression of ethnocentrism and racial solidarity to the comprehensive and sophisticated ideologies of Pan-Negroism or Pan-Africanism. Between these extremes lie many varieties of black nationalism.[3]

Part of the problem of clarifying what is meant by black nationalism stems from the difficulties that exist with the broader concept of nationalism. It has posed enormous descriptive, analytical, and typological problems for scholars because of the wide variety of views over time that are characterized as nationalism. Early expressions of nationalism which contributed to organization of the modern European state system, the nationalism of the Slavs and other ethnic groups of Eastern Europe, and the post-World War II nationalist movements of the then colonial peoples all share some common characteristics as well as substantial differences which make a precise, common definition difficult. Most studies of these varied forms of nationalism suggest that it is a feeling or emotion shared by a group of people who perceive themselves as sharing a common set of experiences and some tangible common bonds, and who frequently but not always share a common homeland.[4] This nationalism, which in some cases may also be viewed as the

---

[1] C. Eric Lincoln, *The Black Muslims in America* (Boston: Beacon Press, 1961); E. U. Essien-Udom, *Black Nationalism, A Search for Identity in America* (New York: Dell, 1962).

[2] Gary Marx, *Protest and Prejudice, A Study of Belief in the Black Community* (New York: Harper & Row, 1967), pp. 106–125.

[3] August Meier, Elliott Rudwick, and John Bracey, *Black Nationalism* (Indianapolis: Bobbs-Merrill, 1970), p. xxvi.

[4] See for example Hans Kohn, *The Idea of Nationalism* (New York: Macmillan, 1960), pp. 3–20; John Kautsky, *Political Change in Underdeveloped Countries: Nationalism and Communism* (New York: Wiley, 1966), 32–48.

development of "ethnic consciousness," frequently includes the aspiration to some form of self-determination albeit this has not always been achieved or even vigorously pursued by the affected group.

These conditions all seem generally applicable to black Americans who share a common bond of race and African origin, a common experience of subordination and exploitation, and a common aspiration for dignity and equality with all other human beings. Du Bois identified precisely these bonds in his observation that

> The so-called American Negro group, . . . while it is in no sense absolutely set off physically from its fellow Americans, has nevertheless a strong, heriditary cultural unity born of slavery, of common suffering, prolonged proscription and curtailment of political and civil rights. . . . Prolonged policies of segregation and discrimination have involuntarily welded the mass almost into a nation within a nation.[5]

Furthermore the aspiration for dignity and equality has been thought by some blacks to require partial or complete self-determination for the group. This feeling is reflected in the persistent advocacy of "separation" of some kind by many black nationalists. It is appropriate therefore that we view black nationalism as *all those expressions and activities by black Americans that emphasize their common origins, experiences, and aspirations and that seek to dignify the race.* This broad definition incorporates the many forms of separatist thought among blacks as well as the rich, varied, and sometimes conflicting body of thought relating more broadly to the black predicament in the United States over time. Of course, it has the disadvantages of vagueness and imprecision, but what is referred to as black nationalism is neither clear nor precise.

Unavoidably, assessment of the character and meaning of black nationalism raises the question of its relationship to the nationalism of the former colonial peoples of Africa, South and Southeast Asia, and the Caribbean. Noting similarities between nationalist sentiments in these areas and those of black Americans, some observers have suggested that they are all part of a single, broad nationalist movement among nonwhite peoples of the "Third World." One strong proponent of this view is John Bracey, who asserts that "black nationalism is a variety of the nationalisms of non-Western peoples in general and of the black peoples of Africa and the West Indies in particular."[6] Bracey's principal argument for this position is that black Americans exist in a colonial status, and like the Afro-Asian world the colonial experience gave birth to black nationalism.

There is little doubt that a strong relationship exists between the nationalism of former colonial peoples and black American nationalism. They

---

[5] Quoted in Carey Williams, *Brothers Under the Skin* (Boston: Little, Brown, 1964), p. 251.

[6] Meier, Rudwick, and Bracey, *op. cit.*, p. lvii.

all can be characterized as "defensive nationalism" having as their basic objective eradication of oppression and exploitation by white Europeans. Thus to some degree they all involve racial struggles. In this regard Gwendolyn Carter's observation about African nationalism in South Africa is applicable to black nationalism in the United States. She observed that "the expressions of African nationalism in South Africa like those in colonial Africa are conditioned by the superior power of white authorities, and a white community whose policies and actions determine the milieu within which Africans must live."[7]

This basic similarity results not only from a degree of similarity in experiences and objectives but from a fairly long-standing pattern of interaction among elites from these areas. Africans and West Indians have benefited from sharing ideas and tactics of struggle developed among black Americans. One example of this sharing is provided by the experience of Africans in South Africa. Although interaction between them and black Americans has not been extensive, A. P. Walshe provides evidence that black Americans were influential both in the development of South African nationalism and in their approach to the struggle against white supremacy in that country.[8] The parallels between the two approaches to this struggle are further demonstrated in Chapter 2 as the basic strategies in the two societies reveal remarkable similarities. On the other hand, black Americans benefited from the contributions of race-conscious intellectuals from the West Indies as well as from the liberation struggles of Africans which provided new incentives and models for action.

In spite of the apparent similarities between black nationalism in the United States and nationalism in African and West Indian societies, there are some distinct characteristics of the phenomenon in the United States that must be noted. Perhaps most significant is the fact that blacks within the United States exist within a larger nation-state to which most claim allegiance; thus theirs is a form of "subgroup nationalism" that has not been primarily concerned with independent nationhood. In fact, while for most African and West Indian groups nationalist aspirations centered around the demand for independence, among black Americans there has been no similar clear-cut objective but an exploration of several possible paths to a dignified and fulfilling existence. This basic difference contributed to the relative complexity of nationalist thought in black America, since there has not been the opportunity to articulate an unambiguous, widely shared goal such as independence from colonial rule. This fact also suggests that while we may refer broadly to "nationalist thought" in black America, we cannot really

[7] Gwendolyn Carter, "African Concepts of Nationalism in South Africa," in Heribert Adam, ed., *South Africa, Sociological Perspectives* (London: Oxford University Press, 1971), p. 104.
[8] A. P. Walshe, "Black American Thought and Nationalism in South Africa," *Review of Politics* (January 1970), 51–77.

equate it with the highly purposive "nationalist movements" that culminated in independent nationhood in other societies.

Second, black nationalism has been shaped by the specific and in some respects unique character of the black experience in the United States. It has ebbed and flowed with the fluctuating conditions of the black population, and its specific content and thrust have been shaped by variations in the attitudes and behavior of white Americans. In view of these distinct features of black nationalism, we may regard it as related to yet distinct from the nationalisms of these other African peoples.

## The Scope of Black Nationalism

Black nationalism has been present throughout most of the black presence in America, but it has not been a consistent stream of thought nor has it maintained a consistently high level of support among blacks. Manifestations of nationalist sentiments have ebbed and flowed over the years and the specific focus of these sentiments has shifted from one major theme to another. Meier, Rudwick, and Bracey suggested that there have been in addition to the present at least three distinct periods of history when nationalist sentiment reached particularly high levels. Furthermore, these periods of heightened nationalism coincided with particularly difficult and disappointing experiences for blacks.[9]

The first of these periods of heightened nationalist expression was between 1790 and 1820. During this time initial optimism surrounding the Declaration of Independence and the birth of a new nation on liberal, democratic principles changed to disillusionment. Not only did these events leave the black condition unaltered but several subsequent events combined to worsen that condition. The modest impetus toward emancipation that was manifest in several Northern states in the aftermath of the revolution quickly subsided. The Fugitive Slave Act of 1793 brought the national government into direct support of the institution of slavery, and Eli Whitney's cotton gin provided a new and compelling rationale for its continuation. Faced with these developments, blacks became more conscious of their separateness from the dominant society and pessimistic about any prospects for improvement of their lot. Establishment of black institutions—primarily all-black churches and social or fraternal organizations—began about this time, along with the first major stirrings of an emigrationist movement. According to Meier, Rudwick, and Bracey, the question of emigration was broached in 1789 but the first positive action in this regard came in 1815 when Paul Cuffe sailed for Sierra Leone with 38 "free Negroes." During this period, the strong identification with Africa which has characterized black nationalism took clear shape.

[9] Meier, Rudwick, and Bracey, *op. cit.*, pp. xxx–lii.

By the 1840s a second major wave of black nationalist thought began to develop. In the two decades prior to this time many blacks were encouraged by the growing antislavery movement. They worked vigorously for the antislavery cause and against persistent efforts to effect their total exclusion from the political community but as the decade of the '40s progressed, reality overcame optimistic sentiments and again blacks looked elsewhere for a solution to their problems. The abolitionist movement had made no real progress toward emancipation and even its white leaders often proved contemptuous of blacks. The intensifying debate about the expansion of slavery and the clear loss of ground in the civil and political rights of blacks in Northern states contributed prominently to a new wave of disillusionment.

Against this background, black spokesmen like Martin Delaney, Alexander Crummell, and Edward Blyden emerged as vigorous exponents of black nationalism and advocates of emigration from the United States. Emphasizing that blacks were Africans in exile and victims of degradation, they urged establishment of a separate black nation to fulfill the yearnings of "every true Negro." Thus black nationalism, fueled by the frustrations and disappointments of the race, reached a new peak by the eve of the Civil War, only to subside once more in the postwar decade when the promise of full citizenship was held out briefly before the black population.

By about 1880 the immediate post-Civil War efforts at inclusion of the black population as full citizens were being sharply reversed. Widespread use of terror tactics including lynching and mob violence, an unsympathetic judiciary, and the rapidly waning interest of a once-sympathetic North combined to usher in a new era of gloom. As in the past, many blacks again resorted to various forms of nationalist expression in response to these developments as they searched for a plausible course of action. This third period of heightened nationalist sentiment lasted until about 1920. During this time Booker Washington emphasized the advisability of "turning inward" to develop a strong economic base for the progress of the race instead of fighting for political and social rights. Du Bois' more aggressive advocacy of continued struggle for full political and social equality for the race, the intellectual and artistic efforts to explore, develop, and popularize the historical and cultural traditions of the race all combined to mark this period as the most productive in the development of black nationalist thought. It culminated with the appearance of Marcus Garvey in 1916 and the rapid development of a large-scale nationalist organization that reached its peak in 1921.

The present era, beginning in the early 1960s, constitutes the fourth period of strong nationalist emphasis. It was not prompted as much by the total failures experienced in earlier periods as by a new impatience with the pace and character of changes and the inevitable rise in expectations stimulated by limited progress. While it is difficult to pinpoint all the factors contributing to the current resurgence of black nationalism, three specific developments deserve mention. First, the post-World War II era has been one of unprecedented economic prosperity for the nation as a whole, but a prosperity in which relatively few blacks participated. Failure to realize improvement in the quality of life in a period of rapid overall growth thus appears to have been one factor in the new black nationalism. Second, generations of quiet suffering with oppression and equally quiet efforts to modify conditions via the courts yielded to vigorous mass action that characterized the decade of the civil rights movement. In addition to the specific legislation it prompted, the movement served as a powerful mobilizing force arousing blacks to the reality of their situation and to the enormity of the obstacles they face. Finally, the emergence of African and Caribbean peoples from centuries of colonial bondage into full nationhood provided a challenge and inspiration and, in some instances, a model to which blacks in America could aspire.

This periodization is inevitably imprecise, since in fact there were no sharp time boundaries separating periods of heightened nationalist activity from periods of low or modest activity. Furthermore, periodization should not obscure the fact that there has been a degree of continuity in nationalist thought over the years. These qualifications notwithstanding, it helps to indicate the ebb-and-flow pattern of black nationalist thought, and emphasizes the direct relationship between black nationalism and the specific conditions to which the black population has been subjected.

A significant concern with respect to the scope of black nationalism is the degree of support it achieved within the black population. Very few efforts have been made to assess the level of support for nationalist programs or ideas at any time. In perhaps the only such attempt, Gary Marx examined support for only the Black Muslims and their program and found very little popular enthusiasm for this form of nationalism. There is virtually no reliable basis for estimates of support for the broader range of nationalist issues; however, one broad pattern can be noted. Until the emergence of the Garvey movement in 1917, black nationalist thought was confined largely to a small elite within the black population. Through newspapers, pamphlets, and conventions which were widespread during the 1830s–1840s, black intellectuals and political activists espoused their nationalist ideas. The churches provided the only substantial channel of these ideas to "the masses."

Larger numbers of people became directly involved in some aspects of "cultural nationalism," but it was with the emergence of Garveyism that a dramatic change occurred. Marcus Garvey, a relatively uneducated but widely traveled Jamaican, arrived in New York in 1916 and with his remarkable oratorical skill soon captured the attention of large numbers of poor, uneducated urban blacks. With uncanny perceptiveness, Garvey recognized and appealed to the fear, insecurity, demoralization, and hopelessness of the urban black masses, most of whom were recent migrants from the South. In large numbers they joined his Universal Negro Improvement Association. [10] They were inspired by a grand vision of a soon-to-be established powerful black nation of Africa. The black elite had by this time redirected its interests into activities like the NAACP and viewed Garvey's mass movement with contempt.

Between the demise of Garveyism in the mid-1920s and the mid-1960s when blacks from all walks of life—particularly the young—were drawn to various nationalist organizations and developed a new pride and consciousness of color, black nationalism remained essentially a lower-class movement. The Black Muslims, first organized in 1935, concentrated on the urban poor in much the same manner of Garveyism and only recently began to broaden their appeal. [11] Today, formally organized nationalist groups continue to be very small, but nationalist programs, attitudes, and aspirations are widespread. It might even be said that to some degree the majority of blacks of all socioeconomic levels now embrace nationalist sentiments in some form. Several factors have contributed to the popularization of nationalist ideas and the bridging of the gap in this area between black elites and masses, but certainly Malcolm X was the most potent single contributor. [12] During his years as the articulate spokesman for the Black Muslims and particularly in the year after his separation from the Muslims, Malcolm X provided a clear, vigorous, and compelling exposition of basic nationalist themes that proved remarkably influential in all segments of the black community.

## The Content of Black Nationalism

We observed earlier that unlike the nationalist movements of the colonial areas, black nationalism has not had a single, widely shared goal toward which the black population could be directed. On the contrary, black nationalism consists of several themes or thrusts, some existing simultaneously and others being identified with a specific time period or set of circumstances. Over the years black nationalism emphasized religious, economic, political, and cultural themes with each one especially prominent during a particular period of time. By 1916, what J. Herman Blake characterizes as "integral nationalism," appeared in the form of a single nationalist movement embracing all these themes. [13] The Garvey movement and the Black Muslims represent this kind

[10] Of the several interesting studies of the Garvey movement the most extensive is that by Edmund D. Cronon, *Black Moses: The Story of Marcus Garvey and the Universal Negro Improvement Association* (Madison: University of Wisconsin Press, 1955).

[11] Essien-Udom, *op. cit.*, pp. 201–231.

[12] For wide-ranging assessment of the impact of Malcolm X see the collection of articles in *Malcolm X, The Man and His Times* (New York: Macmillan, 1969), and J. Herman Blake, "Black Nationalism," *Annals of the American Academy of Political and Social Sciences* 382 (March 1969), 15–25.

[13] *Ibid.*

of approach. We can examine the content of black nationalism by reference to three basic themes or concerns: (1) the search for ways of "making out" in America, (2) the impulse to withdraw or achieve some form of separation from white America, (3) the attempt to identify with the diaspora or blacks scattered throughout the world.

### The Challenge of Making Out in America

To a certain extent all expressions of black nationalism have as a basic objective survival in spite of stultifying and humiliating white racism. Some, however, have been more directly concerned with the problem of adjusting to, surviving in, and struggling against racism and black subordination within the United States. This is the case with the religious, economic and political themes in black nationalism.

What is now referred to as "religious nationalism" includes the emergence of separate black churches and other religious or spiritual organizations, as well as the development of a theology particularly oriented to blacks. Both steps were prompted by the increasing harshness of the segregation of early churches and the obviously self-serving and even sinister utilization of the Bible to reinforce black subordination. The all-black church came into being in about 1790 with the founding of the African Methodist Episcopal Church (AME) as a result of the obvious incongruity of worship in an intensely racist setting. The Reverend Richard Allen (1760–1831), founder of the first black church in America, relates that blacks were forced to withdraw from the white church in Philadelphia after whites not only insisted that blacks sit in the balcony during worship, but actually forcibly ejected a black worshipper during prayer when he failed to conform.[14]

The development of black churches not only constituted a solution to the immediate problem of securing an environment conducive to worship—it became the first visible separatist move executed by blacks and immediately began to contribute vitally to black life. Daniel Payne, in one early history of the AME church, points out that it threw blacks upon their own financial and administrative resources, giving them an opportunity to manage their own affairs. Furthermore, he observes, "the separation of our church from the Methodist Episcopal [white] church has been beneficial to the man of color by giving him an independence of character which he could neither hope for nor attain if he had remained as the ecclesiastical vassal of his white brethren."[15]

The church rapidly became the crucial social institution in black life, serving as the focal point of communication, organization, and "together-

[14] Richard Allen, "The Founding of the African Methodist Episcopal Church," in Meier, Rudwick, and Bracey, *op. cit.,* p. 7.
[15] Daniel A. Payne, *History of the African Methodist Episcopal Church* (Nashville, Tenn.: AME Publishing House, 1891), 13.

ness." In time it became the chief instrument for dissemination of nationalist thought, especially since many of the leading black nationalists were ministers. To a great extent this crucial role of the church has continued to this day, as evidenced by the fact that the most successful nationalist movements among blacks in this century have been in part religious movements with a church at the center.

The development of black churches has been followed by an even more significant expression of religious nationalism, the development of a "black theology."[16] Observers have commented on the use of religion to pacify and soothe the oppressed black population.[17] To an equally great extent religion has served to convey and perpetuate racist values. In addition to its crude utilization by white Americans as evidence of black inferiority, Roger Bastide suggests that Christianity, both Protestantism and Catholicism, "has been accompanied by a symbolism of color."[18] This symbolism is most dramatically represented in the association of goodness or purity with white and evil or sinfulness with blackness and in the practice of depicting divine personages as white.

Black nationalists have sought to counter this negative image of blacks and other nonwhite peoples fostered by traditional Christian theology with one more congruent with black values. This effort is consistent with the efforts of black peoples in Latin America and Africa to associate the divine personages with blackness by depicting them as black. Bastide reports that in colonial Africa there were "efforts on the part of the Africans to free themselves from the dominance of the white missions and to establish black Messiahs as saviors of their own rejected, down-trodden and exploited race."[19] Togolese writer Dr. R. E. G. Armattoe captured this thrust in poetry:[20]

> Our God is black
> Black of eternal blackness
> With large voluptuous lips
> Matted hair and brown liquid eyes . . .
> For in his image are we made
> Our God is black.

Furthermore, rejecting the attitudes of passivity and other-worldliness that has characterized most religious belief, the black theology emphasizes height-

---

[16] A classic early statement reflecting this trend is Henry Turner, "God Is a Negro," in Meier, Rudwick, and Bracey, *op. cit.*, pp. 154–155. For a recent expression of this perspective see James H. Cone, *Black Theology and Black Power* (New York: Seabury, 1969).

[17] A notable example is Gary Marx, *op. cit.*, pp. 94–105.

[18] Roger Bastide, "Color, Racism and Christianity," *Daedalus* (Spring 1967), pp. 313.

[19] *Ibid.*, 317–319.

[20] Ras Khan, The Poetry of Dr. R. E. G. Armattoe. (*Présence Africaine*, February 1957), quoted from Colin Legum, *Pan-Africanism* (New York: Praeger, 1965), p. 18.

ened racial consciousness and the necessity for militant action to induce change.

A similar though somewhat more complex set of factors prompted the widespread advocacy of economic self-reliance or "economic nationalism" by blacks. Although it was urged as early as the 1850s it became a prominent theme after about 1880 as the major reverses of the post-reconstruction era created a new mood of disillusionment among blacks. Economic nationalism thus emerged as an alternative to full social and political involvement in the society by blacks. Its chief proponent was Booker Washington and it was an integral part of his "philosophy of accommodation." The essence of the approach was that in the face of their exclusion from the political arena, blacks should refrain from persisting in the struggle for political rights and instead should strive for economic self-sufficiency for the race. Blacks were urged to develop basic skills and their own business enterprises and to support black economic enterprises.

Washington and the other advocates of economic nationalism considered the strategy vital to the survival of the race because of their limited resources, more so because the influx of European immigrants flooded the labor market, occupying the place in the economy which blacks might otherwise have occupied. Another equally important motive was belief that when blacks became economically strong their inclusion in the society would be assured. This view was expressed by Booker T. Washington in perhaps his most famous public speech, that at the Atlanta Exposition in September 1895:

> The wisest among my race understand that the agitation of questions of social equality is the extremest folly, and that progress in the enjoyment of all the privileges that come to us must be the result of severe and constant struggle rather than of artificial forcing. No race that has anything to contribute to the markets of the world is long in any degree ostracized. It is important and right that all privileges of the law be ours, but it is vastly more important that we be prepared for the exercises of these privileges. The opportunity to earn a dollar in a factory just now is worth infinitely more than the opportunity to spend a dollar in an opera-house.[21]

The advocacy of economic nationalism coincided with and contributed substantially to development of a black "petit-bourgeoisie." White hostility toward blacks especially in the South forced the small group of black businessmen to rely almost entirely on support from blacks. According to Meier, "it is among what we should call this upwardly mobile middle class that the philosophy of racial progress through economic solidarity ... and the philosophy of Booker T. Washington found their greatest support."[22]

[21] In Howard Brotz, ed., *Negro Social and Political Thought, 1850–1900* (New York: Basic Books, 1966), p. 359.
[22] August Meier, "Negro Class Structure and Ideology in the Age of Booker T. Washington," *Phylon* (1962), 260.

Within a short time after its active promulgation its effects began to become apparent. The National Negro Business League, organized in 1900 to encourage black economic self-improvement, reported that in the period 1900–1914 the total number of black business enterprises doubled, going from 20,000 to 40,000, and there were many other signs of economic progress.[23]

Economic nationalism had as a basic objective eventual integration of blacks into the larger society and reflected a willingness to postpone this until economic strength was achieved. The deferral of efforts for social and political equality or full citizenship was too great a compromise for some blacks, notably Monroe Trotter and W. E. B. Du Bois. Not only did they criticize what they regarded as a humiliating acceptance of a subordinate status, but with others similarly opposed to this strategy they organized the short-lived Niagara Movement in 1905.[24] Through this organization and individually these "radical blacks" advocated an alternative strategy, that of unwavering struggle for full citizenship.

The basic differences reflected in an essentially conservative economic nationalism and a more radical commitment to uncompromising struggle for full political rights represented a clash of interests as well as backgrounds. Booker T. Washington's background as a slave whose incredible diligence and patience brought him considerable success brought to the problem a point of view vastly different from that of Du Bois, whose upbringing was far removed from the ordeal of slavery and whose "ivy league" background inculcated a different set of attitudes toward the racial problem. As an intellectual he saw the problem of racism as an evil with which no compromise was possible, whereas Washington's practical experience led him to choose the path of incrementalism, moving stealthily to secure progress for the race while endearing himself to whites with his indications of satisfaction with the "place" accorded blacks.

Part of the effort at making out under the particular condition to which blacks were subject involved the search for the black man's past, his cultural heritage, and his contribution to civilization. These were particularly important because slavery left a largely rootless and demoralized black population constantly bombarded with assertions of their inferiority and only vaguely, if at all, aware of their heritage. This was the task of black "cultural nationalism," a dramatic cultural awakening which got underway during the first decade of this century. By the early 1920s the "Harlem Renaissance" became the focal point of this cultural outburst. It was marked by a new pride in blackness, by a celebration of the creativity and effervescence of the separate black society, by a search for cultural and historical roots, and by the expression in poetry and song of the political attitudes and aspirations of the black peoples of the new world. This rich and exciting era brought international attention to its foremost contributors—the writers Countee Cullen,

[23] *Ibid.*
[24] For a study of this organization see Elliott Rudwick, "The Niagara Movement," *Journal of Negro History* **42**, 3 (July 1957), 177–200.

Langston Hughes, and Claude McKay, among others, and entertainers like Ethel Waters and Bill Robinson—to name a few. It included major steps by black scholars to explore the history and heritage of blacks. Toward this end the Association for the Study of Negro Life and History was organized in 1915 by Professor Carter Woodson and began publishing the *Journal of Negro History*. This cultural nationalism helped blacks in discovering themselves, imbued them with a new degree of pride, dignity, and self-confidence, so much so that the press at the time referred freely to the "New Negro."[25]

Finally, the cultural expressions of the time reflected the political mood of blacks in a variety of ways. The anger and frustration resulting from widespread violence against blacks prompted Claude McKay's immortal statement of resolute defiance:[26]

> If we must die, let it not be like hogs
> Hunted and penned in an inglorious spot,
> While round us bark the mad and hungry dogs,
> Making their mock at our accursèd lot.
> If we must die, O let us nobly die,
> So that our precious blood may not be shed
> In vain; then even the monsters we defy
> Shall be constrained to honor us though dead!
> O kinsmen! we must meet the common foe!
> Though far outnumbered let us show us brave,
> And for their thousand blows deal one deathblow!
> What though before us lies the open grave?
> Like men we'll face the murderous, cowardly pack,
> Pressed to the wall, dying, but fighting back!

The loneliness and alienation felt by many was also reflected in the themes portraying blacks as an alien people hopelessly longing for the motherland.

### Looking Elsewhere—The Emigrationist Impulse

Making out in white America was not the path chosen by all black nationalists. At least as early as 1787 and consistently since that time some blacks have urged complete withdrawal from the United States. The first known effort at withdrawal involved about eighty blacks from Boston who petitioned the state legislature in 1787 for money to migrate to Africa because their circumstances in America were "very disagreeable and disadvantageous." In 1815 Paul Cuffe, a black sea captain, left with 38 "free blacks" for Africa; during the next two decades a few thousand blacks migrated to Canada and Haiti and National Negro Conventions debated the

[25] A representative work of the period is Alain Locke, *The New Negro, An Interpretation* (New York: Boni, 1925), pp. 3–18.
[26] *Selected Poems of Claude McKay* (New York: Twayne, 1953), p. 53.

merits of migration throughout the 1920s and 1930s.[27] The sentiment continues to exist today as a few blacks continue to migrate to Africa in search of a new life; many others speak wistfully of the desire to migrate, and still many others support the idea of some form of separation into black and white societies in the present United States.

The desire to leave the United States was prompted by at least two distinct considerations. First, many blacks were motivated by the recognition that full and equal citizenship could never be achieved by blacks because of the depth and intensity of white racism, and considered their subordinate status an intolerable indignity. Dr. Martin Delaney, one of the remarkably versatile black intellectuals of the nineteenth century, seems representative of this view. In 1852 at the age of 40 Delaney completed his training at the Medical School of Harvard College after having been a successful writer and editor of the *Mystery,* one of the first weekly Negro newspapers and a co-editor with Frederick Douglass of the *Northstar.* He conceded, however, that although he would just as well live among whites as among blacks he was forced to look elsewhere because of the hopelessness of the black situation in America.[28] Having come to this conclusion, he spent several years as a vigorous and articulate exponent of black withdrawal from white America. This approach to separatism meant that whenever there was cause for optimism about the prospects for change in the conditions of black life the separatist impulse would subside. It has accordingly fluctuated with the changing conditions in American race relations. Much of the recent advocacy of withdrawal from the United States is based on this feeling of disillusionment with treatment by whites combined with a conviction that the future holds nothing better.

A second, though not unrelated rationale for withdrawal is reflected in the views of Edward Blyden and Marcus Garvey. For Blyden, if black subordination provided the immediate incentive for withdrawal, the larger and more compelling reason was that it was an inevitable step toward the "fulfillment of the race." In Blyden's view, "the heart of every true Negro yearns after a distinct and separate nationality,"[29] thus it was not of great importance whether or not white attitudes toward blacks changed. The creation of a black nation was a natural aspiration that should be pursued, and black subordination in white America made this undertaking only more urgent.

Both Blyden and later Garvey felt that all the major racial groups possessed sovereign states of which they could be proud, but that there was no such state for people of African origin. Blyden thus urged that blacks need

---

[27] See in this regard Theodore Draper, *The Rediscovery of Black Nationalism* (New York: Viking, 1969), pp. 14–47.

[28] *Ibid.,* p. 24.

[29] Edward Blyden, "The Call of Providence to the Descendants of Africa in America," in Brotz, *op. cit.,* p. 117.

"some African power, some great center of the race where our physical, pecuniary and intellectual strength may be collected."[30]   The first step toward such a power base would come with the mass migration of blacks from America. Several decades later Garvey echoed this theme and made it one of the cornerstones of his nationalist program. By his own account, on becoming familiar with the plight of blacks throughout the new world he began to ask, Where is the black man's country and his emperor? These were indispensable to the achievement of strength and dignity for the race. Thus Garvey's advocacy of mass migration to Africa by blacks was less a desire to escape black subordination here than a desire to build a black empire that would provide strength, dignity, and pride for black people everywhere. The grand migration which Garvey promised never occurred, but he came closer than anyone else to providing a measure of fulfillment to the dream. In a massive world convention in August 1920 that marked the peak of Garvey-ism, Garvey proclaimed himself provisional President of Africa, appointed Knights and other impressive-sounding officers of the new nation (including Duke of the Nile, Knight of the Distinguished Order of Ethiopia, Ashanti, and Mozambique) and with great pomp and pageantry Garvey and his followers paraded through the streets of New York City. One observer provides this description of the scene:

> His Excellency, Marcus Garvey, Provisional President of Africa, led the demonstration bedecked in a dazzling uniform of purple, green, and black, with gold braid, and a thrilling hat with white plumes. . . . He rode in a big, high-mounted black Packard automobile and graciously, but with restraint becoming a sovereign, acknowledged the ovations of the crowds that lined the sidewalks. Behind him rode His Grace, Archbishop McGuire, in silk robes of state, blessing the populace. Then, the Black Nobility and Knight Commanders of the Distinguished Order of the Nile followed, the hierarchy of the state, forms of black and green, trimmed with much gold braid, came the smartly strutting African Legion; and in white, the stretcher-bearing Black Cross nurses. Then came troops of kit-clad Boy and Girl Scouts, trailed by a multitude of bumptious black subjects.[31]

Concern with the positive impact of a powerful black nation is still prominent, although it does not now inspire a widespread desire for physical withdrawal from the United States. At the end of his tour of Africa, Malcolm X observed in a filmed interview that a strong Africa is vital to the future of black people everywhere. He recalled that there was a time when the phrase "you don't have a Chinaman's chance" was widely used and reflected the low esteem in which Chinese were held, but with the emergence of a strong proud People's Republic of China, Chinese everywhere are respected and the expres-

[30] *Ibid.*, p. 116.
[31] Quoted in John Brisbane, *The Black Vanguard* (Valley Forge, Pa.: Judson Press, 1970), 89.

sion is hardly ever used. He suggested that a strong Africa will have a similar impact on black people everywhere.

In spite of the persistent advocacy of withdrawal, blacks were almost unanimously opposed to migration schemes instigated by whites, most of which reflected the desire of slave masters and their sympathizers to get rid of "free blacks" who threatened the stability of the slave system. Thus when the American Society for Colonizing the Free People of Color in the United States (American Colonization Society) was organized by whites in 1816 with substantial government support, it was vigorously opposed by blacks even while they sought their own avenues of escape from the United States. Furthermore, the emigrationists were never in total agreement about a site for resettlement. For a brief period during the 1830s the annual "Negro Conventions" of the time endorsed migration to Canada. Some individuals later urged migration to South or Central America because its proximity to the United States made mass migration feasible. Still others urged Haiti, then the only country in the Western Hemisphere governed by blacks. The greatest sentiment, however, seems to have been for migration to Africa. Even Delaney, who once objected to this, eventually participated in the Niger Valley Exploration undertaken by blacks to find a suitable site in Africa for settlement.[32] Later Garvey committed his movement to migration to Africa because historically it has been the black man's continent and therefore the place to which he is naturally entitled.

Emigration, either under government auspices or independently, clearly was a formidable if not impossible undertaking from the start. Yet the advocacy of withdrawal cannot be seen merely as a form of fantasizing, as Theodore Draper suggests.[33] Rather it represents a genuine expression of frustration and a search for the dignity and freedom to which blacks have always aspired. It must be noted that the idea of withdrawal was criticized by blacks as vigorously as it was propounded. Spokesmen like Frederick Douglass saw it not as a solution to the problem of white racism or the black man's enslavement; on the contrary, he suggested, it was merely an evasion of a difficult problem because when a few freed blacks had withdrawn the slaves would remain with their cause considerably weakened.[34] Furthermore, Douglas and other advocates of continued efforts for improved race relations believed that the racial problem was susceptible to solution and required steadfast work by dedicated individuals, both black and white.

Today the separatist impulse exists but there are important differences in direction. To a growing segment of the black community the basic pattern of race relations has not changed sufficiently to ensure a free and dignified existence, and thus the integrationist dream has not been realized. Actual

---

[32] See Brotz, *op. cit.*, pp. 101–111.
[33] Draper, *op. cit.*, p. 48.
[34] Frederick Douglass, "The Present and Future of the Colored Race in America," in Brotz, *op. cit.*, pp. 267–277.

withdrawal from the United States, however, is seen as a realistic aspiration by very few. Instead, concerned black nationalists advocate self-determination for black people in the communities in which they reside. The desire to control the land, basic resources, and institutions in black communities has become the new burden of nationalists. Thus separatism is being redefined to emphasize a "dynamic pluralism" in which black and white communities interact with mutual respect. For a smaller group there is still the aspiration to an opportunity for complete independence within the present territory of the United States. Reflecting this outlook, the black "agenda" adopted by the National Black Political Convention at Gary, Indiana, in 1972 calls on the United States Government to take steps to permit a separate black state for those who desire it. The Republic of New Africa is the principal advocate of this form of separation.

### Embracing the Black World—The Pan-African Idea

In his autobiography Du Bois wrote: "as I face Africa I ask myself: What is it between us that constitutes a tie which I can feel better than I can explain?" He concluded that the real essence of the kinship with Africa is "its social heritage of slavery; the discrimination and insult; and this heritage binds together not simply the children of Africa, but extends through yellow Asia and into the South Seas."[35] This feeling of which Du Bois speaks was and continues to be felt by many thoughtful black people within the United States and has found poignant expression in the literature of black nationalism and even in the dress and behavior of blacks. In part these feelings which found expression in the Pan African idea were a result of the isolation and alienation felt by the black population, and it represented an attempt to reach out for solace, strength, and a sense of belonging. It was, too, the result of a growing sense of pride in blackness and sorrow at the misfortunes of the race. These and other emotions colored the expressions of black nationalists and prompted participation by some in the Pan-African Movement.

The Pan-African idea took shape around the end of the nineteenth century. Du Bois noted in 1897 that "if the Negro were to be a factor in world history it would be through a Pan-Negro Movement."[36] In 1900 H. Sylvester Williams, a Trinidadian attorney, sponsored a Pan-Africanist Congress in England, and with this a Pan-African Movement was born. Du Bois, in attending this meeting, made the prophetic observation that "the problem of the twentieth century is the problem of the color line—the relation of the darker to the lighter races of men in Asia and Africa, in America and the Island of the Seas."[37] At that conference too was Alexander Walters of the AME

---

[35] W. E. B. Du Bois, *Dusk of Dawn* (New York: Harcourt Brace Jovanovich, 1940), pp. 116–117.
[36] Quoted in Colin Legum, *Pan-Africanism* (New York: Praeger, 1962), p. 24.
[37] *Ibid.*, p. 25.

Zion Church, who became an active participant and a link between the Movement and the black churches. Although Du Bois and others hoped that blacks in the United States would occupy a prominent role in the movement, few indeed became actively involved. The Pan-African idea, however, received wide expression, especially among writers who reflected in many ways the "emotions of the black world." The feelings of being trapped in a strange and hostile world was forcefully conveyed by Claude McKay in his sonnet, *Outcast:*[38]

> For the dim regions whence my fathers came
> My spirit, bondaged by the body, longs.
> Words felt, but never heard, my lips would frame;
> My soul would sing forgotten jungle songs.
> I would go back to darkness and to peace.
> But the great western world holds me in fee,
> And I may never hope for full release
> While to its alien gods I bend my knee
> Something in me is lost, forever lost,
> Some vital thing has gone out of my heart,
> And I must walk the way of life a ghost
> Among the sons of earth, a thing apart.
> For I was born, far from my native clime,
> Under the white man's menace, out of time.

Langston Hughes emphasized the feeling of oneness, the common bond shared throughout the diaspora in these lines:[39]

> We are related—you and I.
> You from the West Indies,
> I from Kentucky.
> We are related—you and I.
> You from Africa,
> I from these States.
> We are brothers—you and I.

The Pan-African Movement continued with about six world conferences up to 1944 and then its emphasis became less one of diasporic unity and more a movement for African Unity. During much of this time, Du Bois served as a leading spirit along with such prominent Pan-Africanists as C. L. R. James and George Padmore. It directed its energies toward three basic concerns: (1) development of feelings of unity among African peoples everywhere and a concern for the motherland, (2) encouragement of racial pride and dignity to which the concept of negritude contributed, and (3) anti-

---

[38] *Selected Poems of Claude McKay, op. cit.,* p. 41.
[39] In Legum, *op. cit.,* p. 16.

colonial agitation. The most significant achievement of the movement may have been the interaction of black intellectuals of the black triangle—Africa, the United States, and the West Indies—which it facilitated, and the inspiration it gave to the independence movement in Africa.

In a sense the Pan-African idea is still a vital part of the thinking of black Americans. The decade of the 1960s witnessed a heightened affection for the African motherland reflected in clothing and hair styles, in academic pursuits, and in increased concern with the political and economic problems of the African peoples. This reidentification with Africa has been a source of considerable pride, but more important it reflects an awareness that, as Malcolm X insisted, black people are not free anywhere until they are free everywhere and particularly in Africa.

## An Appraisal of Black Nationalism

Our review of the scope of black nationalism in the United States suggests that (1) it has been a long-standing component of black political life, and (2) it is a product of the subordinate status of blacks in the society and reflects their efforts to cope with the ordeal of subordination. Although the specific conditions of life in America contribute a degree of distinctiveness, even uniqueness to it, viewed in a larger context black nationalism is one manifestation of the widespread phenomenon of ethnic or subgroup nationalism. One scholar recently identified fifty-six states (apart from the United States) in which there are significant expressions of ethnic nationalism. So widespread is it that that scholar questions whether there might not, in fact, be an "ethnic imperative" similar to the territorial or economic imperatives that allegedly motivate states.[40]

Its virtual universality notwithstanding, nationalism is not universally regarded as an unmixed blessing. Some observers consider it an unfortunate perversion of industrialism and democracy and a detriment to the well-being of mankind. Nationalist sentiment among distinct subgroups in a society has been viewed with even greater concern because it is usually perceived as divisive and a threat to a highly valued national unity. On the other hand, in spite of its negative features nationalism is clearly functional in some important respects. Rupert Emerson suggests that in colonial societies it facilitated mobilization of the colonial peoples for the independence struggle and provided a sense of worth and social solidarity.[41] In concluding our examination of black nationalism, it is essential that we undertake a brief assessment of its role in black life as well as its weaknesses or limitations.

---

[40] Walker Conner, "The Politics of Ethnonationalism," *Journal of International Affairs* 27, 1 (1973), 2.

[41] Rupert Emerson, *From Empire to Nation* (Boston: Beacon, 1960), pp. 60–87.

Functions of Black Nationalism

In spite of the absence of a single, clear, and coherent theme or a consistently high degree of prominence in black political life, nationalist expression has been beneficial to the group in several ways. First, it has been vital in stimulating group identity or consciousness and racial pride. While blacks have always been a visibly distinct group, it required an awareness of this distinctness by group members, and a recognition that their place in the society is defined by reference to group characteristics for the emergence of national consciousness. Such an awareness was stimulated by the various forms of nationalist expressions which emphasized the concept of "us," the oppressed, as opposed to "them," the oppressor. This development of group consciousness is a vital first step in any struggle for liberation and should not necessarily be viewed as routine or automatic. In Stanley Elkins' comparison of the impact of American slavery and of Nazi concentration camps, he observed that in both cases prolonged humiliation by and dependency on a superior power created a confusion of identity as the victim eventually identified with his oppressor rather than with his group.[42] A somewhat similar process was apparent in colonial societies where segments of the indigenous population so thoroughly internalized the attitudes and values of the colonizer that it ceased to identify with the "oppressed group." Because the black population in America was scattered, interaction restricted and specific circumstances different (between slave and nonslave and the over-whelmingly poor and unprivileged majority of blacks and a few well-off and relatively privileged ones), development of a group identity and group perspective did not come routinely. It had to be stimulated by persistent effort over an extended period.

Prolonged subordination and even dehumanization produced a sense of shame and demoralization that is frequently alluded to but is not yet fully understood. Black nationalist activity has been a vital instrument in aiding in the recovery from these conditions and instilling (along with group identity) group pride. This particular contribution of nationalist activity is most vividly manifested in the major nationalist movements of this century such as Garveyism, the Black Muslims, and contemporary revolutionary nationalist groups, as well as in the outburst of cultural nationalism which we described earlier. A common theme in these separate expressions of black nationalism has been the "glorification of blackness." In an incredible variety of ways the "black is beautiful" theme has been espoused by blacks since the first nationalist expressions, but it has been done with new and compelling force during this century and especially since the decade of the 1960s. In the majestic sounding titles bestowed on even the very lowly of Garvey's follow-

---

[42] Stanley Elkins, *Slavery* (Chicago: University of Chicago Press, 1968), pp. 103–115.

ers, in the invocation of a black God to guide the destinies of black people, as well as in thousands of assertions of future glory for the race, Garvey did indeed arouse black pride.  E. Franklin Frazier notes of the Garveyist impact that "a Negro might be a porter during the day, taking his orders from white men, but he was an officer in the Black Army (of Africa) when it assembled at night at Liberty Hall."[43]  An even more intensive and remarkably successful attempt at infusing pride and dignity in blackness characterizes the efforts of Black Muslims.  The theme of pride in blackness is today a pervasive one in black America and is reflected in both attitudes and behavior.

Second, black nationalism has been useful in mobilizing the group for collective action against continued subordination. Even with the emergence of a measure of group consciousness, group activity has not been easy to achieve for at least two reasons: (1) one of the apparent consequences of severe and prolonged oppression such as blacks encountered is immobilism resulting from fragmentation or atomization of the group, and (2) apathy typical of the uneducated and the very poor.[44]  In the face of these circumstances black leaders have had the difficult task of mobilizing the race in support of group goals. Avenues for group mobilization were often lacking or very limited in their capacity to reach large numbers of people. Initially the black church provided the only organized avenue of such mobilization, but later state, regional, and national conferences as well as black-owned newspapers became vital instruments for mobilizing the group. The most effective efforts in this regard occurred within nationalist organizations like the Garvey and Muslim movements and even more so with efforts of nationalist spokesmen during the 1960s. The impact of SNCC leaders Carmichael and Brown during the later "nationalist" years of the organization, and of Imamu Baraka (LeRoi Jones) and Malcolm X, is illustrative as nationalist advocates embraced the slogans of "black power" and "community control," making them common themes throughout black communities.

A third function of black nationalism is that of articulating goals vital to the race. James Lightbody suggests in this connection that one may view ethnic group nationalism "as one expression of a potential spectrum of group demands particularly related to ethnic communities...."[45]  With reference to black Americans, black nationalism involved at one level articulation of some broad, abstract goals such as full citizenship rights or self-determination. On another level, black nationalism has involved the articulation of specific group demands—for improved economic opportunities, increased access to the political system, and improvement in basic services to black communities. Further-

---

[43] E. Franklin Frazier, "The Garvey Movement," in August Meier and Elliott Rudwick, eds., *The Making of Black America II* (New York: Atheneum, 1969), p. 206.

[44] Several scholars have observed that the most oppressed segments of society are among the least likely to rebel or otherwise actively struggle to change their condition. See for example Crane Brinton, *The Anatomy of Revolution* (New York: Norton, 1938).

[45] James Lightbody, "A Note on the Theory of Nationalism as a Function of Ethnic Demands," *Canadian Journal of Political Science* 11, 3 (September 1969), 329.

more, because the level, thrust, and intensity of black nationalism has been so directly related to changes in public policy and the conditions of black life, black nationalist activity may be viewed as a fairly reliable barometer of the level of frustration by the group.

### Weaknesses of Black Nationalism

As is the case with virtually any form of nationalism, black nationalism exhibits important weaknesses which cannot be overlooked. We observed that it involves no widely accepted program of action but is an extremely diverse, often conflicting body of thought lacking a coherent or consistent set of beliefs. Often goals are stated in such broad terms that they provide room for considerable variation in interpretation and emphasis. Although they may be shared by all blacks, their meaning and the approach to their realization remain sources of major controversies. Another complicating factor has been the tendency to link nationalist goals with a disparate assortment of ill-fitting "Socialist" and "Marxist" ideological fragments which further confuse rather than clarify goals.

One consequence of this fragmented and incoherent character of much nationalist thinking is that it possesses a highly divisive potential. Passionate commitment to distinct nationalist viewpoints by some groups or individuals at times becomes a formidable obstacle to united action and instead stimulates mistrust and hostility in black communities. Bitter and occasionally abusive conflict between advocates of opposing strategies for achieving supposedly commonly held goals sometimes replaces constructive united efforts.

Another result of the nationalist tradition is the tendency to encourage a peculiar overindulgence in polemicism and programatic fantasizing when there are many profound and perplexing problems which require pragmatic approaches to solution. Too often, however, this pragmatic approach to problem solving is ignored or disparaged in favor of grand nationalist programs which, while superficially satisfying, are as a practical matter dangerously misleading and irrelevant to the real needs of black people. Matthew Holden's uncompromising critique of some of these grand schemes for "withdrawal" and what he describes as the "ritual of the third world" are illustrative of this tendency.[46] Although this has been costly to black America, it should not be overlooked that it is part of the character of nationalism that its "prophets" often have been dreamers or visionaries rather than political realists.[47] Thus, while black nationalism has made valuable contributions to black political life, it has at times been a negative force.

As one looks toward the future, there is increasing evidence of a willingness among nationalist proponents to accept as legitimate and con-

[46] Matthew Holden, *The Politics of the Black Nation* (San Francisco: Chandler, 1973), pp. 68–114.
[47] See Hans Kohn, *Prophets and Peoples* (New York: Collier, 1946), p. 13.

structive a variety of perspectives and strategies for change. Furthermore, while we are not entirely free of empty posturings, this has been giving away rapidly to a new pragmatism. This new pragmatism is being exhibited in a renewed interest by nationalist spokesmen in participating vigorously in the political process in spite of its limitations. Noting this trend, especially the emphasis on community control, Robert Fogelson has concluded, appropriately, that black nationalism has come of age.[48]

## SELECTED BIBLIOGRAPHY

Andrain, Charles F. "The Pan-African Movement: The Search for Organization and Community." *Phylon* 23, 1 (Spring 1962), 5–17.
Ball, Howard. "Negro Nationalism: A Factor in Emigration Projects, 1858–1861." *Journal of Negro History* 46, 1 (January 1962), 42–53.
Bennett, Lerone, Jr. *Before the Mayflower,* Rev. ed. Baltimore, Md.: Penguin, 1966.
Bennett, Lerone, Jr. *The Negro Mood.* Chicago: Johnson, 1964.
Bontemps, Anna, and Jac, Conroy. *They Seek a City.* Garden City, N.Y.: Doubleday, 1945.
Breitman, George. *The Last Years of Malcolm X: The Evolution of a Revolutionary.* New York: Merit, 1967.
Breitman, George, ed. *Leon Trotsky on Black Nationalism and Self-Determination.* New York: Merit, 1967.
Breitman, George, ed. *Malcolm X Speaks.* New York: Grove, 1965.
Broom, Leonard, and Norval Glenn. *Transformation of the Negro American.* New York: Harper & Row, 1965.
Brotz, Howard. *The Black Jews of Harlem: Negro Nationalism and the Dilemmas of Negro Leadership.* New York: Free Press 1964.
Browne, Robert S. "The Case For Black Separatism." *Ramparts* (December 1967).
Carmichael Stokely. "Pan-Africanism—Land and Power." *Black Scholar* (November 1969), 36–43.
Clarke, John Henrik. "The New Afro-American Nationalism." *Freedomways* (Fall 1961), 285–295.
Cronon, Edmund David. *Black Moses: The Story of Marcus Garvey and the Universal Negro Improvement Association.* Madison: University of Wisconsin Press, 1955.
Du Bois, W. E. B. *Black Reconstruction.* New York: Harcourt Brace Jovanovich, 1935.
Fager, Charles E. *White Reflections on Black Power.* Grand Rapids, Mich.: Eerdman, 1967.
Fanon, Frantz. *The Wretched of the Earth.* New York: Grove, 1963.

[48] Robert Fogelson, "Review Symposium," *American Political Science Review* 43, 4 (December 1969), 1274.

Fauset, Arthur H. *Black Gods of the Metropolis.* Philadelphia: University of Pennsylvania Press, 1944.

Fox, Stephen R. *The Guardian of Boston: William Monroe Trotter.* New York: Atheneum, 1970.

Frazier, E. Franklin. *The Negro Church.* New York: Schocken, 1962.

Fullinwider, S. P. *The Mind and Mood of Black America: 20th-Century Thought.* Homewood, Ill.: Dorsey, 1969.

Gregor, A. James. "Black Nationalism: A Preliminary Analysis of Negro Radicalism." *Science and Society* 27, 4 (Fall 1963), 415–432.

Grimes, Alan. *Equality in America.* New York: Oxford University Press, 1964.

Hale, Frank W., Jr., ed. *The Cry for Freedom.* London: Yoseloff, 1968.

Handlin, Oscar. *Race and Nationality in American Life.* Garden City, N.Y.: Doubleday, 1957.

Hawkins, Hugh, ed. *Booker T. Washington and His Critics: The Problem of Negro Leadership.* Boston: Heath, 1962.

Hill, Herbert, ed. *Soon, One Morning: New Writing by American Negroes 1940–1962.* New York: Knopf, 1963.

Isaacs, Harold. *The New World of Negro Americans.* New York: Day, 1963.

Jacques-Garvey, Amy, ed. *Philosophy and Opinions of Marcus Garvey.* New York: Arno Press, 1969.

Jones, LeRoi. "The Legacy of Malcolm X and the Coming of the Black Nation," in Douglas A. Hughes, ed., *From a Black Perspective.* New York: Holt, Rinehart & Winston, 1970.

Kardiner, Abram, and Lionel Ovesy. *The Mark of Oppression.* New York: Norton, 1951.

Kellogg, Charles F. *NAACP–A History of the National Association for the Advancement of Colored People 1909–1920.* Baltimore, Md.: Johns Hopkins Press, 1969.

Landon, Fred. "The Negro Migration to Canada After the Passing of the Fugitive Slave Act." *Journal of Negro History* 5 (January 1920), 22–36.

Lincoln, E. Eric. *The Black Muslims in America.* Boston: Beacon, 1961.

Lincoln, E. Eric. "Extremist Attitudes in the Black Muslim Movement." *Journal of Social Issues* 19 (April 1963), 75–85.

Lockard, Duane. *Toward Equal Opportunity.* London: Macmillan, 1968.

Love, James H. "A Contemporary Revitalization Movement in American Race Relations: The 'Black Muslims.'" *Social Forces* 42, 3, 315–323.

McColley, Robert. *Slavery and Jeffersonian Virginia.* Urbana: University of Illinois Press, 1964.

McKay, Claude. *A Long Way from Home.* New York: Citadel, 1937.

McPherson, James. *The Struggle for Equality.* Princeton, N.J.: Princeton University Press, 1964.

Marine, Gene. *The Black Panthers.* New York: New American Library, 1969.

Marshall, Ray. *The Negro and Organized Labor.* New York: J. Wiley, 1965.

Mehlinger, Louis R. "The Attitude of the Free Negro Toward African Colonization." *Journal of Negro History* 1 (July 1916), 276–301.

Meier, August. *Negro Thought in America, 1880–1915.* Ann Arbor: University of Michigan Press, 1963.

Meier, August. "Negro Protest Movements and Organizations." *Journal of Negro Education* 32 (Fall 1963), 437–450.

Meier, August. "The Emergence of Negro Nationalism: A Study in Ideologies." *Midwest Journal* 4, 1 (Winter 1951–1952), 96–104; 4, 2 (Summer 1952), 95–111.

Muhammad, Elijah. *Message to the Blackman in America.* Chicago: Muhammad Mosque No. 2, 1965.

Nelson, Bernard. *The Fourteenth Amendment and the Negro Since 1920.* New York: Russell and Russell, 1946.

Parenti, Michael. "The Black Muslims: From Revolution to Institution." *Social Research* 31, 2 (Summer 1964), 175–194.

Patterson, William L. "The Black Panther Party." *Political Affairs* 48, 11 (November 1969), 7–14.

Quarles, Benjamin. *Black Abolitionists.* New York: Oxford University Press, 1969.

Quarles, Benjamin. *Lincoln and the Negro.* New York: Oxford University Press, 1962.

Record, Wilson. "American Racial Ideologies and Organizations in Transition." *Phylon* 26, 4 (Winter 1965), 315–329.

Record, Wilson. "Extremist Movements Among American Negroes." *Phylon* 17, 1 (1956), 17–23.

Record, Wilson. "Intellectuals in Social and Racial Movements." *Phylon* 15, 3 (1954), 231–242.

Record, Wilson. "Negro Intellectual Leadership in the National Association for the Advancement of Colored People." *Phylon* 17, 4 (1956), 375–389.

Redkey, Edwin S. *Black Exodus.* New Haven, Conn.: Yale University Press, 1969.

Rudwick, Elliott. *W. E. B. Du Bois: Propagandist of the Negro Protest.* New York: Atheneum, 1968.

Rudwick, Elliott. "Du Bois vs. Garvey: Racial Propagandists at War." *Journal of Negro Education* 27 (Fall 1959), 421–429.

Rudwick, Elliott, and August Meier. "Organizational Structure and Goal Succession: A Comparative Analysis of the NAACP and CORE, 1964–1968." *Social Science Quarterly* (June 1970), 9–24.

Scott, Benjamin. *The Coming of the Black Man.* Boston: Beacon, 1969.

Shepperson, George. "Notes on Negro American Influence on African Nationalism." *Journal of African History* 1, 2 (1960), 299–312.

Sherrill, Robert. "We Want Georgia, South Carolina, Louisiana, Mississippi, and Alabama—Right Now." *Esquire* (January 1969), 72–75, 146–148.

Sherwood, Henry Noble. "Early Deportation Projects." *Mississippi Valley Historical Review* 2 (March 1916), 484–508.

"The Legacy of Slavery and the Roots of Black Nationalism." *Studies on the Left* 6 (November–December, 1966).

Thornbrough, Emma Lou. "The National Afro-American League,

1887–1908." *The Journal of Southern History* **27**, 4 (November 1961), 494–512.

Tinker, Irene. "Nationalism in a Plural Society: The Case of the American Negro." *Western Political Quarterly* **19**, 1 (March 1966), 112–122.

Warren, Robert Penn. "Malcolm X: Mission and Meaning." *Yale Review* **56**, 2 (December 1966), 161–171.

Weisbord, Robert G. "Marcus Garvey, Pan-Negroist: The View from White-hall." *Race* **11**, 4 (April 1970), 419–427.

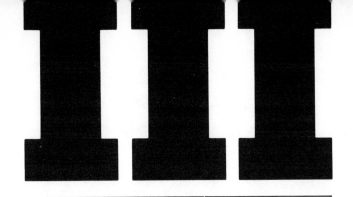

# Blacks in the American Political Arena

"In the past two decades, Negroes have expended more effort in quest of the franchise than they have in all other campaigns combined. Demonstrations, sit-ins and marches, though more spectacular, are dwarfed by the enormous number of man-hours expended to register millions, particularly in the South. Negro organizations from extreme militant to conservative persuasion, Negro leaders who would not even talk to each other, all have been agreed on the key importance of voting. Stokely Carmichael said black power means the vote and Roy Wilkins, while saying black power means black death, also energetically sought the power of the ballot."

". . . The time is short for social science to illuminate this critically important area. If the main thrust of Negro effort has been, and remains, substantially irrelevant, we may be facing an agonizing crisis of tactical theory."

*Martin Luther King, Jr.*
"The Role of the Behavioral Sciences" in the Civil Rights Movement,"
*Journal of Social Issues* **24** (April 1968).

# 7

## Political Attitudes
of Black Americans

The basic thrust of the preceding part of our study is that the status of black people within the United States has been one of the major problems in black political life. Slowly and circuitously they have progressed toward full, formal inclusion into the American political community, but even now this process remains incomplete and highly tentative. Partly as a result of this circumstance blacks have had to wrestle constantly with the question of the character of their status in American society and their place in the political life of the society. The long-term pattern of nationalist thought illustrates the dimensions of this dilemma, and increasing references to "the black nation" either as a reality or an aspiration are indicative of its continued salience.

This disturbing uncertainty about their status notwithstanding, black Americans are inextricably involved in American political life. Recognizing this fact, most blacks have directed their political energies at improving their position within the political system and making it more responsive to their needs. How they feel about government at its various levels, how they feel about themselves as political actors, and the specific forces that shape their political attitudes and values are thus vital concerns. They will be examined in this chapter to the extent that available research findings permit.

### Black America as a Political Subculture

The political attitudes and values of individuals within a society are now of considerable importance to political scientists. This importance derives from a fundamental belief that political behavior is a function of political attitudes and thus provides a reliable basis for explaining and eventually even predicting political behavior. Political scientists use the term "political culture" to designate the generalized political attitudes and values of a society. According to Gabriel Almond and Sidney Verba, the concept refers to "the specifically political orientations, attitudes toward the political system and its various

119

parts, and attitudes toward the role of self in the system."[1] Lucian Pye views it as "the set of attitudes, beliefs, and sentiments which give order and meaning to a political process and which provide the underlying assumptions and rules that govern behavior in the political system. It encompasses both the political ideals and the operating norms of a polity. Political culture is thus the manifestation in aggregate form of the psychological and subjective dimensions of politics. A political culture is both a product of the collective history of a political system and the life histories of the members of that system, and thus it is rooted equally in public events and private experiences."[2]

Although reference is frequently made to *the political culture* of a society, it is clear that there are very few if any culturally homogenous societies. Distinct orientations to politics may be found in different groups or segments within the society as a result of the "private experiences" to which Pye referred or the status they occupy in the society. Where there are identifiable segments of a society sharing political attitudes and values distinct from that of the rest of the society we say a "political subculture" exists. Often these subcultures are products of deep cleavages in a society resulting from discontinuities in the level of economic development, religious, racial, or linguistic differences, or even geographic isolation.[3] Viewed in this way, the study of the political attitudes of blacks may proceed with black America seen as *a distinct political subculture.*

Both Matthew Holden's conception of black America as a separate "nation" within the United States with its own "quasi-government"[4] and Harold Cruse's view of black-America as a "semicolony" emphasize a basic distinction between the political worlds of black and white America. Furthermore, an enormous volume of readily available statistical information confirms the fundamental cleavage between black and white sectors of the society. It shows that the overwhelming majority of blacks are concentrated in the lowest socioeconomic categories within the society and that they are severely limited in access to the goods and services of the society.[5] The subcultural concept here emphasizes this distinct place that blacks occupy as well as the nature of the relationship between the two major racial groups in the society.

[1] Gabriel Almond and Sidney Verba, *The Civic Culture* (Boston: Little, Brown, 1963), pp. 13–14.
[2] Lucian Pye, "Political Culture," *International Encyclopedia of the Social Sciences,* Vol. 12, p. 218.
[3] See for example Juan Linz and Amanda de Miguel, "Within-Nations Differences and Comparisons: The Eight Spains," in Richard Merritt and Stein Rokkan, eds., *Comparing Nations* (New Haven, Conn.: Yale University Press, 1966), pp. 267–319. See also Almond and Verba, *op. cit.,* pp. 26–29.
[4] Matthew Holden, Jr., *The Politics of the Black Nation* (San Francisco: Chandler, 1973), p. 3.
[5] For an examination of the socioeconomic status of blacks in relation to other ethnic groups in the society see Leonard Broom, Cora Woods, and Betty Maynard,

In his empirical study of some political attitudes of blacks, Dwaine Marvick noted that "Negro Americans in many ways are excluded from the dominant political culture of their community and nation and are denied its rewards. Norms and roles are learned in a special Negro subculture."[6] Jewell Prestage more recently reinforced this point of view, observing that "the political world of American blacks is so radically different from the political world of American whites that it might well constitute a "subculture within a dominant or major culture."[7] However, relatively few other political scientists have explicitly identified black America as a separate subculture. Donald Devine, in perhaps the most extensive examination of the American political culture to date, concludes that although there are some differences in level of support among blacks for some basic values of the American political culture, a majority of blacks support all of these values and hence black America does not constitute a distinct subculture, and "race is not an active cleavage in the American political culture."[8]

My own position differs from Devine's in that it takes a much broader view of the subcultural concept. Although there is no widely accepted criteria for determining precisely what conditions must exist before a group can be identified as a subculture, it seems clear that major disagreement on the "central values" of the political system is not an indispensable condition. Consistent and substantial differences in (1) level of support for the central values of the political culture, (2) affect for the political system, and (3) evaluations of the performance of the political system are important indicators of subcultural cleavages. Reference here to a black political subculture should not be confused with the contention that black America is, in a broader sense, a distinct cultural entity apart from an American culture, nor should it be construed as suggesting a massive or total estrangement from the basic political values of the society. It does assume that race forms the basis of one fundamental cleavage in the society which is reflected in virtually every area of political life. Second, it suggests that black Americans are set apart from the dominant political culture by a unique pattern of experiences that define their status in the political system and shape their perception of the system and of themselves as political actors. Third, it implies that black America is

---

"Status Profiles and Ethnic Populations," *Social Science Quarterly* **52**, 2 (September 1971), 379–388. See also St. Clair Drake, "The Social and Economic Status of the Negro in the United States," in Talcott Parsons and Kenneth Clark, *The Negro American* (Boston: Houghton Mifflin, 1965), p. 3–46. Whether this status has changed or not is a topic of heated debate, but no one seriously contends that considerable change has occurred in the relative status of blacks.

[6] Dwaine Marvick, "The Political Socialization of the American Negro," *Annals of the American Academy of Political and Social Science* 361 (September 1965), 113.

[7] Jewell Prestage, "Black Politics and the Kerner Report: Concerns and Directions," in Jack Van Der Slik, *Black Conflict with White America* (Columbus, Ohio: Merrill, 1970), p. 326.

[8] Donald J. Devine, *The American Political Culture* (Boston: Little, Brown, 1972), p. 281.

set apart by a set of objectives that give a distinct character to their politics. These distinguishing characteristics are all directly related to the subordinate status blacks occupy in American society.

More concretely, the differences separating the black political subculture from the dominant white one may be observed in significantly different patterns of orientation to the political system or to specific roles or structures within the system. Furthermore, it is evidenced by the fact that blacks perceive themselves as a distinct community. Thus in spite of important differences among black Americans with respect to several specific issues, there is a strong underlying cohesiveness. Findings by Marvin Olsen[9] and Angus Campbell et al.[10] confirm this cohesiveness. Jan Dizard also convincingly argues that black Americans possess a strong sense of "collective identity," a "primordial bond that links otherwise diverse individuals to one another" resulting from a strong sense of common fate.[11]

References to cohesiveness and collective identity as characterizing the black subculture should not obscure the fact that black America is far from a highly unified community. Despite the broad unifying forces to which reference has been made, there are significant divisions, most of them routine, natural, and healthy, and others peculiar products of black history. E. Franklin Frazier several years ago incisively analyzed one of the more prominent divisions among blacks in his study of the Black Bourgeoisie.[12] He pointed to that stratum whose income, though modest by white standards, sets them apart from the impoverished black masses. This stratum, Frazier noted, held values and attitudes that were not only different from the black masses but in some instances were detrimental to its progress. Holden calls the black masses "the folks," and he too notes that there has been considerable tension between the two groups. Indeed, he suggests that in the black community, "nothing has been more significant a barrier to collective action than the distrust of the black bourgeoisie by the black 'folks.'"[13] Jesse Jackson some time ago spoke of another significant division when he suggested that it was time for the various "tribes" to come together. He spoke of the Southern tribe, the Northern tribe, the Western tribe, and Eastern tribe, emphasizing the regional differences characterizing the black community. Furthermore, a wide range of political and other issues divide individuals within the black community. It is clear therefore that there is no totally homogenous black community with respect to political attitudes and values. What is being undertaken here then is an attempt to identify those basic

[9] Marvin Olsen, "Social and Political Participation of Blacks," *American Sociological Review* 35 (August 1970), 695–696.

[10] Angus Campbell et al., *The American Voter* (New York: Wiley, 1960), p. 316.

[11] Jan Dizard, "Black Identity, Social Class and Black Power," *Psychiatry* 33 (1970), 195–207.

[12] E. Franklin Frazier, *Black Bourgeoisie* (New York: Collier, 1962).

[13] Holden, *op. cit.,* p. 31.

political orientations and values that seem to characterize the black community.

## Attitudes Toward the Political System

In attempting to identify some of the political attitudes of the black subculture we may, for convenience, order our observations within the three broad attitudinal dimensions widely utilized in the political science literature: (a) the cognitive dimension, involving knowledge or awareness of the political system and political issues; (b) the affective dimension, involving feelings toward government such as support or hostility, trust or distrust; (c) the evaluative dimension, involving assessment of the performance of government.[14]

### Knowledge of Politics

The link between knowledge and behavior in politics is obvious. Generally the level and character of an individual's participation in politics is affected by the extent of his knowledge about the political system. In spite of several studies of black political participation, there is virtually no concrete information about the level of information blacks have about political structures and processes. We know that the society as a whole is not very knowledgeable about government,[15] although Almond and Verba reported that Americans exhibit a higher level of information than individuals in other modern democratic polities.[16] We may infer from this that blacks are also not very well informed about politics. Because level of information about politics is usually directly related to the general level of education, we may assume that the black subculture is less knowledgeable about politics than whites in view of the substantial differences between the two in educational levels.

This assumption was confirmed in one very limited examination of this question undertaken by Matthews and Prothro. They found that although the level of information about politics was generally low in the four Southern counties studied, black respondents were decidedly less informed than whites.[17] Sidney Verba et al. provide similar evidence from their more recent national survey.[18] Further evidence of the gap in knowledge of political

---

[14] Almond and Verba, *op. cit.,* p. 15.

[15] The evidence from several surveys is summarized in Devine, *op. cit.,* p. 38.

[16] Almond and Verba, *op. cit.,* pp. 53–57.

[17] Donald Matthews and James Prothro, *Negroes and the New Southern Politics* (New York: Harcourt Brace Jovanovich, 1966), pp. 271–273.

[18] Sidney Verba, Bashiruddin Ahmed, and Anil Bhatt, *Caste, Race and Politics, A Comparative Study of India and the United States* (Beverly Hills, Calif.: Sage, 1971), pp. 105–106.

matters is provided in studies of the political socialization of black and white youth. Kenneth Langton reported in one such study that "white youth score higher on the knowledge scale than do Negroes, and when parents education is controlled, differences persist at all levels."[19] Indications are that the gap is even wider where specialized issue areas such as international affairs are concerned. In his empirical study of the attitudes of various groups toward foreign affairs, Alfred Hero reported that blacks are much less knowledgeable than are whites. This was particularly apparent with respect to Southern blacks, who were reported to be "consistently less informed about virtually all international questions than Southern whites."[20]

Findings of this kind may be of only limited significance, both because of their "patchiness" and because it is not entirely clear to what extent the general information tapped by these surveys is consequential for political behavior. Devine suggests that "contextual" information might be more important, i.e., knowledge of matters directly related to specific types of political activity may be of greater importance for political behavior than a general knowledge of politics.[21]

### Feelings About the Political System

The feelings of individuals or groups toward the political system is perhaps the most crucial attitudinal dimension. Whether one is supportive of or hostile to the political system and whether or not one feels trusting toward the system are vitally related to patterns of political behavior and the strength or stability of government. Especially since the urban revolts of the 1960s, substantial efforts have been made to examine black political attitudes in an effort to explain why the revolt occurred and to suggest possible future patterns of political behavior. It is necessary, however, to approach these findings with considerable caution for at least two reasons. First, political attitudes are extremely complex, and there are still many obstacles to their accurate measurement.[22] With respect to black political attitudes we must still rely on several piecemeal studies that vary widely in quality and that attempt generalizations about the black subculture on the basis of geographically limited surveys. Second, attitudes are not static, and in black America there is every indication of rapid, even dramatic changes within short periods

---

[19] Kenneth Langton, *Political Socialization* (New York: Oxford University Press, 1969), p. 101.

[20] Alfred Hero, Jr., *The Southerner in World Affairs* (Baton Rouge: Louisiana State University Press, 1965), p. 249.

[21] Devine, *op. cit.,* p. 38.

[22] Bernard Hennessy, for example, provides one sobering critique on the study of political attitudes in which he asserts that "study of political attitudes by survey research falls lamentably short of the criteria of empiricism. It is a tissue of assumptions and inferences." Specifically he proposes that political attitudes are an elite phenomenon and are held by only a small segment of the society. "A Headnote on the Existence and

of time. Findings based on data gathered in 1960 or 1968 may therefore have very little relationship to political attitudes in 1974. With these caveats in mind, we will examine reported attitudes of blacks toward the political system.

### Level of Support for the System

One of the notable observations made by Gunnar Myrdal in his 1944 study of American race relations was that blacks are "exaggerated Americans."[23] By this he meant that blacks not only considered themselves Americans and were proud of that fact but they tended to emphasize this supportive posture more than most other Americans. Myrdal's reference was to a broadly supportive attitude toward the United States and the basic values associated with it, what we might call a sense of patriotism or national pride. Several more recent observers also have reported highly supportive attitudes among blacks. From an analysis of 1958 survey data, Donald Stokes concluded that there were then no pronounced feelings of hostility among disadvantaged solidarity groups and that unlike in several other societies there was no "disaffection among Negroes and other ethnic groups in the United States."[24] In his 1964 study, Gary Marx found black Americans overwhelmingly supportive of the political system. He found that a large majority reject separatist appeals and consider themselves Americans and that more than 85 percent of his sample consider the United States "worth fighting for."[25] Consistent with Marx's findings, data from a more extensive survey by Brink and Harris in 1966 indicated that 86 percent of blacks sampled believed that the country was worth fighting for and only 9 percent disagreed.[26]

The mid-1960s saw severe and frequent episodes of rioting that reflected deep-seated dissatisfaction by blacks, but even these do not appear to have reflected a fundamental change in supportive attitudes toward the society and its political values. David Sears concluded from his postriot study of blacks in the Watts area of Los Angeles that there was evidence of dissatisfaction with political incumbents and their policies "rather than a more general loss of attachment to the American political system."[27] Robert

Study of Political Attitudes," *Social Science Quarterly* **51**, 3 (December 1970), 463–476.

[23] Gunnar Myrdal, *An American Dilemma* (New York: McGraw-Hill, 1964), p. 811.

[24] Donald Stokes, "Popular Evaluations of Government: An Empirical Assessment," in Harlan Cleveland and Harold Lasswell, eds., *Ethics and Bigness: Scientific, Academic, Religious, Political and Military* (New York: Harper & Row, 1962), p. 65.

[25] Gary Marx, *Protest and Prejudice* (New York: Harper & Row, 1969), p. 30.

[26] William Brink and Louis Harris, *Black and White: A Study of U.S. Racial Attitudes Today* (New York: Simon & Schuster, 1967), p. 274.

[27] David Sears, "Black Attitudes Toward the Political System in the Aftermath of the Watts Insurrection," *Midwest Journal of Political Science* **23**, 4 (November 1969), 533.

Fogelson also observed in this regard that the pattern of racial violence reflected disapproval of the system's abuses rather than the system. Riots, he believes, were attempts to alert America and not to overturn it, to denounce its practices but not to renounce its principles.[28]  The Kerner Commission took a similar view, asserting that "what the rioters appeared to be seeking was fuller participation in the social order and the material benefits enjoyed by the majority of American citizens. Rather than rejecting the American system, they were anxious to obtain a place for themselves in it."[29]

Although several critical questions may be raised about some of these findings, they are significant in that they reflect consistently what has been a long-standing pattern of support among blacks for the United States and its basic political values. These attitudes, held over a long period, are somewhat paradoxical in view of the actual experience of blacks within the political system, yet several factors appear to have contributed to them. First, very early black political activists found it necessary and desirable to embrace the Constitution and the political values it reflected and to conduct their struggle for liberation within the framework of the political system. Thus, even as Frederick Douglass bitterly criticized white America's hypocrisy for espousing democratic values while keeping blacks in bondage, he called the Constitution "a glorious liberty document."[30]  The long and vigorous struggle by the black abolitionists included unequivocal commitment to the basic political values of the society as they fought against black subordination.

Second, the struggle for inclusion into the American political community, especially after the Civil War, prompted many blacks to emphasize their commitment to America as if to demonstrate their suitability for citizenship. Even in the face of utterly humiliating conditions, blacks gladly marched off to fight America's wars, and those who remained behind took pride in the contributions of the race. Those few who questioned black America's participation in wars for principles they could not enjoy at home were firmly criticized, as in the case of Du Bois on the eve of World War I. Loyalty to America and America's values seemed also to have contributed to the utter failure of Communists to win adherents among the black population in spite of the extravagant programs and policies with which they sought to attract blacks.

The peculiarly vulnerable position of blacks within the society has been a third factor contributing to the highly touted support for the political system. Blacks have been victims of a sustained hostility by white Americans in the face of which the power of the national government has been one of

[28] Robert Fogelson, *Violence as Protest* (Garden City, N.Y.: Doubleday, 1971), pp. 12–13.

[29] United States Commission on Civil Disorders (New York: Bantam, 1968), p. 7.

[30] Frederick Douglass, Oration Delivered in Corinthian Hall, Rochester, July 5, 1852, in Herbert J. Storing, ed., *What Country Have I?* (New York: St. Martin, 1970), p. 37.

the few sources of protection. Not surprisingly, therefore, many blacks see it as the principal instrument by which the goals of justice and equality are to be realized. One 1963 nationwide survey found that "easily the largest amount of Negro confidence in white society resides in the power of government."[31]

Findings that blacks are highly supportive of the political system are significant, but alone they are not sufficiently revealing. American society as a whole is remarkable for its level of pride in and support of the political system. Almond and Verba found that approximately 85 percent of their nationwide sample identified the political system as that aspect of American life about which they were proudest.[32] This level of pride was almost twice as high as any of the other four societies examined. (Of course these results were obtained prior to Vietnam and the Watergate affair.) Important too is the fact that these studies appear to have captured very little of the changes that have been taking place among especially the young and articulate blacks recently. The postriot mood among this sector of black America has been one of increasing tendencies to question the basic structure of power in the society and the desirability of what is perceived as an inhumane capitalist system.

Furthermore, black perceptions of white attitudes undoubtedly help shape their attitudes toward the political system. Several national polls report substantial changes in white attitudes toward blacks and toward a number of racial issues. For example, a relatively small percentage of whites now concede that they consider blacks inferior to whites, and an equally small percentage now openly admit opposition to the integration of most public facilities or to equal job opportunities for blacks, but these reported changes are not apparent to blacks. Instead, blacks are aware only that the cruder forms of racism have yielded to new, more subtle, but equally offensive and injurious ones. Thus they concede that there have been changes in conduct and changes in forms of resistance to black advance, but no fundamental change in attitudes. As recently as 1970, 81 percent of one nationwide black sample felt that whites considered blacks inferior, and 77 percent believed that "whites give blacks a break only when forced to."[33] This perception of whites who are the holders of power in the society undoubtedly colors black attitudes toward the political system. It should also be noted that attitudes toward the national government are highly changeable and depend to a great extent on who occupies the White House and thereby provides national political leadership. A March 1970 Louis Harris poll yielded dramatic evidence of this, reporting that 62 percent of a nationwide black sample felt that

---

[31] William Brink and Louis Harris, *The Negro Revolution in America* (New York: Simon & Schuster, 1964), p. 131.

[32] Almond and Verba, *op. cit.*, p. 64.

[33] *The Harris Survey Yearbook of Public Opinion 1970: A Compendium of Current American Attitudes.* (New York: Louis Harris & Associates, 1970).

## TABLE 7.1

A. Thinking back over the past ten years, do you feel that when Presidents Kennedy and Johnson were in the White House, the federal government could be depended on to help blacks a great deal, some but not a lot, or not much?

B. How about today under President Nixon—do you think the federal government can be depended on to help blacks a great deal, some but not a lot, or not much?

C. And how about in the next five years—do you think the federal government can be depended on to help blacks a great deal, some but not a lot, or not much?

### March
(All figures are percentages)

| | A. Past Ten Years | | | | B. Today | | | | C. Next Five Years | | | |
|---|---|---|---|---|---|---|---|---|---|---|---|---|
| | A Great Deal | Some But Not a Lot | Not Much | Not Sure | A Great Deal | Some But Not a Lot | Not Much | Not Sure | A Great Deal | Some But Not a Lot | Not Much | Not Sure |
| Nationwide Blacks | 62 | 30 | 4 | 4 | 3 | 21 | 66 | 10 | 17 | 26 | 24 | 33 |
| Region | | | | | | | | | | | | |
| South | 73 | 21 | 2 | 4 | 5 | 27 | 57 | 11 | 24 | 26 | 15 | 35 |
| Non-South | 52 | 39 | 6 | 3 | 1 | 14 | 76 | 9 | 9 | 25 | 35 | 31 |
| Size of Community | | | | | | | | | | | | |
| Large urban | 55 | 36 | 6 | 3 | 2 | 17 | 72 | 9 | 11 | 27 | 30 | 32 |
| Small urban | 65 | 29 | 1 | 5 | 4 | 18 | 66 | 12 | 15 | 25 | 24 | 38 |
| Rural | 74 | 20 | 3 | 3 | 6 | 30 | 56 | 8 | 31 | 25 | 15 | 29 |

|  |  |  |  |  |  |  |  |  |  |  |  |  |
|---|---|---|---|---|---|---|---|---|---|---|---|---|
| **Age** |  |  |  |  |  |  |  |  |  |  |  |  |
| 14 to 21 | 58 | 32 | 4 | 6 | 4 | 20 | 67 | 9 | 20 | 26 | 23 | 32 |
| 22 to 29 | 56 | 36 | 4 | 4 | 5 | 20 | 69 | 6 | 11 | 28 | 23 | 38 |
| 30 to 49 | 63 | 32 | 3 | 2 | 2 | 22 | 66 | 10 | 16 | 27 | 27 | 30 |
| 50 and over | 73 | 20 | 4 | 3 | 4 | 19 | 65 | 12 | 19 | 22 | 23 | 36 |
| **Income** |  |  |  |  |  |  |  |  |  |  |  |  |
| Under $3,000 | 72 | 20 | 4 | 4 | 6 | 25 | 60 | 9 | 24 | 24 | 20 | 32 |
| $3,000–$6,999 | 63 | 30 | 4 | 3 | 3 | 19 | 68 | 10 | 15 | 26 | 23 | 36 |
| $7,000–$9,999 | 62 | 33 | 5 |  |  | 13 | 81 | 6 | 12 | 26 | 36 | 26 |
| $10,000 and over | 54 | 41 | 2 | 3 | 2 | 23 | 69 | 6 | 13 | 29 | 29 | 29 |
| **Employment Status** |  |  |  |  |  |  |  |  |  |  |  |  |
| Professional and managerial | 51 | 40 | 5 | 4 | 2 | 19 | 72 | 7 | 13 | 26 | 24 | 37 |
| On welfare | 66 | 27 | 5 | 2 | 4 | 23 | 64 | 9 | 22 | 28 | 20 | 30 |
| **Contact with Whites** |  |  |  |  |  |  |  |  |  |  |  |  |
| Low | 62 | 26 | 6 | 6 | 3 | 23 | 60 | 14 | 14 | 24 | 19 | 43 |
| Medium | 68 | 27 | 3 | 2 | 3 | 20 | 69 | 8 | 19 | 24 | 28 | 29 |
| High | 60 | 34 | 3 | 3 | 4 | 20 | 68 | 8 | 17 | 28 | 25 | 30 |
| Prorevolution and violence | 51 | 35 | 7 | 7 | 1 | 8 | 82 | 9 | 6 | 18 | 36 | 40 |
| Panthers represent own views | 55 | 36 | 5 | 4 | 5 | 20 | 70 | 5 | 21 | 23 | 32 | 24 |

*Source: The Harris Survey Yearbook of Public Opinion 1970.* (New York: Louis Harris & Associates, 1970), p. 250.

"the federal government could be depended on to help blacks a great deal" during the Kennedy and Johnson administrations, but only 3 percent felt this was true during the Nixon administration.

### Level of Trust in the System

It is apparent that while the black subculture, like the society at large, exhibits substantial support for the political system and for the traditional political values of the society, they are aware of its failures and their political attitudes reflect this awareness. A clearer picture of political attitudes among blacks requires that we examine in greater depth evidence concerning the level of trust blacks have in the political system.

One early attempt to explore empirically the question of trust in the political system by blacks is that by Dwaine Marvick. From a secondary analysis of survey data compiled in connection with a comparative study by Almond and Verba, Marvick reported a considerably lower level of trust among blacks than among whites. He found that only 49 percent of his black sample expected fair treatment from government as opposed to 90 percent of a comparable group of whites.[34] More recent studies have confirmed consistently Marvick's findings. For example, in the wake of the Watts riots, David Sears reported a similar pattern of distrust among riot area residents. He reported that 50 percent of his black sample felt that elected officials could be trusted while 45 percent felt that they could not be.[35] This contrasts sharply with the white sample, 79 percent of which trusted their representatives while 17 percent did not.

More recently, one major study focusing on the Detroit area showed that there has been a serious erosion of trust in the political system among blacks, and that this erosion was especially sharp in the period 1967–1971. These investigators found that blacks were consistently less trusting than whites and that distrustful attitudes were not confined to any specific demographic category within the black community but cut across virtually all categories. Much of this distrust was reflected in support for or advocacy of the black power slogan. Of the supporters of black power, the study reports that

> Many are distrustful of government, unimpressed with most of the civic notables and established political leaders of both the black and white communities, and increasingly pessimistic about their chances to achieve a satisfactory life in this country. They have not surrendered the ultimate aim of social equality and social integration, but they have begun to doubt that the goal will be reached in the foreseeable future.[36]

[34] Marvick, *op. cit.,* 118.
[35] Sears, *op. cit.* 521.
[36] Joel Aberback and Jack Walker, "The Meanings of Black Power: A Comparison of White and Black Interpretations of a Political Slogan," *American Political Science Review* **64**, 2 (June 1970), 387.

Studies focusing on the political alienation of blacks provide still further information on black political attitudes and on the bases of some of these attitudes. In spite of the apparent complexity of the concept,[37] Ada Finifter provides a relatively clear explication of its major dimensions and some important findings about the precise nature and extent of black political alienation. The four major dimensions of the concept she identified are (1) political powerlessness or one's feeling that he has no influence over decision making by government; (2) political meaninglessness, involving one's inability to perceive any meaningful political choices available to him; (3) political normlessness; an individual's feelings that the norms governing political relations have broken down and that government violates its own procedures in dealing with people; (4) political isolation, a rejection of the political norms and goals that are shared by other members of the society.[38]

Finifter's study revealed that blacks are consistently more alienated than whites and that this alienation is particularly notable in the powerlessness and normlessness dimensions. Powerlessness, it will be noted, is closely related to the concept of political efficacy defined as an individual's feelings about his capacity to influence public policy by his own effort. Powerlessness would correspond to a low level of political efficacy, and thus this finding is supported by other empirical research which indicates that blacks exhibit a lower level of political efficacy than whites.[39] Notably Finifter finds that educational level is the most potent predictor of level of powerlessness, with the sense of powerlessness highest for those with the lowest educational levels. Race is a significant but less potent predictor; in fact, when educational achievement is controlled there is little difference between blacks and whites on this measure. The implication of this finding is that the relatively low level of education within the black subculture contributes directly to the reported feelings of powerlessness. If this finding is correct it means that the level of political efficacy among blacks will increase with increased education.

A different picture emerges with respect to feelings of normlessness. Not only is race one of the most powerful predictors of normlessness, but it persists even when education and occupation are controlled. Simply put, regardless of their level of education, black people generally perceive government to be failing to live up to its own norms and procedures to a much greater extent than whites, and this contributes to their feelings of estrangement from government.[40]

---

[37] For a thorough exploration of the concept see John S. Jackson, III, "Alienation and Black Political Participation," *Journal of Politics* (November 1973), 849–885.

[38] Ada Finifter, "Dimensions of Political Alienation," *American Political Science Review* 64 (June 1970), 389–391.

[39] For example, among high school students whites reported in one study to score twice as high on the efficacy scale as blacks. Kenneth Langton and M. Kent Jennings, "Political Socialization and the High School Civics Curriculum," *American Political Science Review* 62 (September 1968), 860.

[40] Finifter, *op. cit.*, p. 399.

**TABLE 7.2  Attitude of Blacks Toward the Police**
(Figures are percentages)

|  | Agree | Disagree | Not Sure |
|---|---|---|---|
| Many policemen around here are just as dishonest as the numbers runners and petty thieves | 73 | 12 | 15 |
| When people do some looting in a riot, they are just releasing some of the tension and bitterness built up through years of discrimination | 52 | 31 | 17 |
| Since junkies commit so many crimes, the best thing to do with them is to put them in jail and throw away the key | 22 | 61 | 17 |
| Too many policemen around here are more interested in cracking black heads than in stopping crime | 67 | 18 | 15 |

Source: The Harris Survey Yearbook of Public Opinion 1970. (New York: Louis Harris & Associates, 1970), p. 241.

One of the most recent studies of political attitudes, based on a nationwide sample, provides a clear and startling picture of the dramatic change in black attitudes over the last decade. The study reports that

> In 1958, whites and blacks were virtually no different in affective orientation to government, both groups were overwhelmingly supportive. What follows, however, is a steady but fairly rapid decline in trust for whites, with the greatest change occurring between 1964 and 1968. At the same time, trust among blacks rose between 1958 and 1964, reversed and declined at a rate nearly equal to whites between 1964 and 1968, and then plummeted at an astounding rate that was more than four times that at which distrust was increasing among the white group.[41]

Miller, Brown, and Raine also point out that whereas blacks in low income and occupation brackets were the ones severely estranged from government earlier, by 1972 estrangement among upper-middle and middle-class blacks almost equaled that of lower-class blacks.

The reasons offered for this pattern of estrangement are several. Miller, Brown, and Raine suggest that up to 1958 blacks were convinced that progress could be achieved by hard work and reliance on interested white "liberals." The civil rights era evoked substantial optimism among blacks, but by 1968 the slow pace of change contributed to a general disillusionment.

[41] Arthur Mitchell, Thad Brown, and Alden Raine, "Social Conflict and Political Estrangement, 1958–1972," paper prepared for delivery at the 1973 Midwest Political Science Association Convention, Chicago, 1973, p. 12.

Furthermore, they pointed out, "a growing sense of black pride and identity among blacks that probably promoted identification of middle-class blacks with the majority of the black population for whom system rewards had not expanded noticeably, an upsurge in system blame and, correspondingly, an increased willingness to strike out violently at white-dominated property and institutions,"[42] all operated to precipitate the rapid decline in political trust.

### Evaluations of Government

How individuals feel about government is partly a function of their evaluations of the performance of government. The link between evaluative and affective orientations should be particularly strong for blacks because, as we observed above, their circumstances made reliance on government vital. The extent of that reliance even now was suggested by a study of black political attitudes in the Buffalo area. The investigators reported that

> . . . blacks see their everyday life situations as inextricably tied to governmental performances. The very basics of life—jobs, housing, education—and the good life in general, are seen as being related to positive governmental action. For blacks, the very definition of basic civil liberties involves the providing of opportunities for a better life, and are seen as part of governments' basic responsibilities to help provide.[43]

These high expectations notwithstanding, the experience blacks have had with government is mostly one of failure to respond adequately to black demands and to fulfill for them the most basic obligations of government to its citizens. The chronicle of governmental failure in this regard need not be repeated in depressing detail here. It can be amply illustrated with the single issue of the physical security of blacks in the society.

The obligation of government to protect the individual is basic to our conceptions of government. Thomas Hobbes considered it the primary responsibility of the state, failing which the people were free to withdraw their support from the monarch.[44] Yet the history of lynching in America provides vivid and grotesque evidence of the failure of government at all levels to provide this basic protection to blacks. Lynchings were not merely a few clandestine murders indulged in by social misfits. On the contrary, they were public murders participated in by large numbers of people and routinely reported in the press in a largely successful effort to intimidate, terrorize, and subdue an entire people. The NAACP reported that in the period 1889–1918, 3224 black persons were lynched, often publicly and in circumstances as

---

[42] *Ibid.*, pp. 14–15.

[43] Everett Cataldo, Richard Johnson, and Lyman Kellstadt, "Political Attitudes of Urban Blacks and Whites: Some Implications for Policy Makers," in Van Der Slik, *op. cit.*, p. 61.

[44] Thomas Hobbes, *Leviathan* (New York: Collier, 1962), p. 167.

gruesome and barbaric as the mind could devise, in order to achieve maximum terror among blacks.[45] In the face of these acts, the national government pleaded "states rights" as an obstacle to intervention and the states made no serious efforts to prevent them.

Denials of this basic protection by the state is still a part of black life. Law enforcement in black neighborhoods remains haphazard and ineffective in many areas.[46] One consequence is that blacks are more likely than whites to be victims of violent crimes, and often black communities quickly become cesspools of vices and criminal exploitation of various kinds, with only meager responses from government unless whites and their businesses are threatened. Not all of the blame for this condition rests with the present performance of government, but the absence of effective law enforcement is certainly a major contributor. Complicating the problem is the fact that the police, who do serve in black communities, often become not the protectors of the citizen but an added threat to the physical security of the community. This perception is reflected in the overwhelmingly negative attitudes of blacks toward the police.[47]

There have been very few attempts to tap black evaluations of the performance of government but those undertaken are revealing. As part of the study by the National Advisory Commission on Civil Disorders (The Kerner Commission), Angus Campbell and Howard Schuman undertook a 15-city study of the attitudes of blacks toward the performance of government at the local, state, and national levels. The study found that

> Negroes were consistently less satisfied with the efforts of all three governmental levels than whites, especially of their city mayor. The attitude of Negroes toward their city government is more polarized than white attitudes. Nearly half of the Negro sample feel their mayor is "trying as hard as he can" but a quarter say he is "not trying hard at all."[48]

On specific programs such as federal antipoverty programs, however, blacks emerged as more favorable about the performance of government.

It is noteworthy that while blacks have been much less satisfied than whites with governmental performance, that of the Supreme Court appears to

[45] For a discussion of lynchings and other atrocities committed by whites against blacks see John Brisbane, *The Black Vanguard* (Valley Forge, Pa.: Judson Press, 1970), pp. 75–80.

[46] The role of the police in black neighborhoods was extensively examined in the Report of the National Advisory Commission on Civil Disorders. See Louis Knowles and Kenneth Prewitt, *Institutional Racism in America* (Englewood Cliffs, N.J.: Prentice-Hall, 1969), pp. 59–62, 320–332.

[47] See Burton Levy, "Cops in the Ghetto: A Problem of the Police System," in Louis Masotti and Don R. Bowen, *Riots and Rebellion: Civil Violence in the Urban Community* (Beverly Hills, Calif.: Sage, 1968), pp. 347–358.

[48] Angus Campbell and Howard Schuman, *Negro Attitudes in 15 Cities.* Staff Report to the National Commission on the Causes and Prevention of Violence (Washington, D.C.: Government Printing Office, 1969), p. 41.

have been an exception. Studies focusing on attitudes toward the Court during the 1960s revealed that blacks were much more positive in their evaluation of its performance than whites.[49] This suggests that institutions that have been identified as prominently and directly involved in facilitating the struggle for change will be viewed positively. The Supreme Court's leadership in bringing about certain basic changes in the pattern of race relations is undoubtedly responsible for this favorable evaluation by blacks and at the same time explains the much more negative response especially among Southern whites.

## The Pattern of Black Political Socialization·

The tradition of governmental unresponsiveness to blacks or even complete abdication of its responsibilities help to explain the attitudes now found within the black subculture, but other important factors are also contributors. An individual need not directly experience governmental neglect in order to develop negative attitudes toward government. Political attitudes are acquired by the process of political socialization. There are significant differences among scholars on how they define political socialization, but for our purposes we will view it as the process by which individuals acquire political attitudes, values, and skills relevant to the political system in which they live. In its broad patterns the process is similar for all individuals, but investigators have now convincingly demonstrated that there are significant differences across cultures and across subcultures in the attitudes, values, and skills that are acquired and in precisely how they are acquired. Study of the socialization of blacks in the United States thus may provide further evidence concerning the existence of a black subculture in addition to informing us about how these attitudes are formed.

Unfortunately only a relatively small portion of the now large body of literature on political socialization in the United States focuses on blacks, and even this is limited in some important respects. First, most of the studies rely on analyses of black subsamples of inadequate size and limited geographical location which provide very weak bases for generalizations about black political socialization. Second, like most of the socialization literature, studies of black political socialization focus almost exclusively on children from the very low grades through high school and thus suffer from the many limitations flowing from survey research among children. These limitations notwithstanding, they provide some significant findings and raise several issues for further exploration. Specifically, the studies demonstrate that historical, social and environmental factors combine to provide to black youth political attitudes and values different from those of white youth. In examining these

[49] Herbert Hirsch and Lewis Donohew, "A Note on Negro-White Differences in Attitudes Toward the Supreme Court," *Social Science Quarterly* **49**, 3 (December 1968), 562.

findings we can conveniently focus on the principal agents usually involved in the socialization process—family, school, and environment or social milieu.

### The Family and Black Political Socialization

The crucial role of the family in the socialization process now has been firmly established by extensive research. The intensity and pervasiveness of its impact is suggested in the observation that

> The family provides the major means for transforming the mentally naked infant organism into the adult, fully clothed in his own personality. And most of the individual's personality—his tendencies to think and act in particular ways—have been determined at home, several years before he can take part in politics as an ordinary adult citizen or as a political prominent.[50]

More concrete evidence on the impact of the family in shaping political attitudes is provided in V. O. Key's findings about the transmission of partisan attitudes from parents to children. Key reported from one survey that of those adults who could remember that both their parents supported the same party, 80 percent cast their first vote for that party and 69 percent of all adults claim to support the party of their parents, while only 13 percent support another party.[51]

In view of its potency in the socialization process, substantial attention has been directed at the impact of the black family on the socialization of its youngsters. Findings to date suggest that (a) weaknesses in the structure of the black family limit its effectiveness in transmitting some generally desired political attitudes to its youngsters; (b) the different orientations to politics exhibited by black and white youngsters are traceable in large part to the family.

The high percentage of black homes from which the father is absent is the structural characteristic that has been of greatest concern to investigators. In one of his more notable and controversial addresses, President Lyndon Johnson emphasized this issue before a Howard University audience. He observed that

> Only a minority—less than half of all Negro children—reach the age of 18 having lived all their lives with both of their parents.
> At this moment tonight, little less than two-thirds are at home with both of their parents.
> Probably a majority of all Negro children received federally aided public assistance sometime during their childhood.

[50] James Davies, "The Family's Role in Political Socialization," *Annals of the American Academy of Political and Social Science* 361 (September 1965), 11.

[51] V. O. Key, *Public Opinion and American Democracy* (New York: Knopf, 1961), p. 301.

> The family is the cornerstone of our society. More than any other force it shapes the attitudes, the hopes, the ambitions, and the values of the child.
>
> When the family collapses, it is the children that are usually damaged. When it happens on a massive scale, the entire community itself is crippled.[52]

These remarks by President Johnson were merely the highlights of a major study of the black family by Daniel Patrick Moynihan. In the study Moynihan documents what he perceives as the widespread breakdown in the black family structure, reporting that in the decade 1950–1960 33 percent of the black homes in urban areas were headed by females as opposed to eight percent for whites. The same pattern also prevailed in rural areas with only slight improvement. Furthermore, Moynihan felt this alleged deterioration in black family structure is continuing.[53] This condition is considered to have severe consequences for the security and stability of the home as well as for its ability to contribute effectively to political socialization. James Coleman suggests in this regard that "the weakness of the conjugal bond among Negroes has consequences for the economic stability of the family, its ability to socialize the young, and the entire set of functions that the family provides for its members in modern society."[54] Moynihan's conclusions are not unanimously shared, as several analysts have questioned his analysis of available data and his understanding of black family life. Warren Ten Houten, for example, refutes the assertion that there is a rapid, continuing disintegration of the black family and suggests that the phenomenon of father absence is much more closely associated with economic status than with race.[55]

The precise impact of "father absence" or homes headed by females on political attitudes is still unclear. In one extensive examination of this question Kenneth Langton tested three hypotheses:

1. Males from father-absent families are more likely than females to react to the anxiety of insecure paternal identification with compensatory closed belief systems as measured by the dogmatism scale.
2. The absence of a paternal political stimulant and role model is more likely to retard the political interest of males than females.
3. Maternal dominance will have a more debilitating effect on the feelings of male children than female.[56]

[52] Lyndon Johnson, "Commencement Address at Howard University," in Gary Marx, *Racial Conflict, Tension and Change in American Society* (Boston: Little, Brown, 1971), p. 222.

[53] Daniel Patrick Moynihan, *The Negro Family: The Case for National Action* (Washington, D.C.: U.S. Department of Labor, Office of Policy Planning and Research, 1965).

[54] James Coleman, *Resources for Social Change: Race in the United States* (New York: Wiley, 1971), p. 22.

[55] Warren Ten Houten, "The Black Family: Myth and Reality," *Psychiatry* 33 (May 1970), 145–173.

[56] Langton, *op. cit.,* p. 32.

The hypotheses were confirmed in Langton's study of the role of Jamaican families in political socialization. He found that male children from "fatherless homes" tended to exhibit more authoritarian tendencies, were less interested in politics and less politically efficacious than their counterparts from "nuclear families."

No comparable studies have been conducted with black American families but some extrapolation to the American situation appears appropriate since several studies have identified in black American children the cluster of traits Langton reports from his Jamaica study. For example, strong authoritarian tendencies have been reported among samples of black children. One study of black and white children's attitudes toward authority figures found among black children a greater tendency to idealize authority[57] than is found among whites; and another study reported a similar pattern among black adults in Detroit.[58] The measurement of attitudes toward authority, especially among blacks in the United States is highly problematic and may reflect attitudes toward specific individuals occupying authoritative roles like the presidency, instead of preference for strong authority in general. For example, it is very likely that blacks would respond differently to questions about support for presidential authority during the Kennedy and Johnson administrations than they would to the same questions during the Nixon administration. Taken together the studies do suggest, however, that the style of family life within the black subculture may be an important factor in shaping the distinct political attitudes of blacks.

### The School and Political Socialization

Only the family seems to exceed the school in importance as a socializing agent, and Robert Hess and Judith Torney even suggest that "the public school is the most important and effective agent of political socialization in the United States."[59] Unlike the subtle and pervasive role of the family, the school's major contribution to the political socialization of its charges is usually limited to

1. Providing basic information about government and its role in society
2. Inculcating positive or supportive attitudes toward government
3. Developing the skills necessary for effective participation in political life

[57] Edward S. Greenberg, "Orientations of Black and White Children to Political Authority Figures," *Social Science Quarterly* 51 (December 1970), 561–571.

[58] Roberta Sigel, "Image of the American Presidency: Part III of an Exploration into Popular Views of Presidential Power," *Midwest Journal of Political Science* 10 (February 1966), 123–137.

[59] Robert Hess and Judith Torney, *The Development of Political Attitudes in Children* (Chicago: Aldine, 1967), p. 101.

These may be accomplished through formal training in civics or social studies courses, the "patriotic rituals" such as saluting the flag and the general atmosphere of the classroom or school.

Unfortunately we are without many major studies of the extent of the school's socializing impact on youngsters, although several socialization studies have utilized samples of children of various age levels. One of the few major attempts in this regard does demonstrate some differences between black and white students in the impact of the high school civics curriculum. The investigators found that blacks benefited more (i.e., showed greater increase in information level) from civics courses than did whites, apparently because white students entered the courses with much greater knowledge of government than did black youngsters.[60]

An even more significant finding by Langton is that the civics curriculum appears to have a substantially different impact on the *attitudes* of black and white students. Although both are exposed to the same information, blacks emerge with a strong "subject orientation" to politics rather than a "participant" one. Thus "it appears to inculcate in Negroes the expectation that a good citizen is above all a loyal citizen rather than an active one."[61] The indication is that while the civics curriculum emphasizes both loyalty and participatory attitudes, blacks are less strongly influenced by its participant emphasis. The authors believe that with respect to both knowledge and efficacy the different impact of the civics curriculum on blacks and whites is a result of the earlier impact of the home.

Further light on some specific attitudes of black youngsters is provided in a study of Philadelphia school children conducted by Edward Greenberg. He reports substantial differences between his sample of black and white children, noting that "black and white children diverge significantly with respect to their judgments as to government's benevelence and protection."[62] He also reports that although black and while children begin with similar views about the benevolence of government, blacks tend to see government as less caring, and less to be trusted, as they advance in grade level. Some of this decline in trust is recovered later, but a substantial difference remains between blacks and whites. The difference in feelings of political efficacy reported by Langton and Jennings is also reported by Greenberg, who concluded that compared to white children, "Negroes lag in their development of participant orientations" and they are "less likely than whites to see government leaders as responsive to the demands of the people."[63]

---

[60] Kenneth Langton and M. Kent Jennings, "Political Socialization and the High School Civics Curriculum," *American Political Science Review* 62 (September 1968), 801.

[61] Langton *op. cit.,* pp. 110–111.

[62] Edward S. Greenberg, "Children and Government: A Comparison Across Racial Lines," *Midwest Journal of Political Science* 14 (May 1970), 260.

[63] *Ibid.*

Studies of the impact of schools in the political socialization of young-sters in the United States have been limited almost entirely to the curriculum but there is evidence from a wide range of comparative research that the physical environment and the "atmosphere" of the school are also potent forces in shaping political attitudes.[64] Furthermore, there is evidence that teachers bring to the classroom expectations about the likely roles that children of certain racial or socioeconomic groups will occupy, and these expectations influence the attitudes imparted to students. Since little if any research has been undertaken which would indicate clearly the impact of these factors on black children, we may only conjecture about the impact of the dilapidated, ill-equipped ghetto schools, or different treatment and oppor-tunities accorded to the black minority in many "integrated schools" on their attitudes toward government and toward themselves as political actors.

Environment and Political Socialization

The environment within which an individual lives is another important agent of political socialization. Our knowledge about its exact impact is at best scanty, since researchers have made few serious attempts to assess this. It seems reasonable to expect, however, that the immediate environment within which one lives will affect the socialization process in any or all of the following ways: (1) It may provide an independent source of learning for youngsters as they observe political events and the performance of agents of government in their communities. (2) It may reinforce positive images of government presented in school by providing concrete evidence of the con-cern and benevolence of government regarding the community's well-being. (3) It may contradict the positive image of government inculcated by formal institutions like schools by providing evidence of governmental neglect and unconcern. (4) Community institutions and traditions that are not explicitly political may directly or indirectly affect an individual's political attitudes and values.[65]

Attention to the impact of environment is especially important in studying the political socialization of blacks. Black America is to a large extent physically separate from the larger white society. The environment, especially the decaying urban ghettos in which a large portion of the black population lives, provide black youth with experiences and perceptions of self and government that are substantially different from those of their white counterparts. It is very likely that the view of government as benevolent and

[64] See for example David Koff and George Von der Muhl, "Political Socialization in Kenya and Tanzania: A Comparative Analysis," *Journal of Modern African Studies* 5 (May 1967), 13–52.

[65] Milton D. Morris and Carolyn Cobe, "The Political Socialization of Black Youth: A Survey of Research Findings," *Public Affairs Bulletin* (Southern Illinois University at Carbondale), **4**, 3 (May–June 1972), 5.

responsive is severely challenged as the black child begins to grasp the reality of his surroundings. In sharp contrast to the mostly white-occupied, neat suburban communities with their many evidences of governmental attentiveness, the poverty and decay of urban slums and rural backwaters provide few indications of governmental concern for or involvement in the black child's world. Thus the image of government conveyed by the schools may be in such sharp contrast to reality as seriously to erode the trust in government that schools attempt to inculcate in black children.

There are more concrete ways in which environment appears to contribute distinct political attitudes and values to blacks. In one highly perceptive study, David Schultz provides a view of ghetto life not unlike Kenneth Clarke's depiction of the "dark ghetto" cut off from the rest of society by an "invisible wall." Schultz found that the ghetto imposes demands on its residents unlike the demands on residents of other environments. Family life not only perpetuates the pathology of the ghetto but socializes the young into the distinct values and attitudes that are essential elements of ghetto life.[66]

James Coleman points out another peculiarity of black communities that undoubtedly affect political socialization. He observes in these communities a lack of social cohesion and trust in people that normally characterize communities. Lack of cohesion, Coleman suggests, deprives the community of the capacity to make demands on external social institutions, to enforce internal constraints, and to protect the community from predators.[67] In short, these conditions create a state of powerlessness and sustains a generally low level of political efficacy. Coleman's observations do not seem to apply to the spontaneous warmth and empathy that characterize many black communities, but to the lack of a tradition of organized, institutionalized cooperation for problem-solving. He observes, for example, that lack of trust in black communities results in part from absence of those cooperative institutions that normally facilitate development of trust among members of a community.[68]

An attempt to determine empirically whether and to what extent environment affects the political attitudes of youngsters was undertaken by Schley Lyons. He compared one black and one white group of inner-city low-income residents with similar groups of suburban residents in the Toledo area. Lyons found that regardless of where black children lived they were more cynical about government and felt less efficacious than their white counterparts, but that those children from deprived inner-city slums had, by the fifth grade, become more cynical and less efficacious than children living elsewhere. Thus, although race was the most significant variable, environment

[66] David Schultz, *Coming Up Black: Patterns of Ghetto Socialization* (Englewood Cliffs, N.J.: Prentice-Hall, 1969).
[67] Coleman, *Resources for Social Change, op. cit.,* pp. 27–42.
[68] *Ibid.*

clearly had a substantial impact on the attitudes of both black and white children sampled.[69]

## Explaining Black-White Differences in Political Attitudes

Although they differ considerably in method, scope, and depth, virtually all of the recent research on the political attitudes of the black subculture and the political socialization of youth within the subculture arrive at some common conclusions. Chief among these are that in comparison with whites (1) blacks are less trusting (or more cynical) toward the political system, (2) blacks feel less efficacious or confident about their capacity to influence governmental performance, and (3) blacks tend to be more authoritarian (or deferential toward authority) than are whites. We noted earlier that many of these findings may not be entirely accurate because not enough thorough, well-designed investigations have been undertaken to permit confident generalizations about the black population, and because of overreliance on children, especially in the face of evidence that children often respond to questionnaires on matters about which they have no real attitudes.[70] Nevertheless, the consistency of the findings and the absence of significant conflicting evidence make them convincing. It is useful to inquire further about why the difference between the races in political attitudes.

At one level it is easy to understand why the reported differences exist between the political attitudes of blacks and whites. Their subordinate status in the society and the pattern of governmental performance flowing from this status are clearly the fundamental bases of these differences. It is noteworthy that President Johnson, in his speech on the black family, linked its weaknesses to the history of black oppression and subordination by noting that for "the breakdown of the Negro family structure—white America must accept responsibility. It flows from centuries of oppression and persecution of the Negro man; it flows from the long years of degradation and discrimination which have attacked his dignity and assaulted his ability to produce for his family."[71] In a few cases investigators have attempted to probe this "why" question more deeply and their efforts altogether yield three broad explanatory propositions or "theories"—the subcultural theory, the social deprivation theory, and the political reality theory. In surveying these proposed explanations for the differences in the kinds of political attitudes learned by black and white youngsters we may be able to understand more clearly the impact of race on political attitudes and behavior.

One of the most extensive recent efforts to account for black-white differences in political attitudes is that by Paul Abramson. He identified two

[69] Schley Lyons, "The Political Socialization of Ghetto Children: Efficacy and Cynicism," *Journal of Politics* 32 (May 1970), 258–304.

[70] This problem is discussed in William Schonfield, "The Focus of Political Socialization Research: An Evaluation," *World Politics* 23 (April 1971), 544–578.

[71] Johnson, *op. cit.*, p. 222.

possible explanations for these differences. One is what he calls the "social deprivation theory," which suggests in essence that the political attitudes of blacks differ from those of whites because blacks have been socially deprived. He conceptualizes the link between social deprivation and nonsupportive political attitudes thus:

> Social deprivation contributes to low feelings of self-competence. Feelings of personal self-competence contribute both to feelings of political effectiveness and to feelings of political trust. Because blacks are socially deprived and consequently their feelings of self-competence are low, their low self-competence contributes to low levels of political efficacy and trust.[72]

Abramson did not test this social deprivation theory empirically however, and although each of the closely related propositions upon which it rests has been supported by fairly extensive research, there is room for doubt about whether the relationships postulated exist in fact.[73]

The social deprivation of blacks is clearly obvious, just as the gap between their aspirations for social well-being and their actual achievements or opportunities for achievement is an extensively documented fact of American life. What this theory does, however, is to suggest why the poor—or those in the society who are socially deprived—exhibit low levels of trust and efficacy. It does not appear to explain black-white differences where they exist in spite of socioeconomic status.

As a second approach to explaining black-white differences in political attitudes, Abramson suggests that the negative attitudes of black American youngsters toward the political system may be a reflection of the reality of black political life within the United States. The basic premises on which this approach rests are that blacks have less ability to influence the political system and thus have less reason to trust political leaders than whites. Children become aware of this condition, and this awareness is reflected in their negative attitudes toward government.

Abramson concedes that although the political reality thesis appears highly plausible as an explanation of black-white differences in political attitudes, it is extremely difficult to link empirically children's political attitudes to the powerlessness experienced by their parents. In fact there is evidence that efficacious attitudes might not be among those usually transmitted directly from parents to children. However the process works, Abramson suggests that certain consequences might be expected to flow from the political reality explanation which can be empirically tested and which appear to be supported by some existing research. These are hypothesized thus:

---

[72] Paul R. Abramson, "Political Efficacy and Political Trust Among Black School Children: Two Explanations," *Journal of Politics* 34 (1972), 1249–1250.
[73] See for example, Harrell Rodgers, Jr., "Toward Explanation of the Political Efficacy and Political Cynicism of Black Adolescents: An Exploratory Study," *American Journal of Political Science* 18, 2 (May 1974), pp. 257–282.

1. Feelings of political effectiveness and political trust should be lower among blacks who understand political realities than among blacks who do not.
2. Racial differences on feelings of political efficacy should be reduced or reversed in settings where blacks have political power.
3. Blacks should be more trusting toward political leaders who depend on electoral support from blacks than upon leaders who do not rely on black support.[74]

The political reality thesis is stressed by Joan Laurence in her study of black-white differences in political socialization, but with a somewhat different emphasis from Abramson's. She perceives political reality for blacks as involving real-life encounters with government and indications of governmental concern or unconcern. Thus she suggests that while programs of conscious socialization will have an impact on children, this impact may be mediated by "the reality that the subject perceives around him." At present, Laurence maintains, the political world of black Americans is a fundamentally different one from that of whites, and thus "the black child's position as a black gives him a different reality and a different self-interest."[75]

A broader basis for explaining black-white differences in political attitudes and one that subsumes the social deprivation and political reality theories is the "subculture theory" for explaining differences in black-white political attitudes. Orum and Cohn tested the subcultural theory and found it particularly relevant because "it would explain the similarities in the attitudes of black youth and adults." In particular, it suggests that "such similarities occur because blacks, both young and old, are exposed to the values of the larger black subculture, and partly because black parents transmit such values to their children."[76] In testing the subcultural theory, Orum and Cohn hypothesized that black children who identified most strongly with the black community would also exhibit to the greatest degree the political beliefs and behavior reported in black-white comparisons. In support of the hypothesis they found that "black children who scored high on their identification with the black community were consistently more cynical as well."[77] This finding agrees with the conclusion of Miller, Brown, and Raine that among black adults, increased identification with the black subculture heightened the feelings of distrust and estrangement among blacks, and particularly among those of middle-class backgrounds. Much more rigorous and extensive test of the subculture theory is required, but it appears reasonable to conclude that

[74] Abramson, *op. cit.*, 1262–1264.
[75] Joan Laurence, "White Socialization: Black Reality," *Psychiatry* 33 (May 1970), 176.
[76] Anthony Orum and Roberta Cohen, "The Development of Political Orientations Among Black and White Children," *American Sociological Review,* 38 (February 1973), 70.
[77] *Ibid.*

the tradition of inferiority, deprivation, and oppression are crucial in shaping black political attitudes and values.

The implications for political attitudes of the relationship of the black subculture to the dominant white culture has been suggested by Archie Singham's observation that black America exists as a "marginal group" because it has never been fully accepted into the political community and its basic goals are not shared by other groups in the society. This marginal status, which is similar to our concept of subordinate status, he finds comparable to the status of colonized people in the traditional colonies and it results in similar orientations to politics. He observes:

> The parallel of the situation of the American Negro and the colonial are strikingly similar in many ways. . . . One of the consequences of the dependency induced in the Negro by the system has been his perception of government. Like the colonial, his attitude toward government is often negative. The government is both benefactor and oppressor: the two agencies of government that he has the most contact with are welfare agencies and law enforcement officers, most of whom are white, thus encouraging a we-they concept of government. Thus, not only does he not develop a feeling as a responsible citizen, but he is also ambivalent about "politics," especially since he feels his participation is not likely to result in "capturing" the government.[78]

[78] A. H. Singham, "The Political Socialization of Marginal Groups," *International Journal of Comparative Sociology* 8 (September 1967), 189–190.

# Black Political
# Participation I:
# The Electoral Process

Participation by the public in the political life of its society is now an almost universally shared value. Within the United States it has been one of the fundamental values on which the political system rests. In fact, many American political scientists now regard level of political participation as a crucial indicator of degree of political modernization and adherence to democratic values. Not surprisingly, therefore, an analysis of political participation is essential to any serious examination of politics in the United States. Political participation is especially crucial in studies of the black political experience, since blacks very early accepted the view that the democratic political process—particularly exercise of the franchise—is the source from which all blessings flow, and directed their energies toward getting full access to the political arena as participants.

Black politics has involved, first, a struggle for opportunities to participate fully in the political process and second, development of new participatory techniques in order to influence the policy process when traditional techniques were either unavailable or proved ineffective. For these reasons the bulk of research on black political life focuses on their political participation. Scholars have attempted to describe broad patterns of black political participation, to compare it with participatory activities of whites, and to measure or speculate about its impact on black life as well as on the political system as a whole. Results of these studies are at best mixed. They have been primarily piecemeal studies which focus on limited segments of the black subculture, employ a wide assortment of analytical techniques, and cover various time periods, so that a total picture of black political participation is extremely difficult to obtain. What emerges from these efforts often is inconclusive, conflicting, or even misleading. In this and the following two chapters we attempt a broad examination of black political participation in the hope of contributing a measure of order and clarity to this important aspect of black political life.

146

In political science literature, *political participation* is used to designate a wide range of politically relevant activities in which individuals engage. The breadth of the concept is suggested by Donald Matthews and James Prothro in their assertion that

> Old men talking politics in the shade of a crossroads store, housewives discussing the local schools over a cup of coffee, a farm family attending a campaign barbecue, a Negro student joining the "sit-in" at a drug-store lunch counter, a union member contributing his dollar to a labor political committee—all are taking part in the daily round of democratic politics.[1]

This broad, inclusive view of political participation is influenced by Lester Milbrath's treatment of the concept in which he identifies and arranges in hierarchical order fourteen types of participatory acts ranging from mere exposure of oneself to political stimuli at the bottom to holding public and party office at the top.[2]

Noting that this broadly inclusive use of the concept makes detailed study extremely difficult, one group of scholars suggests a more limited conception of political participation. They define it as "all those activities by private citizens that are more or less directly aimed at influencing the selection of governmental personnel and/or the decisions that they make."[3] The two definitions differ in scope but both include the basic set of activities and behaviors of primary concern to us. For purposes of this study we will rely more on the more limited approach to political participation.

Within any given population one is likely to find considerable differences in the participatory habits of individuals. Some people are apathetic toward politics and do not participate at all; others participate only sporadically and to a limited extent, while still others participate extensively. For analytical purposes, Verba, Nie, and Kim identify four basic types or modes of participation: voting, electoral activities beyond voting, cooperative activities such as group efforts to secure political goals, and citizen-initiated contacts of government officials.[4] These do not cover all conceivable forms of participation, since the categorization omits those participatory acts not directly relevant to the policy process. They include those activities that are most crucial, however, to an understanding of the black political subculture.

For the sake of convenience we divide our discussion of black political participation into three categories instead of the four suggested by Verba, Nie, and Kim. Under the heading of electoral participation we will describe voting and other electoral activities by blacks, including seeking and holding

---

[1] Donald R. Matthews and James Prothro, *Negroes and the New Southern Politics* (New York: Harcourt Brace Jovanovich, 1966), p. 37.
[2] Lester Milbrath, *Political Participation* (Skokie, Ill.: Rand McNally, 1965), pp. 17–19.
[3] Sidney Verba and Norman Nie, *Participation in America: Political Democracy and Social Equality* (New York: Harper & Row, 1972), p. 2.
[4] *Ibid.*, pp. 45–48.

public office. In Chapter 9 we will focus on partisanship and the pattern of support by blacks for the political parties over time. In Chapter 10 we will examine the nonelectoral forms of political participation involving cooperative activities of various kinds. This classification is based primarily on organizational considerations, inasmuch as these forms of political participation are not entirely separable but overlap at several points. Moreover, they must be viewed as a whole in characterizing the pattern of political participation within the black subculture.

## The Pattern of Black Electoral Participation

The electoral process is still the basic avenue through which most individuals participate in politics in this and virtually all other "democratic" societies. It provides the only regular, formal procedure by which qualified members of a society contribute to the policy process. Voting, as the basic participatory act in the electoral process, is the form of participation most widely engaged in by the public. For these reasons, insight into the participatory habits of a society or any segment of that society can be most directly and conveniently obtained by studying the electoral process and the manner and degree of an individual's participation as voter and as activist in other ways. Our concern here is with the participatory habits of the black subculture in the United States, but it is useful to proceed by comparing black-white participatory habits.

Although the many studies of black political participation conducted thus far vary widely in their specific findings, most report substantial differences between the participatory habits of blacks and whites. It is frequently reported and widely accepted that blacks have been generally apathetic politically, participating less than whites do. Charles Silberman, like several other well-meaning observers, has lamented that blacks are victims of "a massive political apathy."[5] Although there are no comprehensive studies that provide a clear picture of the level of black political participation, several limited studies of voting behavior appear to support this point of view. One empirical study, conducted in 1950, revealed that while 11 percent of the white sample could be categorized as "extremely active," only 5 percent of the black sample fell in this category. On the other hand, 60 percent of the black sample was found to be "very inactive" politically compared to 35 percent of whites.[6] Other studies based on scattered, incomplete data from presidential elections since the 1940s also reveal a substantial gap between the levels of political participation of blacks and whites.[7]

---

[5] Charles Silberman, *Crisis in Black and White* (New York: Random House, 1964).
[6] Julian Woodward and Elmo Roper, "Political Activity of American Citizens," *American Political Science Review* 44, 4 (December 1950), 874.
[7] See for example Angus Campbell et al., *The American Voter* (abridged version), (New York: Wiley, 1964), pp. 151–153; James Q. Wilson, "The Negro in American Politics—The Present," in John P. Davis, ed., *The American Negro Reference Book* (Englewood Cliffs, N.J.: Prentice-Hall, 1966).

Findings of this kind raise several important questions for examination. First, we need to know if there are in fact substantial differences between the participatory habits of black and white Americans, and if so to attempt to clarify the extent of these differences. Second, we need to identify the bases of the reported differences in electoral behavior between blacks and whites. In this regard it should be ascertained whether any or all of these differences are entirely racial or may be attributable to nonracial factors. Finally, it is essential that we examine the actual, or predictable impact of black electoral participation of the policy process.

A careful assessment of black political participation over time will indicate that assertions of a massive political apathy within the black subculture do not appear to have been well considered. Such assertions are prompted by an overreliance on uncritical analyses of voting statistics and ignore other factors essential to a thorough evaluation of black electoral participation. The following assertions are consistent with the available evidence on the subject. (1) There is a substantial difference between blacks and whites in their level of voting and this difference has remained relatively constant over a substantial period of time in spite of major developments such as the Voting Rights Act of 1965. (2) The gap between blacks and whites in voting appears to be associated with socioeconomic factors as well as historical circumstances peculiar to blacks. (3) In certain forms of electoral participation beyond voting, the level for blacks comes much closer to and in some instances surpasses the level for whites. (4) The most striking feature of black electoral participation is that it far exceeds the level which their historical experience and socioeconomic status would lead us to expect, and must be partly explained by factors peculiar to the black subculture.

### The Pattern of Voting

As will be shown below, extensive, widespread voting by blacks is fairly recent, although some blacks have always participated in American politics as voters. Only since 1965, with the massive intervention of the federal government in several Southern states, have blacks in that region been free to vote. While it is difficult to make nationwide comparisons of black and white voting, because of the difference between the races in access to the vote, available data reveal some interesting facts. The level of voting for the nation as a whole has not been very high, remaining fairly constant at least since about 1950. About 62 percent of the eligible American adults reported that they voted in the 1952 presidential election; in 1972 the figure was approximately 55 percent, after reaching a peak 64 percent in 1960. A much lower level of voting occurs in Congressional elections, the figure going from just above 40 percent in 1954 to 45 percent in 1970. Among whites the level of voting in presidential elections hovered about 70 percent, declining steadily since 1968 to 65 percent in 1972.

Some studies of black voting behavior in the major urban centers of the

**TABLE 8.1** *Reported Voter Registration for Persons of Voting Age by Region: 1966, 1968, 1970, and 1972*
(Numbers in thousands)

| Subject | Negro | | | | White | | | |
|---|---|---|---|---|---|---|---|---|
| | 1966 | 1968 | 1970 | 1972 | 1966 | 1968 | 1970 | 1972 |
| All persons of voting age | 10,533 | 10,935 | 11,473 | 15,494 | 101,205 | 104,521 | 107,997 | 121,241 |
| North and West | 4,849 | 4,944 | 5,277 | 6,544 | 72,593 | 75,687 | 77,158 | 85,830 |
| South | 5,684 | 5,991 | 6,196 | 6,750 | 28,612 | 28,834 | 30,839 | 35,415 |
| Number who reported they had registered: | | | | | | | | |
| United States | 6,345 | 7,238 | 6,971 | 7,238 | 72,517 | 78,835 | 74,672 | 78,835 |
| North and West | 3,337 | 3,548 | 3,406 | 3,548 | 54,125 | 58,419 | 54,591 | 58,419 |
| South | 3,008 | 3,690 | 3,565 | 3,640 | 18,392 | 20,416 | 20,081 | 20,416 |
| Percent of voting-age population:[a] | | | | | | | | |
| United States | 60 | 66 | 61 | 66 | 72 | 75 | 61 | 73 |
| North and West | 69 | 72 | 65 | 67 | 75 | 77 | 71 | 75 |
| South | 53 | 62 | 58 | 64 | 64 | 71 | 65 | 70 |

[a]Rounded to nearest whole number.
*Source:* U.S. Department of Commerce Current Population Reports, Series P–23, No. 42, 1971 and Series P–20, No. 244, 1972. *The Social and Economic Status of the Black Population in the U.S., 1973* (Washington, D.C.: U.S. Department of Commerce, 1974), p. 121.

**TABLE 8.2**  *Reported Voter Participation and Registration of the Population of Voting Age, by Region: 1964, 1968, and 1972*

(Numbers in Thousands)

| | Black | | | White | | |
|---|---|---|---|---|---|---|
| | 1964 | 1968 | 1972 | 1964 | 1968 | 1972 |
| **Number who reported that they voted:** | | | | | | |
| United States | 6,048 | 6,300 | 7,033 | 70,204 | 72,213 | 78,167 |
| South | [a]2,576 | 3,094 | 3,324 | 15,813 | 17,853 | 20,201 |
| North and West | [a]3,891 | 3,206 | 3,707 | 54,392 | 54,362 | 57,966 |
| **Percent of voting age population who reported that they voted** | | | | | | |
| United States | 58 | 58 | 52 | 71 | 69 | 64 |
| South | [a]44 | 52 | 48 | 59 | 62 | 57 |
| North and West | [a]72 | 65 | 57 | 75 | 72 | 68 |
| **Percent of registered population who reported they voted** | | | | | | |
| United States | (NA) | 87 | 80 | (NA) | 92 | 88 |
| South | (NA) | 84 | 75 | (NA) | 87 | 82 |
| North and West | (NA) | 90 | 85 | (NA) | 93 | 90 |

NA = Not available
[a]Includes persons of "other races."
*Source: The Social and Economic Status of the Black Population in the U.S., 1973*
(Washington, D.C.: U.S. Department of Commerce, 1974), p. 120.

North reveal relatively high levels of participation despite the fact that overall black voting rates have remained between 10 and 13 percentage points below that of whites. In the seven largest Northern cities, excluding New York, Oscar Glantz reported that voting among blacks in 1960 ranged from 61.4 percent to 83.5 percent of those registered.[8] In sharp contrast, Matthews and Prothro reported in 1964 that only 41 percent of adult blacks in the South reported ever having voted.[9] While the voting level of whites has remained fairly constant since 1952, the level among blacks increased sharply between 1952 and 1960. Marvin Olsen reports in this regard that "Negroes were almost twice as likely to vote in 1960 as they were in 1952."[10] However, even with the addition of large numbers of Southern black voters and the increased visibility of black candidates for office, overall voting levels for blacks have not increased significantly since 1960. On the contrary, there has been a decline from a high of 59 percent of those eligible in 1964 to 52 percent in 1972. This seven-point drop represents a sharp decline in voting by Northern blacks, for voting by blacks in the South rose from 42 percent in

[8] Oscar Glantz, "The Negro Voter in Northern Industrial Cities," *Western Political Quarterly* **13** (December 1960), 1004–1006.
[9] Matthews and Prothro, *op. cit.,* p. 44.
[10] Marvin Olsen, "Social and Political Participation of Blacks," *American Sociological Review* **35** (August 1970), 695–696.

1964 to 52 percent in 1968 and in 1972 stood at just under 49 percent of those eligible to vote.

The reasons for the fall-off in voting among blacks are complex. It may be partially related to the decline of major "civil rights" issues since passage of the civil rights bills of the early 1960s, or to the types of presidential candidates in 1968 and 1972, or to a sharp decline in positive black attitudes toward the political system. Indications are that in terms of overall nationwide voting participation, the 1965 Voting Rights Act has not been very effective in closing the gap between the levels of voting by the two races. Furthermore, the chances do not appear very good that this gap will be considerably narrowed in the near future.

### Campaign Activities

Voting is the most widespread form of electoral participation but certainly not the only one. For most adults it is a relatively effortless activity. In fact, Lester Milbrath ranks it next to the bottom above only "exposing oneself to political stimuli" on his fourteen-item hierarchy of participatory activities. In addition to voting, political activists may participate by contributing money to an election campaign, working to help elect a political candidate, or even running for office. These activities would appear to require much more effort and personal sacrifice by the participant, yet blacks compare favorably with whites here—although again they lag behind slightly.

In their study of Southern politics, Matthews and Prothro found a surprisingly high incidence of participation by blacks in political campaign activities. They state that "instead of widening, the gap between Negro and white participation thus decreases startlingly when we shift from voting to campaign activity as a measure of participation."[11] Specifically, they found that black participation dropped to its lowest in the highly visible forms of electoral participation and reached its highest point in such inconspicuous activities as contributing money or buying tickets to candidates' rallies.

The rate and particular form of black electoral participation in the South derive in part from the peculiar constraints under which blacks must function in that region. However, the pattern of high electoral activity is also supported from nationwide data. Matthews and Prothro report that during the 1960 Presidential election, non-Southern Negroes participated more than did whites in almost every aspect of the campaign—more gave money, attended meetings or rallies, engaged in direct campaign work, and reported contact with a party worker.[12] This pattern was confirmed by the Brink and Harris survey which reported that 12 percent of their black sample worked to elect a political candidate as opposed to 11 percent of whites. Their study,

[11] Matthews and Prothro, *op. cit.*, p. 49.
[12] *Ibid.*, p. 50.

however, found 17 percent of the whites contributing money to a candidate or party in comparison to 11 percent blacks.[13] More recently Verba, Ahmed, and Bhatt found that 20 percent of their black sample were very active in party and campaign activities in comparison to 26 percent of whites.[14]

Finally, one recent study of black political participation focusing on college students from three Southern black universities further confirms the trend toward substantial increases in the level of black political participation in activities beyond voting. In that study, John S. Jackson, III reported a remarkably high level of participatory activity among black college students. With the exception of contributing funds to a party or candidate, the black youngsters indicated a participation rate twice as high as that found by Matthews and Prothro among Southern black adults less than a decade earlier.[15] The trend in regard to black electoral participation appears clear. If we examine only levels of voting among blacks and whites on a nationwide basis, whites outperform blacks by several percentage points, but when other forms of electoral participation are included the gap narrows considerably. This picture suggests that while further improvement is clearly desirable, blacks have not been victims of mass apathy toward politics.

### Competing for Public Office

According to Milbrath, running for public office ranks highest among the various participatory activities in which one can engage. It is therefore extremely significant that at this level black political activity has been particularly pronounced. As yet a relatively small percentage of the total black population is engaged in this form of participation; nevertheless the increase in recent years has been dramatic. Between 1964 and 1974 the number of blacks serving in the United States House of Representatives increased from 5 to 17, the number of state legislators from 94 to 239, and the number of black mayors from 29 in 1968 to 108 in 1974. Altogether, in 1974 there were 2,991 blacks holding elective public office in 44 states and the District of Columbia compared to about 914 in 1964.[16] From Table 8.2 it will be observed that most of this growth occurred within the last five years. There are no precise figures available for the number of candidates who actually competed for office but it is reasonable to assume that the propor-

[13] William Brink and Louis Harris, *Black and White* (New York: Simon & Schuster, 1966), pp. 90–91.

[14] Sidney Verba, Bashituddin Ahmed, and Anil Bhatt, *Caste, Race and Politics, A Comparative Study of India and the United States* (Beverly Hills, Calif.: Sage, 1971), p. 122.

[15] John S. Jackson, III, "The Political Behavior and Socio-Economic Backgrounds of Black Students: The Antecedents of Protest," *Midwest Journal of Political Science* 15, 4 (November 1971), 666–668.

[16] *Roster of Black Elected Officials,* Joint Center for Political Studies, IV (April 1974), xiv.

tion of increase in candidates running for office at least equals that of elected officials.

Although participation by blacks as candidates for office began well before the Civil War, it did not represent a significant level of black involvement until the Reconstruction era. Between 1869 and 1900 a total of 22 blacks served as members of the House of Representatives, 2 served in the Senate, and scores served in a variety of elective offices at the state and local level throughout the South. With the rapid rise of Southern whites to political power and the almost total exclusion of blacks from the political system by the turn of the century, very few blacks competed for public office. Blacks virtually disappeared from the scene as officeholders except in a few large cities with substantial black population.

In the initial phase of extensive competition for office by blacks, most black elected officials were in the South with its large concentration of black voters. Starting in the 1920s those elected to office came almost entirely from the North and were confined to a few major urban areas where the

TABLE 8.3  *Black Legislators and Blacks Elected to Other Public Office: 1964, 1968, 1970, 1972, and 1974*

| Subject | 1964 | 1968 | 1970 | 1972 | 1974 |
|---|---|---|---|---|---|
| Total | 103 | 1,125 | 1,860 | 2,625 | 2,991 |
|   United States | – | 1 | 1 | 1 | 1 |
|   South | – | – | – | – | – |
| House of Representatives | | | | | |
|   United States | 5 | 9 | 13 | 15 | 16 |
|   South | – | – | 2 | 4 | 4 |
| State Legislature | | | | | |
|   United States | 94 | 172 | 198 | 238 | 239 |
|   South | 16 | 53 | 70 | 90 | 90 |
| Mayors | | | | | |
|   United States | (NA) | 29 | 81 | 83 | 108 |
|   South | (NA) | 17 | 47 | 49 | 63 |
| Other | | | | | |
|   United States | (NA) | 914 | 1,567 | 2,288 | 2,627 |
|   South | (NA) | 468 | 763 | 1,242 | 1,452 |

*Note:* Figures for the years 1964 and 1968 represent the total number of elected blacks holding office at that time, not just those elected in those years. The 1970, 1972, and 1974 figures represent the number of elected blacks holding office as of the end of March 1971, March 1972, and March 1974, respectively. NA = Not available.

[a]Includes all black elected officials not included in first four categories.

*Source: The Social and Economic Status of the Black Population in the U.S., 1973.* (Washington, D.C.: U.S. Department of Commerce, 1974), p. 125.

black population had been increased by heavy migration from the South and where effective political machines were in operation. This was the case in Chicago, for example, as politicians like Oscar de Priest, Arthur Mitchell, and William Dawson were enabled by the political machines to secure elective office in return for their efforts in delivering black votes. The role of the urban political machine in the rise of black elected officials is not altogether clear. In some cases these machines facilitated election of blacks by (1) providing the organizational framework within which black politicians operated (thus avoiding debilitating political fragmentation common in cities without such machines), (2) helping to mobilize the otherwise largely apathetic black population through the organizational resources of the machine as well as the incentives (patronage) at its disposal, (3) providing a ready mechanism through which blacks could have a voice, albeit a limited one, on the white-controlled city government. On the other hand, the urban machines often made independent political effort all but impossible, thus controlling both the selection and the number of black candidates. Some observers note too that the capacity of the machines to provide valuable payoffs had seriously declined when blacks entered the cities, and that its principal favors were low-echelon positions and the protection of black gangsters and petty criminals.[17]

It would appear that the factor which unquestionably contributed to the rise of the black politician or at least encouraged office seeking by blacks is the rapid growth of the black electorate—first through mass migration from the South to Northern urban areas and later through the effect of civil rights laws in the South. James Q. Wilson has shown that as the black population in the major cities expanded, the number of seats available to blacks at the local, state, and national level increased. He asserts that "other things being equal, Negro political strength in city organizations tends to be directly proportionate to the size and density of the Negro population and inversely proportional to the size of the basic political unit."[18] The importance of the size of the black electorate is reflected in the fact that in only four of the 16 constituencies represented by blacks in the House of Representatives is there a white majority, and in all but one constituency the black population exceeds 40 percent of the total population. Similarly, in the case of the black mayors elected to date, most come from communities that either have black majorities or a black population in excess of 30 percent.

A significant fact in the pattern of black competition for office is that the greatest increases have occurred in the Southern states, notably Alabama, Louisiana, Mississippi, Arkansas, and Georgia. Joe Feagan and Harlan Hahn reported that 44 percent of all the elective offices held by blacks in the South

[17] See studies by James Q. Wilson, *Negro Politics: The Search for Leadership* (New York: Free Press 1960), pp. 21–76; Hanes Walton, *Black Politics* (Philadelphia: Lippincott, 1972).

[18] Wilson, *Negro Politics, op. cit.*, p. 27.

up to 1969 were won in these states. In 1973 this had risen to 45 percent as the regional breakdown in Table 8.3 shows. They suggested further that although the number of elected officials throughout the South has increased sharply, "they have been disproportionately represented in a limited number of local offices." The largest number of elected black officeholders, for example, were municipal officials; but 93 percent of these positions were on city councils. In addition, 83 percent of the black law enforcement officials were justices of the peace or constables.[19]  On the other hand, outside the South, black office seekers have been more successful in securing national or statewide office.

The activities of blacks in seeking office have not been free of obstacles. A variety of factors, some deliberately contrived, have operated as impediments. Wilson points out, for example, that the structure of representation in Northern cities, i.e., the size of constituencies or mode of candidate selection determined the likelihood of blacks being elected to office.[20]  In some instances constituencies were deliberately "gerrymandered" to prevent the election of blacks or to reduce the number of those elected. One blatant attempt at redrawing the boundaries of the city of Tuskegee, Alabama in

**TABLE 8.4**   *1974 Distribution of Blacks and Black Elected Officials by Region* *

|  | Black Population | Percent of Total Black Population | Black Elected Officials | Percent of Total Black Elected Officials |
|---|---|---|---|---|
| South | 11,957,055 | 53 | 1,609 | 54 |
| North Central | 4,565,413 | 20 | 691 | 23 |
| Northeast | 4,336,913 | 19 | 497 | 17 |
| West | 1,690,434 | 8 | 194 | 6 |
| Total | 22,549,815 | 100 | 2,991 | 100 |

*Source: National Roster of Black Elected Officials*, Vol. 8 (Washington, D.C.: Joint Center for Political Studies, 1974).

*U.S. regions as defined by the U.S. Department of Commerce/Social and Economic Statistics Administration are: WEST: Alaska, Arizona, California, Colorado, Hawaii, Idaho, Montana, Nevada, New Mexico, Oregon, Utah, Washington, and Wyoming; NORTH CENTRAL: Illinois, Indiana, Iowa, Kansas, Michigan, Minnesota, Missouri, Nebraska, North Dakota, Ohio, South Dakota, and Wisconsin; SOUTH: Alabama, Arkansas, Delaware, District of Columbia, Florida, Georgia, Kentucky, Louisiana, Maryland, Mississippi, North Carolina, Oklahoma, South Carolina, Tennessee, Texas, Virginia, and West Virginia; NORTHEAST: Connecticut, Maine, Massachusetts, New Hampshire, New Jersey, New York, Pennsylvania, Rhode Island, and Vermont.
*Source: National Roster of Black Elected Officials*, Vol. 4 (Washington, D.C.: Joint Center for Political Studies, 1974), p. xvi.

[19] Joe Feagan and Harlan Hahn, "The Second Reconstruction: Black Political Strength in the South," *Social Science Quarterly* **51**, 1 (June 1970), 51.
[20] Wilson, *Negro Politics, op. cit.*, pp. 25–26.

order to eliminate the electoral effect of a black majority was declared unconstitutional by the Supreme Court in *Gomillian vs. Lightfoot.* Throughout the South the obstacles have been even greater and more varied. The United States Civil Rights Commission reported that in the aftermath of the 1965 Voting Rights Act several steps were taken to prevent blacks from becoming candidates. Among them were

> . . . abolishing elected offices, extending the terms of incumbent white officials, substituting appointment for elections, increasing filing fees, and otherwise stiffening the requirements for getting on the ballot. In addition, Negroes elected to county office in Mississippi have encountered difficulty in securing the bonds which under state law they must obtain before assuming office.[21]

It is in spite of obstacles such as these that thousands of black candidates nevertheless compete for office and several hundred have secured election.

## Constraints on Black Electoral Participation

Why individuals participate or fail to participate in politics is a long-standing concern of political scientists and considerable efforts have been made to identify those factors that explain participatory behavior. While much remains to be learned in this regard, investigators have been able to demonstrate significant links between participatory behavior and socioeconomic, psychological, ecological, and political factors. It has been convincingly demonstrated for example that (1) the higher one's socioeconomic status the greater his propensity to participate in politics; (2) the stronger one's feelings are about his capacity to influence public policy by his activities the more likely he is to participate; (3) where one lives—the size of the community, whether it is rural or urban or even the racial distribution—affects participatory behavior.[22] These findings suggest directions in which we may look in examining some of the bases for existing participation patterns within the black subculture. Prior to exploring them, however, it is necessary to examine the unique experience of blacks as victims of a pattern of deliberate, systematic exclusion from the political arena over several decades, for clearly it has contributed to present participatory habits.

### A History of Planned Exclusion

Widespread, productive, political participation by a community does not come about overnight. Rather it is the result of extensive practice over

---

[21] *Political Participation* (Washington, D.C.: U.S. Commission on Civil Rights, 1968), p. 40.

[22] Verba and Nie, *op. cit.,* pp. 123–263.

long periods of time. It is not coincidental that those societies with a record of high levels of effective political participation have had long experience with widespread, if not universal, participation and an even longer acceptance of such participation as necessary and legitimate. This has not been the case with black America, as a complex array of historical forces combined to deny them such an experience.

In an earlier chapter we reported that blacks were for a long time excluded from the political community, and that only after 1865 were first steps taken to facilitate their inclusion. Throughout most of the colonial era and up to 1865 a few blacks participated as voters and activists in political parties, and occasionally offered themselves as candidates for office. The terms of such participation varied from one colony or state to the next as several states imposed major restrictions on voting by blacks and some prohibited their voting altogether.[23] Prior to the Civil War, in only five states—Maine, Massachusetts, New Hampshire, Vermont, and Rhode Island— were there no specific conditions limiting black participation. Apparently, local attitudes toward race determined the degree of participation permitted blacks in each case. What is clear and crucial to the case is that such participation was the exception rather than the rule. Blacks clearly were not participants in the development of a "democratic or participant tradition" in the United States.

After the Civil War, when they were suddenly invested with the right to vote, to hold office, and to otherwise participate fully in Southern politics, most blacks in the South—as former slaves—faced the twin problems of illiteracy and lack of familiarity with the participatory role. Many were keenly aware of the power their new status conferred and in large numbers they voted—many held local, state, and national elective offices—but this participation did not become the norm. Its legitimacy was conceded by very few. Their role as participants was vigorously opposed by white Southerners, blatantly exploited by white Northerners, and accepted with considerable discomfort by blacks themselves. Circumstances for blacks outside the South were not considerably better; they were in fact worse in several states and localities as blacks continued to be denied access to the political system in many areas.

This initial opportunity for full participation in politics rapidly began to disappear in the face of widespread and often unchecked resort to terror and intimidation by white Southerners before it could become habitual. Thus, unlike white Americans, including virtually all immigrant groups, most Blacks developed no strong convictions about their role as participants in the political system. On the contrary, the lynchings and other terror tactics

---

[23] G. James Fleming, "The Negro in American Politics: The Past," in Davis, *op. cit.,* pp. 414–418.

employed against them may have contributed to a lasting disinclination to participate. The extent of this disinclination is apparent in Booker T. Washington's virtual surrender of any immediate claim to political rights for blacks. Although a vocal black elite including Du Bois, Trotter, and the Niagara group opposed it, indications are that large segments of the black population acquiesced in this course of action.

An equally significant impediment to development of participatory habits among blacks is the pattern of official state action respecting their role in the political system. The most powerful of the immediate post-Civil War obstacles to participation were private or informal actions by whites motivated by a conviction that blacks should not have, and would not be accorded, a participatory role in the political system. The Fourteenth and Fifteenth Amendments appeared to preclude state action in this connection but Southern state governments, again in the full control of white Southerners, found effective devices to achieve this end. Through constitutional provisions, statutes, and administrative practices these states developed and applied three basic exclusionary tools: literacy and other subjective tests, the poll tax, and the white primary.

One of the most extensive studies of black suffrage in the South is that by Paul Lewinson. He points out that denying the suffrage to blacks was one of the most compelling and pervasive passions in Southern politics. If the broad objective was maintenance of black subordination, the specific or immediate motivations were (1) belief that a large black electorate in alliance with other discontented segments of the region would conceivably wrest power from the privileged group which controlled Democratic Party politics in the South as the Populist movement tried to do, and (2) belief that any concession of political equality would inevitably lead to social equality. Lewinson demonstrates the extremes to which this point was taken in what he terms "the post-prandial non sequitur—if you let them vote, you've got to let them marry your daughter."[24]

### Literacy Tests as an Obstacle

Reflecting this preoccupation, constitutional conventions in several Southern states after 1890 adapted the concept of a qualified suffrage, based on the tested fitness of the voter, to this vital task of excluding blacks as voters. This effort began in about 1890 when the Mississippi Constitutional Convention adopted a provision requiring that an individual be able to read and provide a "reasonable" interpretation of any portion of the Constitution before he could be registered to vote.[25] By 1910 eight Southern states had

---

[24] Paul Lewinson, *Race, Class and Party: A History of Negro Suffrage and White Politics in the South* (New York: Grosset & Dunlap, 1965), p. 87.

[25] "Federal Protection of Negro Voting Rights," *Virginia Law Review* 51, 6 (October 1965), 1051–1074.

adopted such measures, and other states had adopted statutes to achieve the same purpose. Application of "literacy" and "understanding" clauses in an evenhanded manner would have meant mass disfranchisement of blacks, since 57.1 percent of the black population was illiterate in 1890.[26] The objective, however, was total disfranchisement through the discriminatory application of the provisions by voting registrars, as one Virginia legislator emphasized:

> The committee is not blind to the fact that this is not an ideal test. . . . But it would not be frank of me, Mr. Chairman, if I did not say that I do not expect it to be administered with any degree of friendship by the white man to the suffrage of the black man. I expect the examination with which the black man will be confronted to be inspired with the same spirit that inspires every man in this convention.[27]

Numerous modifications to this basic strategy were adopted in most Southern states. In many cases a "property test" requiring the prospective voter to show ownership of real property valued at at least $300, and "good character" tests supplemented the basic literacy tests.

Because even the most generous application of the literacy tests would have excluded large numbers of illiterate whites, some states adopted "grandfather clauses" providing that a prospective voter need not pass the literacy test if his ancestors were eligible to vote prior to 1860. Throughout the South a wide range of constitutional and statutory innovations thus developed in order to ensure the exclusion of blacks from the political arena. The extent of their effectiveness is dramatically reflected in Louisiana, where the black vote dropped from 130,344 in 1897 to 730 in 1910.[28] In 1915, in the case of *Guinn vs. United States,* the Supreme Court invalidated Oklahoma's Grandfather Clause as a violation of the Fifteenth Amendment, but it was quickly replaced by other equally effective devices in the states where it was used. In one form of the other these subjective, literacy, and character tests proved the most formidable obstacles to black electoral participation. They continued in use until the entrance of federal registrars in 1965.

### The Poll Tax as an Obstacle

The poll tax, the origin of which is not altogether clear, was not devised exclusively as an instrument for the exclusion of blacks from the polls. It appears to have been a remnant of the notion that only propertied individuals should participate in the political process. Ironically, it was devised as an alternative to the possession of property in an attempt to

---

[26] Lewinson, *op. cit.,* p. 83.
[27] Quoted in Lewinson, *op. cit.,* p. 85.
[28] "Federal Protection of Negro Voting Rights," *op. cit.*

broaden the electorate. However, it quickly became one more obstacle to be overcome by blacks. The most obstructive features of the tax were (1) it imposed a fee that many poor, including most blacks, could not afford; (2) receipts indicating that the fee had been paid had to be produced on demand when an individual sought to vote, and the demand could be selectively made so as to screen out all blacks except those who had managed to save receipts; (3) the tax was required long in advance of an election and thus could easily be overlooked. In spite of these features it was upheld by the Supreme Court in *Breedlove vs. Suttle* (1937). The end of the poll tax occurred recently after decades of opposition to it by the NAACP and other groups as discriminatory toward the poor. Largely in response to this, its use in connection with federal elections was outlawed by the Twenty-Fourth Amendment and the Supreme Court declared it unconstitutional in all other elections in *Harper vs. Virginia State Board of Education* in 1965.

### The White Primary as an Obstacle

A third major obstacle to political participation by blacks in the South—the white primary—came into widespread use in 1921. The use of the primary in this way constitutes one more of the grosser perversions of a legitimate and progressive political innovation because, as initially conceived, it was a device for further democratizing the leadership selection process. The primary, which grew out of the concern that candidates for public office were selected by "undemocratic" party procedures, was designed to bring the people more directly into the candidate selection process. In the hands of Southern whites, however, it became an instrument for reinforcing the barricades against blacks.

In essence, the white primary was a procedure in which the political party conducted a primary election from which blacks were excluded to choose candidates for office. Because throughout the South the Democratic Party operated without opposition, the primary was, for all practical purposes, the election. The winner was always unopposed in the regular election and hence automatically elected to office. Exclusion of blacks from the primary meant exclusion from the electoral process. In its first test in the courts, the Supreme Court upheld the practice in *Newberry vs. United States* (1924), ruling that the primary was not part of the electoral process and thus discrimination against blacks was not unconstitutional. Over the next twenty-three years the white primary was fought in the courts—until the Supreme Court's decision in *Smith vs. Allwright* in 1944 declaring the practice unconstitutional. Prior to this decision, in rulings in *Nixon vs. Herndon* (1927) and *Nixon vs. Condon* (1932) growing out of challenges in the state of Texas, the Supreme Court maintained that the white primary was unconstitutional when operated on the basis of direct or indirect state action. In *Grovey vs. Townsend* (1935), however, it sanctioned the practice when no state action was involved. The ground for *Smith vs. Allwright* was prepared by a 1941 Court ruling in *United States vs. Classic* asserting that primaries could be regulated by the government where it was clearly an integral part of the procedure of choice in an election.

The impact of the invalidation of the white primary on black voting participation was immediate and dramatic. Professor Hugh Price examined its impact in Florida in the decade after the 1944 decision. He found that black registration increased from 20,000 in 1944 to 128,329 in 1954. Furthermore, all of the 20,000 registrants up to 1944 were Republicans (since blacks were not permitted to register as Democrats), while in 1954, 119,975 blacks were registered as Democrats.[29] The pattern was similar throughout the South. In 1940 there were only 250,000 blacks registered to vote, 5 percent of the total voting age black population, whereas by 1956 this had climbed to 1,238,038 and 25 percent.[30]

The obstacles noted here by which blacks were effectively excluded from the political arena do not exhaust the arsenal of such techniques. Furthermore, the many and varied obstacles persisted in spite of several minor efforts by the federal government to alter the situation, simply because the states constantly modified the techniques employed to "legally" evade these federal efforts. These barriers erected and administered by states and local governments yielded only after the sweeping Voting Rights Act of 1965, which drastically limited the power of state governments to enact and enforce discriminatory legislation and considerably expanded the power of the federal government to intervene where a pattern of discrimination has been observed.[31]

The full impact of such systematic exclusion over so long a period cannot be easily ascertained. Glimpses of the impact can be obtained by observing the performance of the large numbers of migrants from the South to the major urban centers of the North. Although they encountered few if any formal obstacles, they remained politically ineffective because of their naiveté and lack of experience in political matters and their widespread apathy. Although attention centered on the vote, it is apparent that the exclusion had considerable impact on all areas of political life. Representatives elected without black votes were not responsible to the black community and thus had no need to be responsive to them. Furthermore, this exclusion contributed heavily to the "we-they" view of government, for

[29] Hugh Price, "The Negro and Florida Politics 1944–1954," *Journal of Politics* 17 (May 1955), 200. For an evaluation of the impact of *Smith vs. Allwright* in Texas see Donald Strong, "The Rise of Negro Voting in Texas," *American Political Science Review* 17, 3 (June 1948), 516–522.

[30] Matthews and Prothro, *op. cit.*

[31] For an extensive analysis of the Voting Rights Act, see "Federal Protection of Negro Voting Rights," *op. cit.*, pp. 1053–1213.

blacks had little if any basis for regarding themselves as influentials or potential influentials.

The pattern of deliberate and systematic exclusion outlined here is interesting as history, but more significant for our purposes are its implications for black political participation even today. Such exclusion denied to blacks the opportunity to develop through practice the skills vital to effective political participation. It denied them the development of strong convictions about the legitimacy of their role as participants, and it undermined the development and transmission of participatory attitudes and values to very large segments of the black population. Removal of most of these obstacles by legislation cannot therefore be expected to bring about immediate, total transformation of the participatory habits of blacks. Rather, the impact of this history of exclusion can be expected to continue for an indefinite period.

### Social, Economic, and Psychological Obstacles to Participation

The several formal and informal obstacles to extensive participation constitutes only one of several sets of factors which together explain the pattern of black participation in the electoral process. James Q. Wilson wisely observed some time ago that "even if discriminatory practices were ended, the low socioeconomic status of the Negro would result in relatively low registration and voter turnout figures."[32] The study by Matthews and Prothro clearly confirmed this impression.[33] Starkly put, the black dilemma has been that throughout the nation, but particularly in the South, blacks are concentrated at the bottom of the economic scale in terms of annual income and they are concentrated at the bottom of the educational scale. The two conditions are interrelated and they are the grim consequences of a history of subordination and exploitation. To a substantial degree they adversely affect the inclination to participate in politics.

The link between socioeconomic status and political participation is beyond serious challenge. A large body of empirical research has demonstrated that in general, the propensity to participate in politics increases as one moves up the socioeconomic scale. In this regard Verba and Nie have convincingly demonstrated that "political participation is predominantly the activity of wealthier, better educated citizens with high-status occupations."[34] It is apparent, therefore, that for a variety of reasons, not all of which are clear, the segment of the society with the lowest income and the lowest education tends to exhibit the lowest level of participation. This

[32] Wilson, "The Negro In American Politics—The Present," *op. cit.*, p. 434.
[33] Matthews and Prothro, "Social and Economic Factors and Negro Voter Registration in the South," *American Political Science Review* 57 (March 1963), 25–44.
[34] Verba and Nie, *op. cit.*, p. 150.

means that with all other factors equal, a smaller proportion of the black population can be expected to participate in politics than that among whites.

The extent of the impact of the socioeconomic factor is reflected in studies by Marvin Olsen and Jack Walker. Olsen found that although as a whole blacks are less active as political participants, the difference between the two races virtually disappears when socioeconomic status is controlled.[35] In other words, when samples of blacks and whites of equal educational and economic status are compared, there is no difference between them in level of participation. In a study of voting behavior in Atlanta, Walker found that when socioeconomic status is controlled, blacks exhibited a higher level of participation in virtually every type of election.[36] These findings indicate that the differences between the socioeconomic status of blacks and whites contribute substantially to their reported differences in levels of political participation. The full impact of the black subculture on the political system may therefore depend on the speed with which the present wide gap between the socioeconomic status of blacks and whites is narrowed or altogether eliminated.

Just as important as socioeconomic status in determining one's inclination to participate in politics are certain psychological or attitudinal factors. These have to do with level of interest in politics, feelings of competence as a political actor, conviction that actions can influence public policy, and faith and trust in government. The relationship of these psychological factors to political participation is clearly demonstrated in an extensive body of research and undoubtedly are of importance in accounting for the level of participation among blacks. In the preceding chapter we observed that although blacks were generally supportive of the political system, they tended to be less trusting than whites, were less knowledgeable about politics, and were less confident about their capacity to influence government. Distrust or alienation from government often leads to a disinclination to participate, and in the case of blacks appears to inhibit political participation.

Not only is there evidence of a more "subject orientation" to politics among blacks than among whites, but apparently blacks now lack faith in the electoral process to a much greater extent than whites. The study by Miller, Brown, and Raine discussed earlier indicates that blacks' attitudes toward parties, elections, and representatives have changed drastically:

> In 1964, blacks had placed more faith in Congressmen, parties and elections than did whites. However, in 1968, blacks were somewhat less trusting of Congressmen, but still slightly more confident in parties and elections than whites. By 1972 blacks had completely lost faith in

[35] Olsen, *op. cit.,* p. 686.
[36] Jack Walker, "Negro Voting in Atlanta: 1953–1961," *Phylon* **24,** 4 (Winter 1964), 379–387.

Congressmen and their confidence in both parties and elections plunged even more decidedly.[37]

It is conceivable that where black candidates run for office this estrangement from the electoral process is reduced, since blacks have consistently shown greater electoral support for, and trust in, candidates of their own race.[38]

## Factors Contributing to Black Electoral Participation

Although, as we have observed, the level of voting by blacks is below that of whites, when all forms of electoral activities are considered the overall level of black political participation is close to that of whites. Given the pattern of deliberate, systematic exclusion of blacks from the political arena, their socioeconomic status, and their psychological orientations to politics, it is remarkable that they have maintained this level of participation. Indeed, Verba and Nie provide evidence that the level of black political participation exceeds that predicted by their socioeconomic status (SES). Although 36 percent of the bottom one-sixth of the SES scale are black, only 16 percent of those in the bottom one-sixth of the participation scale are black. On the other hand, while only 2 percent of the top one-sixth of the SES scale are black, 11 percent of the top one-sixth of the participation scale are black.[39]
In evaluating black political participation it is important to account for this feature and identify those forces that propel blacks into the political arena to participate to the extent that we have observed. At this point we can only be speculative, but three factors appear operative.

First, over the years the black subculture has come to attach special significance to political participation beyond that normally associated with it in a "democratic polity." Because their long experience of exploitation and subordination is so closely related to exclusion from the political arena, political participation has important symbolic significance in the struggle for freedom and equality. Acquisition of the right to participate represented a tangible victory in the struggle for full citizenship. This is not surprising, since Southern whites also viewed political participation in symbolic terms. Gunnar Myrdal noted in this connection that

> Already in the ante-bellum elections, political campaigning and voting had acquired a ceremonial significance as marking off a distinct sphere of power and responsibility for the free citizen. From Recon-

[37] Arthur Miller, Thad Brown, and Alden Raine, "Social Conflict and Political Estrangement 1958–72," paper prepared for delivery at the Midwest Political Science Association Convention, May 1973, p. 64.
[38] See for example David Sears, "Black Attitudes Toward the Political System in the Aftermath of the Watts Insurrection," *Midwest Journal of Political Science* 23, 4 (November 1969), 528–530.
[39] Verba and Nie, *op. cit.*, pp. 153–154.

struction on, voting remained to the white Southerner more than a mere action; it was, and still is, a symbol of superiority.[40]

For blacks, however, voting has been more than symbolic. The admonition by Kwame Nkrumah, first president of Ghana, to "seek ye first the political kingdom and all things will be added thereto" has been a guiding principle for blacks long before Nkrumah. Voting for them has not been merely the performance of a civic duty or a conscious or unconscious effort at "system maintenance," it is one vital dimension of an all-consuming struggle for change. Regardless of how they cast their votes, the overriding concern among blacks appears to be whether and to what extent the vote will contribute to the struggle for change. This preoccupation is apparent in the virtual disregard by blacks for such issue areas as foreign policy even when identifiable black interests are involved.[41] The almost total commitment to self-improvement led Brink and Harris to observe that at the polls blacks were preoccupied almost always with a single issue: "Would the candidate help or hurt the cause of civil rights?"[42] Under these conditions, such factors as low socioeconomic status may be less of an obstacle to political participation than is ordinarily the case. In this emphasis on self-improvement there is the danger that too much will be expected of electoral participation, especially in view of its limitations as a procedure for achieving change; nevertheless black participation in politics is highly purposive to a greater extent than among whites.

A third factor that may help to explain the level of participation by blacks is that for them, as for virtually all subordinate groups in a "democratic polity," participation is fraught with special problems. Often outnumbered in the political arena, their most vital objectives are shared only by the group and often vigorously opposed by the dominant group. According to Verba, Ahmed, and Bhatt these obstacles can be overcome only by intensive mobilization based on group identity and group cohesiveness.[43] In this situation, members of the subordinate group may be motivated to participate because failure to do so constitutes to some degree a betrayal of group solidarity.

The operation of this factor is readily apparent in the pattern of black political participation. Several studies of black voting behavior identify a high degree of cohesiveness and solidarity among blacks; Verba, Ahmed, and Bhatt concluded from their study that "for blacks there is an association between most forms of (political) activity and group consciousness. Black voting is associated with group consciousness."[44] The impact of group consciousness

---

[40] Gunnar Myrdal, *An American Dilemma* (New York: Harper & Row, 1944), pp. 448–449.

[41] In this regard see Milton D. Morris, "Blacks and the Foreign Policy Process: The Case of Africa," *Western Political Quarterly* 25, 3 (September 1972), 451–463.

[42] Brink and Harris, *op. cit.*, p. 77.

[43] Verba, Ahmed, and Bhatt, *op. cit.*, p. 25.

[44] *Ibid.*

on black political participation was tested by Verba and Nie and they report that "Blacks who do not mention race in response to our questions participate substantially less than the average white. But those who mention race—once or more—participate a bit above the average white. Consciousness of race as a problem or a basis of conflict appears to bring those blacks who are conscious up to a level of participation equivalent to that of whites."[45]

Finally, black political participation has been affected by the vigorous mass mobilization efforts of the last two decades. While they were never content with their status, there appeared to have been a sense of hopelessness and resignation in a large segment of the black population. The era of protest from 1956 to 1963 aroused the black population perhaps to an even greater extent than it did whites. By projecting a new sense of urgency and commitment to change, the "protest era" stimulated blacks to participate in the struggle in some manner. Besides this general mobilizing effort, more direct and intensive efforts at drawing blacks into the political arena have been undertaken throughout the nation. Voter registration and voter education projects throughout the South, though costing the lives and freedom of several individuals, were instrumental in bringing blacks into the political arena. The passage of several federal civil rights bills contributed to this effort by providing incentives for further political activity.

These do not entirely account for the present levels of participation; improvement in the educational and economic status of a substantial segment of the black population during the last decade also has been influential. The fact is, however, that there have been forces at work within the black subculture that have made powerful contributions to widespread participation in politics. Indications are that they are still at work and that today many blacks look with considerable hope to the political arena in their efforts to improve the quality of their lives and their overall status in the society.

### The Impact of Black Electoral Participation

Lucius Amerson, recently elected sheriff of Macon County, Alabama, has asserted that "in active and effective and unhindered political participation by Negroes and all other citizens of the United States lie our future and our hopes for progress and mutual welfare."[46] This observation is central to the democratic political process where individuals believe, or are asked to believe, that their actions determine the policy choices made by government. It deserves particular emphasis here because the participation of blacks in the electoral process as voters, campaign activists, and candidates for office is motivated primarily by the desire to achieve goals considered vital by them.

---

[45] Verba and Nie, *op. cit.,* p. 158.

[46] Lucius D. Amerson, "The First and Second Times Around," in Mervyn M. Dymally, *The Black Politician: His Struggle for Power* (N. Scituate, Mass.: Duxbury Press, 1971), p. 9.

In completing this portion of the study it is essential that we attempt to assess whether and to what extent these participatory efforts have been—or promise to be—productive.

Several problems exist in attempting such an undertaking; at best we can make only tentative observations about the impact of black electoral participation. First, the attempt is somewhat premature since extensive, wide-ranging participation by the entire black population is only now becoming possible and much more time is required before any clear indication of its impact can be obtained. Second, it is difficult and in some cases perhaps impossible to establish causal links between specific political activities by the public and policy outcomes, for the simple reason that the public does not decide on policies through the electoral process—only on who shall make public policy. At best therefore, impact on public policy is indirect. Third, it is difficult to identify precisely the specific goals or objectives of blacks within the political system. This difficulty is suggested here because it complicates attempts at evaluating impact on public policy, but it should be noted that the electorate as a whole has at best only vague ideas about what policy outcomes it desires to achieve by voting.[47]

With respect to goals, we stated earlier that the fundamental goal of blacks within the society is to alter their subordinate status in the society. In operational terms this implies (1) a desire to eradicate all of the rituals and symbols within the society that suggest black inferiority or status subordination, and (2) improvement of the quality of life for blacks so that blacks are enabled to achieve a socioeconomic status comparable to that of whites. These objectives are consistent with what James Q. Wilson characterized as the two basic "race ends" sought by blacks. Wilson identified "status ends" as "those which seek the integration of the Negro into all phases of the community on the principle of equality . . . ," and "welfare ends" as "those which look to the tangible improvement of the community or some individuals in it through the provision of better services, living conditions or positions."[48] Wilson's analysis focused on Chicago but may be extrapolated to the entire black subculture.

On this level of generality, there is little disagreement among blacks about goals, even though small but significant groups of blacks reject what may be construed as their "integrationist" implications. Attempts to identify or pursue specific objectives reveal substantial disagreements with respect to both the objectives and the methods by which they are to be pursued. Nevertheless these broad goals appear to be basic to the political activity of blacks, and in examining the impact of black electoral participation they serve as useful if imprecise reference points.

[47] John C. Wahlke, "Policy Demands and System Support: The Role of the Represented," in Gerhard Loewenberg, *Modern Parliaments, Change or Decline* (Chicago: Aldine, 1971), pp. 141–171.

[48] Wilson, *Negro Politics, op. cit.,* p. 185.

The impact of black electoral activity may be viewed first in broad symbolic terms and then in relation to policy processes affecting the lives of individuals at the local and national levels. Extensive participation by blacks in virtually all aspects of political life by itself constitutes an important gain in view of the historical attitudes of both blacks and whites toward political participation. We observed earlier that exclusion of blacks from political activity was, for both races, a glaring symbol of their inferior or second-class status. Election of black councilmen, sheriffs, mayors, and state and national legislators undoubtedly constitutes strong symbolic assurance of progress toward full inclusion into the political community or full citizenship. In turn, this appearance may heighten the interest of blacks in the political arena and hopefully their level of confidence in the political system.

Important as this symbolic impact is, however, individuals also antici- pate significant policies beneficial to them and their communities. The Southern Regional Council's Voter Education Project emphasized this in its observation that "increased political participation is a feasible means of bettering the living conditions of deprived groups. The implicit assumption is that the political process is a primary means by which the benefits of society are distributed."[49] It is with this aspect of the question that we are most concerned.

William Keech has explored the extent to which voting can indeed facilitate achievement of policy objectives considered important to blacks. His focus was on two Southern communities, but the basic findings appear to have much broader implications. In Tuskegee, Alabama, where blacks had a voting majority, Keech found that voting achieved remarkable gains in "eras- ing most of the existing mechanisms of discrimination in that city."

> Negro votes were obviously instrumental in securing a very exten- sive turnover among those who are elected to public office, including the election of many Negroes. Negro votes brought a radical change in the distribution of public services, including garbage collection, street paving and recreational facilities. Negroes were hired for the first time to municipal service positions and appointed to boards and commis- sions as a result of Negro votes, and those votes were also instrumental in bringing about the passage of local public accommodations and fair employment ordinances. Negro votes played a somewhat lesser role in eliminating discrimination in hospitals, and discrimination in schools and jury selection was dealt with through court suits initiated before Negro voting had reached sufficient strength to secure them. Still it is likely that none of these things would have been beyond the influence of Negro votes in contemporary Tuskegee were they left to that process for resolution.[50]

[49] Quoted in Feagan and Hahn, *op. cit.,* p. 53.
[50] William Keech, *The Impact of Negro Voting: The Role of the Vote in the Quest for Equality* (Skokie, Ill.: Rand McNally, 1968), p. 2.

The impact of the vote was not as clear or extensive in the second community, Durham, North Carolina, where black voters constitute less than a majority of the total electorate. Nevertheless Keech found that "the vote was relevant to influence over the outcome of elections, to securing equal treatment by law enforcement agencies, to equal distribution of such public goods as parks and fire stations, to employment of Negroes in municipal service and to appointments to boards and commissions."[51]

Just as significant as the positive impact of the vote in these communities are the important limitations observed by Keech. He found (1) that while the vote aided in preventing continued discriminatory policies, it was not very effective in correcting the effects of past discrimination; (2) the vote was not very effective in preventing discrimination in the private sector; (3) the vote is more influential in securing incremental change than in providing new programs; (4) the vote is much more effective in removing the "cruder forms" of discrimination than it is with the more subtle forms. Perhaps Keech's most notable finding has to do with the impact of the vote in the quest for equality. Observing that it was more instrumental in achieving "legal equality" than "social equality" and that those legal rights so protected are those that are firmly rooted in the political culture, Keech concludes that "the prospect that votes will help eliminate basic inequalities in the life chances of Negroes is contingent on the degree to which appropriate programs fit within the value structure of elites and voting majorities."[52] In other words, the vote will contribute to the achievement of social equality only to the extent that whites are willing to concede such equality.

Since Keech's study, black electoral participation has resulted in the election of black mayors in several major cities throughout the nation—Cleveland, Ohio; Gary, Indiana; Newark, New Jersey; Los Angeles, California; Atlanta, Georgia, and Detroit, Michigan among them. These events have dramatized both the changing racial composition of the cities and the impact of the black vote. They are hailed by many as evidences of a new era in the political activity of blacks and as a major step toward black power. While their symbolic value is obvious, their overall impact especially in terms of the basic goals we identified are not as clear. Studies of these mayoralties to date indicate that they have been beneficial in the following ways: (1) they have increased substantially the level of interest and participation in politics by blacks; (2) they have increased somewhat the level of trust in local government; (3) they have provided limited improvements in community services and facilitated a more equitable distribution of public goods and services in the community.

These political "breakthroughs" have been limited in their impact on black life, however, because of three basic factors. First, almost all of the

[51] *Ibid.*, p. 93.
[52] *Ibid.*, p. 94.

cities that have elected black mayors are rapidly decaying communities with very limited resources and demands that far exceed their resources. Second, although highly visible, mayorships frequently confer little real power; the principal opportunity is one of community leadership and persuasion of influentials in state government or local power cliques. Third, as Wilson points out, many problems faced by blacks are simply not susceptible to resolution by political means.[53] The result therefore is that black electoral activity in major urban communities will achieve at best limited payoffs even when black mayors are elected. This is demonstrated in a case study of Gary in which William Nelson, Jr., concludes that

> A Black mayor catapulted into office on the back of a Black power thrust can assuage the anxieties produced in some quarters of the Black community through the energetic and sagacious mobilization of governmental concern and resources behind salient Black needs and interests. By doing so, he can also build for himself a reputation in the Black community of sufficient esteem as to make him a formidable candidate in local elections.
>
> But such a response will be inevitably unsatisfactory to politically minded Black citizens who seek not only temporary relief, but long-term instrumental benefits for the Black community as a whole. The failure on the part of the Black mayor to seriously address himself to the concerns of this group will produce a level of disunity in the Black community which may, over the long run, significantly hamper the achievement of both short- and long-term Black political goals.[54]

The problems and limitations with which black mayors are faced certainly should not detract from the opportunities open to them for community leadership. Although less visible than mayoralties, the growing numbers of blacks who are elected to local boards, councils, and law enforcement positions as well as to state legislatures provide opportunities for the articulation of black interests and preferences and thus are vital to the overall objective of bringing about change in the status of blacks.

Assessment of the impact of the black vote at the national level is considerably more difficult than at the local community level. The national arena is much more complex; the forces at work are many and varied and the overall weight of blacks more diluted than in the local situation. Nevertheless, some general observations here might be beneficial. The Presidency and the Congress are the two national institutions on which black electoral influence can be most directly brought to bear. We are therefore concerned with whether and to what extent black participation, particularly in voting and competing for office, enhances the interests of blacks through these institutions.

[53] Wilson, *Negro Politics, loc. cit.*
[54] William Nelson, Jr., *Black Power in Gary* (Washington, D.C.: Joint Center for Political Studies, 1972), p. 37.

With respect to the Presidency, the black electorate has been credited with playing a crucial role. Because blacks are heavily concentrated in a few large and pivotal states in the North, their support has been regarded as crucial by most Presidential candidates and by analysts of American voting behavior. The basis for this becomes apparent when it is observed that since 1936 no Presidential candidate aside from Richard Nixon has managed to secure election to office without substantial support from blacks. President John Kennedy's victory over Richard Nixon in 1960 has been widely attributed to heavy support from blacks. Scammon and Wattenberg report that had black voting in the North not fallen off considerably in 1968, Hubert Humphrey would have received a greater popular vote than Nixon.[55] The impact on specific Presidential elections is discussed at length elsewhere, but it is almost universally conceded that barring extraordinary circumstances the black vote is crucial. This fact has had two kinds of consequences for the policy process. First, in attempting to appeal to the black electorate, Presidential candidates have found it increasingly necessary to adopt and espouse policies consistent with the interests of blacks or at least to refrain from expressions of hostility to these interests. Second, in office Presidents have found it necessary to pursue, and encourage pursuit of, policies that may be perceived as beneficial to blacks. These may include proposal of civil rights or other social programs aimed at blacks, the appointment of blacks to "visible" public offices, or simply exertion of positive leadership in resolving racial conflicts in other arenas. At this point we are not making judgments about the sincerity or long-term significance of these gestures. We are emphasizing that they appear to be calculated to influence a crucial sector of the electorate and reflect one kind of impact blacks have on the policy process at the national level.

In Congress the impact of the black vote is becoming increasingly apparent although, again, the extent to which it affects the policy process is unclear. It is estimated that blacks now constitute at least 30 percent of the electorate in more than 60 Congressional districts and they are a majority in about 13. (The constituencies with black majorities are still this few because of widespread "racial" gerrymandering.) To varying degrees this should affect the conduct of legislators from these districts. Walter Fauntroy, Representative of the District of Columbia in Congress, once pointed to at least one way in which increased voting by blacks brings about change in the Congress. He noted that for a long time Senator Strom Thurmond referred to blacks in his state as "them Nigras," but after the Voting Rights Act he began to speak politely of his "colored constituents." Fauntroy predicted that as more blacks register Thurmond would eventually be rising on the Senate floor to speak on behalf of his "black brothers."

[55] Richard Scammon and Ben Wattenberg, *The Real Majority* (New York: Coward, McCann & Geoghegan, 1971), p. 56.

In articulating the interests of blacks in the legislature, a convenient indicator of black influence in Congress is the number and activities of black legislators. The steady increase in the number of blacks elected to Congress is one of the clear indications of the growth and increasing effectiveness of the black electorate. There is little doubt but that growth will continue as the size of the black electorate increases in the urban areas. Furthermore, there are growing indications that strong black candidates in astutely run campaigns can win in districts without a black majority. It is also significant that almost all of the blacks now in Congress come from what may be characterized as "safe districts"; that is, they win by majorities of over 55 percent of the votes cast. In 1972 the only exceptions to this were Ronald Dellums, Andrew Young, and William Clay.

Although each legislator has his own constituency as a primary responsibility, the 16 black legislators have been willing to accept a somewhat broader view of their role, regarding themselves as representatives of black and poor people throughout the nation. In attempting to fulfill this broad role they organized the Congressional Black Caucus in 1969. Through the Caucus, their various committee assignments, and their other activities in Congress the black legislators have been vigorously seeking to influence the policy process in a variety of ways. The Caucus, as an informal body, has no formal status in the legislature but it provides a mechanism through which a coherent and consistent common effort can be made in pursuing what it perceives as the interests of the black population. Its early confrontation with President Nixon and the extensive list of issues it brought to his attention is illustrative of its efforts.[56] Furthermore, it has attempted investigations of a wide range of issues such as racism in the armed forces and blacks and the communications media and has lobbied in behalf of legislative proposals it considers vital to blacks. Although its activities have tapered off somewhat, it is notable that President Ford made his "goodwill gesture" to the black community by conferring at the White House with the Caucus almost immediately after coming to office.

The committee structure appears to provide even greater opportunities for influence by black legislators. Up to now few black legislators have been able to climb the seniority ladder to prominence, but where this has occurred it has been beneficial to blacks. Adam Clayton Powell's chairmanship of the House Committee on Health, Education and Welfare enabled him to shape important social legislation beneficial to blacks. More recently Charles Diggs, as Chairman of the House Foreign Affairs Subcommittee on Africa, has been an effective and persistent watchdog of United States policies toward Africa and a critic of the more blatant manifestations of racism in United States foreign policy. Diggs' subcommittee has no decisive influence on the conduct

[56] See "Congressional Black Caucus' Recommendations to President Nixon," *Congressional Record,* 92nd Cong., 1st Sess., Mar. 30, 1971.

**TABLE 8.5** *Congressional Districts with 25 Percent or More Black Population* *

| State | Total Number of Congressional Districts | Congressional District Number | Percent Black Population of District | Percent Black Voting Age Population | Congressional Representative |
|---|---|---|---|---|---|
| Alabama | 7 | 1 | 32.7 | 28 | Jack Edwards (R) |
| | | 2 | 29.8 | 25 | William L. Dickinson (R) |
| | | 3 | 31.3 | 26 | Bill Nichols (D) |
| | | 6 | 30.0 | 27 | John Buchanan (R) |
| | | 7 | 37.9 | 32 | Walter Flowers (D) |
| Arkansas | 4 | 4 | 31.3 | 27 | Ray Thornton (D) |
| California | 43 | 7 | 25.5 | 21 | Ronald Dellums (D)[a] |
| | | 21 | 54.2 | 49 | Augustus Hawkins (D)[a] |
| | | 37 | 50.7 | 45 | Yvonne Burke (D)[a] |
| Florida | 15 | 2 | 28.0 | 24 | Don Fuqua (D) |
| | | 3 | 26.0 | 23 | Charles E. Bennett (D) |
| Georgia | 10 | 1 | 33.6 | 29 | Bo Ginn (D) |
| | | 2 | 36.8 | 31 | Dawson Mathis (D) |
| | | 3 | 32.0 | 28 | Jack Brinkley (D) |
| | | 5 | 44.2 | 39 | Andrew Young (D)[a] |
| | | 8 | 31.0 | 27 | W.S. Stuckey (D) |
| | | 10 | 32.8 | 28 | Robert Stephens (D) |
| Illinois | 24 | 1 | 88.9 | 85 | Ralph H. Metcalfe (D)[a] |
| | | 2 | 40.0 | 34 | Morgan F. Murphy (D) |
| | | 5 | 31.1 | 26 | John C. Kluczynski (D) |
| | | 7 | 54.9 | 46 | Cardiss Collins (D)[a] |
| Louisiana | 8 | 1 | 31.2 | 26 | F. Edward Hebert (D) |
| | | 2 | 39.7 | 35 | Corinne Boggs (D) |
| | | 4 | 31.2 | 27 | Joe Waggoner, Jr. (D) |
| | | 5 | 34.5 | 29 | Otto E. Passman (D) |
| | | 6 | 29.7 | 26 | John Rarick (D) |
| | | 8 | 36.2 | 32 | Gillis W. Long (D) |
| Maryland | 8 | 7 | 74.0 | 68 | Parren J. Mitchell (D)[a] |
| Michigan | 19 | 1 | 70.0 | 64 | John Conyers, Jr. (D)[a] |
| | | 13 | 65.8 | 59 | Charles C. Diggs (D)[a] |

| State | | District | % | | Congressman |
|---|---|---|---|---|---|
| Mississippi | 5 | 1 | 35.5 | 29 | Jamie L. Whitten (D) |
| | | 2 | 45.9 | 39 | David Bowen (D) |
| | | 3 | 40.4 | 34 | G.V. Montgomery (D) |
| | | 4 | 43.1 | 37 | W. Thad Cochran (R) |
| Missouri | 10 | 1 | 54.3 | 48 | William Clay (D)[a] |
| New Jersey | 15 | 10 | 51.8 | 45 | Peter W. Rodino, Jr. (D) |
| New York | 39 | 7 | 36.5 | 31 | Joseph F. Addabbo (D-L) |
| | | 12 | 77.1 | 76 | Shirley Chisholm (D-L)[a] |
| | | 19 | 58.7 | 57 | Charles Rangel (D-R-L)[a] |
| | | 21 | 41.7 | 41 | Herman Badillo (D-L) |
| North Carolina | 11 | 1 | 35.8 | 30 | Walter B. Jones (D) |
| | | 2 | 40.1 | 34 | L.H. Fountain (D) |
| | | 3 | 26.7 | 23 | David N. Henderson (D) |
| | | 7 | 25.6 | 22 | Charles G. Rose (D) |
| Ohio | 23 | 21 | 66.3 | 60 | Louis L. Stokes (D)[a] |
| Pennsylvania | 25 | 1 | 39.2 | 34 | William A. Barrett (D) |
| | | 2 | 65.0 | 58 | Robert N. C. Nix (D)[a] |
| | | 3 | 28.5 | 24 | William J. Green (D) |
| South Carolina | 6 | 1 | 34.0 | 29 | Mendel Davis (D) |
| | | 2 | 33.8 | 29 | Floyd Spence (R) |
| | | 5 | 31.6 | 27 | Tom Gettys (D) |
| | | 6 | 42.2 | 36 | Edward Young (R) |
| Tennessee | 8 | 8 | 47.5 | 41 | Dan Kuykendall (R) |
| Texas | 24 | 18 | 41.6 | 37 | Barbara Jordan (D)[a] |
| Virginia | 10 | 1 | 30.1 | 27 | Thomas Downing (D) |
| | | 3 | 26.2 | 24 | Robert Satterfield (D) |
| | | 4 | 37.1 | 33 | Robert Daniel (R) |
| | | 5 | 29.0 | 25 | W.C. (Dan) Daniel (D) |

[a]Black Congressmen.

Source: U.S. Bureau of the Census, 1970 Census of Population; Congressional Quarterly. Potential Black Voter Influence in Congressional Districts (Washington, D.C.: Joint Center for Political Studies, March 1973).
*This table is based on data from the 1970 census and includes members of the 93rd Congress. Recent reapportionment in some states and results of the November 1974 Congressional elections are not reflected.

**TABLE 8.6** *Black Representatives in Congress\**

| Name | District | Year Elected | Percent of Vote in Last Election | Constituency Racial Composition in Percent | | Committee Assignments |
|------|----------|--------------|----------------------------------|---------------|---------------|------------------------|
| | | | | *White* | *Black* | |
| Yvonne B. Burke | 37th District California | 1972 | 73.0 | 58.0 | 42.0 | Interior and Insular Affairs Public Works |
| Shirley A. Chisholm | 12th District New York | 1968 | 66.5 | 32.4 | 65.9 | Education and Labor |
| William L. Clay | 1st District Missouri | 1968 | 64.1 | 45.3 | 54.3 | Education and Labor Post Office and Civil Service |
| Cardiss Collins | 7th District Illinois | 1973 | N.A. | 57.0 | 42.3 | Government Operations Public Works |
| John Conyers | 1st District Michigan | 1964 | 83.6 | 24.1 | 75.2 | Government Operations Judiciary |
| Ronald V. Dellums | 7th District California | 1970 | 57.3 | 66.5 | 23.7 | Armed Services District of Columbia |
| Charles C. Diggs, Jr. | 13th District Michigan | 1954 | 65.8 | 28.4 | 70.2 | Chairman, District of Columbia Foreign Affairs |
| Augustus F. Hawkins | 21st District California | 1962 | 84.5 | 21.7 | 75.7 | Education and Labor House Administration |
| Walter Fauntroy | District of Columbia (Nonvoting) | 1971 | N.A. | 29.0 | 71.0 | District of Columbia Banking and Currency |

| | | | | | | |
|---|---|---|---|---|---|---|
| Barbara Jordan | 18th District Texas | 1972 | 81.0 | 55.1 | 44.0 | Judiciary |
| Ralph H. Metcalfe | 1st District Illinois | 1970 | 91.0 | 3.9 | 95.5 | Interstate and Foreign Commerce<br>Merchant Marine and Fisheries |
| Parren J. Mitchell | 7th District Maryland | 1970 | 58.7 | 25.6 | 74.0 | Banking and Currency<br>Select Committee on Small Business |
| Robert N.C. Nix | 4th District Pennsylvania | 1958 | 72.6 | 34.3 | 65.0 | Foreign Affairs<br>Post Office and Civil Service |
| Charles B. Rangel | 18th District New York | 1970 | 86.8 | 25.4 | 72.4 | District of Columbia<br>Judiciary |
| Louis D. Stokes | 21st District Ohio | 1968 | 74.7 | 37.8 | 61.5 | Appropriations |
| Andrew Young | 5th District Georgia | 1972 | 53 | 60.5 | 39.1 | Banking and Currency |
| Edward Brooke | Senator Massachusetts | 1966 | 66 | 96.9 | 3.1 | Banking, Housing and Urban Affairs<br>Appropriations<br>Select Standard and Conduct<br>Special Committee on Aging |

*Data is for the 93rd Congress. The table does not reflect results of the 1974 Congressional elections. In that election Harold Ford of Tennessee's 8th District defeated Dan Kuykendall to become the sixteenth black representative. The Democratic Caucus has tentatively decided on several changes in committee assignments for black representatives. Yvonne Burke will join the Appropriations Committee, Charles Rangel and Andrew Young will become the first black members of the Ways and Means and Rules committees respectively.

of foreign policy but he has used it in at least three important ways: (1) to undertake extensive research and investigation that emphasize and publicize the problems and failings of present United States policies; (2) to generate increased popular concern with the problem facing African countries and especially those directly affected by white minority rule; (3) to increase contact and communication with African countries through visits to these countries and through cooperation with representatives of African countries in the United States. Diggs' recent appointment to the chairmanship of the House Committee on the District of Columbia can be expected to provide an energetic and concerned advocate for the now overwhelmingly black population of the District.

In summary, the electoral process does not guarantee to any portion of the electorate clear, direct impact on the policy process and it is even less likely in the case of blacks. As a minority with some interests not generally shared by the dominant group, blacks face particularly formidable obstacles in seeking to achieve their basic goals through electoral activity. However, the experience to date suggests that while they cannot realistically expect spectacular or rapid results, the electoral process indeed provides opportunities for some influence. This influence can be expected to grow as the level of participation increases and as the black subculture becomes increasingly sophisticated in devising tactics to maximize their impact.

# 9

# Black Political Participation II: Party Politics

Political parties are among the most vigorously criticized of American political institutions. The Watergate scandal has tarnished their image even further. Nevertheless, political parties are vital institutions in the United States as well as in virtually all other political systems. The precise role of parties vary from one polity to the next, from one era to the next, and even from one observer to the next.

For the purposes of our study, however, we need to emphasize a few particularly crucial functions which they perform in American political life. (1) Political parties are the structures through which political leaders are usually selected. As one scholar suggests, they structure the struggle for power. (2) Political parties accommodate and aggregate a wide range of conflicting interests within a society, formulating from them a coherent set of objectives or policy proposals. (3) Political parties are often able to bridge the gaps or divisions within a society and thus facilitate a measure of "national integration."[1]

The foregoing functions refer to the political system as a whole, but equally important functions are performed for the individual. (1) The party serves as a "reference group," aiding the individual in appraising and taking a stand on sometimes complex public issues. (2) It helps to educate the individual with respect to specific issues and stimulates interest in politics generally.[2]

This wide range of crucial functions performed by political parties make them a logical focus of special attention in examining the political

---

[1] See for example Clinton Rossiter, *Parties and Politics in America* (Ithaca, N.Y.: Cornell University Press, 1960); Samuel J. Eldersveld, *Political Parties: A Behavioral Analysis* (Skokie, Ill.: Rand McNally, 1964), p. 22; Frank Sorauf, *Political Parties in the American System* (Boston: Little, Brown, 1964), pp. 165–166.

[2] Marion Irish and James Prothro, *The Politics of American Democracy* (Englewood Cliffs, N.J.: Prentice-Hall, 1971), pp. 224–225.

179

experience of blacks and particularly their participation in the political system. Clearly, the pattern of activities in and support for political parties over time constitutes a vital dimension of the participatory activities of blacks. Furthermore, the impact of race on American political life and the dilemmas blacks face in attempting to influence public policy are nowhere more starkly manifested than in the activities of the political parties. In this chapter we describe the contemporary pattern of support among blacks for the political parties and their participation in the structure of party decision making. We also review the historical relationship of blacks with the major parties, the treatment of racial issues by the parties, and some of the tactical problems involved in continued partisan activities.

## Partisanship Among Blacks

In the highly competitive atmosphere of American party politics where parties are overwhelmingly pragmatic and nonideological, no significant sector of the electorate escapes careful scrutiny and extensive courtship by the parties. However, it would appear that the black subculture has received more attention than any other subgroup in the society, and this attention continues to increase as the subculture becomes larger and thus constitutes a more potent political force. Not only are ambitious white politicians and party officials extremely attentive to black attitudes toward the parties; black leaders and commentators are even more attentive as they contemplate ways in which blacks may maximize their impact on the political system. Of greatest concern in this regard are the perceptions blacks have of the political parties, the extent and depth of their attachment to the parties, and the implications of these for black influence in the political system.

### Black Democrats: The Pattern of Partisan Identification

The observation that the black vote is overwhelmingly and almost unalterably Democratic has been made so frequently that it is now unquestioningly accepted. From this acceptance, observers then proceed to the question of how to change this pattern so that blacks become more discriminating and thus more influential participants. The perception of the black vote as "unerringly loyal to one party," to use Chuck Stone's expression,[3] is supported by two kinds of evidence: self-identification as Democrats and level of electoral support given to the Democratic party.

A number of surveys indicate that blacks overwhelmingly regard themselves as Democrats and consider the Democratic party more sympathetic to their interests. From their nationwide survey, William Brink and Louis Harris

[3]Chuck Stone, *Black Political Power in America* (Indianapolis: Bobbs-Merrill, 1968), p. 44.

reported the following breakdown in response to the question: "Which political party will do more for Negroes"?[4]

**TABLE 9.1**

|  | Percent | |
|---|---|---|
|  | *1966* | *1963* |
| Democrats | 69 | 63 |
| Republicans | 3 | 4 |
| Other parties | – | – |
| No difference | 14 | 18 |
| Not sure | 14 | 15 |

Other research findings differ in detail but reflect a similar pattern. Data from the University of Michigan's Survey Research Center in 1968 show that 95 percent of black adults identify with the Democratic party and only 2 percent with the Republican party.[5] In a 1970 Louis Harris survey 63 percent of the black respondents agreed that "the Democrats usually can be trusted to help blacks, while the Republicans don't care much." Nineteen percent disagreed, while 18 percent were unsure.[6] Matthews and Prothro found a similar pattern of support for the Democratic party among Southern blacks. They reported that "by 1964 ninety-four percent of Southern Negroes with party images had generally favorable attitudes toward the Democratic Party whereas only three percent had pro-Republican images."[7]

The high level of support for the Democratic party reflected in these varied surveys is matched by remarkably strong support for the party at the polls. We have available systematic national studies of voting only since 1952, but these data indicate that black voting support for Democratic Presidential candidates has increased steadily since that time. According to Robert Axelrod, in 1952 7 percent of the Democratic party's electoral support came from blacks, and by 1968 this had risen to 19 percent, the largest single source of support for the party. Furthermore, over the same period loyalty to the Democratic party by blacks has been consistently and substantially higher than that for the nation as a whole.[8] Viewed another way, black support for Democratic Presidential candidates rose from 60 percent of the total black vote in 1956 to a peak of 94 percent in 1964.

[4] William Brink and Louis Harris, *Black and White* (New York: Simon & Schuster, 1966), p. 92.

[5] See Frank Sorauf, *Party Politics in America,* 2nd ed. (Boston: Little, Brown, 1972), p. 159.

[6] *The Harris Survey Yearbook of Public Opinion 1970. A Compendium of Current American Attitudes* (New York: Louis Harris & Associates, 1970).

[7] Donald Matthews and James Prothro, *Negroes and the New Southern Politics* (New York: Harcourt Brace Jovanovich, 1966), p. 385.

[8] Robert Axelrod, "Where the Votes Come from: An Analysis of Electoral Coalitions, 1952–1968," *American Political Science Review* 66, 1 (March 1972), 14–15.

**TABLE 9.2** *Party Identification of American Adults, 1952–1968*
(Figures Are Percentages)

| Identification | October 1952 | October 1956 | October 1960 | October 1964 | October 1968 |
|---|---|---|---|---|---|
| Strong Democrats | 22 | 21 | 21 | 27 | 20 |
| Weak Democrats | 25 | 23 | 25 | 25 | 25 |
| Independents | 22 | 24 | 23 | 23 | 29 |
| Weak Republicans | 14 | 14 | 13 | 13 | 14 |
| Strong Republicans | 13 | 15 | 14 | 11 | 10 |
| Others | 4 | 3 | 4 | 2 | 2 |

*Source:* Survey Research Center of the University of Michigan, data made available through the Inter-University Consortium for Political Research. Sorauf, *Political Parties in the American System,* 2nd ed., (Boston: Little, Brown 1972). Copyright © 1968, 1972 by Little, Brown and Company (Inc.). Reprinted by permission.

Although the attachment of blacks to the Democratic party is strong, its inflexibility should not be uncritically assumed, nor should it be viewed as an unfortunate aberration requiring immediate correction. Close scrutiny of black voting behavior and that of the society as a whole will reveal that (1) blacks are not really unique with respect to their heavily Democratic preference; (2) their Democratic preference does not actually reflect inflexibility in partisanship at the polls; (3) the particular pattern of partisan support exhibited by blacks is entirely consistent with the circumstances in which they find themselves as participants.

There is considerable evidence that the favorable image of the Democratic party held by blacks is shared by a substantial majority of the total adult population. Data from the Survey Research Center indicate that almost twice as many adults identified themselves as Democrats compared with those who identified themselves as Republicans in the period 1952–1968. Thus, although blacks are more supportive of the Democratic party than the electorate as a whole, they share the basic pattern of partisanship of the total society.

Furthermore, several other distinct social groups also indicate overwhelming preference for the Democratic party, although the proportion of Democratic identifiers in these groups is not as great as among blacks. Axelrod indicates that the Democratic party is a coalition of blacks, the poor, union members, Catholics, and central city residents.[9] All of these groups report overwhelming preference for the Democratic party and support the party heavily at the polls.

The high level of black support for the Democratic party need not be construed as unusual inflexibility because there have been substantial, sometimes drastic changes in the level of support for Democratic candidates. Harry Truman's election in 1948 was made possible in large part by the overwhelming support given him by blacks but by 1956 Adlai Stevenson, the

[9] *Ibid.*

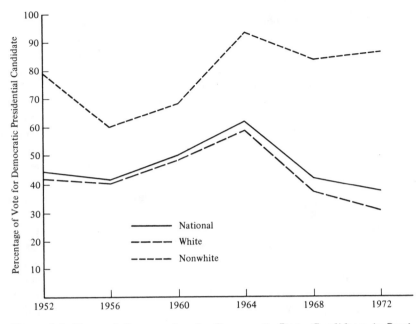

**Figure 9.1** *Electoral Support for the Democratic Party Candidates in Presidential Elections, 1952–1972*

Source: Based on Gallup Poll Survey Data in The Gallup Opinion Index, March 1974, p. 23.

Democratic candidate, secured only about 60 percent of their votes to almost 40 percent for Dwight Eisenhower. John Kennedy did somewhat better in 1960, approaching 70 percent to Richard Nixon's 30 percent. Lyndon Johnson's 94 percent to Barry Goldwater's 6 percent in 1964 and Hubert Humphrey's 85 percent to Nixon's 12 percent in 1968 are dramatic increases in black support for Democratic Presidential candidates. Substantial support for Republican Eisenhower in 1956 was nationwide but was heaviest in the South, where Eisenhower won majorities in four major cities.[10] Although the reasons for the shift to the Republican party are not all clear, an attractive candidate and absence of a strong civil rights stand by the Democrats combined to affect the vote.

Perhaps the strongest evidence refuting the notion of the black vote as inflexibly Democratic is offered by Brink and Harris in their examination of voting patterns among blacks on both national and state levels. They report that the black vote has shifted between parties at almost twice the rate of the white vote on both levels. After their resounding 94 percent vote for Democrat Johnson in 1964, 25 percent of the black vote shifted in 1966 to support

[10] According to Henry Lee Moon, Eisenhower won majorities in Atlanta, Ga., of 85.3 percent; Memphis, Tenn., 54 percent; New Orleans, La., 55.1 percent; Richmond, Va., 73.0 percent. "The Negro Vote in the Presidential Election in 1956." *Journal of Negro Education,* **26** (Summer 1957), 224.

Republican candidates whereas the shift for whites was only 11 percent. The shift in some particular state elections was even more dramatic according to Brink and Harris. Two years after 94 percent of Maryland's black votes had been cast for Democrats, George Mahoney, the Democratic candidate for governor, received only 6 percent of their votes. Exactly the reverse occurred in Massachusetts where the black vote for black Republican Senator Edward Brooke was 83 percent in 1966 while Goldwater received only 6 percent two years earlier. The pattern was similar in several other states, as black voters responded to the candidates and the salient issues rather than the party.[11] According to Brink and Harris, the crucial question in each case was the candidate's attitude toward civil rights.

Finally, there is strong evidence of a fundamental change in the level of partisanship among blacks. According to Miller, Brown, and Raine there has been a general decline in the level of partisanship in the society as a whole. Between 1964 and 1972 the political independents increased from 8 to 13 percent of the electorate, not including the newly enfranchised 18–20-year-olds. The decline in partisanship among blacks, however, was considerably greater than for the nation as a whole. Among blacks the independents increased from 4 percent in 1964 to 11.5 percent in 1972. Furthermore they found "a precipitous drop in Strong Democrats among blacks from 56.1 percent in 1968 to 37.7 percent in 1972, a decline of more than 18 percentage points in four years."[12]

The reasons for this decline are complex. It appears partly related to the sharp decline exhibited by blacks in trust in the political system, especially trust in political parties, the electoral process, and elected representatives. Another reason suggested by one group of scholars is that attachment to the Democratic party among blacks is relatively recent and, especially in the South, has not been very firm. Philip Converse concludes, for example, that in the South "Negro partisanship was weakly developed and remarkably labile. White partisanship was rigidly crystalized."[13] Significantly the most drastic decline in Democratic identification has occurred in the South, "dropping from 91 percent in 1968 to 66 percent in 1972," while independents increased from 6 to 28 percent. Outside the South there has been virtually no change in black partisan identification.[14] These findings suggest that rapid changes are taking place among blacks, although they do not amount to a reversal of the earlier pattern and there continues to be firm evidence of

[11] Brink and Harris, *op. cit.*, pp. 75–77.

[12] Arthur Miller, Thad Brown, and Alden Raine, "Social Conflict and Political Estrangement 1958–1972," paper prepared for delivery at the Midwest Political Science Association Convention, May 1973.

[13] Philip E. Converse, "Change in the American Electorate," in Angus Campbell and Philip E. Converse, *The Human Meaning of Social Change* (New York: Russell Sage, 1972), p. 312.

[14] Arthur Miller et al., "A Majority Party in Disarray: Policy Polarization in the 1972 Election," paper prepared for delivery at the annual meeting of the American Political Science Association, September 1973, p. 86.

overwhelming support among blacks for the Democratic party as is reflected in their voting records. Indeed, in spite of the decline in identification with the party, blacks again overwhelmingly supported the Democratic candidate for President in 1972.

### Determinants of Black Partisanship

An important consideration here then is, What explains the overwhelming preference for the Democratic party among blacks, and what are the consequences of this preference? According to Frank Sorauf, two factors are crucial in determining the pattern of party identification in the electorate. They are political socialization and socioeconomic status.[15] Political scientists have demonstrated that partisan attitudes are learned and that the family is the most potent factor in transmitting partisan attitudes.[16] Sorauf points out, however, that political socialization has to do with *how* attitudes are learned, not *why*. The "why" question is answered primarily by reference to socioeconomic status. The two political parties clearly are perceived as representing the interests of distinct socioeconomic classes in the society. Sorauf suggests that intensification of the SES lines between the two parties was the revolution which Franklin D. Roosevelt achieved in 1936. It is not coincidental that it is at this time that a large-scale shift of blacks to the Democratic party occurred.

The importance of the socioeconomic factor in explaining partisanship among blacks is obvious. Support for the Democratic party is highest among the lowest socioeconomic groups in the society, as is demonstrated by Table 9.3. Because a disproportionately large percentage of the black population clusters at the lowest levels of the socioeconomic scale, the Democratic party has proven more attractive to them. This should not suggest that blacks are Democrats only because they are poor, but it does go a long way to explain this preference.

The fact that the Democratic party has been more closely identified with the cause of civil rights in the post-World War II period is a second major factor explaining identification of blacks with that party. Although both parties enunciated strong commitment to civil rights for blacks, it was the Democratic party that emerged as the more vigorous advocate. President Truman took several highly visible actions in the area of racial discrimination, appointing a commission to study race relations, ordering desegregation of the armed forces, and proposing comprehensive civil rights legislation. The adoption of a strong civil rights plank in the 1948 Democratic party platform over the vigorous objection of Southern Democrats further heightened the

[15] Sorauf, *Party Politics in America*, pp. 134–140.
[16] See for example V. O. Key, *Public Opinion and American Democracy* (New York: Knopf, 1961), p. 301; M. Kent Jennings and Richard Niemi, "Family Structure and the Transmission of Political Values from Parents to Child," *American Political Science Review* 62 (March 1968), 172–173.

TABLE 9.3  Social Characteristics of Party Identifiers: 1968

| | Strong Democrat | Weak Democrat | Independent | Weak Republican | Strong Republican | Others | Totals |
|---|---|---|---|---|---|---|---|
| Race | | | | | | | |
| White | 16.1% | 24.8 | 31.0 | 16.1 | 10.5 | 1.4 | 99.9% |
| Negro | 55.7% | 28.9 | 10.1 | .7 | 1.3 | 3.4 | 100.1% |
| Others | 21.7% | 39.1 | 34.8 | 0 | 4.3 | 0 | 99.9% |
| Occupation | | | | | | | |
| Professional | 11.6% | 18.1 | 37.1 | 20.3 | 12.9 | 0 | 100.0% |
| Manager, official | 17.1% | 22.0 | 33.6 | 16.6 | 9.3 | 1.5 | 100.1% |
| Clerical, sales | 15.3% | 23.5 | 32.3 | 17.6 | 11.2 | 0 | 99.9% |
| Skilled, semiskilled | 18.3% | 29.7 | 30.3 | 12.7 | 7.3 | 1.6 | 99.9% |
| Unskilled, service | 33.3% | 26.2 | 24.3 | 6.0 | 7.1 | 3.0 | 99.9% |
| Farmer | 25.7% | 27.0 | 10.9 | 23.0 | 12.2 | 1.4 | 100.2% |
| Other (retired, etc.) | 28.0% | 27.0 | 19.0 | 10.6 | 11.6 | 3.7 | 99.9% |
| Income | | | | | | | |
| 0–$1,999 | 29.4% | 28.7 | 17.7 | 10.3 | 10.3 | 3.7 | 100.1% |
| $2,000–3,999 | 28.2% | 25.8 | 24.0 | 10.8 | 8.9 | 2.3 | 100.0% |
| $4,000–5,999 | 19.8% | 25.7 | 29.7 | 11.9 | 9.9 | 3.0 | 100.0% |
| $6,000–9,999 | 18.6% | 25.3 | 30.8 | 13.9 | 10.1 | 1.3 | 100.0% |
| $10,000–14,999 | 17.7% | 28.0 | 30.5 | 15.8 | 7.7 | .3 | 100.0% |
| $15,000 and over | 9.4% | 16.5 | 39.5 | 24.1 | 10.0 | .6 | 100.1% |
| Education | | | | | | | |
| None-8 grades | 31.0% | 31.8 | 15.9 | 10.6 | 7.5 | 3.1 | 100.1% |
| 9–12 grades | 19.2% | 27.3 | 28.9 | 14.6 | 8.3 | 1.7 | 100.0% |
| Some college | 10.8% | 18.8 | 42.5 | 15.7 | 11.7 | .4 | 99.9% |
| Baccalaureate degree | 10.0% | 15.7 | 37.1 | 20.7 | 16.4 | 0 | 99.9% |
| Advanced degree | 21.0% | 12.9 | 40.3 | 12.9 | 12.9 | 9 | 100.0% |
| Religion | | | | | | | |
| Protestants | 19.1% | 24.1 | 26.9 | 16.3 | 11.5 | 1.9 | 99.8% |
| Catholics | 23.1% | 29.4 | 31.2 | 9.5 | 5.6 | 1.2 | 100.0% |
| Jews | 33.3% | 19.0 | 42.9 | 4.8 | 0 | 0 | 100.0% |

From Frank Sorauf, Party Politics in America 2nd ed., (Boston: Little, Brown, 1972), Table 4, p. 149. Source: Survey Research Center of the University of Michigan; data made available through the Inter-University Consortium for Political Research. Copyright © 1968, 1972 by Little, Brown and Company (Inc.). Reprinted by permission.

party's image as champion of civil rights. The Brown decision in 1954, its subsequent enforcement with troops by Republican Eisenhower, and passage of the first civil rights act in 1957 failed to alter fundamentally the more negative image of the Republicans on this issue. Thus the issue of civil rights, which has been the most salient one for blacks, has operated to the advantage of the Democratic party.

Another crucial element in explaining both the high level and the persistence of Democratic identification is the operation of group cohesiveness. We earlier observed that the black subculture exhibits the highest level of group cohesiveness in its political behavior. This cohesiveness operates to enhance the level and persistence of identification with the Democratic party. Angus Campbell et al. explain the impact of group cohesiveness in this way:

> If group influence leads the identified member to take on identification with the party, then little renewal of interest is needed. The individual has, as it were, acceded to a self-steering mechanism, that will keep him politically "safe" from the point of view of group standards. He will respond to new stimuli as a party member and code them properly. As time passes, his identification with the party will increase of its own accord, because the individual will find that event after event demonstrates—in nongroup matters as well as group matters now—the rectitude of his own party and the obnoxiousness of its opponent.[17]

This would appear to suggest that where one party manages to project an image of pursuing policies consistent with black objectives, black support is likely to be very heavy, and furthermore it is likely that this support will be persistent.

A different situation obtains when the distinctions between the parties are not clear, especially when highly visible black leaders appear divided. This was particularly apparent in 1956. Dissatisfaction with the obstruction of civil rights legislation by Democratic legislators, the attractiveness of the Republican candidate, and the general uncertainty about the commitment of the Democratic candidates to civil rights combined to produce considerable ambivalence among blacks. Reflecting this ambivalence, the two black members of Congress at the time were divided—Adam Clayton Powell of New York supporting the Republicans while William Dawson of Chicago supported the Democrats. Campbell et al. suggested that this division contributed substantially to the 60–40 percent split rather than more decisive support for the Democratic ticket.[18]

### Partisanship and the Problem of Strategy

As growing numbers of blacks turn to the political arena in their efforts to achieve basic race goals, partisan attitudes within the subculture become a

[17] Angus Campbell et al., *The American Voter* (New York: Wiley, 1964), p. 328.
[18] *Ibid.*

source of increasing concern. The primary consideration is how blacks can use their numbers in the electoral process to achieve goals which have thus far eluded them. Virtually all analyses of this issue look toward a highly flexible black electorate rather than a solidly partisan one. Chuck Stone, one of the more prominent of these analysts, believes that at present "because of its controlled habits, the black vote can expect to be nothing more than an occasional and minimal influence in national, state and local elections."[19] Stone suggests that this vote can be truly influential only when three conditions exist—voting cohesion (bloc voting), an evenly divided white vote, and oscillation of black votes between the two parties. The last point he considers most important because, he observes, "once the Negro vote has been taken for granted—as it has been nationally since the New Deal—it loses its bargaining power."

Stone's desire to see the black vote "swing back and forth periodically between the two parties" is a widely shared one. The same view is succinctly expressed by Representative William Clay of Missouri in his observation that blacks should have "no permanent friends, just permanent interests." In view of the pattern of partisanship we just observed, it is necessary to inquire whether this desire is realistic. My impression is that although the prospect is tantalizing, it is unrealistic. Advocates of this strategy seem to have failed to consider the nature of the electoral process and the political behavior of individuals. Frequent massive shifting of the black vote between the two parties is unrealistic for at least two important reasons: (1) on the basis of what is known about the behavior of the electorate, party identification tends to be fairly stable and frequent shifts on the scale contemplated are extremely unlikely if not impossible, except in such limited cases as we described earlier; (2) important benefits accrue from firm partisan identification the loss of which would be even more damaging than the present situation.

In the United States as in many other societies, there are strong indications of the stability and persistence of party identification. A substantial body of research appears to support Sorauf's contention that it "develops early and lingers late."[20] Socialization studies reveal that children by the fourth grade have begun to develop partisan attitudes, although they are unable to relate general policies or issue orientations to the parties until much later. There is no evidence that this pattern is absent from the black subculture; indeed, fragmentary evidence tends to confirm its existence, suggesting that partisan attitudes among blacks will ordinarily be as stable as among whites. According to Sorauf,

> . . . party identification may be weakened or altered during adulthood by cataclysmic events, such as the Civil War or the great depression of the 1930s, which alter basic social interests and upset patterns of social attitudes. While changes in occupation alone seem not to

[19] Stone, *op. cit.,* p. 43.
[20] Sorauf, *Party Politics in America,* p. 140.

affect party identification, a general change in life style and peer groups—such as those changes associated with drastic upward social mobility—often does.[21]

Among blacks, drastic shifts in policies on racial matters or the nomination of candidates clearly hostile to black interests will evoke shifts in party identification. If, however, the parties continue to take generally similar stands on issues that are salient for blacks there is little reason to expect that a significantly greater level of shifting back and forth will occur among blacks. A much more likely basis for change in the pattern of partisanship is rapid improvement in socioeconomic status.

In spite of these expectations and our suggestion that socioeconomic status is an important determinant of black partisanship, recent voting patterns provide no indication of such a shift. According to one analysis in the 1972 Presidential election,

> McGovern received 97 percent of the black college-educated vote, 85 percent of the black high-school educated vote, and 80 percent of the black grade-school educated vote. McGovern also received nearly unanimous support, among blacks, from those under 30 (95%), from those with relatively higher incomes and from white collar workers.[22]

Indications are, therefore, that change in partisan attachment among blacks will continue to be determined by which candidate or party appears more likely to facilitate black advancement.

Comments on partisan attitudes among blacks often fail to consider some of the positive contributions of partisanship for political participation. Verba and Nie have examined the impact of partisan affiliation on levels of political participation and report that (1) levels of political participation are substantially higher for partisans than for nonpartisans, (2) party affiliation has an effect on participation that is over and above that predicted by the social status of the individual, and (3) with respect to voting participation, "partisan affiliation greatly reduces the participation-rate gap among the social levels." Verba and Nie conclude that as far as voting is concerned, "lower status citizens receive more of a participatory boost from partisan identification than do upper-status citizens."[23] Given their generally low social status, it is very likely that partisanship is an important contributor to the existing levels of participation among blacks. Furthermore, they suggest that lower-status individuals are more likely to be strong identifiers than higher-status ones. If Verba and Nie are correct, attempts to alter or discourage present high levels of partisanship among blacks will substantially reduce their overall level of participation.

[21] *Ibid.*, p. 145.

[22] Miller et al., "A Majority Party in Disarray," *op. cit.*, p. 83.

[23] Sidney Verba and Norman Nie, *Participation in America: Political Democracy and Social Equality* (New York: Harper & Row, 1972), pp. 208–247.

## Blacks and the Major Political Parties

The salience of race in American political life is very clearly evidenced in the activities of the two major political parties. No other single issue has dominated party politics as thoroughly and as persistently as the race issue—or more specifically, *attitudes toward blacks*. As an issue, blacks have never really disappeared from the political scene. Busing to achieve racial integration in the 1970s, civil rights legislation in the 1960s, fair employment practices in the 1940s, lynching in the 1920s, citizenship rights in the Reconstruction era, and the issue of slavery in the pre-Civil War era are among the compelling issues which have shaped the fortunes or misfortunes of the political parties. The rapid rise of the Republican party to capture the Presidency in 1860 may be credited in part to the astute handling of the question of slavery. In fact, the vicissitudes of the two parties over the past hundred years appear directly linked to their treatment of the race issue and the level of black support they managed to attract.

Today's widespread support for the Democratic party by blacks constitutes a sharp reversal of the picture of approximately one hundred years ago when politically active blacks, with few exceptions, were Republicans. It is interesting to note that all 22 blacks elected to serve in Congress up to 1890 were Republicans, while among the 16 blacks now in Congress all except Senator Edward Brooke of Massachusetts are Democrats. Under the still controversial McGovern reform rules, just over 15 percent of the delegates to the 1972 Democratic National Convention were black compared to an approximately similar percentage at Republican conventions prior to 1892. Between these two peak periods of party activity are decades of marginal involvement by blacks whose support was sought by the parties—but mainly via the back door.

### Blacks and the Republican Party

When blacks in large numbers first entered the electoral arena in 1868 they entered as solid Republicans. The few who held the franchise in Northern states supported the Republican party even before this time, but black Republicanism became a significant part of American politics with enfranchisement of millions of former slaves, almost all residing in the South. Their adherence to the Republican party is understandable, having been prompted by several factors. First the emancipation proclamation was made by a Republican president and subsequent adoption of the Thirteenth Amendment completely abolishing slavery resulted from Republican effort. It did not matter that Lincoln was motivated more by expediency than conviction in issuing the emancipation proclamation. He received the adulation of blacks and his party benefited by decades of grateful support from blacks. Second, the Republican party emerged as the champion of "Negro rights" in the South during the Reconstruction era. To be exact, "Radical Republicans" who controlled the Congress championed black rights, making them citizens by legislation in 1866 and by constitutional amendment in 1868, and providing special guarantees of the franchise through the Fifteenth Amendment in 1870. Again, it didn't really matter that Republican presidents Lincoln and his successor Andrew Johnson opposed these moves vigorously—Lincoln looking vaguely toward repatriation of blacks to Africa and Johnson using all his powers to prevent extension of citizenship rights to them. Third, the Republican party made vigorous efforts to enlist the support of blacks, employing its organizational resources to ensure their voting and competition for office. In this way, the Republican party inducted the black population into the business of state and national politics on a large scale.

There are varying interpretations of the motives of Radical Republicans in this involvement of blacks. We discussed earlier the alleged desire to solidify Republican control by developing a solid base of support among blacks in the South. We wrote of the desire to punish the seemingly unrepentant South by imposing on it a powerful black electorate, and we mentioned the larger struggle between the executive and legislative branches out of which advantages flowed to the black community. Although deciding on motivations may be difficult, it can be readily observed that at best Republican efforts were mutually beneficial for blacks and the party, and in the long run appeared more self-serving than motivated by genuine concern.

Republican interest in Southern blacks declined sharply after 1876 and when, fourteen years later, widespread disfranchisement of blacks was being undertaken, the Republican party in the South split into "lily-white" and "black-and-tan" factions. The "lily-white" movement is said to have begun in 1888 among Texas Republicans and was so named by black Republican leader Morris Cuney after whites, at the party convention, allegedly precipitated riots in order to eliminate black members. In part it was motivated by the desire to develop a "respectable Republican party" in the South that could effectively compete with the Democratic party for white votes at a time when black voting strength was declining and hostility to black participation among whites was increasing. Blacks were charged with corruption, with being concerned only with getting patronage positions, and with virtually any misdeed that could be dredged up by hostile whites. Within a short time, "lily-white" organizations sprung up in every Southern state except West Virginia and Kentucky. The "black-and-tan" Republicans, as loyalists, were faced with vigorous opposition from "lily-whites;" there was competition for patronage over which blacks had effective control, and at the national party conventions their delegations were challenged by "lily-whites" in a way that calls to mind the recent challenges between regular Mississippi Democrats and the Mississippi Freedom Democratic Party.

The Party's response to the racial split in its Southern ranks was never decisive. At times it was tolerated, but eventually the courtship of whites prompted support for "lily-white" organizations over "black-and-tans."

Prominent black party officials like Benjamin Davis of Georgia and Perry Howard of Mississippi were dismissed from their party positions, Howard being eventually indicted (but not convicted) for the sale of public office. Encouragement of the lily-white organizations was especially vigorous in Herbert Hoover's campaign of 1928. Lewinson reports that after Hoover's election the new President came out in favor of the "lily-whites,"[24] but lily-white Republicanism failed in the South because the party was unable to generate enough support among whites to challenge the entrenched Democratic party; moreover, it alienated and eventually lost the support of most of the small black electorate.

The circumstances and environment in the North were substantially different, although black Republicans were affected by the growing conservatism on the race issue within the Republican party. In fact, blacks outside the South were kept in the Party as a result of the powerful Republican party machines in several large cities and the strong hostility of the Democratic party to support from blacks up to 1932. Because they were not wanted in the Democratic party, most blacks continued to vote Republican. There were exceptions, of course, most notably the brief and disappointing experience with Woodrow Wilson, who lured black support with vague promises only to later usher in a new era of racism in the federal government. It is noteworthy, however, that the payoffs for their support were minimal. Northern blacks failed to achieve anything comparable to the prominence and visibility achieved by Southern blacks in the party. Among blacks North and South an estrangement from Republicanism began to set in by 1928. It is reported that Roscoe Conklin Simmons, prominent black Republican leader and leading orator of his day, dramatized black discontent by standing beneath Herbert Hoover's window at the White House while he implored, "Speak Mr. President, speak. Tell us Lincoln still lives."[25] Hoover did not answer, for the spirit of Lincoln had indeed died as far as blacks were concerned.

### Blacks and the Democratic Party

Black support for the Democratic party is usually traced to the New Deal era, beginning in 1932 with the election of Franklin D. Roosevelt. However, the switch to the Democratic party was not a sudden one and its immediate causes have not been entirely clear. Up to this time the Democratic party, unlike the Republican party, did virtually nothing to justify support of blacks. On the contrary the party deliberately attempted in several ways to discourage black support. Throughout the South it developed as an

[24] Paul Lewinson, *Race, Class and Party: A History of Negro Suffrage and White Politics in the South* (New York: Grosset & Dunlap, 1965), pp. 173–174.

[25] G. James Fleming, "The Negro in American Politics: The Past," in John P. Davis, ed., *The American Negro Reference Book* (Englewood Cliffs, N.J.: Prentice-Hall, 1966), p. 428.

alternative to the so-called "niggerism" of the Republicans; it vigorously opposed the franchise for blacks and in many areas was closely associated with the atrocities inflicted on blacks to discourage their electoral activities. So obsessed was the party in the South with opposition to blacks that it rarely concerned itself with national political issues. The only real issue was race and the forces unifying the white South solidly in the Party's ranks was fear of and hostility toward blacks.

Outside the South the party's image was not considerably better as far as the race question was concerned. In Congress it provided opposition to much of the reconstruction program. Its members were easily the most persistent purveyors of racism in national politics. Aside from a few rare exceptions the party did not select blacks to run for office. It was not until 1924 that the first black delegate attended the Party's national convention as an alternate. In most cases party platforms cannot be taken seriously, but they are useful as indicators of what groups or sectors of the society the party seeks to appeal to for support. It is significant, then, that while the Republicans continued to include statements favoring antilynching legislation, equal economic and political opportunities, and similar measures, the Democratic party included no mention of these issues until 1940.

In spite of these conditions a small number of blacks voted for Democratic candidates well before the New Deal. During this era of Republican dominance, two Democrats won the Presidency. In both cases a substantial portion of the black electorate supported the Democratic candidate. Especially in the increasingly competitive environment of the North, the black vote was becoming crucial to electoral success; both Democratic candidates wooed the black vote—albeit in an extremely discreet, even clandestine manner—in order not to antagonize regular party supporters.

The first of these Democratic candidates, Grover Cleveland, did little to alter the position of blacks. He continued the few patronage positions to which blacks had been accustomed under Republican presidents. Thus while no ground was gained, little was lost. A different experience occurred with Woodrow Wilson in 1912. More than any of his predecessors Wilson needed and sought the support of blacks. Although he maintained a discreet distance and made no specific pledges, he uttered vague, lofty generalities with enough sincerity to convince large numbers of blacks, including a wary Du Bois, that black people would benefit from his leadership. But with his election, black hopes quickly turned to nightmares. His passionate commitment to democracy and self-determination was confined to the caucasian peoples of Europe and did not include black people in the United States. Not only did Wilson eliminate virtually all of the traditional black patronage positions but he went to considerable length to order the segregation of the federal bureaucracy and the District of Columbia. Thus Wilson, who sought to pass himself off as the conscience of the world, shattered the black man's dream at home and sent them back to the Republican party for the want of a plausible alternative.

Widespread support for Roosevelt was understandably hesitant and more cautious among black people than in the rest of the voting community. Up to the time of his candidacy in 1932, Roosevelt had done little to win the trust of blacks. He was a member of the distasteful Wilson administration; later as a Vice-Presidential candidate he criticized his Republican opponents for catering to black support, and he made no explicit commitment to the policy interests of blacks. The party platform ignored civil rights and related issues entirely, thus providing little direct attraction to blacks. Nevertheless Roosevelt received substantial support from blacks, carrying four of fifteen large wards in nine states later surveyed by Gunnar Myrdal.[26] Although he ran behind Hoover in most communities, the showing was good and by 1936 he had won 11 of these 15 wards and by 1940 14 of them. Thus in the eight years between 1932 and 1940 Roosevelt brought into the Democratic party the overwhelming majority of black voters. According to Wilson, the shift to the Democratic party was earliest and most pronounced in cities with powerful Democratic party organizations. Furthermore, middle-class blacks shifted to the Democratic party and the New Deal before lower-class blacks, as Harold Gosnell demonstrated in Chicago.[27]

This movement into the Democratic party represented a response to the vigorous economic initiatives undertaken by the Roosevelt administration and was consistent with the dramatic swing of the remaining urban political machines to the Democrats. It should not be overlooked, however, that while as a whole the New Deal proved beneficial to them, blacks continued to be victimized, and President Roosevelt remained reluctant to support legislation on their behalf. John Davis complained in one early evaluation of the New Deal program that blacks were in many cases worse off than they were before, and even where there were benefits, they were dispensed in grossly discriminatory fashion.[28] Furthermore, up to 1936 Roosevelt refused to urge passage of antilynching legislation because it would infuriate Southern legislators and thus impede his programs in Congress. Discontent with the first New Deal administration and serious division among blacks about whether to support Roosevelt's reelection are very clearly reflected in the proceedings of the First National Negro Congress held in Chicago in February 1936.[29] The party's gesture of including 30 blacks as delegates to its national convention and including a black to make one of the seconding speeches in the nominations of Roosevelt helped a little in assuaging the chagrin over neglect of blacks and the blatant discrimination they experienced in various New Deal programs.

[26] Gunnar Myrdal, *An American Dilemma* (New York: Harper & Row, 1944), pp. 494–496.

[27] Harold Gosnell, *Negro Politicians* (Chicago: University of Chicago Press, 1935), pp. 34–35.

[28] John Davis, "A Black Inventory of the New Deal," *Crisis* 43, 3 (1935), 141–145.

[29] Their deliberations are discussed in James A. Harrell, "Negro Leadership in the Election Year 1936," *Journal of Southern History,* 34, 4 (November 1968), 546–564.

The activities of Eleanor Roosevelt and the efforts of several bureaucrats in the Roosevelt administration helped create a positive image for the administration in black communities. In addition to well-known bureaucrats like Harold Ickes (considered one of the principal advocates of black interests in the Roosevelt administration), a group of blacks served as advisers on policy matters. Although he had to be pushed by the threat of a mass march on Washington, D.C., Roosevelt's establishment of a Fair Employment Practices Commission by Executive Order represented the first direct Presidential response to black demands. Even though it did not really solve the basic problems of job discrimination against blacks, its symbolic significance cannot be overlooked. Furthermore, for the first time the Democratic platform recognized the presence of blacks as part of the new majority, asserting that "We shall continue to strive for full legislative safeguards against discrimination in government services and benefits and in the national defense forces. We pledge to uphold due process and the equal protection of the laws for every citizen, regardless of race, creed or color."[30] The 1944 platform went a bit further:

> We believe that racial and religious minorities have the right to live, develop and vote equally with all citizens and share the rights that are guaranteed by our constitution. Congress shall exert its full constitutional powers to protect those rights.[31]

In this election, blacks supported the Democratic ticket in even larger numbers than in 1940, although the party's overall support was sharply reduced nationwide. Thus the transition from the Republican to the Democratic party was completed for the overwhelming majority of blacks by 1944. The vigorous resistance of Southern Democrats continued, but these strange bedfellows—starting with diametrically opposed objectives—came to claim a common partisanship. In fact, the continued influence of these Southern Democrats as chairmen of important Congressional Committees depended (and still does) on black support of the party.

After an initial skepticism about his attitude, Harry Truman (who became President on the death of Roosevelt) further strengthened black support for the Democratic party. Making good some of the party's platform pronouncements, Truman commissioned a study of race relations in the United States. Its findings, published under the title *To Secure These Rights*, provided the basis for the first comprehensive legislative program on civil rights submitted to Congress by a president. His Executive Order calling for the desegregation of the armed forces further identified Truman and the Democrats with the cause of civil rights. But it was primarily a Democratic Congress which frustrated the efforts for civil rights, and thus one should not go too far in emphasizing Truman's activities. They do suggest, however,

[30] *National Party Platforms 1840–1964* (Urbana: University of Illinois Press, 1966), p. 387.
[31] *Ibid.*, p. 404.

some of the forces and circumstances that help to account for the present partisanship among blacks.

During the 1940s the Republicans tried to recover the support the party lost among blacks. With Eisenhower's candidacy in 1952 and 1956 it managed to make substantial inroads. This temporary gain has not been maintained, however, for several reasons. First, the increasing identification of the Democratic party with support for civil rights reduced considerably its appeal to whites in the South, and the Republican party has concentrated on catering to this new Southern vote. The 1964 Presidential elections dramatized this new orientation as Republican candidate Barry Goldwater repudiated the civil rights efforts of the federal government and seemed to endorse conservative "extremism." The continuation of this "Southern strategy" was apparent in both the 1968 and 1972 campaigns by Richard Nixon. Second, while the Republican party has maintained a generally conservative posture, the pattern of black voting has been progressive. Moon some time ago commented on this trend, observing that the political maturity of the black population is fully demonstrated in their consistency in supporting progressive candidates. He suggests that especially since the New Deal blacks have, in spite of pressures and blandishments, usually been found on the side of those candidates who not only advocate equal rights for blacks but who also stand for progressive labor and social legislation.[32] Third, the class factor we discussed earlier operates among blacks more heavily in favor of the Democratic party than the Republican. Comprising an overwhelmingly lower-class community, blacks find a variety of specific class incentives to support the Democratic party. The prospect of significant Republican inroads into the black vote thus appear to be hinged on the growth of the middle-class sector of the black population as well as the party's ability to develop a more progressive posture in the area of economic and social policies.

## Blacks and the Minor Parties

The relationship between blacks and the two major political parties, as we have described it, points up some of the major problems that have faced blacks. The political parties reflect the interest of the white society, and their success depends on the extent to which they are able to generate support among whites. For blacks, who form a relatively small segment of the total electorate, it is extremely difficult to influence the posture adopted by the party with respect to race issues or the candidates selected to represent the party. Black participation in these parties is therefore always a matter of accepting considerably less than desired and at times receiving nothing in

[32] Henry Lee Moon, *Balance of Power: The Negro Vote* (Garden City, N.Y.: Doubleday, 1948).

terms of influence. The pattern of party activities suggests that they respond to blacks only when the electorate is divided in such a way as to make black support essential to the party's success. In short, when black votes are clearly vital in determining the outcome of elections, the parties will actively seek to court them. Secondly, the evidence suggests that the capacity of the parties to respond to blacks is extremely limited. Responses must not be sufficiently far-reaching to alienate the white electorate, and hence the parties yield grudgingly to black demands. In this regard it is significant to note that prior to the 1940s the only direct payoffs to the black community by the major parties came in the form of minor patronage positions. In addition to some clerical positions, a few prestigious-sounding but relatively uninfluential posts were reserved for blacks. These included ambassadorships to Liberia and Haiti—the all-black nations—and minor positions like Recorder of Deeds, Marshall of the District of Columbia and Register of the Treasury.

To an extent these problems are intrinsic to the two-party system of politics and affect other groups in the society as well. They are felt more keenly by blacks, however, because of the pervasiveness of racial hostility to blacks and because more than any other group blacks possess interests that are not widely held outside the group. There is the further problem that the parties are not "responsible" in the sense that they can be counted on to deliver on the promises they make to the electorate. There is therefore no clear relationship between commitments made and policies initiated. The result is that even when blacks play a crucial role in the electoral outcome the rewards for their support may not be forthcoming. For these and several other reasons blacks have, from time to time, despaired of traditional party politics and have sought alternatives to the two major parties. The record of black electoral activity therefore includes considerable activities within minor political parties.

We are using the term "minor parties" instead of "third parties" because these parties in fact rarely posed serious challenges to the two major parties and because, at times, several of them existed simultaneously. For convenience we may divide these minor parties into (1) protest parties, those organized around a specific issue or set of issues; (2) ideological parties which seek to win adherence to a particular set of ideological beliefs as a basis for political action; (3) all-black parties. To some extent blacks have been associated with all of these types of parties in efforts to achieve goals that seemed unachievable in the context of the two major parties.

There is some plausibility to the involvement of blacks in minor parties. Political scientists agree that while two-party systems appear to facilitate political stability, they do not usually provide for effective representation of citizen interests, since one is constantly compelled to choose between the lesser of two evils. On the other hand, multiparty systems, while sometimes associated with political instability, provide a greater range of choices for the voter. With respect to the American political scene, minor parties have not been successful in gaining control of government but some have managed to influence public policy, sometimes considerably. Specifically these parties focus attention on clear-cut issues that might otherwise have been ignored by the major parties; they have been the principal sources of innovation in the policy arena since eventually their ideas, initially rejected by the major parties, were absorbed into the program of the major parties; and finally, they provide an outlet for the citizen outraged by the unresponsiveness of government.

### Blacks and the Protest Parties—Abolitionists, Populists, and Progressives

There have been numerous minor political parties of the protest type in United States political history. The Liberty, Populist, Progressive, Prohibitionist, Dixiecrat, and American Independent parties are but a few. In a few cases like the Liberty and Dixiecrat parties, race constituted the principal issue and raison d'être, while in other cases race became a peripheral concern dealt with in such a way as to maximize the party's appeal. In either case blacks were involved in several of these protest parties. Three of them—the Liberty, Populist, and Progressive parties—deserve special attention, either because of the scale of black participation in them or the distinct lessons this participation provided.

The Liberty Party, organized in April 1840 at Albany, New York, was one of the earliest protest parties whose primary focus was race. Its principal objective was abolition of slavery through regular political means. It included in its membership most of the prominent abolitionists of the time. In fact, one might describe it as the political arm of the abolition movement. It was organized by whites but soon included many prominent black abolitionists like Henry Highland Garnett, Samuel Ward, and William Wells Brown. A few blacks, notably Frederick Douglass, expressed reservations about participation in the party because it encouraged reliance on political rather than moral suasion in seeking abolition of slavery. Two years after its founding, however, its strong stand against slavery and for citizenship rights for blacks resulted in its endorsement by a Colored State Convention meeting at Rochester, New York. The following year several blacks were elected to prominent roles in the party as it swung its doors open to blacks—inviting them, as one of its resolutions put it, "to fraternity with us in the Liberty Party, in its great contest to secure the rights of mankind and the religion of our common country."[33]

The party was short-lived. By 1848 divisions seriously weakened it and the Free Soil Party emerged alongside it. By 1860 it was dead. Nevertheless, the Liberty Party was important to blacks because (1) it provided the first opportunity for leadership roles for blacks in an American political party,

[33] Quoted in Charles Wesley, "The Participation of Negroes in Anti-Slavery Political Parties," *The Journal of Negro History* 29, 1 (January 1944), 45.

(2) it rekindled a spirit of political activism among blacks as reflected in the annual conventions by blacks during much of the 1840s, and (3) it extended the first unqualified invitation to blacks to enter the political arena.

The conditions of black involvement in the Populist movement were substantially different from those of the Liberty party. The central theme of Populism was economics.[34] The impoverished farmers of the West and South sought to improve their lot through political action. In the South, the efforts of Populists to achieve political power rested on an alliance between blacks and mostly poor whites of the region. The episode is interesting because it was the first attempt at a "class-based political movement" seeking to cut across racial lines. The alliance rested on the proposition that blacks and poor whites had their poverty in common and both would benefit from coopera-tive political action. This informal political alliance between blacks and whites proved beneficial to both races at the outset. For the reform-minded whites of the region it made them a formidable political force with the prospect of gaining political power in the South. The alliance permitted blacks to hold prominent positions in the party and compete for office in many areas. It appeared much more likely to support black efforts for change than either of the major parties. However, by 1896 the alliance crumbled in complete failure.

Evaluations of this abortive alliance and opinions on the reason for its failure vary widely, but two basic and highly significant reasons for its downfall stand out. The first has to do with the problem of objectives. The program of Populism focused mainly on the economic interests of the whites in which it was assumed that blacks would share. It included vague assurances of protection of the franchise for blacks, access to free schooling, and protection against lynching—but it contained no firm commitments to these and other issues that were most salient for blacks. One scholar states the problem thus:

> The Populists in the South failed to formulate a program that would meet the special grievances of Negroes. The emphasis in Populist program was on the need of property-owning farmers whose interests were threatened by Eastern capital. But little attention was given to the need of agrarians who owned no land, who were caught in the trap of sharecropping and who had practically no cash income. Much of the Negro South found itself in this situation.[35]

Furthermore, Populist leaders vigorously opposed some of the issues most vital to blacks—notably the Force Bill that sought to provide federal protec-

---

[34] For a discussion of the economic pressures resulting in a massive agrarian movement of which the Populists were a prominent part, see James L. Sundquist, *Dynamics of the Party System* (Washington, D.C.: Brookings Institution, 1973), pp. 94–141.

[35] Herbert Shapiro, "The Populist and the Negro: A Reconsideration," in *The Making of Black America*, Vol. II (New York: Atheneum, 1969), pp. 27–30.

tion of voting rights for blacks—and, like the rest of the South, they resented even such relatively trivial gestures as President Cleveland's invitation of Booker T. Washington to a White House reception. Thus it appears that black gains from the alliance were to be minute, secondary to those of whites.

The second reason is not entirely separable from the first: white people's overpowering fear and resentment of black people. As Populism gathered momentum, Democratic party leaders became concerned and began to publicize the prospect of black control, thereby creating a wave of racist hysteria. Whites were urged to remain loyal to the Democratic party or lose their supremacy. Put another way, lower-class whites were made to believe that they had to choose between giving political power to blacks to be used to dominate whites and maintaining the status quo. They chose the latter. The process of disfranchisement, already begun, was rapidly intensified in the name of White Supremacy. The implications are chilling for contemporary advocates of a "class approach" to American politics without regard to race.

Under the leadership of Theodore Roosevelt the Progressive party appeared in 1912, and it, too, actively sought the support of blacks. Black support for Progressivism, though not overwhelming, was substantial. Throughout several of the black population centers, progressive organizations appeared; some blacks even traveled the country speaking on behalf of Progressives. This support by blacks is somewhat paradoxical because Teddy Roosevelt in his first term did much to infuriate blacks. He gave his support to the "lily-white" Republicans in the South, he arbitrarily dismissed "without honor" three companies of black soldiers for allegedly participating in the Brownsville riot. He once virtually defended lynching by blaming it on black misconduct. Furthermore, the Progressive party failed to incorporate in its program anything of direct interest to blacks. Roosevelt eventually announced that while he was seeking black support in the North, he was not seeking their support in the South out of deference to white Southerners. It was clear that in this case—as with the Populists—white racism would not be compromised in any respect even while black electoral support was actively sought.

The pattern of black involvement in minor protest parties indicates that while their generally liberal posture appealed to blacks, participation brought very few payoffs. The black vote, where it existed, was often self-servingly sought after with little regard for the interests of the group. One also senses among blacks an unfortunate gullibility not uncommon to people who are desperate. Blacks yielded to the blandishments of every seemingly "progressive" party or politician yet had little to show for their vacillation.

### Blacks and the Ideological Parties

Ideological parties hold a clearly defined set of beliefs as a basis for interpreting social and political reality and for formulating programs of action in these areas. This type of party has not fared well in the United States although it has managed to survive for much longer than the protest-type party. The two well-known ideological parties in America are the Socialist and Communist parties, both of which, while not having the race issue as central themes, have had to deal extensively with the race question in seeking support of blacks. Wilson Record suggests three reasons for the involvement of the ideological parties with blacks:

> First, such movements usually seek to establish a working class base, and the Negro is a significant portion of the labor force. Second, Negroes suffer more than any other racial group from social and economic exploitation and their special plight is posited as a manifestation of the fundamental characteristics of capitalism. Third, because Negroes are numerically important and especially exploited, they are regarded as either an important resource or a distinct liability for those who would reconstruct American society along radical lines. . . .[36]

The Socialist party was the earlier of the two "radical" ideological parties, beginning its activities in about 1901. The party soon succumbed to factionalism and so has existed as a weak group of splinter organizations rather than as a cohesive organization. Race, while not central, was an unavoidable issue. The party's first platform in 1901 dealt at length with the class-based exploitation of the Negro, declared the identity of the interests and struggles of Negroes and the working class of all lands, and invited them to "membership and fellowship with us in the world movement for economic emancipation by which equal liberty and opportunity shall be secured to every man and fraternity become the order of the world." Despite this initial posture, the Socialists failed to vigorously seek black political support. Furthermore, Record observes that blacks, with a highly pragmatic orientation to politics, took a dim view of a party professing concern for them while seeking to be the spokesman for highly prejudiced craft unions. Its success was thus confined to a few black intellectuals and labor leaders like Chandler Owen and A. Philip Randolph.

The Communist Party differs sharply from the Socialists in that its efforts to secure the support of blacks have been extensive and persistent. The Party's activities over time are interesting more because of the novelty of their programs and strategies than for their success in winning black adherents to the Party. In this latter respect it has been an almost total failure.

A full grasp of the Party's activities and programs for black Americans can be gained most clearly if viewed from an international perspective. One of the principal themes of the Bolsheviks, especially after the failure of other revolutions in Europe, was the "colonial question." Lenin had identified the colonies as a primary reason for the continued strength of capitalism; he saw the breakup of the colonial empires as crucial to the defeat of capitalism.[37] The black peoples of colonized Africa, South Africa, and America were

[36] Wilson Record, *The Negro and the Communist Party* (Chapel Hill: University of North Carolina Press, 1951), p. 16.

[37] V. I. Lenin, *Imperialism, the Highest Stage of Capitalism* (Moscow: Progress Publishers, 1966).

Phalanx

therefore early concerns of the Party's international organs. Very early it advocated vigorous activities among them. Black America at this time was important to the Communists in two respects. First the Party viewed the racial problem, especially in view of a rising race consciousness among blacks, as an American weakness that could be effectively exploited to the Party's advantage. The Party's experience with the "national question" (it developed a broad set of policies and a federal structure designed to facilitate inclusion of the many ethnic groups) in the Soviet Union heightened its confidence in this regard. Second, the Bolsheviks hoped that after they had won the support of black Americans, these blacks could become ambassadors of Communism among Africans.[38]

It is usually assumed that the poor, the exploited and the discontented lower classes are most likely to succumb to the appeals of Communism, but

[38] See Walter Kolarz, "The West African Scene," *Problems of Communism* 10, 6 (November–December 1961), 16.

this has not been the case for blacks. In spite of their obvious poverty and discontent, Communist efforts to win them failed completely. Such efforts, in fact, appear to have been an unbroken series of misadventures as the Party stumbled from one ill-considered initiative to the next. Behind this failure are several important factors, some having to do with the Party and others with the character of the black subculture at the time.

Like the Socialists, the Communists approached the race question as another manifestation of class conflict. The economic system of capitalism, they suggested, is basically responsible for the exploitation of blacks, although they did concede certain departures from the classical model of oppression. They began by urging that blacks join the revolutionary struggle of the working classes against capitalism. By 1935 the Party had shifted its approach somewhat, urging instead the creation by blacks of a "black-belt republic" with socialist ideology in the Southeastern United States. This strategy, apparently formulated by officials of Comintern (the organ of world Communism at that time) who were far removed from the scene, had little relationship to reality and failed to generate interest among blacks. Thus the first problem the party encountered was its failure to formulate a realistic program with genuine appeal for blacks.

A second and somewhat related problem was the Party's failure to attract the attention and interest of blacks. It had attempted to do this by infiltrating black labor and protest organizations, by visibly engaging in the struggle for black causes, by attempting to lure blacks through complete social acceptance and the awarding of prominent positions with the party, and by adopting forthright, comprehensive party platforms in support of full equality of blacks. Even here, however, the efforts were seriously flawed. The attempted infiltration of black labor ranks, the UNIA, and especially the NAACP to which considerable effort was directed, was a conspicuous failure. The Party's efforts stumbled on an apparent inability to comprehend the nature of the black struggle or the aspirations of black people at that time. This is reflected in the uneasy shifting between support and hostility for Garveyism and what Harold Cruse regards as their complete misconception about the character of black nationalism in America.[39]

The Party's failures also stemmed from distinctive features of the black subculture, although exactly what these features are is not altogether clear. Unquestionably, though, black loyalty to or support for the political system was a formidable obstacle to Communist success. Not only were blacks firmly committed to the Democratic creed and to aspirations of success in a capitalist system, but they felt that their complete loyalty was an important factor in favor of eventual inclusion. Myrdal has pointed to the strong influence of religion and the church in black life as perhaps a second major obstacle to Communist infiltration.[40] Finally, black leaders were overwhelm-

---

[39] Harold Cruse, "Revolutionary Nationalism and the Afro-American," *Studies on the Left* **2**, 3 (1962), 12–25.

[40] Myrdal, *op. cit.*, pp. 508–510.

ingly drawn from the ranks of the middle class and were generally conservative. They saw Communism as a threat rather than an ally. There were notable exceptions like George Padmore, originally from the West Indies, who after radical protest activities against racism in the United States joined the Party and quickly climbed to the highest levels of the international Communist organization before rejecting it in disgust in the 1930s. Du Bois, while resisting Communism for most of his active life, embraced it in his last years and a few other prominent blacks even migrated to the Soviet Union in the belief that that kind of society represented an alternative to racism and black subordination in America. It was no such alternative and so most of them returned to the United States. There have been a scattering of other expressions of interest by blacks but except for episodes like the recent Angela Davis case in which her persecution appeared related to her color and Communist affiliation, the Party is virtually nonexistent for blacks.

The failure of Communist efforts among blacks has not ended concern with the basic ideological posture the party espoused, especially the link between capitalism and black exploitation. During the 1960s the widespread hostility to capitalism and imperialism through most of the third world contributed to a reemphasis of these themes in black America. Several vocal black commentators have found in the views and experiences of personalities like Fidel Castro and Mao Tse-tung ideas and strategies they consider relevant to black America. Unfortunately, the experience of those who saw capitalism as the basic enemy of blacks and who saw in some form of socialism the answers to black subordination provide little support for today's proponents of these views. The fact is that racism exists without regard to ideology or to the "mode of production."

### Black Political Parties

We have recounted the pattern of black involvement in the two major parties as well as in some minor ones. The recounting clearly suggests that the tangible rewards for their involvement have been few. A consistent theme running throughout these years of party activities is dissatisfaction and frustration with the performance of the parties and their commitment to the interest of blacks. Occasionally, frustration led to the advocacy of black political parties, and on several occasions attempts have been made to organize such parties. The idea is still prominent among politically active blacks. At the 1972 National Black Political Convention at Gary, Indiana, this sentiment was a powerful undercurrent, pushed as an alternative to support of either of the major parties by blacks.

In spite of its long and frequent discussion, initiatives for a black political party operating nationally have been very few. The attempts made thus far can hardly be regarded as serious or significant. Black political parties have not enjoyed the leadership of nationally prominent black politicians, have not managed to attract the attention of a substantial segment of the black electorate, and have not been able to survive for more than brief periods. Nevertheless, it is one of the many roads which blacks have traveled in search of political influence, and the fact that virtually all serious contemplations of future political strategy by blacks include formation of an all-black party makes it worthy of attention.

In order to have a noticeable impact on American politics, parties need to operate on a national basis or at least maintain a strong regional base. They must transcend district and state boundaries. Few such party efforts have been undertaken by blacks. Walton reports that the first attempt at a national black party occurred in July 1904 when delegates from 36 states met at the Douglas Hotel in St. Louis, Missouri, and formed the National Liberty Party. The new party selected George Edwin Taylor as its candidate for president, but according to Walton the effort soon fell apart and was replaced by several "nonpartisan groups" such as the National Negro American Political League, the National Independent Political League, the National Labor Congress, and the National Negro Congress.[41] Since that time other modest beginnings of black parties have been made, among them the Afro-American Party organized in Alabama in 1960, the Freedom Now Party in 1964, the National Civil Rights Party in 1963, and the Peace and Freedom Party (sponsored by the Black Panthers) in 1968. These parties all faded shortly after organization, however, with no indication of significant support even among blacks.

At the state and local levels, there have been more black parties and they seem to have fared a bit better. Such local parties date back to 1883 when the Colored Independent Party was formed in Pennsylvania, followed by the Negro Protective Party of 1897 in Ohio. The more recent attempts at organizing local parties have been almost wholly confined to the South, where blacks experienced considerable difficulty in gaining access to the existing parties in anything but token fashion. In some of these Southern states the party effort began when "black-and-tan" Republicans fielded their own candidates for state and local office, sometimes receiving substantial local support. In other cases, black party organizations emerged to challenge the all-white Democratic organization by selecting delegates to the party's national convention in an effort to have them seated instead of regular all-white delegations. One such attempt was that of the South Carolina Progressive Democratic Party in 1944, which although failing to replace the white state delegation, fielded its own local candidates and continued its efforts to be recognized by the Democratic party up to 1956. The Mississippi Freedom Democratic Party organized at Jackson, Mississippi, in April 1964 is the best known and most successful of these local party efforts. It has challenged both the seating of all-white Democratic delegates at the party's convention and the seating in Congress of individuals elected to that body by

[41] Hanes Walton, *Black Politics* (Philadelphia: Lippincott, 1972), p. 126.

an all-white party. At the state level it managed to win at least five county posts in cooperation with the NAACP. Throughout the South other such organizations have appeared periodically; some, like the party of Christian Democrats in Georgia, were confined to a single legislative district.

Altogether the black parties have, in some cases, managed to focus attention on the exclusion of blacks from regular party organization and have spearheaded efforts for greater participation by blacks in the national party organizations and the national conventions. For example, the vigorous efforts by the Mississippi Freedom Democratic Party to replace the segregationist regular Democratic party's delegates at the party's 1964 national convention provided the impetus for major reform that facilitated more extensive black participation in the 1972 convention. Although it failed to secure its objective of replacing the regular Democrats, the convention responded by adopting a resolution which made the seating of delegates to future conventions contingent on the absence of discriminatory practices in the state party's affairs. In implementing this resolution, a special Equal Rights Committee in 1966 adopted a set of six antidiscrimination standards to be followed by all state parties. These were adopted by the Democratic National Committee in 1968 and were included as part of the McGovern Commission's reforms.[42]

In some cases black parties appear to have had important mobilizational impact among blacks. Unfortunately they have not been sufficiently broad based, well-funded, or supported to give effective voice to issues of concern to blacks or to sufficiently threaten the major parties into greater responsiveness to blacks. Do black parties have a place in black political life in the future? The question is highly debatable. Past efforts point up major problems that must be overcome—such as the difficulty of finding bases for agreement among blacks—but other vital concerns must be faced. A highly successful black party effort of the future could simply remove from the two major parties the need to compete for black votes and thus the need to be attentive or responsive to blacks. It should be borne in mind that over the years minor parties have been most useful in bringing to public attention important issues that the major parties have overlooked. The issue of race certainly has not been overlooked, and thus party effort in this regard might be of marginal value. Efforts to form a new nonracial alliance of the poor and oppressed, or efforts to influence the priorities of the major parties by vigorous and persistent involvement, may be more plausible courses of action.

---

[42] *Mandate for Reform* (Washington, D.C.: Democratic National Committee, 1970), pp. 39–40. Largely as a result of this effort substantial improvement has occurred in the level of black participation in the Democratic National Convention. In 1964 only 2.4 percent of the delegates to the Convention were black, with 1.9 percent actually voting delegates. In 1968 black representation climbed to 5.5 percent, and, under the new rules applied, in 1972 it reached 15 percent.

# 10

# Black Political Participation III: Group Activities

The forms of political participation described in the preceding two chapters are those routinely engaged in by individuals in democratic societies. As we observed, blacks have regarded these activities as vital in their persistent struggle to fundamentally alter their subordinate status within the society. The evidence indicates that their participatory activities in these areas have been impeded by a wide range of social, economic, and psychological factors as well as by deliberate and systematic attempts to exclude them from the political arena. Furthermore, while these "traditional" forms of political participation may be satisfactory to individuals who benefit from or are satisfied with the status quo, they have not been adequate for blacks—or for any group which desires far-reaching change—because they rarely facilitate more than minor modifications in the status quo. Not surprisingly therefore a vital dimension of black participatory activity involves their cooperative efforts within an assortment of organized social and political groups and at times in spontaneous group activities. A total picture of the participatory activities of blacks requires therefore that we examine the various forms of "nontraditional" political activities undertaken within these organized groups.

The pattern of black participation in organized social groups is important for two reasons. First, there is substantial evidence that participation of this kind is closely related to the inclination to participate in politics and so is reflective of the group's level of "participant orientation."[1] Second, organized groups often are instruments of direct political activity or are agencies for educating and mobilizing individuals for political action. This has been particularly true of black America, where organized groups of various kinds

[1] See for example Norman Nie, G. Bingham Powell, and Kenneth Prewitt, "Social Structure and Political Participation: Developmental Relationships, II," *American Political Science Review* 63, 3 (September 1969), 811–813.

have been especially prominent in a wide range of political activities. For example, Floyd Hunter reported in his study of the power structure of Atlanta that the major associational groups in the black community "have a political content not found in the larger community."[2]

Some attempts have been made to compare the level of overall participation in organized social groups for blacks and whites. The results are not altogether consistent but they strongly suggest that the rate of this form of activity among blacks may be higher than among whites. Gunnar Myrdal noted that blacks belonged to far more organized social groups than did whites[3] and, although one more recent empirical study reported evidence to the contrary,[4] a number of studies have supported Myrdal's initial observation to some extent. Some studies report that when socioeconomic status is controlled, blacks have been found consistently more likely to participate in organized groups than whites, although one study of a single city revealed higher levels of organized group participation among blacks than among whites regardless of the socioeconomic factor.[5]

Comparisons of black-white involvement in organized groups are not considerably enlightening taken alone, but they do suggest the relative prominence of this form of activity. For our purposes the facts to be emphasized from these several studies are that black involvement in organized groups is widespread, long-standing, and directly related to the distinct characteristics of the group and its subordinate status. In our earlier discussion of black nationalist activity we observed that a variety of all-black organizations— churches, fraternal, economic and cultural organizations—emerged as a direct result of white hostility and the need for collective struggle against oppression. In commenting on the prevalence of organized groups among blacks and the high level of participation in them, Gunnar Myrdal concluded that discrimination by the white society has encouraged blacks to resort to "within-group" activities as an alternative to interaction with whites. Babchuck and Thomspon arrived at a similar conclusion, suggesting that "regarding participation, the rank and file Negro adult finds in his formal voluntary associations, in the same way that he finds in his church, release from his restrictive social environments."[6] In a more directly political context, the

[2] Floyd Hunter, *Community Power Structure: A Study of Decision Makers*, (Chapel Hill: University of North Carolina Press, 1953), pp. 114–115.

[3] Gunnar Myrdal, *An American Dilemma*, rev. ed. (New York: Harper & Row, 1962), pp. 952–953.

[4] Charles R. Wright and Herbert Hyman, "Voluntary Association Memberships of American Adults: Evidence from National Sample Surveys," *American Sociological Review* 23, 3 (June 1958), 284–294.

[5] Anthony Orum, "A Reappraisal of the Social and Political Participation of Negroes" in Russell Endo and William Strawbridge, *Perspectives on Black America* (Englewood Cliffs, N.J.: Prentice-Hall, 1970), pp. 42–60; Nicholas Babchuck and Ralph Thompson, "Voluntary Associations of Negroes," *American Sociological Review* 27 (October 1962), 647–655.

[6] *Ibid.*, p. 649.

overwhelming array of formal and informal impediments to their direct participation in politics has contributed to the need to rely on group involvement. One prominent group of scholars observe in this regard that "organizational involvement may represent an alternative channel for political participation for socially disadvantaged groups. The rural peasant, the industrial laborer, the disadvantaged black, may become politically active through his organizational involvement even though he may otherwise lack the status resources for political participation."[7]

Clearly, participation by blacks in organized groups has not been confined to all-black organizations, but the bulk of their activities has been in these organizations or in those having vital black interests as their primary objectives. Altogether these groups represent a wide variety of sometimes overlapping interests and activities, but for our purposes we may place them in three categories: (1) primarily social and religious organizations, (2) organizations for economic betterment of the group, and (3) protest or political action organizations. In different ways all of these three types have contributed to the struggle for change through vigorous political activity, but the third type has been most directly involved in political action and will be the focus of attention in this chapter.

## Development of Organized Political Action Groups

The first noteworthy feature of organized group activities by blacks is that it began to develop very early, well before "interest group activity" became a prominent element of American political life. While most organized group activity developed as a supplemental technique to increase the influence of distinct segments in the society, it was for blacks the principal—and in some respects the only—avenue by which the policy interests of the group could be effectively articulated. One might place the beginnings of these organized group activities at the 1790s when attempts were first made by small groups of free blacks to secure the franchise by petitioning state legislatures. This effort gradually developed in scope and was directed toward the federal Congress; the issue was joined by the demand for an end to slavery. The twin issues of slavery and the franchise occupied black organizations up to the Civil War. Periodic national or state conferences of "free blacks" became the principal organizational forum for drafting and submitting these petitions to government and for seeking avenues to the liberation of black people. So widespread were these efforts, especially in the decade 1835–1845, that several scholars refer to a "convention movement" among blacks.[8]

These early group activities gave the satisfaction of struggle to the participants and facilitated an ongoing debate about the problems facing the

[7] Nie, Powell, and Prewitt, *op. cit.,* p. 819.
[8] Howard Bell, "National Negro Conventions of the Middle 1840s: Moral Suasion vs. Political Action," *Journal of Negro History* **52,** 4 (October 1957), 247–260.

race, but they had virtually no policy impact. Their ineffectiveness was partly a result of the lack of political resources with which to influence policymakers and their necessary reliance solely on appeals to the moral values of Americans. These early efforts may have been further stymied by the inability of the participants to achieve a consensus on specific goals or on the strategy to be employed in pursuing these goals. After the Civil War, extensive political group activity subsided somewhat except for a few statewide or local groups as blacks in large numbers were admitted to the political arena throughout the South, where they became active in political parties and in state and local government. Later, as their political activity was drastically curtailed, new attempts at organized group activity began to reappear. The politically active Colored Farmers Alliance was organized in Texas in 1886 and grew rapidly throughout the South, eventually effecting a brief alliance with the Populists. In Chicago the short-lived National Afro-American League was organized in 1890, but neither it nor the scattering of other local groups managed to wield considerable influence.

Vigorous protest and political action organizations began to appear during the first decade of the present century. One of the first was the Niagara Movement, organized in July 1905 after Du Bois issued a call to participants from about 17 states to meet near Niagara, New York. Its initial impetus came from resolute opposition to the program of Booker T. Washington who had, since the Atlanta Exposition speech, urged that blacks forgo efforts for political and social equality and concentrate on acquiring skills for economic self-improvement. The group therefore included the most articulate opponents of Washington's viewpoint and issued an impressive list of basic objectives embracing a wide range of political, legal, and social issues. Their official statement asserted that

> [We] believe that this class of American citizens [Negroes] should protest emphatically and continually against the curtailment of their political rights. We believe in manhood suffrage; we believe that no man is so good, intelligent or wealthy as to be entrusted wholly with the welfare of his neighbor.
> We believe also in protest against the curtailment of our civil rights. All American citizens have the right to equal treatment in places of public entertainment according to their behavior and deserts.
> We demand upright judges in courts, juries selected without discrimination on account of color and the same measure of punishment and the same efforts at reformation for black as for white offenders. . . .
> We protest against the "Jim Crow" car, since its effect is and must be to make us pay first-class fare for third-class accommodations, render us open to insults and discomfort and to crucify wantonly our manhood, womanhood and self-respect. . . .
> At the same time we want to acknowledge with deep thankfulness the help of our fellowmen from the Abolitionist down to those

who today still stand for equal opportunity and who have given and still give of their wealth and of their poverty for our advancement.[9]

As Robert Brisbane suggests, however, the movement "failed to become more than an annual round table conference of young Negro intellectuals."[10] Among the reasons for the failure were (1) lack of funds or permanent organization, (2) internal divisions such as that between Du Bois and Monroe Trotter, and (3) the overwhelming influence of Booker T. Washington.

As the Niagara Movement faltered, a new and different kind of organization, the National Association for the Advancement of Colored People (NAACP) emerged. It was formally organized at a meeting held in New York City in the early summer of 1909 as a result of the efforts of William E. Walling, Mary White Ovington, Henry Moskovitz, and Oswald Garrison Villard. The new organization drew heavily on the spirit of the Niagara Movement as several of the Niagara group participated and Du Bois, the only nonwhite officer in the organization, served as its publicity and research secretary. Organization of the NAACP reflected a concern among its founders with a general deterioration in race relations and the exclusion of blacks from the political process, but the most urgent concern, and the factor prompting creation of the organization, was the widespread violence against blacks. The Springfield riot of 1908 in which several blacks were killed or wounded by white mobs actually triggered the move to create the NAACP. The new organization grew rapidly to include a large supporting membership and quickly developed a vigorous and many-sided program designed to

> Promote equality and eradicate caste or race prejudice among the citizens of the United States; to advance the interest of colored citizens; to secure for them impartial suffrage; and to increase their opportunities for securing justice in the courts, education for their children, employment according to their ability, and complete equality before the law.[11]

One year after the formation of the NAACP, three organizations working in New York City to alleviate the suffering and job discrimination experienced by blacks migrating to the city from the South, merged to form the National League on Urban Conditions Among Negroes (Urban League). The leading spirits behind this organization included several of those who a year earlier had helped organize the NAACP, but here their objectives were more limited. They were concerned almost exclusively with aiding blacks settle in the cities and helping them find jobs in industry. As with the NAACP, the Urban League's growth was rapid and its activities quickly

[9] Quoted in *Freedom to the Free, Century of Emancipation* (Washington, D.C.: Government Printing Office, 1963), p. 78.
[10] Robert Brisbane, *The Black Vanguard* (Valley Forge, Pa.: Judson Press, 1970), p. 41.
[11] Quoted in *Freedom to the Free, op. cit.*, p. 81.

spread to almost all major cities outside the South. It remained a relatively conservative organization almost entirely occupied with social activities until 1961 when, under the leadership of Whitney Young, former Dean of Atlanta University's School of Social Work, it adopted a more activist, political posture while continuing its traditional social activities. Despite the efforts of these organizations, the situation of blacks deteriorated everywhere with the end of World War I, and throughout the nation economic hardship was accompanied by savage physical attacks by white lynch mobs and urban rioters. Partly as a result of these conditions the first major nationalist organization—The United Negro Improvement Association—emerged, followed later by a few other nationalist and religious organizations, among them the Nation of Islam or Black Muslims organized in 1935.

The first of the essentially modern "protest organizations," The Congress of Racial Equality (CORE) started in 1942 as an outgrowth of a small pacifist organization, the Fellowship of Reconciliation (FOR) in which James Farmer was an active member. Its initial emphasis was on opposing racial discrimination in Chicago by the use of nonviolent protest. It thus pioneered in adapting to the racial struggle Ghandian principles of nonviolent protest. In 1957 it was joined by the Southern Christian Leadership Conference (SCLC), a loose coordinating agency of mostly Southern church groups growing out of the Montgomery Bus Boycott of 1956. The third of the major protest organizations, the Student Non-Violent Coordinating Committee (SNCC), came into being in April 1960, bringing into active struggle a young and largely college-student group. During the mid-1960s several smaller "nationalist" or "revolutionary" groups emerged, expressing a willingness to resort to violence if and when it became necessary in order to defend themselves and to bring about basic changes in the pattern of race relations. The most notable of these is the Black Panther Party, organized at Oakland, California, in 1966. Thus gradually an array of political action groups emerged among blacks reflecting a variety of tactical preferences. Yet all were engaged in efforts to improve the undesirable conditions experienced by blacks and ultimately to end their subordinate status in the society.

Although these organizations differed in some substantial respects, it is important to note that almost all of those formed up to 1960 shared some similar characteristics. First, aside from the Niagara and the nationalist groups, they were all interracial organizations. The extent of white involvement varied but was in no case insignificant. The white presence was particularly prominent in the NAACP and the Urban League, for both were founded by "liberal whites" and depended upon whites for a substantial portion of their membership and leadership. Thus in a small but significant way the organizations brought together the concerned elements of both races to work together for change in race relations. This interracial character of the organizations appears to have had an important bearing on the strategies adopted by the groups and the kind of support they evoked among blacks. Second, virtually all of these organizations were primarily elitist in that the founders and principal activists were highly educated, professional people. Meier and Rudwick point out, for example, that most of the founders of CORE, both black and white, were either students of the Federated Theological Seminary of the University of Chicago or college graduates engaged in white-collar occupations.[12] The NAACP and Urban League were similarly elitist, especially at the leadership level.[13]

A third feature of these organizations is the extent of their reliance on white individuals and philanthropic organizations for financial support. The NAACP is the only one of these organizations with a large, mostly black, dues-paying membership which provides a reliable source of income. Nevertheless a substantial portion of the organization's income comes from gifts by white individual and institutional contributors. Most of the other groups have been even more dependent on such white financial support than has the NAACP. Corporations and foundations provide virtually all of the operating budget of the Urban League, while the Southern Christian Leadership Conference depends heavily on mail solicitation for support. The point here is that, at least during the early years, the black population lacked the resources to sustain these organizations and thus depended heavily on the financial support of "liberal whites." This fact has undoubtedly further influenced the activities of these organizations.

One respect in which these political action groups have been very different is their organizational structure. It is apparent that the style, effectiveness, and stability of a group is in large part a function of its organizational structure. While the Niagara Movement crumbled—partly because of a lack of effective organization—the NAACP developed from the outset a tightly organized structure. Most of the other groups have fallen somewhere between these two extremes. The SCLC does not maintain a national membership in local chapters; individuals join indirectly through affiliated churches and civic organizations. Because of this its organizational structure is relatively simple, confined to a small staff and a governing board of thirty-three members, most of whom are ministers. CORE, during its period of greatest activity, maintained a large number of local chapters across the nation but with a highly decentralized structure. In one interesting study, Rudwick and Meier compared the organizational structure of the NAACP and CORE in an attempt to test their hypothesis that the centralized, highly bureaucratized structure of the NAACP contributed to that organization's "stability in ideology and goals," while the decentralized structure of CORE made it susceptible to radical transformation. Rudwick and Meier suggest that the NAACP's corporate structure permitted firm control over local chapters

---

[12] August Meier and Elliott Rudwick, "How CORE Began," *Social Science Quarterly* 49 (March 1969), 790–791.

[13] Wilson Record, "Negro Intellectual Leadership in the National Association for the Advancement of Colored People," *Phylon* 17, 4 (1956), 375–389.

by the national organization. Furthermore, the complex process by which members of the organization's Board of Directors is elected assures continuity at the policy-making level and a well-organized and stable bureaucracy added to overall stability or perhaps inflexibility. On the contrary, CORE's "federational" style of organization provided greater freedom for local groups and greater internal democracy, which in turn made the organization susceptible to drastic changes in philosophy and strategy.[14] Of course the differences between the two organizations and particularly their different responses toward changing attitudes among blacks go well beyond organizational differences and require still further thoughtful examination.

## The Pattern of Organized Group Political Action by Blacks

The many political action organizations, their limitations notwithstanding, have been the principal agents through which black cooperative efforts have been made to influence public policies at various levels throughout the political system. It is difficult to determine with any degree of accuracy the extent of actual participation by blacks in the various groups. Membership figures are not very useful in this regard. Although the NAACP maintains careful record of membership, which now stands at 487,000, few other organizations do. Furthermore, the activities of these groups permit considerable opportunity for participation without the need to formally join as a member. The available evidence indicates that the degree of actual cooperation by blacks has varied widely with the particular organization and action strategy employed, but there is no doubt that in the decades of struggle by these organizations large segments of the black population have been directly or indirectly involved.

In viewing this aspect of black political participation we will focus on the three basic strategies or types of activities in which organized groups of blacks have been engaged. The first involves the use of litigative and lobbying techniques whereby efforts were directed (a) at the courts through a series of lawsuits designed to alter public policies and (b) at the Congress, to secure enactment into law of specific, desired policies. The second—nonviolent protest and civil disobedience—involved attempts to mobilize public concern and sympathy for the injustices experienced by blacks through massive protest activities. A third type of group activity is "political violence" which involved sporadic, symbolic resort to violence or spontaneous outbursts of racial violence. As was suggested in Chapter 3, these activities represent a progression of gradually intensifying efforts aimed at achieving fundamental change in the subordinate-superordinate structure of the society. These types of activities have been associated with specific organizations and reflect a distinct choice of strategies although there have been some overlaps.

[14] Elliott Rudwick and August Meier, "Organizational Structure and Goal Succession: A Comparative Analysis of the NAACP and CORE, 1964–1968," *Social Science Quarterly* 51, 1 (June 1970), 9–24.

Litigation and Lobbying as Group Strategies

Organized, systematic litigative and lobbying activities to achieve fundamental change in the status of blacks have been undertaken primarily by the NAACP and the NAACP Legal Defense and Educational Fund (NAACP/ LDF). By lobbying we mean persistent organized efforts to influence legislative decision making through informal contact with legislators and other public officials or groups capable of influencing the decision-making process. Litigation, on the other hand, is the somewhat more formal process of petitioning the courts for the redress of grievances and for the formulation of policy in areas within its authority. Because of its extensive reliance on these activities, the discussion will focus on the NAACP and NAACP/LDF. It should not be overlooked, however, that other groups and individuals have also utilized these techniques for the same purpose.

### *Litigation for "Civil Rights"*
One of the most memorable decisions by the United States Supreme Court is that rendered in *Brown vs. Board of Education of Topeka, Kansas* (1954). It is remembered primarily because the Court ruled that segregated schooling in fact had detrimental consequences for black children and thus violated the equal protection principle of the Fourteenth Amendment. The ruling was followed by a directive from the Court one year later (in Brown II) that public schools discontinue segregation of black and white students, "with all deliberate speed."[15]

The decision had much broader implications than the drastic change in public education that it initiated, however, because by reversing an earlier Supreme Court ruling in *Plessy vs. Ferguson* (1896) which declared separation of the races constitutional as long as the facilities available to each race were equal, it provided a new constitutional basis for the struggle against black subordination. This memorable case was prepared by the NAACP/LDF and argued before the Supreme Court by its chief counsel Thurgood Marshall. It represented the high point in decades of vigorous and largely successful litigative effort by the Organization on issues relating to racial discrimination.

Several factors appear to have influenced the NAACP's decision to rely on litigation as one of the principal methods for achieving its objectives. First, it was clear that blacks lacked the resources necessary to secure favorable responses from the legislature, especially since their goals were not widely shared throughout the society. On the other hand, the resources essential for litigation—money, legal expertise and suitable cases to which it could become party—were readily available to the organization. Second, the founders and subsequent leaders of the NAACP were highly supportive of the political system and apparently reluctant to undertake any activity that appeared to threaten that system. It should be noted, however, that especially during its

---

[15] 347 U.S. 483 (1954). For what is frequently referred to as *Brown II* which actually ordered desegregation, see 349 U.S. 294 (1955).

early years the organization was widely viewed as radical, and a radical strategy might have been counterproductive. Third, leaders of the NAACP have been firmly committed to the view that law is a potent instrument of social change and hence can be utilized to alter the subordinate status of blacks.[16] This belief was further supported by the assessment that the issues involved were "peculiarly suited to adjudication."

The NAACP's litigative effort began almost immediately after the Organization's founding as a legal committee was organized and later placed under the leadership of Arthur Spingharm. Its first appearance before the Supreme Court occurred in 1915 as a "friend-of-the Court" (amicus curiae) in *Guinn vs. United States*[17] which successfully challenged Oklahoma's "grandfather clause." Although the organization participated in several important court cases and appeared before the Supreme Court about seven times by 1930, it was after this time that a concerted, systematic program of litigation began. The Legal Defense and Educational Fund was established as an autonomous arm of the NAACP and its efforts were directed at developing a substantial body of judicial rulings in the area of civil rights. It is not altogether clear whether, as part of well-developed strategy, a carefully chosen series of cases were utilized in attacking several major issue areas. According to Jeane Hahn, former Chief Counsel Marshall suggests that a clear-cut strategy was impossible because of the need to take cases as they developed.[18] In spite of this, the NAACP/LDF pursued a course of action in which cases which broke new constitutional ground on such issues as equal educational opportunities, "open" housing, and the right to vote were argued and favorable decisions obtained.

The issue of educational opportunities provides an illustration of the NAACP's use of the litigative strategy. Starting in 1938 in the case *Missouri ex rel Gaines vs. Canada,*[19] the NAACP/LDF began to petition the Supreme Court to ensure that in implementation of the separate-but-equal principle, education for blacks was indeed equal. As a practical matter, equality was never seriously contemplated by whites and existed nowhere, but specific abuses were attacked by the LDF. In the Missouri case, it challenged that states' practice of excluding blacks from its law schools and instead offering to pay for their attendance at out-of-state law schools. The Supreme Court invalidated the practice.

In a second major effort eleven years later, the issue was Texas' provision of an all-black law school which was obviously inferior to that

---

[16] This point of view is articulately stated by the NAACP/LDF's General Counsel, Jack Greenberg, *Race Relations and American Law* (New York: Columbia University Press, 1969).

[17] 238 U.S. 347 (1915).

[18] Jeane Hahn, "The NAACP Legal Defense and Educational Fund: Its Judicial Strategy and Tactics," in Stephen Wasby, *American Government and Politics* (New York: Scribner, 1973), p. 393.

[19] 305 U.S. 337 (1938).

available to whites. The Court ruled in *Sweatt vs. Painter* (1949)[20] that this was unconstitutional and ordered the state to admit blacks to its regular law school. Another discriminatory tactic employed against blacks and challenged in the courts was Oklahoma's practice of segregating black students in its graduate schools. This practice was invalidated by the Supreme Court in *McLaurin vs. Oklahoma State Regents* (1950).[21] In these challenges to discriminatory policies the NAACP left unchallenged the basic separate-but-equal principle. That step, taken after extensive debate and meticulous preparation of unprecedented proportions, resulted in the Court's favorable ruling in 1954. The NAACP's efforts in the area of education have not ended with the Brown decision but continue in a variety of complex issues ranging from the assignment of teachers in desegregated school systems to the issue of busing. The post-Brown efforts have been of two kinds: (1) efforts to ensure adequate implementation of the Supreme Court's decisions, and (2) resolving a variety of problems relating to the implementation of the Court's decisions.

Equal educational opportunity is only one of the many issues with which the NAACP/LDF has been concerned. Just as vigorously it sought to ensure the right of blacks in the South to vote, challenging a number of specific discriminatory practices and participating in challenges to the white primary before the courts. By 1950 it had argued about 49 cases before the Supreme Court and had secured favorable judgments in 42. With the wide-ranging activities of the 1960s its litigative activities increased further. According to Benjamin Muse, in 1963 alone the Fund's sixteen full-time attorneys and 102 cooperating attorneys across the country defended 10,487 citizens arrested in civil rights demonstrations and represented blacks in 30 cases before the Supreme Court.

These efforts, particularly those in the area of education, reveal at once the strengths and weaknesses of litigation as a means of inducing change. In its favor is the fact that it is highly system-supportive, nondisruptive and nonthreatening to most whites and thus did not arouse the immediate and widespread hostility from whites which other kinds of efforts might have evoked. This was important, especially when the level of public white hostility to any black advancement prior to the 1960s is considered. Second, litigation is a strategy that utilized effectively the kind of resources the organization had at its command—money and a strong legal staff—and the successes in terms of favorable court decisions have been frequent and consistent. Third, as Hahn suggests, through these activities the organization led in the development of a body of jurisprudence where none existed, thus providing a strong constitutional basis for further efforts by blacks to alter their subordinate status.[22] In a broader context the NAACP/LDF pioneered in developing a strategy whereby the politically weak minorities in the society

[20] 339 U.S. 629 (1950).
[21] 339 U.S. 737 (1950).
[22] Hahn, *op. cit.*, pp. 393–395.

can achieve desired policy decisions by petitioning the courts. Thus they have contributed markedly to the development of the Court's role as "national policy maker" and to the use of litigation as a form of lobbying.[23]

The drawbacks of the litigative effort are several. First, it is a slow and tedious process ill-suited to matters of great urgency. For example, in the area of voting rights the major assault against the white primary began in 1927, but it was not until 1944 that the practice was finally invalidated by the Court. Second, Court victories, in the short run at least, are often paper victories, since implementation of its decision may be delayed, circumvented, or even ignored for years. The Brown decision is a case in point: its basic principle remained unimplemented for years afterward because of both official and private hostility. Thus, while victories in the courts have been loudly applauded, often they have had very little impact on the lives of black people for a long time after.

Its shortcomings notwithstanding, the litigative effort of the NAACP has been vital to the overall struggle for change. Its most noteworthy contribution has been the gradual erosion of the constitutional "legitimacy" enjoyed by some of the most blatant and stultifying forms of racial oppression. Recognition by whites of this far-reaching impact led to vigorous legal attacks on the organization in several Southern states in an effort to end its litigative activities. These efforts were particularly prominent in Virginia where, according to Jeane Hahn, "new laws were passed and old laws amended, among which were the offenses of barratry, maintenance and champerty, or the unnecessary stirring up of litigation and judicial proceedings, the solicitation of litigants, and the intervention of third parties in litigation with an eye to pecuniary gain."[24] All of these challenges to the Organization eventually failed but they were nonetheless highly disruptive.

### Lobbying for Civil Rights

Simultaneous with its efforts on the judicial front, the NAACP has also pursued a vigorous program of lobbying in an effort to secure favorable legislative action on a wide range of issues of interest to blacks. It has attempted to meet directly with and persuade legislators, utilized its legal and regular field staff to help draft legislation in which it is interested, tried to influence the Congress indirectly by mobilizing supportive public opinion, and secured the support of other sympathetic interest groups. These efforts, which probably reached their peak with consideration of the Civil Rights Act on 1964

[23] For a discussion of the Court's role as policy maker see Robert A. Dahl, "Decision-making in a Democracy: The Supreme Court as a National Policy-Maker," *Journal of Public Law* **6**, 2 (1957), 279–295. For consideration of the NAACP's role see Clement E. Vose, "Litigation as a Form of Pressure Group Activity," *Annals of the American Academy of Political and Social Sciences* **319** (September 1958), 20–31.

[24] Hahn, *op. cit.* For a discussion of the barratry and other anti-NAACP laws of several Southern states, see Richard Bardolph, *The Civil Rights Record, Black Americans and the Law, 1849–1970* (New York: Crowell, 1970), pp. 383–386.

and the Voting Rights Act of 1965, began in earnest in 1921 as the organization undertook a vigorous campaign to secure federal antilynching legislation.

The NAACP, we have seen, came into existence largely in response to the widespread violence against blacks, but it soon became apparent that protection against lynching required federal legislative intervention, since state and local law enforcement agencies consistently ignored the problem. Following the introduction of an antilynching bill in the House of Representatives by Representative L. C. Dyer of Missouri at the urging of the NAACP, the Organization worked vigorously for its adoption. Their effort resulted in favorable House action but the bill failed in the Senate. For the next twenty years the NAACP worked sedulously for adoption of an antilynching bill without success.

Lobbying proved more successful in the NAACP's effort to prevent the confirmation of Judge John C. Parker of North Carolina as a justice of the Supreme Court in 1930. As a judge in North Carolina, Parker had been vocally hostile to blacks, at one time asserting that "the participation of the Negro in politics is a source of evil and danger to both races and is not desired by the wise men of either race or by the Republican Party of North Carolina." Viewing his appointment to the Court as a formidable threat to black advancement, the NAACP launched a massive and eventually successful campaign against Judge Parker.[25] A similar situation occurred when President Nixon nominated another Southern judge, G. Harrold Carswell, to a seat on the Supreme Court. Like Parker, Carswell had vigorously opposed black participation in politics and had participated in decisions which reflected an attitude hostile to blacks. In conjunction with several other groups, the NAACP successfully fought against Carswell's nomination. Other lobbying efforts such as those to ensure fair employment practices for blacks in the 1940s and to end the poll taxes and other obstacles to voting rights for blacks, proved much less successful, however.

Lobbying is a prominent and legitimate part of American political life and is utilized by a number of groups in the society, but blacks have had to face some rather formidable obstacles in utilizing it. One is the decentralized power structure of the Congress in which Southern legislators hold a large number of key positions of influence and have used them skillfully to frustrate black efforts to secure favorable legislation. Another is the Senate rule permitting unlimited debate which has been used often to obstruct the efforts of blacks in the Congress. Partly because of these obstacles it has been much easier for lobbyists on behalf of blacks to block action it considers unfavorable than to secure passage of favorable legislation.

The NAACP's lobbying efforts embrace a wide variety of issues from strictly civil rights legislation to personnel appointments requiring Senate confirmation or to United States relations with Africa. Appropriately its

[25] Gilbert Ware, "Lobbying as a Means of Protest: The NAACP as an Agent of Equality," *Journal of Negro Education* **33** (Spring 1964), 103–107.

techniques have varied from quiet advocacy (for example, its efforts to have the State Department increase its employment of blacks in key policy-making positions) to direct and indirect efforts or influencing legislation before the Congress. Since 1938 these efforts have been directed from the Organization's Washington, D.C., office headed by Clarence Mitchell III. Compared with other major lobbies, it is a modest operation. In order to maximize its impact—especially on traditional civil rights issues—it joined forces with a number of other lobbies in 1949 to form the Leadership Conference on Civil Rights. At the outset 20 major groups belonged to the Conference but by 1967 it had grown to 113 and included all the civil rights organizations, several labor organizations, church groups, and other bodies like the Americans for Democratic Action and the American Civil Liberties Union. Although this coalition proved very effective in working for general antidiscriminatory laws, it proved much less effective on issues like equal employment opportunities. The Nixon Administration's Philadelphia Plan, designed to improve employment opportunities for blacks in the construction and craft unions, was fought by organized labor, but supported by the NAACP.

In the legislative arena it is often difficult to assess victory and defeat in clear-cut, concrete terms. Issues are rarely resolved in terms of unequivocal decisions for or against one party but in terms of compromises, incremental gains, or degrees of success and failure. For example, over twenty years of effort to enact an antilynching bill failed, but it is more than coincidental that after the vigorous national debate of the issue in 1922, cases of lynching dropped sharply. The record of the NAACP in this arena must be seen as generally effective though certainly imperfect, and a crucial element in the political activities of blacks. A new dimension to lobbying by blacks has been added with emergence of the Congressional Black Caucus whose tactics, while different from those of the NAACP, are also geared to influence the policy process in areas of concern to blacks.

Evaluations of the NAACP and its years of efforts have been mixed. It is hardly contested that in spite of its diligence and effectiveness in pursuing its litigative and lobbying efforts, the broad strategy has important limitations. Some observers have been critical of the organization's unwillingness to consider alternatives to the struggle for total inclusion into the dominant white society. Others have been concerned with the elitist character of the organization which at times has evoked the suspicion and mistrust of the masses of blacks instead of their support. Two broader and more consequential shortcomings should also be observed. First, the organization's inflexible commitment to litigative and lobbying activities resulted in undue satisfaction with "formal victories," even though in most instances implementation was extremely slow in coming. Second, because most of its activities occurred out of public view it failed to contribute to the mobilization of the black population for political action.

Nonviolent Protest as Group Strategy

The NAACP has steadfastly maintained its firm commitment to the strategies it developed over the several decades of its existence despite a variety of pressures to reevaluate its basic goals and methods. Even while it still basked in the satisfaction of the *Brown* decision, a complex array of forces were propelling blacks toward new forms of organized and spontaneous group activities to achieve goals that continued to elude the race. The spark that ignited this new thrust was the arrest in Birmingham, Alabama, of Rosa Parks, a proud black woman who refused to yield her place on the city's segregated bus to a white person in 1955. Responding to this resolute defiance by Mrs. Parks, blacks undertook a boycott of the city's buses to force abolition of some of the indignities imposed on blacks on the segregated buses. The lengthy and occasionally bloody struggle which followed was resolved only after attorneys for the NAACP won a court order prohibiting racial segregation on public transportation, but the incident changed the mood of blacks. It created a new sense of determination and cohesiveness. Under the leadership of a then relatively unknown Reverend Dr. Martin Luther King, the "civil rights movement" came into being.

Actually, the utility of massive nonviolent demonstrations for the black struggle had been demonstrated more than a decade earlier when, in 1941, blacks led by A. Philip Randolph threatened a massive march on Washington, D.C., to protest their exclusion from jobs in war-related industries. In the face of this threat a reluctant Franklin D. Roosevelt responded with an Executive Order prohibiting racial discrimination in industries serving the federal government and established a Fair Employment Practices Commission to implement the order. A year later CORE began to undertake limited protest action against racial discrimination. It was, however, the Montgomery incident that established the viability of massive nonviolent direct action for basic civil rights. Out of the incident the Southern Christian Leadership Conference (SCLC) emerged under the leadership of Dr. King and became active in challenging a variety of long-standing discriminatory policies and practices throughout the South.

By 1960 another dimension was added to this new form of struggle as young blacks, mostly college students, quickly followed the lead of four students from North Carolina Agricultural and Technical State University who took their seats at the lunch counter of a local Woolworth store in Greensboro, North Carolina, and refused to leave until they were served. Subsequently "sit-ins," as they were called, became an important part of the nonviolent, direct-action movement. The scope of the effort is reflected in a report by the Southern Regional Council that between February 1960 and September 1961 sit-ins occurred in 20 states and more than 100 cities in Southern and border states and about 70,000 blacks and whites participated with 3,600 of them arrested.[26] The Student Non-violent Coordinating Committee, organized in April 1960, took the initiative in the sit-in activities. Another technique of nonviolent protest which emerged at this time was the "freedom ride." Here too thousands of black and white college students from all areas of the country challenged the segregation laws enforced in hundreds of bus terminals across the South by defying them. Thus these protest organizations together with the SCLC quickly and dramatically shifted the struggle for black rights from the state and federal courtrooms and from the cloakrooms of Congress to the streets, lunch counters, public parks, swimming pools, and bathing beaches of the Southern states. The direct confrontation between blacks determined to end the various offensive and crippling forms of discrimination and white mobs and law enforcement officials determined to preserve the status quo vividly dramatized to the entire population the dilemma of blacks and the dimensions of the injustices they experience. In hundreds of areas across the South the grim and often bloody confrontations occurred as the strategy of nonviolent protest was pitted against institutions and practices that had hitherto been immune to both judicial and legislative efforts.

The movement developed momentum rapidly, drawing into its ranks thousands of blacks and substantial numbers of whites from all over the country in a common struggle. In August 1963 it reached its peak when over 300,000 individuals joined in a dramatic pilgrimage to Washington, D.C., to demand justice and equality. Standing beneath the shadow of the Lincoln Memorial, Dr. King, at his most eloquent, articulated the profound optimism that characterized the struggle up to this point:

> I have a dream that one day this nation will rise up and live out the true meaning of its creed: "We hold these truths to be self-evident, that all men are created equal. . . ."
>
> I have a dream that one day on the red hills of Georgia the sons of former slaves and the sons of former slaveholders will be able to sit down together at the table of brotherhood.
>
> I have a dream that one day even the state of Mississippi, a state sweltering with the people's injustice, sweltering with the heat of oppression, will be transformed into an oasis of freedom and justice.
>
> I have a dream that my four little children will one day live in a nation where they will not be judged by the color of their skin, but by the content of their character.
>
> This is our hope. This is the faith that I go back to the South with. With this faith we will be able to hew out of the mountain of despair a stone of hope.[27]

[26] Lester A. Sobel, *Civil Rights, 1960–1966* (New York: Facts on File, 1967), p. 79.

[27] Quoted in Benjamin Muse, *The American Negro Revolution* (Bloomington: Indiana University Press, 1968), p. 16.

Emergence of the nonviolent protest movement was not accidental. It was an inevitable consequence of the increasing restiveness of the black population with their continued subordination in spite of decades of patient, largely quiet efforts for change and the lack of adequate resources with which to compel substantial change. In resorting to nonviolent protest blacks were utilizing a strategy uniquely adapted to their relative powerlessness and their deep conviction about the consistency of their objectives with the beliefs and values embraced by the society. Its effectiveness under these conditions had been demonstrated by the Indian leader, Mahatma Ghandi, in leading India's struggle against British colonial rule. In adapting the strategy to the situation in the United States Dr. King combined a moral commitment to nonviolence with a deep religious conviction about the positive power of love for the opponent even while engaged in struggle against him. Finally, the Movement was predicated on a firm belief in the basic morality and sense of justice of white America and on the conviction that, when confronted with the reality of their behavior and the extent of black oppression, whites would alter their behavior toward blacks. These and other basic premises of the movement were expressed by Dr. King thus:

1. Non-violent resistance is not a method for cowards; it does resist. If one uses this method because he lacks the instruments of violence, he is not truly non-violent. . . .
2. Non-violence does not seek to defeat or humiliate the opponent, but to win his friendship and understanding. . . . The end is redemption and reconciliation. . . .
3. A characteristic of this method is that attack is directed against forces of evil rather than against persons who happen to be doing the evil. . . .
4. Non-violent resistance is characterized by a willingness to accept suffering without retaliation, to accept blows from the opponent without striking back. . . .
5. Non-violent resistance avoids not only external physical violence but also internal violence of spirit. The non-violent resister not only refuses to shoot his opponent but he also refuses to hate him. . . .
6. Non-violent resistance is based on the conviction that the universe is on the side of justice. Consequently the believer in non-violence has deep faith in the future. . . .[28]

Although Dr. King managed to infuse large segments of the Movement with his philosophy of nonviolent resistance, there were those who embraced nonviolence primarily for tactical reasons, i.e., because the preponderance of power possessed by whites made resort to violence suicidal. In either case the strategy exacted enormous sacrifices from those who participated. Physical

[28] Martin Luther King, Jr., *Stride Toward Freedom* (New York: Harper & Row, 1958), pp. 102–107.

and verbal attacks by white mobs and the almost unrestrained brutality of police forces inflicted considerable pain and often loss of life but the movement persisted.

Inseparable from the nonviolent posture was the direct challenge to existing laws that were clearly designed to perpetuate black subordination through civil disobedience, a conscious, deliberate disobedience to these laws. Most of the peaceful demonstrations, sit-ins, and other forms of protest activity were in direct violation of local ordinances and challenged patterns of behavior that had long acquired the protection of the law. Such civil disobedience has a long and controversial history in Western social thought and, not surprisingly, proved equally controversial in the context of the civil rights struggle. The classic statement justifying the willingness and even the necessity to deliberately violate laws in the black struggle is a statement by Dr. King in response to a letter from a group of Alabama clergymen challenging his support for civil disobedience.

> You express a great deal of anxiety over our willingness to break laws. This is certainly a legitimate concern. Since we so diligently urge people to obey the Supreme Court's decision of 1954 outlawing segregation in the public schools, at first glance it may seem rather paradoxical for us consciously to break laws. One may well ask: "How can you advocate breaking some laws and obeying others?" The answer lies in the fact that there are two types of laws: just and unjust. I would be the first to advocate obeying just laws. Conversely, one has a moral responsibility to disobey unjust laws. I would agree with St. Augustine that "an unjust law is no law at all."
>
> Now, what is the difference between the two? How does one determine whether a law is just or unjust? A just law is a man-made code that squares with the moral law or the law of God. An unjust law is a code that is out of harmony with the moral law. To put it in the terms of St. Thomas Aquinas: An unjust law is a human law that is not rooted in eternal law and natural law. Any law that uplifts human personality is just. Any law that degrades human personality is unjust. All segregation statutes are unjust because segregation distorts the soul and damages the personality. It gives the segregator a false sense of superiority and the segregated a false sense of inferiority. Segregation, to use the terminology of the Jewish philosopher Martin Buber, substitutes an "I-it" relationship for an "I-thou" relationship and ends up relegating persons to the status of things. Hence segregation is not only politically, economically and sociologically unsound, it is morally wrong and sinful. Paul Tillich has said that sin is separation. Is not segregation an existential expression of man's tragic separation, his awful estrangement, his terrible sinfulness? Thus it is that I can urge men to obey the 1954 decision of the Supreme Court, for it is morally right; and I can urge them to disobey segregation ordinances, for they are morally wrong.

Let us consider a more concrete example of just and unjust laws. An unjust law is a code that a numerical or power majority group compels a minority group to obey but does not make binding on itself. This is *difference* made legal. By the same token a just law is a code that a majority compels a minority to follow and that it is willing to follow itself. This is sameness made legal.

Let me give another explanation. A law is unjust if it is inflicted on a minority that, as a result of being denied the right to vote, had no part in enacting or devising the law. Who can say that the legislature of Alabama which set up that state's segregation laws was democratically elected? Throughout Alabama all sorts of devious methods are used to prevent Negroes from becoming registered voters, and there are some counties in which, even though Negroes constitute a majority of the population, not a single Negro is registered. Can any law enacted under such circumstances be considered democratically structured?

Sometimes a law is just on its face and unjust in its application. For instance, I have been arrested on a charge of parading without a permit. Now, there is nothing wrong in having an ordinance which requires a permit for a parade. But such an ordinance becomes unjust when it is used to maintain segregation and to deny citizens the First-Amendment privilege of peaceful assembly and protest.

I hope you are able to see the distinction I am trying to point out. In no sense do I advocate evading or defying the law, as would the rabid segregationist. That would lead to anarchy. One who breaks an unjust law must do so openly, lovingly, and with a willingness to accept the penalty. I submit that an individual who breaks a law that conscience tells him is unjust, and who willingly accepts the penalty of imprisonment in order to arouse the conscience of the community over its injustice, is in reality expressing the highest respect for law.[29]

Undoubtedly the civil rights movement, emphasizing nonviolent protests in its various forms, dramatically altered the pattern of black-white conflict and contributed to far-reaching changes in race relations. In directly challenging specific and blatant forms of injustice, evoking ruthless repressive responses by local white law enforcement officials often in the view of national television audiences, the strategy aroused and embarrassed a hitherto unattentive public. Thus the first major effect of nonviolent protest was to mobilize whites into opposition to the excesses of Southern racists. A second effect of nonviolent protests was to transform what were traditionally "local issues" protected by the constitutional prerogatives of the states into urgent national issues requiring prompt federal responses. A third effect of nonviolent protest was to mobilize the black population to vigorous, determined participation in the struggle for the first time. Up to this time the black

[29] "Letter from Birmingham Jail," in *Why We Can't Wait* (New York: Signet, 1968), pp. 82–84.

masses were largely apathetic and uninvolved in efforts to induce change—in part because the arena of conflict was far removed from public view and unsuited to mass involvement. The extent of this new mass involvement is reflected in a nationwide survey in 1963 reported by *Newsweek* which indicated that 40 percent of blacks claim to have taken part in a sit-in, marched in a mass protest, or picketed a store.[30] Finally, the nonviolent protest effort resulted in the emergence of a new type of charismatic race leader to articulate the goals of the black struggle and to maintain a high level of continuing public attention to, and concern for, the struggle.

By 1965 the Civil Rights Movement, characterized by reliance on nonviolent protest in its various forms, began to decline rapidly, yielding to a new, more strident posture among blacks reflected in the controversial advocacy of "black power." Initially the new posture was repudiated by many—blacks as well as whites—as a distasteful form of black racism more detrimental than helpful to the black cause, but it was not to be dismissed. There were other evidences too that the movement and its principal leaders no longer had the impact of earlier years. While the reasons for this decline in the nonviolent protest are many and complex, a few of the more obvious ones can be suggested here.

First, the character of the movement was one reason for the change. The most blatant forms of racial discrimination existed in the South, and it was against these highly visible and humiliating symbols of subordination that the protests were directed. The movement was thus almost entirely a Southern movement geared to struggle against Southern style racism. This left untouched the ordeal of millions of blacks in the many urban centers of the North for whom poverty and social decay remained stark realities. To its credit, the SCLC recognized and attempted to remedy this situation by taking to cities like Chicago the strategies perfected in the South, but after repeated and largely unsuccessful efforts in Chicago and the creation of a subsidiary called "Operation Breadbasket," the problem remained largely unchanged, apparently not susceptible to protest techniques.

Second, the success of the protest effort may have contributed to its own decline. The leading protest organizations were very loosely organized and depended for their effectiveness on a high level of public involvement in, and commitment to, nonviolent action but public attitudes were changing rapidly. Between 1956, when the protest activities began, and late 1965, four civil rights bills were enacted into law at the national level and countless barriers to lunch counters, restaurants, and other public facilities were broken down. In these developments nonviolent protest activities played an important, in some cases, decisive role. To many whites the battle was over; for many others the gains already seemed too large, and to most of these individuals further protest activities were beginning to evoke boredom and

---

[30] Cited in Muse, *op. cit.,* p. 32.

even the type of hostility known as "white backlash." In sharp contrast to these attitudes, most concerned blacks were becoming increasingly disillusioned with the fruits of their efforts. It had become painfully apparent that the civil rights laws and other so-called victories would not immediately or substantially alter the plight of the impoverished and oppressed black masses. A painful reassessment of the situation and prospects for the future were thus inevitable. The clamor for black power was the first step toward a redefinition of their situation and the shift toward a new posture by concerned blacks.

Third, the Civil Rights Movement coincided with and contributed to a rapidly growing sense of identity, pride, and confidence among blacks. This new "sense of blackness" may be seen as part of the post-World War II development of nationalist consciousness among the nonwhite peoples of the world and particularly among black people. Several observers have suggested that the independence movement in Africa and the prominence of black statesmen on the international scene stimulated black Americans to greater efforts on their own behalf and to increased racial pride. The years of vigorous protest activities undoubtedly heightened this sense of pride and race consciousness among blacks, reflected in the reemergence of nationalist feelings and in the many themes of black pride and black self-reliance that became prominent at this time. This new set of emotions precipitated impatience with the shallowness of responses to blacks thus far and stressed the need for more extensive changes in the character of black-white relations. Thus this second major form of organized group effort set the stage for a third form.

### Violence and the Struggle for Change

Stokely Carmichael's initial advocacy of "black power" on June 25, 1966, as the immediate goal for blacks highlighted the severe internal strains which were developing in the nonviolent movement since the March on Washington. The black power concept, then still inadequately defined, represented a search by the younger and less patient elements of the Movement for new approaches to the struggle for change. Roy Wilkins, the NAACP's General Secretary, vigorously repudiated it, however, claiming that it was something that "can mean in the end only black death." Leaders of the Urban League and Southern Christian Leadership Conference refrained from a similar public display of hostility but clearly indicated their uneasiness with the concept. This controversy was only one reflection of the growing disenchantment with the civil rights movement among large segments of the black population. Another was the widespread urban violence that began in 1964 and by 1966 had transformed the character of the black struggle.

The most far-reaching civil rights law had just been enacted and national political leaders had hardly completed their self-congratulations when on July 16, 1964, Harlem erupted in two days of bloody riots. Similar outbursts soon followed in other cities and by the end of that summer fourteen cities had experienced serious racial disorders. There is no reliable single source of information on exactly how many such incidents have occurred since that time, but one source suggests that by the Summer of 1968 there had been about 329 major incidents of racial violence in 257 cities. During these incidents 52,629 participants were arrested and 220, mostly blacks, lost their lives.[31] Civil rights leaders found themselves no longer engaged in aggressive challenges to the racial order but were struggling to contain the sudden shift by blacks from relatively "circumspect" forms of group political activity to widespread civil disorders.

Most of the episodes of violence were spontaneous, triggered by encounters with the police in many cases. In almost all of these cases the violence was directed at the police and other symbols of governmental authority and at white-owned property in the ghettos. These spontaneous outbursts were followed later by sporadic, small-scale, calculated use of violence in response to specific grievances (such as police atrocities) and also reflecting a willingness to explore the feasibility of armed insurrection to achieve fundamental change. Almost as ominous as the actual violence, a rhetoric of violence gained prominence among young blacks. It emphasized America's tradition of violence within the society and asserted the determination to resort to violence if necessary to protect the black community and to secure fundamental change.

Expressions of willingness to resort to violence in pursuit of desired goals by groups like the Black Panthers, and the actual episodes of violence were shocking but certainly not new to American society. Scattered over the almost 400 years of black-white contact in America are countless episodes of violence by whites against blacks as well as by blacks who sought to alter their status in the society. Furthermore, as some studies have shown, blacks had, for a long time, asserted a willingness to resort to defensive violence. [32] Racial violence is only one of the many forms of essentially political violence in the society's history as several different groups at different times during the nation's history resorted to violence to achieve what they considered vital. This historical pattern notwithstanding, the society reacted with shock and anger to the outbursts of racial violence because they were unexpected, but also because of what was widely regarded as important strides forward by blacks.

We are not attempting here a detailed examination of the phenomenon of racial violence, the theoretical and conceptual aspects of which were examined in Chapter 2. Instead we will examine briefly some perceptions of

[31] Joe Feagan and Harlan Hahn, *Ghetto Revolts* (New York: Macmillan, 1973), p. 102.
[32] August Meier and Elliott Rudwick, "Black Violence in the 20th Century: A Study in Rhetoric and Retaliation," in Edward Greenberg et al., eds., *Black Politics* (New York: Holt, Rinehart & Winston, 1971), pp. 299–309.

the violence and some of its consequences for the black struggle. From a wide variety of sources an enormous literature on the racial violence of the last decade has developed and with it a variety of perspectives on why it occurred, what it means, and the kind of implications it is likely to have. Unfortunately, serious appraisals of how government has actually responded to the violence have been scarce and at best tentative.

### Perceptions of Racial Violence

The character and meaning of the racial violence has proved a particularly perplexing issue for both official investigators and the many individual scholars who have attempted analyses. For convenience we will place the many interpretations of racial violence of the last decade into three broad categories. First are those which attribute racial violence to the irresponsible, irrational behavior of a very few renegades, and rootless troublemakers or the "riff-raff" of the black community. This point of view was forcefully asserted by the McCone Commission, established to investigate racial upheavals in Los Angeles in 1965.[33] By attempting to separate the violence from "decent, law-abiding" members of the black community this approach depoliticized the violence, absolved the society at large of any responsibility for them and made them merely problems of law enforcement. This "riff-raff" theory of the violence was quickly repudiated by overwhelming evidence that actual participation in racial disorders was widespread and included a large proportion of serious, stable community members and that an even larger segment of the black population sympathized with the disorders and their participants.

The second approach attributes racial violence to certain characteristics of the society which evoke this form of response. At one level this approach focused on the specific surroundings in which blacks live, such as the lack of adequate housing, employment, and recreational facilities, as well as racial composition of the police force. The fact that violence occurred in widely differing communities without any apparent consistency in local characteristics suggested the need to focus on fundamental characteristics of the society as a whole. Thus some analysts have pointed to the pervasive racism within the society which systematically obstructs the efforts of blacks to improve their lot in the society. This interpretation does not dismiss the disorders as senseless, meaningless outbursts but views them as responses to conditions in which the entire society is implicated. Racial violence is thus perceived as a form of protest against these conditions.

Not surprisingly blacks and whites diverge sharply in their response to these interpretations. Several surveys of blacks who actually experienced racial disorders as well as larger samples of blacks overwhelmingly attribute the disorders to racial discrimination and deprivation while only a small

---

[33] Governer's Commission on the Los Angeles Riots, *Violence in the City*, p. 3. For a review of this interpretation see Feagan and Hahn, *op. cit.*, pp. 6–10.

fraction of whites shared this view. On the contrary, most whites attributed the violence to black extremists, criminals, and outside agitators.

The third view of the racial violence is primarily the product of an ideological posture held by a relatively small segment of the black population. It regards the racial violence as a form of rebellion similar to the colonial rebellions which resulted in independence for many former colonies. Thus the violence was not a demand for full inclusion into the society and correction of specific indignities, but for separation from it. Expressing this view, Robert Blauner observes that for blacks the riots were "an inchoate attempt to gain control over their community or turf," to rid themselves of the alien white presence in their communities.[34] This perspective is consistent with the perception of black America as an internal colony.

The first view of the violence has been thoroughly discredited by the accumulated evidence, but neither of the others can be dismissed in their entirety. It is apparent from surveys of the riot participants and of other blacks that they anticipated improvement in their situation and in race relations generally as a result of the violence. There is little evidence that the violence was perceived in revolutionary terms, and little reason to view the riots as revolutionary uprisings even if such an interpretation now appears attractive. They must be seen as part of the total process of struggle to alter the subordinate status of blacks within the society. However, the resort to violence by blacks is of special significance and cannot be viewed merely as protest with a tactical twist.

The racial violence of the 1960s represented first the full entrance of the ignored urban black masses outside the South into the struggle for a better life. The activities of the NAACP, we observed, involved primarily the black elite and middle class while the protest movement remained largely a Southern movement, neither being attentive to the problems of urban blacks. Second, the racial violence reflected a level of racial consciousness and sense of deprivation not hitherto experienced by the black masses. The nonviolent movement and the achievement of nationhood by the black peoples of Africa and the Caribbean contributed to this heightened consciousness of color and sense of deprivation. In conjunction with this attitudinal change there began to develop a sense of futility about efforts to secure change through the political system by those means considered legitimate by the society. The violence appears to have been, in part at least, a product of these forces. Finally, racial violence did in fact represent a qualitative change in the aspirations of many blacks. It was accompanied by the first widespread questioning by blacks of the long-standing aspiration for inclusion on virtually any terms. The rapid, widespread support for the black power concept and the pervasive demands accompanying the riots for greater autonomy for black

[34] Robert Blauner, "Internal Colonialism and Ghetto Revolt," *Social Problems* 16, 4 (Spring 1969), 399.

communities and the institutions that serve these communities are illustrative of this qualitative change among blacks. While it does not appear that the overthrow of "colonial control" and complete self-determination was a widely held objective, undoubtedly a critical view of white society and a desire to achieve far-reaching system changes became prominent aspects of the new viewpoint of blacks and were associated with the violence.

These observations suggest that outbreaks of racial violence of the past decade were essentially political events. Direct political implications have not been adequately examined, in large part because social scientists have persistently tended to view violence of this kind as uncharacteristic breakdowns in the system. In this regard David Olson observes that political scientists have persistently tended to equate successful democracy with stable democracy and thus view racial upheavals as aberrations rather than as political expressions.[35] Increasingly, if belatedly, anomic group behavior as well as the planned, largely symbolic uses of violence such as we have described are being given serious attention by social scientists as important forms of political activity.

### Official Responses to Racial Violence

It has been conceded by several scholars that political violence such as the racial upheavals may have important beneficial consequences for the political system and for the groups using it. Lewis Coser suggests, for example, that this kind of violence may be beneficial to a political system in three ways: it may serve as (1) a source of achievement to the participants; (2) as a signal to the society that there are dangerous discontents that must be remedied; (3) as a catalyst to achieve desired actions.[36] It has been much more difficult to assess its actual contribution to the black struggle, especially since there is little clear evidence of the extent and character of governmental responses to the violence. Unlike the litigative and protest efforts in which court decisions or legislative enactments were easily identified, responses to the violence have been more difficult to identify and evaluate.

In one of the very few thoughtful accountings of governmental responses to the riots, Joe Feagan and Harlan Hahn identify three basic types of official responses undertaken at the national, state, and local levels.[37] The first type of response has been establishment of investigatory boards or commissions, a step taken after every major period of racial violence during this century. Studies of these riot commissions—from that set up by Congress to investigate the East St. Louis Riot in 1917 to the National Advisory Commission on the Causes and Prevention of Violence established in 1968

---

[35] David J. Olson, "Black Violence as Political Protest" in Greenberg et al., *op. cit.*, pp. 274–275.

[36] Lewis Coser, "Some Social Functions of Violence," *Annals of the American Academy of Political and Social Sciences* 364 (March 1966), 8–18.

[37] Feagan and Hahn, *op. cit.*, pp. 239–259.

and including several state investigatory bodies—indicate that they have been remarkably similar in character, composed of lawyers and primarily present or former public employees.[38] While they have been helpful in gathering useful information about the upheavals, stimulating discussion of issues relating to the violence and offering recommendations for reform, there is doubt about their overall contributions to black advancement or to the improvement of race relations. One scholar suggests that these commissions may have served the interests of the dominant group and its entrenched elite by (1) helping politicians to avoid pressures to act promptly in response to riots, (2) giving to the public an impression that action is being taken, (3) whitewashing public institutions implicated in the disorders, (4) reaffirming public belief in the basic soundness of existing arrangements, and (5) supporting official inclination to respond to the violence with repression.[39]

The second type of response involves a wide range of steps of a repressive nature. These steps include creation of special units within the national government to cope with or prevent further disorders. The Directorate of Civil Disturbance and Planning within the Pentagon and the Civil Disturbance Group in the Justice Department are examples. Special programs for training national guardsmen and police in antiriot techniques, purchase of sophisticated law enforcement equipment, and the passage of antiriot legislation are other additional elements in the development of an apparatus of repression. At the national level, the addition of an antiriot section to the Civil Rights Act of 1968 and passage of an Omnibus Crime Control and Safe Streets Act of 1968 were the principal legislative steps to control riots. The Law Enforcement Assistance Administration (LEAA) created under the latter act administers a wide-ranging, lavishly financed nationwide program designed to inhibit further outbreaks of violence.

The third type of response to the violence involves social and economic programs to remedy conditions associated with the violence. In this area officials at all levels have been much less energetic in adopting new programs. Feagan and Hahn report in this connection that there have been very few new programs, and most visible responses have been primarily in terms of modest increases in existing programs like the Model Cities and Office of Economic Opportunity programs. Furthermore, they suggest, governmental responses have been haphazard and inconsistent even in expanding these programs in riot areas. While sharp increases in Model Cities and OEO programs were experienced in areas like Watts, indications are that some affected cities received only slightly increased aid and others even experienced declines. Thus, when the spate of public commitments to improvement subsided, there was little evidence of constructive responses by government. In fact, the

---

[38] Anthony Platt, "The Politics of Riot Commissions, 1917–1970: An Overview," in Anthony Platt, ed., *The Politics of Riot Commissions 1917–1970* (New York: Macmillan, 1971), pp. 11–19.

[39] Feagan and Hahn, *op. cit.*, p. 225.

destruction of several years ago remain, even in the Nation's capital, as grim monuments to official inaction.

Although the vast majority of whites were critical of, even hostile toward the racial upheavals, several of the few imaginative attempts to find solutions to some of the problems identified as a result of the violence came from the private sector. Several major national corporations attempted to assist in relieving the economic hardships of the ghettos. Robert Allen identifies among these efforts like the following: (1) The Xerox Corporation's sponsorship of a black self-help organization, FIGHT; (2) establishment of branch factories in black ghettos by Crown-Zellerbach Corporation, Aero-jet General, and Avco; (3) loans to black businesses from groups like Bank of America, Chrysler Corporation, and Prudential Insurance.[40] Scores of other private initiatives helped temporarily to ease the conditions in some areas in the aftermath of the riots. Unfortunately, most of these efforts were both limited and short-lived. They provided, at most, immediate sops to the discontented, and while the basic conditions remained unchanged the improvements soon disappeared.

Students of the black experience differ considerably in their appraisal of the varied forms of organized group activities we have described. Indeed, among concerned blacks, differences regarding the merits of these types of activities and the specific goals toward which they are directed have been a longstanding source of conflict. However, they need not be evaluated on purely ideological bases or viewed in "either-or" terms. Instead, they can be seen most profitably for our purposes as an interdependent sequence of political activities all aimed at altering the subordinate status of black people in America. They required commitment of somewhat different types of resources but there can be no doubt about the earnestness of the participants in each case and the value of their efforts. It is patently absurd for example to view the efforts of James Farmer or Stokely Carmichael, protest leaders, as "greater," "more meaningful," or "more productive" than those of Thurgood Marshall as NAACP/LDF legal counsel or Clarence Young III as lobbyist. The rights for which Farmer and Carmichael marched or otherwise agitated were initially affirmed in constitutional terms through the efforts of Marshall and were later made operational through legislation in which Mitchell's role was vital.

Although we have attempted to identify some of the strengths and weaknesses of these forms of group activity, it is difficult to assess with any precision the relative effectiveness of each one. It is sufficient to observe that they all contributed vitally to the degree of change achieved thus far. In addition to their contributions to the black struggle they must be credited with generally improving the quality of government for the entire society in at least two fundamental respects. First, they pioneered in developing tech-

[40] *Ibid.*, pp. 245–246.

niques by which powerless groups in the society can influence public policy. Through its persistent and imaginative litigative efforts, for example, the NAACP/LDF contributed to shaping the Supreme Court's role as national policy-maker and as a forum for the articulation of specialized interests. Today's widespread use of class-action suits is one of the major legacies of the Organization.[41] Second, the group activities of blacks have helped to significantly alter the structure of federalism. Specifically, they aided in breaking down the artificial barriers imposed by federalism to the dissemination of desired national norms and practices.

## SELECTED BIBLIOGRAPHY

Abramowitz, Jack. "The Negro in the Populist Movement." *Journal of Negro History,* 38 (July 1953), 257–289.
Aiken, Charles, ed. *The Negro Voter.* San Francisco: Chandler, 1962.
Anderson, William A. "The Reorganization of Protest: Civil Disturbances and Social Change in the Black Community." *American Behavioral Scientist* 16 (January–February 1973), 426.
Andrews, E. F. "Socialism and the Negro." *International Socialist Review* (March 1905), 524–526.
Barnes, Elizabeth. "Independent Politics: The Significance of the Black Panther Party." *Young Socialist* (Oct. 13, 1966).
Bell, Howard. "National Negro Conventions of the Middle 1840's: Moral Suasion vs. Political Action." *Journal of Negro History* 52, 4 (October 1957), 247–260.
Bell, Inge. *Core and the Strategy of Non-violence.* New York: Random House, 1968.
Beth, L. P. "The White Primary and the Judicial Function in the United States." *Political Quarterly* 29 (October–December 1958), 366–377.
Bickel, Alexander M. "The Voting Rights Bill Is Tough." *New Republic* 152 (Apr. 3, 1965), 16–18.
Black, Earl. "Southern Governors and Political Change: Campaign Stances on Racial Segregation and Economic Development, 1950–1969." *Journal of Politics* 33, 3 (August 1971), 703–733.
Blumenthal, Henry. "Woodrow Wilson and the Race Question." *Journal of Negro History* 48 (January 1963), 1–21.
Brewer, William M. "The Poll Tax and the Poll Taxers." *Journal of Negro History* 29 (July 1944), 260–299.
Brittain, J. M. "Some Reflections on Negro Suffrage in Alabama—Past and Present." *Journal of Negro History* 47 (April 1962), 127–138.
Buni, Andrew. *The Negro in Virginia Politics, 1902–1965.* Charlottesville: University Press of Virginia, 1967.
Burns, W. Hayword. *The Voices of Negro Protest in America.* New York: Oxford University Press, 1963.
Callcott, Margaret Law. *The Negro in Maryland Politics, 1870–1912.* Baltimore, Md.: Johns Hopkins Press, 1969.

---

[41] See Daniel Berman, *It Is So Ordered* (New York: Norton, 1966), pp. 30–32.

**Campbell, Angus.** *White Attitudes Toward Black People.* Ann Arbor, Mich.: Institute for Social Research, 1971.

**Carmichael, Stokely,** and **John Hulett.** *The Black Panther Party.* New York: Merit, 1966.

**Chafe, William.** "The Negro and Populism: A Kansas Case Study." *Journal of Southern History* 34, 3 (August 1968), 402–419.

**Clark, Kenneth B.** "The Civil Rights Movement: Momentums and Organization." *Daedalus* 96 (Winter 1966), 239–267.

**Clarke, James.** "Family Structure and Political Socialization Among Urban Black Children." *American Journal of Political Science* 17, 2 (May 1973), 302–315.

**Clubock, Alfred B., John M. DeGrove,** and **Charles D. Farris.** "The Manipulated Negro Vote: Some Preconditions and Consequences." *Journal of Politics* 26, 1 (February 1964), 112–129.

**Coates, Joseph F.** "Urban Violence—The Pattern of Disorder." *Annals of the American Academy of Political and Social Science* 405 (January 1973), 25–40.

**Cook, B.** "Black Representation in the Third Branch." *Black Law Journal* 260 (Winter 1971).

**Cornwell, Elmer E., Jr.** "Bosses, Machines and Ethnic Groups." *Annals of the American Academy of Political and Social Sciences* 353 (May 1964), 27–34.

**Coulter, E. Morton.** *Negro Legislators in Georgia During the Reconstruction Period.* Athens, Ga.: *Historical Quarterly,* 1968.

**Cox, LaWanda,** and **John H. Cox.** "Negro Suffrage and Republican Politics: The Problem of Motivation in Reconstruction Historiography." *Journal of Southern History* 33, 3 (August 1967), 303–330.

**Daniel, Johnnie.** "Changes in Negro Political Mobilization and Its Relationship to Community Socio-economic Structure." *Journal of Social and Behavioral Science* 13 (Fall 1968), 41–46.

**Daniel, Johnnie.** "Negro Political Behavior and Community Political and Socio-economic Structural Factors." *Social Forces* 47, 3 (March 1969), 274–280.

**De Santis, Vincent P.** "The Republican Party and the Southern Negro, 1877–1897." *Journal of Negro History* 45 (April 1960), 71–87.

**De Santis, Vincent P.** "Negro Dissatisfaction with Republican Policy in the South, 1882–1884." *Journal of Negro History* 36 (April 1951), 148–159.

**Douglas, Paul H.** "Trends and Developments. The 1960 Voting Rights Bill: The Struggle, the Final Results, and the Reason." *Journal of Intergroup Relations* 1 (Summer 1960), 86–88.

**Dunn, Charles W.** "Black Caucuses and Political Machines in Legislative Bodies." *American Journal of Political Science* 17 (February 1973), 148–158.

**Dyer, Brainerd.** "One Hundred Years of Negro Suffrage." *Pacific Historical Review* 37 (February 1968), 1–20.

**Ekstrom, Charles A.,** and **Thomas J. Kiel.** "Public Attachment in Black Philadelphia: Does 'Public Regardingness' Apply?" *Urban Affairs Quarterly* 8 (June 1973), 489–506.

Ellis, William W. *White Ethics and Black Power.* Chicago: Aldine, 1969.

Engstrom, Richard L. "Race and Compliance: Differential Political Socialization." *Polity* 3 (Fall 1970), 100–111.

Fenton, John, and Kenneth Vines. "Negro Registration in Louisiana." *American Political Science Review* 51 (September 1957), 704–713.

Form, William H., and Joan Huber. "Income, Race, and the Ideology of Political Efficacy." *Journal of Politics* 33, 4 (August 1971), 659–688.

Garfinkel, Herbert. *When Negroes March.* New York: Atheneum, 1969.

Gauntlett, John H., and John B. McConaughy. "Some Observations on the Influence of the Income Factor on Urban Negro Voting in South Carolina." *Journal of Negro Education* 31 (Winter 1962), 78–82.

Gauntlett, John, and J. B. McConaughy. "Survey of Urban Negro Voting Behavior in South Carolina." *South Carolina Law Quarterly* (Spring 1962), 365.

Gelb, Joyce. "Black Republicans in New York: A Minority Group in a Minority Party." *Urban Affairs Quarterly* 5, 4 (June 1970), 454–473.

Geschwender, Barbara, and James Geschwender. "Relative Deprivation and Participation in the Civil Rights Movement." *Social Science Quarterly* 45, 2 (September 1973), 403–411.

Gillette, William. *The Right to Vote: Politics and the Passage of the Fifteenth Amendment.* Baltimore, Md.: Johns Hopkins Press, 1969.

Gosnell, Harold F., and Robert E. Martin. "The Negro as Voters and Office Holders." *Journal of Negro Education* 32 (Fall 1963), 415–425.

Greenstone, David, and Paul Peterson. *Race and Authority in Urban Politics, Community Participation and the War on Poverty.* New York: Basic Books, 1973.

Greer, Edward. "The 'Liberation' of Gary, Indiana." *trans*action, 8 (January 1971), 30–39.

Grier, William H., and M. Cobbs Price. *Black Rage.* New York: Basic Books, 1968.

Hadden, Jeffrey, Louis Masotti and Victor Triesman. "The Making of the Negro Mayors, 1967." *trans*action 5, 3 (January–February 1968), 21–30.

Hainsworth, Robert W. "The Negro and the Texas Primaries." *Journal of Negro History* 18 (October 1933), 426–450.

Hamilton, Charles V. "Blacks and the Crisis of Political Participation." *The Public Interest* 34 (Winter 1974), 188–210.

Hannerz, Ulf. *Soulside: Inquiries into Ghetto Culture and Community.* New York: Columbia University Press, 1970.

Helmreich, William B. *The Black Crusaders: A Case Study of a Black Militant Organization.* New York: Harper & Row, 1973.

Holland, Lynwood M., and Joseph L. Bernd. "Recent Restrictions upon Negro Suffrage: The Case of Georgia." *Journal of Politics* 21 (August 1959), 487–513.

Holloway, Harry, and David M. Olson. "Electoral Participation by White and Negro in a Southern City." *Midwest Journal of Political Science* 10, 1 (February 1966), 99–122.

Houston, David G. "A Negro Senator." *Journal of Negro History* 7, 3 (July 1922), 243–256.

Jennings, M. Kent, and Harmon Zeigler. "Class, Party and Race in Four Types of Elections: The Case of Atlanta." *Journal of Politics* 28, 2 (May 1966), 391–407.

Kellogg, Charles F. *NAACP: A History of the National Association for the Advancement of Colored People.* Vol. 1, 1909–1920. Baltimore, Md.: Johns Hopkins Press, 1967.

Korolyova, A. "USA: Elections and the Black Movement." *International Affairs* (USSR) No. 10 (October 1972), 85–88.

Larson, Calvin J. "Socioeconomic Status and the Perception of Local Problems in a Black Urban Neighborhood." *Urban Affairs Quarterly* 7 (June 1973), 507–514.

Leggett, John C. "Working Class Consciousness, Race, and Political Choice." *American Journal of Sociology* 69 (September 1963), 171–176.

Lewis, Roscoe E. "The Role of Pressure Groups in Maintaining Morale Among Negroes." *Journal of Negro Education* 12 (Summer 1943), 646–673.

Linden, Glenn. "A Note on Negro Suffrage and Republican Politics." *Journal of Southern History* 36, 3 (August 1970), 411–420.

Litchfield, Edward H. "A Case Study of Negro Political Behavior in Detroit." *Public Opinion Quarterly* 5, 2 (June 1941), 267–274.

Lopata, Helena. "The Function of Voluntary Associations in an Ethnic Community: 'Polonia'," in Ernest Burgess and Donald Bogue, *Contributions to Urban Sociology.* Chicago: University of Chicago Press, 1964. pp. 203–223.

Lubell, Samuel. *White and Black: Test of a Nation.* New York: Harper & Row, 1963.

McLonaughy, John B., and John Gauntlett. "The Influence of the S Factor Upon the Voting Behavior of South Carolina Urban Negroes." *Western Political Quarterly* 16, 4 (December 1963), 985–1006.

Madron, Thomas. "Some Notes on the Negro as a Voter in a Small Southern City." *Public Opinion Quarterly* 30, 2 (Summer 1962), 279–284.

Matthews, Donald R., and James W. Prothro. *Negroes and the New Southern Politics.* New York: Harcourt Brace Jovanovich, 1966.

Matthews, Donald, and James Prothro. "Political Factors and Negro Voter Registration in the South." *American Poitical Science Review* 57 (June 1963), 355–367.

Matthews, Donald, and James Prothro. "Social and Economic Factors and Negro Voter Registration in the South." *American Political Science Review* 57 (March 1963), 24–44.

Meier, August. "Negro Protest Movements and Organizations." *Journal of Negro Education* 32 (Fall 1963), 437–450.

Meier, August. "On the Role of Martin Luther King." *New Politics* 4 (Winter 1964), 52–59.

Meier, August. "The Negro and the Democratic Party, 1875–1915." *Phylon* 17 (1956), 173–191.

Middleton, Russell. "The Civil Rights Issue and Presidential Voting Among Southern Negroes and Whites." *Social Forces* 40 (March 1962), 209–215.

**Minnis, Jack.** "The Mississippi Freedom Democratic Party." *Freedomways* 5 (Spring 1965), 264–278.

**Moon, Henry Lee.** *Balance of Power: The Negro Vote.* Garden City, N.Y.: Doubleday, 1948.

**Ogden, Frederick D.** *The Poll Tax in the South.* University: University of Alabama Press, 1958.

**Orbell, John.** "Protest Participation Among Southern Negro College Students." *American Political Science Review* **61**, 2 (1967), 446–456.

**Overacker, Louise.** "The Negro's Struggle for Participation in Primary Elections." *Journal of Negro History* **30** (January 1945), 54–61.

**Patterson, Beeman C.** "Political Action of Negroes in Los Angeles: A Case Study in the Attainment of Councilmanic Representation." *Phylon* (Summer 1969), 170–183.

**Pfantz, Harold W.** "The Power Structure of the Negro Sub-Community: A Case Study and a Comparative View." *Phylon* **23**, 2 (Summer 1962), 156–166.

**Pierce, John C., William P. Avery,** and **Addison Carey, Jr.,** "Sex Differences in Black Political Beliefs and Behavior." *American Journal of Political Science* **17**, 2 (May 1973), 423–430.

**Pierce, John C.,** and **Addison Carey, Jr.** "Efficacy and Participation: A Study of Black Political Behavior." *Journal of Black Studies.* (December 1971), 201–223.

**Pinard, Maurice, Jerome Kirk,** and **Donal Von Eschen.** "Processes of Recruitment in the Sit-In Movement," *Public Opinion Quarterly* **23** (Fall 1969), 355–369.

**Record, Wilson.** "Intellectuals in Social and Racial Movements." *Phylon* **15**, 3 (1954), 231–242.

**Record, Wilson.** "Negro Intellectual Leadership in the National Association for the Advancement of Colored People." *Phylon* **17**, 4 (1956), 375–389.

**Record, Wilson.** "The Development of the Communist Position on the Negro Question in the United States." *Phylon* **19** (1958) 306–326.

**Riddleberger, Patrick W.** "The Break in the Radical Ranks: Liberals vs. Stalwarts in the Election of 1872." *Journal of Negro History* **44** (April 1959), 136–157.

**Ross, Jack,** and **Raymond Wheeler.** "Structural Sources of Threat to Negro Membership in Militant Voluntary Associations." *Social Forces* **45**, 4 (June 1967), 583–586.

**Rudwick, Elliott M.** "The Niagara Movement." *Journal of Negro History* **42** (July 1957), 177–200.

**Salamon, Lester M.,** and **Stephen Van Evera.** "Fear, Apathy and Discrimination: A Test of Three Explanations of Political Participation." *American Political Science Review* **67**, 4 (December 1973), 1288–1306.

**Saunders, Robert J.,** and **Ronald L. Coccari.** "Racial Earnings Differentials: Some Economic Factors." *American Journal of Economics and Sociology* **32** (July 1973), 225–234.

**Seasholes, Bradbury.** "Political Socialization of Negroes: Image Development of Self and Polity," in William Kvaraceus, ed., *Negro Self-Concept:*

*Implications for School and Citizenship.* New York: McGraw-Hill, 1965.

Shaskolsky, Leon. "The Negro Protest Movement—Revolt or Reform." *Phylon* (Summer 1968), 156–166.

Sherman, Richard B. "Republicans and Negroes: The Lessons of Normalcy." *Phylon* 27 (1966), 63–79.

Sigel, Roberta. "Race and Religion as Factors in the Kennedy Victory in Detroit, 1960." *Journal of Negro Education* 31 (Fall 1962), 436–437.

Sloan, Lee, and Robert M. French. "Black Rule in Urban South?" *transaction* 9 (November–December 1971), 29–34.

Spicer, George W. "The Federal Judiciary and Political Change in the South." *Journal of Politics* 26 (February 1964), 154–176.

Strickland, Arvach E. *History of the Chicago Urban League.* Urbana: University of Illinois Press, 1966.

Strong, Donald S. "The Rise of Negro Voting in Texas." *American Political Science Review* 42, 3 (June 1948), 518–522.

Surace, Samuel, and Melvin Seeman. "Some Correlates of Civil Rights Activism." *Social Forces* 46, 2 (December 1967), 197–207.

Taylor, Alrutheus A. "Negro Congressmen, A Generation After." *Journal of Negro History* 7, 2 (April 1922), 127–171.

Taylor, Joseph H. "Populism and Disfranchisement in Alabama." *Journal of Negro History* 34 (October 1949), 410–424.

Tussman, Joseph, ed. *The Supreme Court on Racial Discrimination.* New York: Oxford University Press, 1967.

Van der Zandan, James. "The Non-Violent Resistance Movement Against Segregation." *American Journal of Sociology* 68 (March 1963), 544–550.

Von Eschen, Donald, Jerome Kirk, and Maurice Pinard. "The Disintegration of the Negro Non-violent Movement." *Journal of Peace Research* 3 (1969), 215–234.

Vose, Clement E. *Caucasians Only: The Supreme Court, the NAACP, and the Restrictive Covenant Cases.* Berkeley: University of California Press, 1959.

Walton, Hanes, Jr. *Black Political Parties: A Historical and Political Analysis.* New York: Free Press, 1972.

Walton, Hanes, Jr. *The Negro in Third Party Politics.* Philadelphia: Dorrance, 1969.

Walton, Hanes, Jr. "Black and Conservative Political Movements in the U.S.A." *Political Science Review* 10 (July–December 1971), 102–111.

Ware, Gilbert. "Lobbying as a Means of Protest: The NAACP as an Agent of Equality." *Journal of Negro Education* 33 (Winter 1964), 103–110.

Watson, Richard L., Jr. "The Defeat of Judge Parker: A Case Study in Pressure Groups and Politics." *Mississippi Historical Review* 50 (September 1963), 213–234.

Watters, Pat, and Cleghorn Reese. *Climbing Jacob's Ladder: The Arrival of Negroes in Southern Politics.* New York: Harcourt Brace Jovanovich, 1967.

Weeks, O. Douglas. "The White Primary, 1944–48." *American Political Science Review* (June 1948), 500–510.

Wehr, Paul E. "Nonviolence and Differentiation in the Equal Rights Movement." *Sociological Inquiry* 38 (Winter 1968), 65–76.

Williams, Allen Jr., Nicholas Babchuck, and David R. Johnson. "Voluntary Associations and Minority Status: A Comparative Status of Anglo, Black, and Mexican Americans." *American Sociological Review* 38, 5 (October 1973), 637–646.

Wolgemuth, Kathleen L. "Woodrow Wilson and Federal Segregation." *Journal of Negro History* 44 (April 1959), 158–173.

Wood, Forrest G. *Black Scare: The Racist Response to Emancipation and Reconstruction.* Berkeley: University of California Press, 1968.

Woodward, C. Vann. "Tom Watson and the Negro in Agrarian Politics." *Journal of Southern History* 4 (1958), 14–33.

Zangrando, Robert L. "The NAACP and a Federal Anti-lynching Bill, 1934–1940." *Journal of Negro History* 50 (April 1965), 106–117.

Zeitz, Leonard. "Survey of Negro Attitudes to Law." *Rutgers Law Review* 19, 2 (Winter 1965), 288–315.

Zinn, Howard. *SNCC: The New Abolitionists.* Boston: Beacon, 1965.

# Blacks and the Political System: Responses and Challenges

# 11

# Black Americans
# and the Policy Process:
# The Pattern of Response

Important changes have been taking place in many aspects of race relations in the society, and especially since 1957. Most of the rituals and symbols of black subordination have disappeared so that exclusion of blacks from public eating places, parks, theaters, and other public facilities is now more the exception than the rule. The major obstacles to black participation in the electoral process of the Southern states have now been largely removed and Governor George Wallace, who defiantly stood in the entrance to the University of Alabama to prevent admission of two black students a decade ago, participated in crowning that university's black homecoming queen in November 1973.

Observers disagree about the significance of these changes, especially since blacks still occupy the very bottom of the socioeconomic scale in the society and so have made little progress in improving the overall quality of life in relation to that of the entire society. Nevertheless, the changes are important and they reflect substantial successes of the many and varied forms of political activities in which blacks have been engaged over time. The objectives of this chapter are to examine briefly the way government has responded to the efforts by blacks to alter their subordinate status and to identify some of the obstacles to more profound change.

## The Pattern of Governmental Responses to Blacks

The difficulties involved in attempting to achieve far-reaching changes in the pattern of race relations in a society like the United States are enormous and probably have not been sufficiently emphasized. The pervasive and deep-seated character of racism within the society and a highly complex political system geared to preservation of the status quo in areas such as race relations are formidable obstacles to change. When these conditions are combined with the many disabilities under which blacks have participated in politics, deep and permanent change becomes even more difficult to achieve.

In reviewing the pattern of governmental responses to blacks, a few broad features of these responses must be emphasized at the outset. First, the federal structure of the political system and the relative autonomy of the three major branches of the national government shape both the character of black political activity and the manner in which racial issues are treated by the political system. We observed earlier that the basic structure of black subordination was maintained primarily by the power of state government while the national government indulged in a benign acquiescence. Black political activities to induce change in this structure of subordination have been directed at both levels of government, but the primary emphasis has been at the national level and has thus required modification in the distribution of power between the two levels of government. Furthermore, the complex issues surrounding black subordination involved several major constitutional questions that required judicial action as well as a wide range of legislative and executive or administrative actions. Often it has been necessary to approach each of these branches of the government separately and with specialized techniques in order to induce desired policy changes.

Second, although the efforts of blacks and sympathetic whites have been vital in bringing about change, these efforts have been most successful when aided by regional or partisan divisions in the white society. For example, the civil rights laws enacted since 1957 by Congress succeeded largely because they were perceived as applicable only, or primarily, in the South. When the issues changed from voting rights, discrimination in public facilities, and other "civil rights" issues traditionally associated with the South to effective integration of the public schools across the nation, attitudes changed rapidly. Traditional "friends of civil rights" quickly became vigorous opponents of "forced busing" and staunch advocates of the sacredness of the "neighborhood school." A quick review of national legislative action on issues involving race since the Civil War will reveal that in almost every case a North-South cleavage facilitated enactment.

Third, responses by government to demands for change in race relations have been primarily incremental adjustments to the status quo rather than full, decisive correction of clearly identified injustices. The long list of civil rights laws passed since 1957 demonstrates this pattern of incrementalism. Although the nature and extent of the problems to which blacks sought remedies were fully apparent well before 1957 when the first legislative action was undertaken, it required four subsequent attempts to respond in barely adequate fashion to the situation. In each instance, when severely pressured, policy makers responded by granting the minimum concessions considered feasible rather than by taking the actions necessary to solve the problem. Although this strategy of incrementalism can be viewed as a politically pragmatic approach to achieving change when public support is not clear and widespread, it may also be viewed as a classic technique of resistance to demand for change. Sufficient action is taken to temporarily mollify the discontent of those seeking change and convey to the public the image of a responsive government while in actuality the basic issues remain unresolved.

Finally, governmental responses to demands by blacks for change in the pattern of race relations have not been systematic and carefully planned, so that change is often hampered by administrative inefficiency, disorganization, and even deliberate bungling. These conditions are partly a result of the incrementalist approach whereby policies, and the provision for their implementation, are made in piecemeal fashion. One result of these conditions is that actual changes often lag far behind formal policy changes. Although these conditions are probably most apparent with respect to racial issues, they are reflective of the character of the political system and thus extend well beyond purely racial issues. Political systems generally, and the American political system in particular, routinely operate to preserve the status quo and to prevent change. Thus while it is relatively easy to obstruct efforts for change, it is considerably more difficult to secure extensive changes through the orderly operation of the political system. The struggle by blacks to achieve desired changes in public policies is thus of broader interest than is the black political experience; it sheds light on a vital and still problematic aspect of political life.

Except in a few trivial respects, the federal government remained unresponsive to blacks for generations. This changed gradually as each of the three major branches of government began to respond at different times and in different ways. In order to delineate the pattern and the limits of governmental responses, this chapter describes the activities of the three branches of government in contributing to policy changes, and explores some of the problems that limit the effectiveness of blacks in influencing the policy process. Finally, the chapter examines the enactment of the 1964 Civil Rights Act as a case in governmental response.

### Judicial Responses to Blacks

The federal courts occupy a prominent role in American society, resolving a wide range of controversies from the purely legal to those relating to vital social and political issues. This prominent and wide-ranging role is particularly apparent in the area of race relations and the struggle of blacks to alter their subordinate status in the society. The Court's involvement in the black struggle is of long duration, beginning prior to the Civil War and continuing to the present time. Its contributions to the struggle have not been consistently helpful, but during much of this century and especially since about 1938 it has been clearly responsive to the demands of blacks. Its responsiveness was particularly prominent during what has now been termed the "Warren Court"—that period of the Supreme Court between 1953 and about 1968 when Earl Warren served as Chief Justice.[1] What is particularly significant about the Court is that it began to respond to black demands well before blacks had significant access to the other branches of government.

The entire federal court system has been involved in the black struggle to varying degrees,[2] but for our purposes we will focus on the Supreme Court as the highest judicial body and the final authority in determining the scope and character of judicial action. Basic to our discussion is the view that the Court is a formidable force for inducing social change in the society even though its primary responsibility is to resolve disputes by the application of law. Concerned scholars are sharply divided about the extent to which law and judicial bodies can and do serve to induce social change. Some scholars view the law as a passive set of rules reflecting clearly established mores and values in the society, while others view it as a dynamic body of rules reflecting societal attitudes and values but also inducing changes in these attitudes and values.[3] With respect to the Supreme Court, most scholars agree that it does have considerable impact on the society and is a powerful agent of social change, although they concede considerable difficulties in ascertaining the full range of its impact.[4] These perspectives unavoidably affect perceptions of the role of the Court in bringing about change in race relations. The activities of the NAACP have been based on a strong conviction that law and the courts are powerful instruments of social change, and indications are that this view is now widely held throughout the society.[5]

Several characteristics of the Supreme Court contribute to its capacity to respond in significant ways to blacks and to serve as an instrument of change. The first of these is the formidable power (of judicial review) it possesses to interpret the constitution and to rule on the constitutionality of the acts of the other branches of the federal government and of the states. Vital to the alteration of their status in the society is the full application of

---

[1] Studies of the Warren Court are numerous. See for example Harold J. Spaeth, "Race Relations and the Warren Court," *University of Detroit Law Journal* 43 (1965), 255–272.

[2] Federal District Courts and Appeals Courts play a much more vital role in issue areas like civil rights and civil liberties than is often recognized. In the area of civil rights, for example, they apply the broad decisions of the Supreme Court to the specific controversies in their jurisdiction and thus control the speed and the degree to which Supreme Court decisions are implemented. For rather thorough examinations of the varied role of Federal Courts, especially in the South, see J. W. Peltason, *Fifty-Eight Lonely Men, Southern Federal Judges and School Desegregation* (Urbana: University of Illinois Press, 1971); Charles V. Hamilton, "Southern Judges and Negro Voting Rights: The Judicial Approach to the Solution of Controversial Social Problems," *Wisconsin Law Review* (Winter 1965), 72–102.

[3] These views are extensively explored in Joel B. Grossman and Mary H. Grossman, *Law and Change in Modern America* (Pacific Palisades, Calif.: Goodyear, 1971).

[4] For an extensive examination of the question of impact, see Stephen L. Wasby, *The Impact of the United States Supreme Court: Some Perspectives* (Homewood, Ill.: Dorsey, 1970), p. 14.

[5] Jack Greenberg, *Race Relations and American Law* (New York: Columbia University Press, 1959).

the rights, privileges, and protections of the Constitution to blacks, and in this respect the Court is uniquely qualified to respond through impartial interpretation of the constitution. Furthermore, the Court, more than any other political institution, possesses the capacity to protect the constitutional rights and interests of individuals and minority groups in the society when these rights are threatened.

Conditions under which the Supreme Court makes its decisions are a second factor of importance in its response to blacks. The Court is relatively isolated from the rigors of competitive politics (since its members are appointed and can be removed only for misconduct) and thus enjoys substantial freedom to make decisions on the merits of the issue rather than in response to direct political pressures—as is usually the case with elected officials like the President or members of Congress. This independence also enables the Court to be bolder than the more politically vulnerable institutions in seeking to change public attitudes and values when such changes clearly serve the interest of justice. Not that the Court can safely ignore public sentiment in its decision making; on the contrary, its effectiveness is enhanced by its ability to remain sensitive to public attitudes. Indeed there is considerable evidence that the Court's decisions are often shaped by its perception of public attitudes.[6] Clearly, however, it need not yield to the prejudices of the masses to the detriment of substantial segments of the society. Other equally important conditions of decision making are the strict decorum of the Court, the presentation of contending views in a formal, apolitical manner, and the absence of devices for obstructing final decision making.

The extraordinarily high level of prestige enjoyed by the Supreme Court is a third factor contributing to its capacity to induce change in race relations. There have been periodic criticisms of the Court and some of its decisions (the "Impeach Earl Warren" campaigns is an example) but respect for the Court as an institution has remained high and its decisions generally have been accorded a large measure of public support. In this regard Wasby observes that "tradition and its high place within the government have over time given the Supreme Court an aura of sanctity."[7] With this kind of prestige, its pronouncements on racial issues have considerable force even when, as in the Brown decision, they are sometimes resisted.

These distinct characteristics of the Court contributed to its relatively early favorable responses to blacks. By favorable responses we mean judgments affirming the position of black litigants on important constitutional and policy questions. One of the first of these in this century was *Guinn vs. United States* when it invalidated the Grandfather Clause.[8] Since that time,

---

[6] Robert Dahl has demonstrated that the Court usually is both attentive to and responsive to the policy views of the lawmaking elites. "Decision-making in a Democracy: The Supreme Court as a National Policy Maker," *Journal of Public Law* 6 (1958), 187–196.

[7] Wasby, *op. cit.*, p. 14.

[8] *Guinn vs. United States* 238 U.S. 347 (1915).

and especially since the Gaines decision in 1938, it has rendered a long series of favorable decisions in areas such as voting rights, discrimination in education, and the housing market. The cumulative effect of these decisions was to substantially alter national policies on segregation and racial discrimination. These favorable actions were particularly noteworthy because the Court provided the only national policy-making arena then available to blacks.

Gradually, the Court developed what came to be widely perceived as an activist posture on racial issues as well as on a broad range of other social issues. With this recent background of social activism, its role as a "champion of civil rights" has been firmly established in the public view, especially among blacks. Studies of public perceptions and evaluations of the Court are still largely fragmentary but there are indications that especially during the early 1960s blacks were overwhelmingly favorable in their evaluations of its role on civil rights. One national survey reveals that in 1963, 80 percent of the black sample perceived the Court's role on civil rights as helpful while only 2 percent disagreed. By 1966 those evaluating it positively had dropped to 65 percent, probably reflecting the shift in civil rights activity to the legislative arena.[9] More recent studies continue to find among blacks a highly positive image of the Court,[10] although one of the most penetrating studies of public attitudes toward the Court found that a large proportion of the black population are unaware of its role in civil rights.[11]

In spite of its recent record and public image, one must be careful not to gravely overestimate the total performance of the Supreme Court in facilitating black advancement. Its responsiveness to blacks is impressive only when viewed against the early performance of the executive and legislative branches of government. A responsible appraisal of its contributions requires that we note at least two important caveats. First, although its responsiveness to blacks since 1915 is commendable, the Court has merely been undoing, slowly and equivocally, the enormous damage it inflicted on blacks for decades prior to that time. It should be borne in mind that, with awesome finality, it permanently barred blacks from membership in the political community in its *Dred Scott* decision of 1858 (discussed in Chapter 5). In a series of decisions starting shortly after the Civil War the Court diligently and methodically emasculated the Fourteenth Amendment as it related to blacks and stymied efforts of the national government to protect the rights and the person of blacks. In *Slaughter House* it rendered the privileges and immunities

---

[9] William Brink and Louis Harris, *Black and White America* (New York: Simon & Schuster, 1967), p. 127.

[10] Herbert Hirsch and Lewis Bowman, "A Note on Negro-White Differences in Attitudes Toward the Supreme Court," *Social Science Quarterly* 49, 3 (December 1968), pp. 557–562.

[11] Walter F. Murphy and Joseph Tanenhaus, "Public Opinion and the United States Supreme Court: A Preliminary Mapping of Some Prerequisites for Court Legitimation of Regime Change," in Joel B. Grossman and Joseph Tanenhaus, *Frontiers of Judicial Research* (New York: Wiley, 1969), pp. 284–285.

section of the Fourteenth Amendment ineffective in protecting blacks from discrimination by state governments, and continued this trend in the Civil Rights Cases by denying to Congress the power to legislate against discrimination in public accommodations. In *United States vs. Harris 1883* the Court held the equal protection principle of the Fourteenth Amendment to be limited to prohibiting discriminatory state action only but not requiring a state to prevent discrimination,[12] and in *Plessy* it affirmed the constitutionality of "separate but equal" laws. Clearly therefore what the Court has been doing on behalf of blacks—or more precisely its greater willingness in recent years to extend basic constitutional protection to blacks—is merely an undoing of the formidable obstacles to black advancement which it helped to erect.

A second caveat which must be emphasized is that even when the Court's decisions have been favorable to blacks, these decisions sometimes remain ineffective for a long time because of inadequate implementation. Because it lacks the capability to enforce its decisions, the Court must rely on lower federal and state courts as well as state and local administrators and law enforcement officials for implementation of its decisions. Often these bodies deliberately attempt to delay or circumvent unpopular decisions, thereby nullifying the impact of the Court's decision. An equally significant impediment to effective enforcement is the unjustified hesitancy and equivocation of the Court in ordering compliance with its decisions.

The 1954 *Brown* decision, which was still uninforced in most of the affected school districts more than a decade later, demonstrates the operation of all of these factors. Having found "separate educational facilities inherently unequal" and a violation of the constitutional right of blacks, the Court failed to forthrightly order an end to the practice. Instead it placed enforcement responsibility in the hands of school officials and local federal district courts, merely requiring them to proceed with "all deliberate speed." This course of action rested on the assumption that Southern school officials who had so diligently created and defended the segregated school systems would proceed in good faith to dismantle these systems and integrate the schools. It also assumed that local federal district court judges in the South would conscientiously enforce the decision. Both assumptions were clearly unfounded. Like most Southern school officials, the judges are in most cases committed defenders of a segregated society. Unlike Supreme Court judges who are drawn from across the nation largely at the discretion of the President and examined by the Senate with substantial care before confirmation, federal district judges are usually local individuals recommended by a state's senior senator. This process, known as "senatorial courtesy," ensures that only individuals acceptable to local politicians are appointed to the federal courts.

[12] *United States vs. Harris* 92 U.S. 214 (1876).

The Court's equivocation along with popular hostility to the decision resulted in almost twenty years of delay and subterfuge throughout the nation. The classic case of resistance was that in Virginia, where the state government, local courts, and school officials all cooperated in delaying implementation by permitting the governor to close integrated schools, abolishing compulsory school attendance rules, and in the case of Prince Edward County, completely closing the public schools for years while white children attended private schools.[13] The Court eventually firmed up its position on the question of school desegregation in the South and in *Alexander vs. Holmes* (1969)[14] held that a standard of "all deliberate speed" for desegregation is no longer permissible. This ruling came, however, after substantial progress had been achieved through administration of Title VI of the 1964 Civil Rights Act. In dealing with so-called *de jure* racial segregation outside the South (segregation allegedly resulting not from specific policy decisions but from residential patterns) it was again slow in taking a definitive stand, finally doing so in *Swann vs. Charlotte-Mecklenberg*, ruling that school authorities were required to do whatever is necessary, including busing to end segregation in the schools.[15]

In one early, forthright criticism of the Court's role on racial matters Lewis M. Steel, a former NAACP/LDF attorney, observes that the Supreme Court has been unnecessarily timid in its rulings, being more attentive to the sensitivities of whites (who are fearful that equality for blacks will affect them adversely) than it is to the rights of blacks. Steel points out that in equally controversial nonracial issues such as malapportionment and religion in the public schools it has been consistently more forthright. On racial issues, however, the Court "has waltzed in time to the music of the white majority— one step forward, one step backward and sidestep, sidestep."[16] Thus, even though the Court's role in the black struggle is a vital, and on balance positive one, its powers certainly have not been consistently and fully utilized to induce fundamental change in the status of blacks.

It should be noted that discussions of the role of the Courts in the black struggle can easily be misleading if we ignore the part played by the lower federal courts. Their role is clearly vital in issue areas like civil rights and civil liberties, for they apply the broad decisions of the Supreme Court to specific controversies in their jurisdiction and thus control the speed and degree to which Supreme Court decisions are implemented. In numerous instances their decisions stand, since relatively few cases are appealed to the Supreme Court. Blacks have been much less successful in these lower courts than is generally assumed. Jack Peltason's study of these courts in the South

[13] See Bob Smith, *They Closed Their Schools: Prince Edward County, Virginia 1951–1964* (Chapel Hill: University of North Carolina Press, 1965).
[14] *Alexander vs. Holmes* 396 U.S. 19 (1969).
[15] *Swann vs. Charlotte-Mecklenberg Board of Education* 402 U.S.1 (1971).
[16] Lewis M. Steel, "Nine Men in Black Who Think White," in Barry Schwartz and Robert Disch, eds., *White Racism* (New York: Dell, 1970), pp. 362–372.

indicate that just over 50 percent of the cases on racial issues brought before Southern federal courts were resolved in favor of blacks. He found that the local background of judges and their religious and political party affiliation affected their responses to racial issues.[17]

### Executive Responses to Blacks

A considerable part of the political activities of blacks has been directed toward the executive branch of government. The rationale for this focus is obvious because the Presidency, and the bureaucracy within its jurisdiction, are vital elements in the policy process. Not only is the Executive charged with responsibility for the enforcement or implementation of public policy, it is also a vital part of the policy-making process, providing most of the initiative and expertise necessary in policy formulation. With this recognition, black political activity focused on the Executive even before any serious efforts to utilize the courts were contemplated. In assessing the extent and character of Executive responses to blacks we will, for convenience, distinguish between those directly involving the Presidency and those involving the federal bureaucracy.

### *The Presidency*

The Presidency is clearly a pivotal institution in the efforts by blacks to achieve fundamental change in the society. Except for that brief post-Civil War period ending in 1880 when the Congress was actively involved in the problems of reconstruction in the South, those blacks who possessed the right to vote focused their attention on Presidential elections. They searched, often in vain, for indications of a sympathetic attitude toward them and their problems in the remarks of Presidential candidates or sought eagerly for minor patronage posts as rewards for their electoral support. As the discussion in Chapter 9 indicates, although blacks were overwhelmingly Republicans, they at times deserted the party to support a Presidential candidate who appeared sympathetic. Until quite recently, however, Presidential responses to blacks were limited to relatively insignificant patronage appointments or the occasional gesture of meeting with groups of "prominent" blacks. Efforts to enlist Presidential support for specific policy changes failed consistently. For example, in 1940 FDR rejected appeals by blacks to support antilynching legislation in Congress. His 1941 Executive Order creating a Fair Employment Practices Commission was the first direct Presidential response to blacks, and it came about in the face of a threat by A. Philip Randolph to lead a massive march on Washington, D.C., to protest racial discrimination in wartime industries.

Over the years presidents became gradually more attentive and respon-

---

[17] Kenneth Vines, "Federal District Judges and Race Relations Cases in the South," *Journal of Politics* 26, 2 (May 1964), 337–357.

sive to blacks. It was not, however, until the Truman administration that a president managed to forthrightly assert his commitment to "equality" for blacks. Like several national politicians before him, Truman had sought earlier to limit his concern to "the constitutional rights of Negroes," considered then to include only "legal" and "political" rights, not full social equality. In this connection he told a 1940 meeting of the NAACP that "I wish to make clear that I am not appealing for social equality of the Negro. The Negro himself knows better than that, and the highest types of Negro leaders say quite frankly that they prefer the society of their own people. Negroes want justice, not social relations."[18]   By 1947, as President, he appeared to go further, suggesting to the 38th NAACP Annual Conference that "Our immediate task is to remove the last remnants of the barriers which stand between millions of our citizens and their birthright. There is no justifiable reason for discrimination because of ancestry, or religion, or race, or color."[19] Eisenhower equivocated on the subject, refusing even to publicly endorse the Supreme Court's *Brown* decision. After a surprisingly long period of equivocating, John F. Kennedy clearly and forthrightly presented the case for full equal rights for blacks, noting in a February 1963 message to Congress that

> Race discrimination hampers our economic growth by preventing the maximum development and utilization of our manpower. It hampers our world leadership by contradicting at home the message we preach abroad. It mars the atmosphere of a united and classless society in which this nation rose to greatness. It increases the costs of public welfare, crime, delinquency and disorder. Above all it is wrong.
> Therefore, let it be clear, in our hearts and minds, that it is not merely because of the Cold War, and not merely because of the economic waste of discrimination, that we are committed to achieving true equality of opportunity. The basic reason is because it is right.[20]

Presidential rhetoric can often be safely dismissed as empty, self-serving assertions, but when Presidential expressions on the race issue are examined over several decades, they do reflect a pattern of painfully slow but significant change in attitudes toward blacks. We can observe the slow transition from the outright hostility of Andrew Johnson toward any change in the legal status of blacks to the aloof indifference of Cleveland, Teddy Roosevelt, and Wilson through the mild endorsement of carefully stipulated *legal rights* from Harding to Franklin Roosevelt, to the more forthright stances of Kennedy and Johnson for full equality.

[18] Quoted in William C. Berman, *The Politics of Civil Rights in the Truman Administration* (Columbus: Ohio State University Press, 1970), p. 12.
[19] *Public Papers of the President of the United States: Harry S. Truman, 1945–1953* (Washington, D.C.: Government Printing Office) [8 vols., 1961–1966]; 1947, p. 311.
[20] *Congressional Record*, 88th Cong., 1st Sess., Feb. 28, 1963, p. 3245.

Table **11.1** *Population Distribution and Change, Inside and Outside Metropolitan Areas: 1960, 1970, and 1973*
(Numbers in Thousands)

| Area | Black | | | White | | |
|---|---|---|---|---|---|---|
| | *1960* | *1970* | *1973[a]* | *1960* | *1970* | *1973[a]* |
| United States | 18,872 | 22,580 | 23,189 | 158,832 | 177,749 | 179,574 |
| Metropolitan areas | 12,741 | 16,771 | 17,619 | 105,829 | 120,579 | 120,631 |
| Inside central cities | 9,874 | 13,140 | 13,868 | 49,415 | 49,430 | 47,206 |
| Outside central cities | 2,866 | 3,630 | 3,751 | 56,414 | 71,148 | 73,425 |
| Nonmetropolitan areas | 6,131 | 5,810 | 5,570 | 53,003 | 57,170 | 58,943 |
| Percent Distribution | | | | | | |
| United States | 100 | 100 | 100 | 100 | 100 | 100 |
| Metropolitan areas | 68 | 74 | 76 | 67 | 68 | 67 |
| Inside central cities | 52 | 58 | 60 | 31 | 28 | 26 |
| Outside central cities | 15 | 16 | 16 | 36 | 40 | 41 |
| Nonmetropolitan areas | 32 | 26 | 24 | 33 | 32 | 33 |

[a] Five quarter average centered on April 1973. Quarterly estimates for the months of October 1972, and January, April, July, and October 1973 were used. These figures do not include annexations since 1970. See "Definitions and Explanations" section for more details.
Source: *The Social and Economic Status of the Black Population in the U.S., 1973* (Washington, D.C.: U.S. Department of Commerce, 1974), p. 11.

While the forces contributing to this gradual change are many and complex, a few are prominent and worthy of note. First is the steady increase in the size and strategic location of the black voting population. With the exception of Richard Nixon, the publicly expressed attitudes of major Presidential candidates toward blacks appears to have improved steadily as black votes became more crucial to the outcome of Presidential elections. Second are changes in the international system, especially the emergence of the largely nonwhite Third World, where the United States sought to develop and maintain its influence in the face of vigorous competition from the Communist world for the friendship and support of these people. These prompted Presidential concern with the embarrassing political problems of continued black subordination. Third are the initiatives by the Supreme Court, the increasing determination of blacks, and the threats that continued subordination posed to domestic tranquility which made it essential that the President take a forthright stand in support of the aspirations of blacks. Largely as a result of these developments, presidents have been more willing to utilize the tools at their disposal in response to blacks.

The Executive Order, first used reluctantly in 1941, has become one important instrument by which presidents have sought to induce limited policy changes. Between June 1941 and September 1965, Executive Orders were used fourteen times on matters relating to the rights of blacks, notably to increase employment opportunities in industries performing services for the government and to reduce discrimination against blacks in the sale or rental of certain types of housing. Perhaps the most far-reaching use of the Executive Order was in the official desegregation of the Armed Forces by President Truman in 1948.[21] Executive Orders have been particularly useful because they require decision by the President only and do not involve lengthy and, as far as some presidents are concerned, politically dangerous deliberation by the Congress. The Executive Order is a very limited instrument, however, because it can be utilized only with respect to issues in which the President already possesses broad constitutional or statutory powers to act.

The increasingly prominent leadership role of the President in the legislative arena has also provided opportunities for significant contributions on race-related public policies. I suggested earlier that Presidential candidates increasingly have found it advantageous to express support for policies designed to improve the status of blacks in the society. Campaign or platform statements rarely are transformed into policy after elections, but they set the level and tone of national debate on policy issues and thus indirectly prepare the way for desired action afterward. More significantly, through regular messages to Congress such as the annual State of the Union and Economic Messages or through special messages identifying specific national problems and proposing legislative action, the President can place before the Congress policy proposals vital to blacks. No president undertook such an effort, however, until Harry Truman's February 2, 1948 message to Congress in which he offered eight specific civil rights proposals stemming from the report of the Truman Commission established in 1946 to investigate race relations.[22]

The President's role in the legislative process goes beyond merely proposing issues for action by Congress to include mobilizing Congressional support for his proposals. Thus, depending on the extent of his commitment to his policy proposals, the President may attempt to secure favorable legislative action by enlisting the support of party loyalists, trading specific favors for legislative support, and utilizing the resources of the bureaucracy in lobbying for favorable action. This is demonstrated in the activities of Presidents Kennedy and Johnson. Kennedy relied heavily on the lobbying activities of his brother Robert and on other Justice Department officials, while Johnson utilized his now legendary skill in prodding and persuading Congress in seeking favorable legislative action on civil rights.

The President's appointive powers provide another important resource that may be utilized to aid the struggle by blacks. The quality and orientation of his judicial and bureaucratic appointees determine in several crucial re-

---

[21] *Public Papers of the President of the United States: Harry S. Truman 1948*, p. 122. For a discussion of this see William C. Berman, *The Politics of Civil Rights, op. cit.*, pp. 79–136.
[22] *Ibid.*

### "YOU CAN'T HAVE A BALANCED COURT IF THEY *ALL* BELIEVE IN CIVIL RIGHTS."
2/13/70

from *Herblock's State of the Union* (Simon & Schuster, 1972)

spects the character of actual governmental responses to blacks. When individuals are appointed who are insensitive or hostile to the rights and interests of blacks they make it considerably more difficult for blacks to achieve policy changes or to have these changes implemented. This has been most notable with respect to judicial appointments at all levels of the federal court system. President Nixon's appointment of Clement Haynsworth and G. Harrold Carswell were vigorously fought by the NAACP and other interested groups in part because the past statements and judicial record of these appointees revealed clear insensitivity or even hostility to the rights of blacks.[23] President Kennedy's appointment of federal district judges in the South like Harold H. Cox of Mississippi and E. Gordon West of Louisiana are sad examples of the negative impact of the appointive power when used injudiciously. Of course, such appointments are often not entirely the Presi-

---

[23] See Joel Grossman and Stephen Wasby, "Haynsworth and Parker: History Does Live Again," *South Carolina Law Review* 23, 3 (1971), 345–359. See also Joel Grossman and Stephen Wasby, "The Senate and Supreme Court Nominations: Some Reflections," *Duke Law Journal* 1972, 3 (August 1972), 557–594.

dent's doing. In Kennedy's case he was clearly a victim of the principle of Senatorial courtesy which permitted Senators from the states involved to have the preponderant voice in the appointments.

Another dimension of the use of the appointive power involves the appointment of blacks to influential judicial and bureaucratic roles. Such appointments are crucial to blacks because they provide evidence that, even to a modest extent, they are part of the political community. More importantly black appointees bring to the decision-making arena the interests and perspectives of blacks. Until recently presidents flinched from such appointments largely out of deference to the racist sentiment of the society, traditional opposition from Southerners (when confirmation is required) and their own lack of sensitivity to the importance of significant and visible black involvement in the policy process. Thus only since the 1960s—especially since 1964—have blacks achieved a number of "breakthroughs" in appointments in the national government.

The informal influence and leadership potential of the Presidency is perhaps the most difficult to evaluate of the tools at the disposal of the President, although it is no less important than the more formal, constitutionally based powers. The leadership potential of the office has grown steadily over time and the vigor and effectiveness with which it is used often has depended on the individual occupying the office. Without doubt, however, the Presidency is the most prestigious public office in the society (assuming that it recovers from Watergate) and the one with the greatest capacity to provide national leadership. Thus it ordinarily provides a uniquely prominent base from which to lead the nation out of the morass of ignorance, irrational hate or blind unconcern that combine to perpetuate black subordination. By his own action in the conduct of the nation's business and through public exhortations, the President may therefore contribute significantly to the end of black subordination.

That the capacity of the Presidency has not been fully exploited on behalf of blacks is obvious. For a long time presidents flatly refused to undertake anything more than the most inconspicuous kinds of action sought by blacks. Even within recent years when the black electorate has become a vital element in national politics presidents often have substituted impressive public statements for decisive action. For example, in his campaign for the Presidency in 1960, John F. Kennedy promised to end discrimination in all federally assisted housing "with the stroke of the Presidential pen." However, after being elected to office with crucial support from blacks, he avoided any such action for almost two years. When he finally issued an Executive Order on November 20, 1962, he acted after prodding by civil rights leaders (an "Ink for Jack" campaign was mounted by some groups in which the White House was deluged with bottles of ink for the Presidential pen) and by the United States Commission on Civil Rights. Even then, the Order was much more restricted than that recommended by the Commission.

**LATEST COMMUNIQUÉ FROM
THE WHITE HOUSE SHELTER**
3/5/70

from *Herblock's State of the Union* (Simon & Schuster, 1972)

Evidently, while powerful resources are at the disposal of the President, there are also a number of constraints on his utilization of these resources on behalf of blacks. (1) Most presidents by virtue of their background and experiences have been either entirely unaware of the character and extent of the black dilemma or accord it a very low level of priority, and it is thus difficult to arouse them to positive action. (2) The President's election by a national electorate ensures that his perspectives are likely to be broader and perhaps more "liberal" than those of most legislators, but he is nevertheless extremely sensitive to "the national mood" on major public issues and thus avoids pursuing policies to which there is widespread public hostility. (3) Situated at the pinnacle of the policy process, the President is susceptible to a variety of conflicting demands and counterpressures on racial issues as well as on virtually every other significant issue, and is thus often required to urge partial or compromise solutions rather than full ones. (4) Although the President has a large bureaucracy under his general supervision, it is often difficult for him to exert control over its activities because of its unwieldly size and mostly permanent staff and so might not actually control the level or quality of policy enforcement. (5) The President shares many of the powers identified here with the Congress and rarely wins complete Congressional support for his proposals. In fact, he may, as in the case of Kennedy, try to avoid action which would tend to create Congressional hostility.

The above observations are not intended to absolve the President of responsibility for the lack of more forthright responses to blacks, but they do point up the very real difficulties which blacks encounter in seeking favorable executive action. A further problem faced by presidents, and one that has grown steadily more important, is that of coordinating executive programs and policies on racial matters. A recent Civil Rights Commission report observes in this connection that at a minimum the President needs mechanisms that can provide him with accurate and prompt information on what is happening around the country and in the government, convey information to the bureaucracy concerning administration civil rights policy, and evaluate agency action and stimulate more forceful action to carry out his policies. [24]

Before the Kennedy administration, no regular organizational or staffing arrangements were made within the White House to meet these needs. Some presidents relied on informal efforts by trusted bureaucrats to serve as informal liaison with black leaders and as advisers on racial matters. FDR's use of Harold Ickes (a former president of the Chicago chapter of the NAACP), and his wife Eleanor, as informal liaisons is an example of this approach. President Kennedy took the first organizational steps to facilitate more systematic White House involvement with these issues. Soon after taking office he appointed a Special Assistant for Civil Rights and shortly thereafter he created a Sub-Cabinet Group on Civil Rights which consisted of ranking representatives of the major agencies of government and was headed by White House staff members. Because actual decision making on racial issues was left primarily to Robert Kennedy at the Justice Department, the group lacked policy-making power but served nevertheless as a valuable clearinghouse for information and a communications channel for the President's policies on civil rights.

With passage of the 1964 Civil Rights Act, a second step was taken to coordinate civil rights policies in the White House as President Johnson created the President's Council on Equal Opportunity. This council, headed by Vice-President Hubert Humphrey and consisting of representatives from sixteen federal agencies, seemed a promising coordinating device but was abolished six months after its inauguration in March 1965, most of its activities being transferred to the Justice Department. The apparent objective at this time was to make the Justice Department the center for coordinating civil rights matters. Between 1965 and 1969 civil rights issues were dealt with

[24] *Federal Civil Rights Enforcement Effort: A Report of the U.S. Commission on Civil Rights 1971*, p. 332.

in the White House on *ad hoc* basis. President Nixon attempted to return to the White House some coordinating responsibility for civil rights and assigned several staff members directly to Minority Group Affairs. After reorganization in March 1970 civil rights matters were placed under the broad umbrella of the Council on Domestic Affairs headed by John Ehrlichman.

What is apparent from the organization and treatment of civil rights or minority group issues in the White House is an absence of clear, well-defined mechanisms for dealing with these problems in an organized way. This may be the case because of the relatively low priority which most presidents accord to it as an issue area and the inclination for the White House to respond only to special problems or crises. Another reason for this situation may have been the perception of civil rights as a controversial and politically dangerous issue, close identification with which could be damaging to the President's influence in Congress and his popularity nationwide. This thinking seemed most pronounced during the Kennedy Administration. Clearly, therefore, although the Presidency is so vital to the aspirations of blacks for policy change, and although presidents constantly assert an interest, this area ranks relatively low at the White House.

### The Bureaucracy

Treatment of racial issues at the White House is crucial because ultimately it is there that policy choices are examined and proposals are made, and it is there too that the tempo of overall bureaucratic conduct is set. However, a vital part of the total policy process rests with the larger federal bureaucracy. Its consideration here is essential to a total picture of Executive responses to blacks. Court decisions, intricate, wide-ranging legislation, Executive Orders, and other Presidential edicts have resulted in considerably increased responsibilities for the federal bureaucracy. In meeting these new responsibilities, organizational changes have been undertaken, either by explicit legislative directive or by decisions of the major departments of government, in order to cope efficiently with their tasks on civil rights or minority group issues. It is not possible to describe or evaluate the total bureaucratic effort here, nevertheless we will look at some aspects of this effort, particularly the role of the Justice Department, and identify some important characteristics of the overall enforcement effort by the federal bureaucracy.

The Justice Department is only one of the several departments and agencies of government with responsibility for implementing federal civil rights policies. In the complex and controversial area of school desegregation, the principal responsibility for implementing the many judicial rulings and statutory provisions rests with the Civil Rights Office of the Department of Health, Education and Welfare. Enforcement of antidiscrimination policies in employment is shared by three units: The Civil Service Commission has responsibility for employment by the federal government; the Office of Federal Contract Compliance within the Department of Labor has responsibility for hiring practices of federal contractors; and the Equal Employment Opportunities Commission (EEOC), established by the 1964 Civil Rights Act, is responsible for employment practices in the private sector. Investigative and data gathering responsibilities relative to the federal civil rights effort are undertaken by the Civil Rights Commission, established by the 1957 Civil Rights Act. Both the Department of Housing and Urban Development and the Federal Housing Authority share responsibility for ensuring nondiscriminatory policies in housing.

The Justice Department occupies perhaps the most crucial role in the overall administration and implementation of laws in the area of race relations. Its statutory role as the law enforcement arm of the federal government or "the government's lawyer" requires it to play a large part in enforcing these laws. In this regard the Civil Rights Commission recently observed that "the Attorney General has become the most important single figure in the government's civil rights program."[25] Before 1957 the Justice Department's role in protecting the civil rights of blacks was not a very strong one. Starting in 1939, the few civil rights cases handled by the Department were handled by a Civil Rights Unit within the Criminal Division. In addition to its small size, the unit had virtually no statutory provisions on which to act and it was hampered by a relatively conservative federal court system. With passage of the Civil Rights Act of 1957 a separate Civil Rights Division was created, headed by an Assistant Attorney General. In 1966 the Community Relations Service, created by the 1964 Civil Rights Act and located in the Department of Commerce, was transferred to the Justice Department and with it the task of helping to resolve difficulties which communities face in implementing civil rights laws and court orders. The principal role of the Justice Department in the enforcement of civil rights laws is undertaken by the Civil Rights Division. These responsibilities as initially outlined in 1957 were

(a) Enforcement of all federal statutes affecting civil rights, and authorization of such enforcement, including criminal prosecutions, and civil actions and proceedings on behalf of the government; and appellate proceedings in all such cases.

(b) Requesting, directing, and reviewing of investigations arising from reports or complaints of public officials or private citizens with respect to matters affecting civil rights.

(c) Conferring with individuals and groups who call upon the Department in connection with civil rights matter, advising such individuals and groups thereon, and initiating action appropriate thereto.

(d) Coordination within the Department of Justice of all matters affecting civil rights.

(e) Consultation with and assistance to other federal departments and agencies and state and local agencies on matters affecting civil rights.

[25] *Ibid.*, p. 324.

(f) Research on civil rights matters, and the making of recommendations to the Attorney General as to proposed policies and legislation therefor.

(g) Upon their request, assisting the Commission on Civil Rights and
other similar federal bodies in carrying out research and formulating recommendations.[26]

The enforcement responsibilities of the Division have broadened considerably since 1957 to include portions of the 1960, 1964, and 1968 Civil
Rights Acts, the 1965 Voting Rights Act, and the Jury Selection and Service
Act of 1968. With these added responsibilities the size of the Division has
grown steadily from fourteen attorneys in 1958 to a staff of 95 attorneys and
101 clerical workers in 1966, and a total of 288 employees, including 136
attorneys as of 1970. This staff is organized along subject-matter lines with
the following five sections: (1) Employment, (2) Education, (3) Housing,
(4) Voting and Public Accommodations and Facilities, and (5) the Criminal
Section.

Its wide-ranging responsibilities mean that the Justice Department
through the Civil Rights Division has a crucial role in shaping the level of
compliance with the laws and court decisions on civil rights. Its role has been
especially prominent since the 1960s, although its performance has been
impaired by a number of factors. Up to 1964 one factor was ineffective
handling of many of the problems blacks encountered. For example, the
Division was forced to utilize the laborious case-by-case approach to voter
discrimination and the assortment of other discriminatory practices faced by
blacks in the South. This approach was slow, inefficient, and clearly inadequate to cope with the formidable structure of institutional racism in the
South. In spite of conscientious efforts by Burke Marshall and John Doar, top
officials in the Division, very little was accomplished. What was needed was
strong legislative action to permit new kinds of efforts for change. This began
to become available with the Civil Rights Act of 1964.

A second limitation on the Civil Rights Division's performance has to
do with the level of priority actually attached to the effort within the Justice
Department. Even during the Kennedy administration when a clear decision
was made to rely on litigation to bring about change in race relations instead
of working for new legislation, the commitment was less than complete.
Victor Navasky's study of Robert Kennedy's tenure as Attorney General
reveals that while Kennedy felt sympathetic toward civil rights, he was not
very aggressive on the issue. For example, the vigor and passion with which he
pursued organized crime was not present in his enforcement of civil rights.
Navasky observes that Kennedy put the "thinkers" in the Civil Rights
Division and the "doers" in the "get-Hoffa effort."[27]

[26] "Report of Assistant Attorney General W. Wilson White in Charge of the Civil
Rights Division," in *Report of the Attorney General—1958* (Washington, D.C.: Government Printing Office, 1958), p. 171.

[27] Victor Navasky, *Kennedy Justice* (New York: Atheneum, 1971), p. 53.

The reluctance of the FBI to vigorously investigate violations of blacks' civil rights by Southern whites also limited the effectiveness of the Justice Department's civil rights efforts. The FBI's role in civil rights activities has been a source of controversy since J. Edgar Hoover's vicious verbal attack on Dr. Martin Luther King when the latter complained about the approach taken by FBI agents in investigating racial disorders in the South. Navasky's study indicates that very often the FBI shaped Justice Department responses to racial problems by its approach to investigations, and that in many instances the Bureau's efforts left much to be desired.[28]

Even with the passage of several civil rights acts, the Division's effort continued to be limited by staff shortages as its responsibilities grew faster than the staff. It also has been hampered by the overlapping enforcement responsibilities within the federal government and the lack of any real capability to supervise or coordinate overall government enforcement efforts.

In one evaluation of the civil rights enforcement effort by the federal government, the Civil Rights Commission concluded that "the focus of civil rights must shift from the halls of Congress to the corridors of the federal bureaucracies that administer these laws." This conclusion emphasizes both the importance of the enforcement effort at this time and the lack of adequate enforcement effort. Effective performance would appear to require, at the very least, a rational organization of enforcement responsibility to end the disorganization which now exists. It also would require much more vigorous and visible commitment to the efforts by the President, Department, and Agency heads and the Congress—which must finance the enforcement effort.

### Congressional Responses to Blacks

To an even greater extent than the Courts or the Executive Branch, the Congress is involved in the policy-making process. Particularly important in its many-faceted role are the formulation or legitimation of public policy and the education of the public through its investigations, debates, and widely disseminated public records. The vital role of the legislature in national politics requires that blacks strive to influence its activities and the manner and extent of its response to their efforts to improve their subordinate status. With this recognition, black political activities have been directed at influencing the decision-making process in Congress through traditional lobbying techniques and through increasing the number of black members of that body or at least members sympathetic to the interests and aspirations of blacks.

Within recent years blacks have encountered some success in bringing before the Congress issues of great importance to them and in securing some favorable responses. On issues directly related to the civil rights of blacks, the Congress has responded, albeit reluctantly, with a series of Civil Rights Acts

[28] *Ibid.,* pp. 100–135.

starting in 1957. After more than a decade of piecemeal legislative responses, basic statutory protection of blacks against the more blatant and damaging forms of racial discrimination has been secured. This situation has not come about easily, however, and the experience of blacks in the legislative arena demonstrates starkly both the peculiar capacity of the Congress to resist demands for significant change through legislative action and the specific problems the efforts encounter.

It should be noted that the reluctant responsiveness of the Congress since 1957 was preceded by decades of firm resistance to all efforts by blacks to obtain favorable legislative action. In discussing the lobbying efforts of the NAACP in the preceding chapter we noted that a systematic campaign began about 1920 to secure federal legislation which would protect blacks from lynching. The effort continued through the 1940s without favorable action by the Congress. Equally vigorous efforts were made in the 1940s to secure legislation which would end job discrimination against blacks by contractors for the federal government through the establishment of an effective Fair Employment Practices Commission, but these efforts also failed. Thus, except for the unusual two decades immediately following the Civil War when a "radical Congress" took the initiative in securing adoption of the Fourteenth and Fifteenth Amendments and enacted several laws aimed at protecting the rights and interests of blacks, Congress has been the last of the three branches to respond to blacks through significant policy decisions.

Without attempting to describe each failure, we will identify some of the more formidable obstacles that blacks have encountered in trying to influence the Congress. The obstacles are of two basic kinds. One involves structural and procedural characteristics of the Congress which can stymie action of almost any kind but which have been particularly effective in obstructing civil rights legislation. One important structural characteristic in this regard is the division of power among standing committees of the Congress. These standing committees, organized along subject-matter lines, are useful in several respects. Ordinarily they increase the efficiency of the Congress by facilitating the development of expertise among legislators and by sharing the task of in-depth study of legislative proposals to be acted upon by the Congress. Often, however, these committees possess almost unlimited power over legislative proposals assigned to them, and are able to block or to significantly alter these proposals.

Related to the powers held by Committees is the practice of selecting committee chairmen by "seniority." This means that in each standing committee the member of the majority party with the longest unbroken term of service becomes chairman. One result of this procedure is that older legislators from areas of relatively low partisan competition frequently become committee chairmen. With the Democratic party as the majority party, most important committee chairmanships have gone to Southern legislators whose hostility to civil rights laws cannot be exaggerated. This is especially important because committee chairmen exercise considerable power within their committees. In the House of Representatives the Judiciary Committee which usually considers civil rights proposals was headed by a New York Democrat, Emanuel Celler. Celler's sympathy for such legislation aided favorable action but in the complex procedures of the House these bills require the permission of the House Rules Committee before they can be brought up for final action by the full House. Traditionally, this crucial "gatekeeping" committee has been headed by a conservative Southern legislator with considerable influence over when the action is taken by the committee and even the conditions under which the action is taken. During much of the 1960s for example, the committee was chaired by Representative Howard Smith of Virginia, an implacable foe of civil rights legislation who would simply make himself unavailable for convening meetings of the Rules Committee when such legislation was to be considered. Smith lost his seat in Congress eventually but the committee chairmanship went to William Comer of Mississippi, himself no champion of civil rights. In the Senate, the Judiciary Committee, headed by James Eastland of Mississippi, has proven a virtual graveyard for civil rights bills since they are never reported out for action by the full Senate. Senate action on such bills has required the circumvention of that committee. When this was accomplished in 1957 the Judiciary Committee had fifteen civil rights bills on which it had taken no action.

The obstructive role of standing committees is not confined to major civil rights legislation but involves, at times, the appropriations process through which actions authorized by the Congress are actually funded. The appropriations process can be effectively used to restrict implementation of laws passed by Congress by appropriating less than is essential for effective implementation. For example, the Civil Rights Division of the Justice Department is established by Congress and entrusted with sweeping responsibilities, but it is restrained in part by the level of funding provided by the Congress. Most of the basic funding decisions are made by standing committees and routinely ratified by the full House.

In addition to the role of standing committees in the Senate, the rules of debate in that chamber have provided an effective weapon against legislation beneficial to blacks. Unlike the House, where debate is carefully limited both with respect to each member's speaking time and to the pertinence of his remarks, the Senate imposes no such restraints. When a legislative proposal appears to have majority support and all other devices for obstruction have been exhausted, opponents may seek to prevent action by a "filibuster" or prolonged speaking which may consume so much time that supporters of the legislation finally give up. These filibusters, have been used on several occasions to obstruct passage of civil rights bills or at least to secure major modifications of the bills before final action is taken. The technique has been very effective because the procedure for terminating debate (cloture) spelled out in Senate rule XXII is a cumbersome one requiring that a 2/3 majority vote in favor of ending the filibuster. It has been so difficult to obtain the

TABLE 11.12  *Civil Rights Cloture Votes*

| Issue | Date | Vote | Yea Votes Needed |
|---|---|---|---|
| Antilynching | January 27, 1938 | 37–51 | 59 |
| Antilynching | February 27, 1938 | 42–46 | 59 |
| Antipoll tax | November 23, 1942 | 37–41 | 52 |
| Antipoll tax | May 15, 1944 | 36–44 | 54 |
| FEPC[b] | February 9, 1946 | 48–36 | 56 |
| Antipoll tax | July 31, 1946 | 39–33 | 48 |
| FEPC[b] | May 19, 1950 | 52–32 | 64[a] |
| FEPC[b] | July 12, 1950 | 55–33 | 64[a] |
| Civil Rights Act | March 10, 1960 | 42–53 | 64 |
| Literacy tests | May 9, 1962 | 43–53 | 64 |
| Literacy tests | May 14, 1962 | 42–52 | 63 |
| Civil Rights Act | June 10, 1964 | 71–29 | 67 |
| Voting Rights | May 25, 1965 | 70–23 | 67 |
| Civil Rights Act | September 14, 1966 | 54–42 | 64 |
| Civil Rights Act | September 19, 1966 | 52–41 | 62 |
| Civil Rights Act | February 20, 1968 | 55–37 | 62 |
| Civil Rights Act | February 26, 1968 | 56–36 | 62 |
| Civil Rights Act | March 1, 1968 | 59–35 | 63 |
| Civil Rights Act | March 4, 1968 | 65–32 | 65 |

[a]Between 1949 and 1959 the cloture rule required the affirmative vote of two-thirds of the Senate membership rather than two-thirds of those Senators who voted.
[b]Fair Employment Practices Commission.
*Source: Revolution in Civil Rights* (Washington, D.C.: Congressional Quarterly 1968), p. 59.

required 2/3 majority to terminate debate that Howard Shuman calls Rule XXII "the grave digger in the Senate graveyard for civil rights."[29]

The importance of Rule XXII in obstructing favorable legislative response to blacks is emphasized by Raymond Wolfinger, who notes that "filibusters essentially are for bills involving salient and emotional issues, of which the prime contemporary example is civil rights."[30] He observes further that because of its close association with civil rights struggles, efforts to change the rule by which filibusters are ended have been treated in the same way as substantive rights bills.

The second major set of obstacles to favorable legislative responses to blacks results from the influence of social background and constituency preferences on legislators. Political scientists are generally agreed that the socioeconomic background of legislators substantially affects their perception of public issues and thus their vote on these issues. It is noteworthy therefore that not only have there been very few blacks in the legislature, but the

[29] Howard E. Shuman, "Senate Rules and the Civil Rights Bill: A Case Study," *American Political Science Review* 51 (December 1957), 957.
[30] Raymond E. Wolfinger, "Filibuster: Majority Rule, Presidential Leadership and Senate Norms," in *Readings on Congress* (Englewood Cliffs, N.J.: Prentice-Hall, 1971), p. 294.

backgrounds of legislators are such as to limit their understanding of, or interest in, the concerns of blacks. On the basis of a large body of literature dealing with the backgrounds of legislators Leroy Rieselbach concludes that

> In terms of their family origins, then, it appears that members of Congress are not typical Americans. Much more than those they represent, senators and representatives are born and raised in America, in affluence, and away from the major metropolitan centers around which swirl so much conflict and controversy in modern life. They grow up in short in atypical families, and it should not surprise us therefore, if they learn atypical views in those families. It is these views, that, in all likelihood, many Congressmen bring with them to their legislative service and which help to determine how they approach their jobs.[31]

It must be conceded that we are not sure of the extent to which this kind of background contributes to unresponsiveness to blacks, we may only assume that its impact is significant. An even more potent factor affecting legislative responses to blacks are the constituency pressures that shape the behavior of legislators. In studying the relationship between constituents and representatives, scholars have distinguished between (1) the "Burkean model," of representation in which the representative acts as his own knowledge and understanding dictate, and (2) the "instructed delegate model," in which the representative merely registers the wishes of his constituents. Most observers conclude that American legislators fall somewhere between these two models in what is referred to as the "responsible party model." One study suggests, however, that the model adopted by the legislator is a function of the kind of issue involved. In the area of foreign affairs the representative is relatively free to vote as he chooses, in the Burkean model. In the domain of social welfare policies, he comes closest to the "responsible party model" but, the study concludes, "the issue domain in which the relation of Congressman to constituency most nearly conforms to the instructed delegate model is that of civil rights."[32] The point here is that legislators, especially members of the House of Representatives, tend to follow constituency attitudes closely on racial issues in Congress, and these attitudes have been deeply racist. This helps to explain why a supposedly learned and liberal senator like William Fulbright of Arkansas fumes with rage about injustices to the Vietnamese people while he consistently votes against legislation to provide a modicum of justice for black Americans.

The result of these various factors is that the American Congress has been extremely reluctant to respond to blacks and it has responded only in the face of massive pressure from blacks, from sympathetic whites, and from the Executive. Furthermore, the legislature has yielded only grudgingly to

---

[31] Leroy Rieselbach, *Congressional Politics* (New York: McGraw-Hill, 1973), 30.
[32] Warren Miller and Donald Stokes, "Constituency Influence in Congress," *American Political Science Review* 57 (1963), 56.

those massive pressures while indulging in a gigantic ritual of resistance with each legislative proposal. The result is a demoralizing process of pleading by blacks and rejoicing for embarrassingly small morsels of a loaf that in fact belongs to them.

## The 1964 Civil Rights Bill—A Case of Governmental Response to Blacks

Thus far we have described separately some of the ways in which the major branches of the national government have responded to the efforts of blacks to improve their status in the society. We noted that each branch began to provide favorable responses of a limited kind at different times and in different ways. Obviously, however, these responses do not always occur independently of one another but often are inextricably interrelated. Furthermore, fundamental, wide-ranging change requires closely coordinated, often simultaneous efforts at policy formulation. Passage of the 1964 Civil Rights Act provides one opportunity to observe the contributions of all three branches of government in a single policy-making effort, and demonstrates the contributions of several forms of black political activities to the effort. Passage of the Act also illustrates the constraints under which the various branches of government operate in dealing with racial matters. The 1964 Civil Rights Act was easily one of the most elaborate and controversial decision-making undertakings in American political life and thus cannot be described fully and definitively here. Nevertheless, examination of some aspects of the case can be highly instructive with respect to the kinds of forces that shape decision making on major racial issues.

### Running the Obstacle Course

When Everett Dirksen, Republican Senator from Illinois and Minority Leader in the Senate, finally gave his support to the Civil Rights Bill he declared that "no army is stronger than an idea whose time has come. . . . Civil Rights—here is an idea whose time has come. Let editors rave at will and states fulminate at will, but the time has come, and it can't be stopped." [33] To a considerable extent Dirksen was responding to the pressures that had been developing from the massive, intense political activities by blacks and a rapidly growing group of sympathetic whites. The nonviolent armies which, in hundreds of communities across the nation, had dramatized the plight of blacks and the ugliness of white racism, succeeded in creating tensions to which government was forced to respond. In fact, what became the Civil Rights Act was submitted to Congress on June 19, 1963 by President John

[33] This and much of the discussion which follows relies on "Revolution" in *Civil Rights* (Washington, D.C.: Congressional Quarterly Service, 1968), pp. 50–65.

Kennedy eight days after widespread and often bloody protests prompted him to comment in a nationwide television address that "the fires of frustration and discord are burning in every city, North and South, where legal remedies are not at hand. . . . Redress is sought in the streets, in demonstrations, parades and protests which create tensions and threaten violence—and threaten lives."

It is noteworthy that although black voters played a vital part in ensuring the election of John Kennedy, and although his campaign speeches appeared to promise substantial activism, the first two years of his Presidency passed without effort on his part to promote obviously needed legislation to protect rights of blacks who were being trampled upon with impunity. According to Navasky, Kennedy's civil rights strategy to the extent that there was one, was to push litigation, not legislation.[34] Thus only the tensions to which he referred prompted his initiative in proposing legislation. This fact is especially important because the Congress rarely has taken the initiative in acting on major policy issues, had never done so in the area of civil rights and seemed both unwilling and unable to act without the President's leadership.

Efforts by the Executive on behalf of the Bill went beyond drafting and recommending its adoption by Congress. They included an attempt to mobilize public support for the bill through his television address and the attempt to win the support of leaders of several organizations representing crucial segments of the society. To this end President Kennedy held a series of meetings at the White House with labor and religious leaders, lawyers, and representatives of women's organizations to solicit their support for the bill. Furthermore, several cabinet members including the Secretary of State and Attorney General; top members of the Civil Rights Division of the Justice Department were made available to testify and otherwise work for a set of proposals which the Kennedy Administration considered likely to win wide Congressional approval.

All of this effort was necessary and might not have been enough, for in spite of substantial support for the bill among members of Congress, opposition was also substantial and the opportunities for obstruction many. Throughout the summer of 1963 the bill remained in Committees in both chambers of the Congress. It was well received by the House Judiciary Committee chaired by Emanuel Celler of New York, and after months of extensive public hearings in which hundreds of individuals and group representatives appeared to support or criticize it, Sub-Committee 5 of the Judiciary Committee (which actually did basic work on the Bill) produced a stronger, more inclusive bill than that proposed by the President. Fearing defeat for this stronger version, Robert Kennedy and his assistants from the Justice Department negotiated a compromise version that was weaker than the Committee's proposal but stronger than that initially submitted by the President.

[34] Navasky, *op. cit.*, pp. 96–100.

No such sympathetic attitude existed in the Senate Judiciary Committee and so, on its arrival at the Senate, the bill was divided and the section prohibiting racial discrimination in public accommodations was assigned to the Commerce Committee and the remainder to the Judiciary Committee. The official rationale for this was that the Commerce Clause formed the constitutional basis for the public accommodations section and thus it was of concern to the Commerce Committee. The Judiciary's record of never having reported out a civil rights bill and the apparent determination of Committee Chairman, Senator Eastland, that this record remain intact were, of course, more compelling considerations. Not surprisingly the Commerce Committee acted with dispatch in holding extensive hearings and reporting out its part of the Bill while the Judiciary Committee heard one witness over an eleven-day period and took no further action on the bill.

Two days before the tragic assassination of President Kennedy, the Civil Rights Bill was reported out of the House Judiciary Committee. It was stalled, however, as Representative Howard Smith, Chairman of the Rules Committee, tried to block final action by refusing to have his committee meet to approve consideration of the bill on the floor of the House. The assassination of President Kennedy became a major factor in facilitating passage as President Johnson urged immediate passage as the only fitting monument to Kennedy's memory. Even more important than the invocation of Kennedy's memory, however, was the degree of legislative skill and personal influence that President Johnson brought to the effort.

President Johnson's first major effort on the bill's behalf was to secure its release from the Rules Committee by pressuring members to undertake the rare and cumbersome step of forcing the bill out of the Rules Committee. When it became apparent that this procedure would succeed, Representative Smith agreed to act and on January 30, 1964, more than nine months after submission, the Rules Committee cleared the bill for debate, thus removing a major obstacle to House action. On February 10, after nine full days of debate during which 122 amendments were offered and all but 28 (mostly technical) were defeated, the House passed the bill by a vote of 290 to 130.

This favorable action by the House represented a major boost to the bill and by any measure was a significant achievement, yet it was not entirely precedent-setting. After all, the House had acted favorably on bills designed to aid blacks only to have the Senate stymie final action by filibuster on at least eleven occasions previously. Thus the final, decisive battle remained ahead in the Senate. The Senate waited for passage of the House bill because that action would improve its chances in the Senate. Then Senate Majority Leader Mike Mansfield invoked a rarely used tactic to bring the bill before the Senate. Instead of the routine practice of having a bill from the House go directly to the appropriate Senate committee (in this case Judiciary), it was "intercepted at the door" and taken directly to the Senate floor, thus preventing its burial in the Judiciary Committee. An indignant Senator

Richard Russell of Georgia objected to the procedure, but it was sustained by a 54–37 vote. Senator Mike Mansfield's March 9 motion to make the bill the pending business before the Senate was adopted on March 26 after a lengthy wrangling which confirmed the determination of its opponents to prevent its adoption. Four days later these opponents, almost all Southerners, turned to their weapon of last resort—the filibuster. The tactic is a crude, even somewhat embarrassing one for the nation but it had been effective on several occasions in the past. Furthermore, cloture—the process by which filibusters are terminated—is a cumbersome one that had succeeded on only a few occasions up to this point and never against a race-related issue.

Supporters of the bill had three options in the face of the filibuster: (1) to give up the effort altogether thus giving opponents of the bill a complete victory; (2) to bargain with the opponents to secure a compromise acceptable to both sides; (3) to work to secure the 67 votes necessary to end the filibuster. The first option was clearly out and neither side appeared to seriously consider the second option both because of the extent of the gap between them and because the opponents were confident of total victory. Thus by mid-May intense negotiations began between leading supporters of the bill, notably Hubert Humphrey who served skillfully as its floor manager, and a few publicly uncommitted leaders whose support was crucial to imposition of cloture. The central figure in this connection was Everett Dirksen, the astute, gravelly-voiced Minority Leader from Illinois, who was opposed primarily to the equal employment and public accommodations sections. As the price for his pivotal support, several portions of the bill were rewritten, and although most of the changes he demanded were technical, some modified substantially the scope of the bill and the limits of governmental enforcement authority. However, with these concessions made, a cloture motion was filed on June 8 and when called up for the vote on June 10, the motion carried by a margin of 71–29, four more than the required two-thirds. It was the first time that cloture was successfully invoked on a race-related issue.

After accepting the negotiated amendments, the Senate quickly defeated 99 other proposed amendments, mostly from Southerners, and on June 19 the Senate passed the amended bill by a 73–27 roll-call vote. Because the Senate bill differed from that enacted by the House earlier, it was necessary that the House vote on whether to accept the Senate version or not. This provided one more opportunity for obstruction by Representative Smith of the Rules Committee, since that Committee's approval was required before the issue could formally come before the House for a vote. The massive momentum built up by deliberations thus far completely overwhelmed Smith, however, and final House passage came on July 2. A few hours later, before a national television audience and a gathering of legislative leaders and civil rights activists assembled in the East Room of the White House, President Johnson signed the bill into law. In its final form the bill contained these ten sections or titles:

1. *Voting Rights*—prohibited several forms of voting discrimination and established new conditions under which literacy tests were administered and processed.
2. *Public Accommodations*—prohibited discrimination on grounds of race, color, religion or national origin in most forms of public accommodations facilities and provided legal recourse for victims of discrimination in these facilities.
3. *Desegregation of Public Facilities*—permitted Justice Department to sue to force desegregation of state or locally owned public facilities after receiving written complaints.
4. *Desegregation of Public Education*—permitted the Office of Education to provide technical and financial assistance to school systems to aid in school desegregation and empowered the Justice Department to sue to desegregate schools and colleges when it receives a signed complaint.
5. *Civil Rights Commission*—extended the life of the Civil Rights Commission for four years and broadened its responsibilities to include investigation of vote fraud.
6. *Nondiscrimination in Federally Assisted Programs*—barred discrimination under any program receiving federal assistance and permitted termination of assistance to any program failing to comply.
7. *Equal Employment Opportunity*—prohibited several forms of discriminatory employment practices with gradual implementation over a five-year period to begin one year after passage and created a five-member Equal Employment Opportunity Commission with limited enforcement powers.
8. *Registration and Voting Statistics*—directed the Census Bureau to gather registration and voting statistics based on race, color, and national origin as recommended by the Civil Rights Commission.
9. *Intervention and Removal of Cases*—permitted the Justice Department to intervene in private suits alleging denial of equal protection of the laws which it considered of general public importance.
10. *Community Relations Service*—created a Community Relations Service in the Department of Commerce to help communities resolve disputes relating to racial discrimination.

## Overcoming the Obstacles: The Lobbying Effort

Just over one year had elapsed between the introduction of the basic bill and final action enacting it into law, even though the major issues in the bill had been topics of national debate for decades. Moreover, passage was not nearly as simple as the foregoing brief description might suggest. It came about only after the most massive, complex lobbying effort in Congressional history combined with constant pressures from outside the legislative arena itself. In addition it required a corps of dedicated, resourceful leaders in both houses to formulate and pursue the strategy by which passage was secured.

The fires of frustration and discontent to which John Kennedy alluded in proposing the legislation did not subside with his action. Instead it intensified as increasing numbers of whites from all walks of life united with the rapidly growing black army to articulate with increasing forcefulness and determination the demand for strong affirmative action from government. This effort reached a grand crescendo in October 1963 when several hundred thousand people converged on Washington, D.C., to demand action to alleviate the agony of blacks in the society. In the face of these massive protests, Congressional response was unavoidable.

Within the legislative arena itself a different but no less impressive army was beginning to assemble to ensure passage of the bill. To an extent, the lobbying effort represents the high point in the black-white liberal alliance on behalf of civil rights. Well over a hundred labor, religious, civic, and other organizations associated within the Leadership Conference on Civil Rights and led by Clarence Mitchell, III of the NAACP provided the funds and the manpower for the massive job of persuading and prodding the Congress. A second part of the lobbying effort involved the Justice Department's contingent from the Civil Rights Division and at crucial points included the Attorney General. In the House, the Democratic Study Group, a loose coalition of liberal Congressmen, formed the third part of the lobbying group.

The lobbying effort can, for convenience, be divided into three kinds of tasks: (1) testifying on behalf of the bill in Committee and contacting and persuading uncommitted or reluctant legislators; (2) maintaining close scrutiny over all proposed amendments in an effort to fend off potentially crippling changes or changes that would sharply reduce support for the bill; (3) ensuring the presence of friendly legislators especially for crucial votes on substantive as well as procedural issues. Efforts in the first category continued for the several months of public hearings by the Committee and throughout debate. One measure of the effectiveness of this effort comes, ironically, from the bitter complaint of Senator Russell, leader of the opposition to the Bill in the Senate, that "during the course of the debate we have seen cardinals, bishops, elders stated clerks, common preachers, priests and rabbis come to Washington to press for the passage of the bill. They have sought to make its passage a great moral issue."

Protecting the bill against crippling amendments required primarily readily available expertise both with respect to the procedures of the chamber and the issues involved in the bill. To provide this expertise, Justice Department officials and Leadership Conference leaders remained in the House Gallery throughout the debates, available for hurried consultations with floor leaders. This procedure, in addition to daily strategy sessions by these individuals and White House representatives, helped to avoid the many pitfalls of the amending process.

Making sure the votes were always present required extensive planning and substantial personnel. Attempt was made to know the whereabouts of every potentially friendly legislator during debate on the bill. When votes were to be taken the members absent from the floor were contacted in order to ensure that a favorable majority would be present at voting. The elaborate watch on attendance worked well with the aid of the Democratic Study Group, but was viewed by some legislators as overly restrictive and perhaps not entirely necessary.

Who were the principal opponents of the bill? This bill, as is true of virtually all other civil rights bills enacted or considered by Congress, focused on aspects of racism that were most prominent in the South. Southern legislators, reflecting attitudes widespread in the area, were thus its principal opponents. In fact, Southern resistance was so automatic and so unyielding that they perceived all civil rights bills as calculated assaults on the South and the Southern way of life rather than as merely an important legislative issue in which they had a strong interest. The voting, however, was not entirely regional but reflected an alliance of Southern Democrats and conservative Northern Republicans in opposition, while support came almost entirely from Northern Democrats and Republicans.

Altogether, in the House 152 Democrats voted for the bill with 11 of these coming from the South and 96 voted against, with four of the negative votes from Northern Democrats. Among Republicans, 138 voted for the Bill and 34 voted against, with 22 of these from the North. In the Senate six Republicans, including Barry Goldwater, joined 21 Southern Democrats to oppose the bill. Off the floor, there was relatively little organized opposition as the Coordinating Committee for Fundamental American Freedoms, an umbrella organization of conservative groups, provided the only major lobbying against the bill. It maintained a relatively low profile but reported total expenditures on the effort of $452,825.

By 1964 the rhetoric of resistance had changed substantially so that the crude racist arguments which in earlier times justified obstruction to any change in the status of blacks now gave way to mostly constitutional ones. Thus most opponents did not seriously defend or justify the injustices to which the bill was a remedy; they emphasized that there was no clear constitutional basis for action or that in correcting the injustices against blacks the constitutional rights of white racists were being violated. Others, like Barry Goldwater, raised the specter of a fundamentally changed society in which a vast federal police force would emerge. In this instance these arguments were not persuasive.

### The Role of the Courts

Although the Civil Rights Act was now the law, it faced one crucial, final hurdle. The constitutionality of the Act had been questioned during Congressional debate. As expected, it was promptly challenged in the Courts as unconstitutional. A final, authoritative determination of its constitutionality had to be made by the Supreme Court, and decision of that body could invalidate all or parts of the bill. The first challenges were directed at Title II, the public accommodations section of the Act, because it was one of the first segments to go into force and also because it represented the core of the Act. The challenges reached the Supreme Court in two cases, *Heart of Atlanta Motel vs. United States* and *Katzenbach vs. McClung* on direct appeal from Federal District courts. The first case involved the Heart of Atlanta Motel's policy of excluding blacks as guests, that had been enjoined from such discrimination by the district court in Georgia under Title II. The second one involved Ollie's Barbecue, a Birmingham restaurant which also refused to serve blacks and whose refusal was sustained by district court in Alabama which ruled the Act unconstitutional as applied to Ollie's.

The Court summarized the arguments against Title II of the Act in the *Heart of Atlanta* petition thus:

> The appellant contends that Congress in passing the Act exceeded its power to regulate commerce under Article 1, Clause 3 of the Constitution of the United States; that the Act violates the Fifth Amendment because appellant is deprived of the right to choose its customers and operate its business as it wishes, resulting in a taking of its liberty and property without due process of law and a taking of its property without just compensation; and finally, that by requiring appellant to rent available rooms to Negroes against its will, Congress is subjecting it to involuntary servitude in contravention of the Thirteenth Amendment.[35]

The Court rejected the complaints and upheld the constitutionality of the Act by finding that the power of Congress to regulate interstate commerce was adequate constitutional basis for the Act. In its ruling it distinguished between the 1964 Act and the 1875 Act which was declared unconstitutional by noting that unlike the earlier Act which "broadly proscribed discrimination in 'inns, public conveyances on land or water, theaters and other places of public amusement' without limiting the categories of affected businesses to those impinging upon interstate commerce, the applicability of Title II is carefully limited to enterprises having a direct and substantial relation to the interstate flow of goods and people, except where state action is involved."

The Court proceeded further to elaborate on the contemporary scope of the interstate power by relying on Chief Justice Marshall's opinion in *Gibbon vs. Ogden* that "the determinative test of the exercise of power by the Congress under the Commerce Clause is simply whether the activity sought to be regulated is 'commerce which concerns more states than one' and has a real and substantial relation to the national interest." It went on to assert that the increased complexity and mobility of the society requires broad application of those principles to today's conditions; thus not only is it reasonable to consider discrimination against blacks a hindrance to interstate commerce but the power of Congress in this regard includes regulation of

[35] *Heart of Atlanta Motel vs. United States* 379 U.S. 241 (1964).

"local incidents thereof, including local activities in both the states of origin and destination, which might have a substantial and harmful effect upon that commerce." With this decision, direct, blatant segregation in most public facilities came to an end.

### Some Implications of the Act

The 1964 Civil Rights Act should not have been necessary and is itself eloquent testimony to the subordinate status of blacks. Furthermore, when viewed against the enormity of the discrimination with which blacks lived up to this time, the Act was an extremely modest corrective. The ineffectiveness of some provisions like that on voting rights was clearly apparent when the Act was passed; and the enforcement of others, like the equal employment provision, was delayed even though their urgency was evident. Nevertheless, by almost any measure the Act represented a vital step forward for blacks and a major turning point in the pattern of black-white relations. Its significance cannot be confined to the specific provisions only but must include the circumstances surrounding its passage.

The most tangible immediate impact of the Civil Rights Act was the prohibition of discrimination in most public facilities, thereby eliminating one of the most visible and humiliating symbols of black subordination. In spite of a few notable resisters like Lester Maddox, who chose to close his Pickwick Restaurant rather than serve blacks, the society complied with the new law without significant incidents. Because the provisions of the equal employment segment of the bill became effective gradually over several years, its impact appeared less dramatic but was nonetheless substantial. Thus the bill had a clearly positive impact on the pattern of race relations, and particularly on blacks, even though it fell short of their expectations.

Passage of the Act was important in two other respects. First, it breached an hitherto impenetrable barrier to significant positive legislative action on racial matters. Although civil rights acts had been passed in 1957 and 1960, they were almost entirely empty gestures and their passage was aided considerably by their lack of significant potential policy impact. In spite of its serious shortcomings, however, the 1964 Act clearly was substantively significant and succeeded in spite of resolute efforts by Southern legislators to defeat it. Actual passage of the bill in the face of this opposition and the first successful application of cloture to a civil rights bill quite conceivably paved the way for passage of other vital civil rights legislation in 1965 and 1968. Second, the passionate involvement of a vast army of white supporters and the intense national debate the bill evoked reflected a desire among many not merely to secure passage of the bill but to register a massive national affirmation of the commitment to full equality for blacks. While it was no such sweeping affirmation, it undoubtedly was a major step in that direction.

With particular reference to black political activities, passage of the Act provided some important lessons. It demonstrated the utility of massive, persistent, and varied political activities in achieving broad political objectives. It demonstrated the necessity of alliances in achieving these objectives. On the other hand, however, the experience pointed up the difficulties which blacks face in attempting to secure favorable legislative action. The massive effort required to ensure passage of the bill was far from comforting, since it is reflective of the indifference and the hostility within the Congress with respect to black advancement. These implications are especially grave because as broad civil rights acts have given way to other, more specific goals such as greater occupational and educational opportunities, the "liberal allies" who contributed to success have all but disappeared and in some cases have become vigorous opponents. Furthermore, while enactment of policy is crucial, the quality of bureaucratic performance in interpreting and administering the policy is equally crucial. For all of these reasons the successes in securing policy changes through civil rights legislation make more important the need for blacks to influence the policy process.

# 12

Black Politics and
the Problem of Influence –
Looking Ahead

This study has attempted to examine the development of black subordination
in America and the persistent and varied political efforts by blacks to alter
their subordinate status. It is appropriate to conclude by assessing some
salient aspects of this centuries-old struggle, particularly the quality of governmental responses to the efforts for change and their implications for the
future of blacks in the society. The effort is somewhat risky because there
exist no entirely reliable bases for such an assessment, and because its
essentially subjective character provides considerable room for disagreement.
Nevertheless, it is necessary because of the sheer importance of the struggle
by blacks for themselves, for society, and conceivably for the entire effort of
human beings to live together harmoniously in spite of racial or ethnic
differences.

## The Quality of Governmental Response to Blacks

The racial cleavage in American society is easily the single most crucial
characteristic of the society. Its impact, especially on the political system, has
been far greater than any other factor in American life. Thus while conflicts
with foreign powers and the emergence of competing ideologies have been
deeply disruptive and threatening, neither of these has approached the racial
issue in its potential to undermine and ultimately even destroy society. In the
face of its overwhelming importance, overall governmental approaches to the
racial issue have been little short of shocking.

In several societies with major racial or ethnic cleavages, considerable
thought and careful planning went into the formulation of policies and the
creation of political institutions to accommodate or cope with the cleavages.
Thus the first years of the new Soviet state were spent in vigorous policy
debates at the national level on how the ethnic diversity within the society

277

would be handled. The somewhat reluctant resort to a federal system and the specific character of the federal structure were motivated by this ethnic diversity.[1] It must be conceded that especially during the Stalin era these formal structures were effectively undermined but the very serious attempt to deal with the problem remains significant. In newly independent India there is also evidence of a national effort to modify some political structures in order to ensure adequate participation by the Harijans or untouchables who had long been excluded from significant participation in politics. The electoral system has been organized to guarantee Harijans a minimum level of representation in the national parliament.[2] Again, the substantive impact of this adjustment is not altogether clear but the structural adaptation to meet the problem of low-caste Harijans is significant.

India and the Soviet Union are only two of several examples of responsible national planning to cope with major cleavages in the society.[3] Within the United States there is little evidence of such an approach to the racial problem. On the contrary, there is a conspicuous lack of systematic planning or willingness to undertake such structural adaptations in the interest of a harmonious multiracial society. The two constitutional amendments undertaken in the immediate aftermath of the Civil War represent the most far-reaching responses by the political system to the racial issue. The Fifteenth Amendment was easily and flagrantly circumvented, Section 2 of the Fourteenth Amendment was never actually utilized, and other important provisions of the Fourteenth were quickly nullified by subsequent governmental actions. The bulk of governmental responses to the racial issue has thus come about at the statutory and administrative levels after permissive interpretations of the Constitution by the Supreme Court.

This apparent casualness with which the racial issue has been treated by government is disturbing because it reflects a failure to recognize the enormity of the issue and to come to terms with it. Furthermore, it makes extremely tenuous the political status of black people in the society. Most of the changes that have occurred in the situation of blacks have come about, we have pointed out, as a result of favorable Supreme Court decisions for which the Court was often criticized. It is entirely possible that a drastically transformed Court could undo much of its recent actions on behalf of blacks. Indeed precisely such a transformation was encouraged by President Richard

---

[1] See E. H. Carr, *The Bolshevik Revolution 1, 1917–1923* (Baltimore, Md.: Pelican, 1969), pp. 278–291; Vernon Aspaturian, "Nationalism and the Political System," in Richard Cornell, ed., *The Soviet Political System* (Englewood Cliffs, N.J.: Prentice-Hall, 1970), pp. 72–91.

[2] L. M. Singhvi, "Parliament in the Indian Political System," in Allan Kornberg and Lloyd Musolf, eds., *Legislatures in Developmental Perspective* (Durham, N.C.: Duke University Press, 1970), p. 185.

[3] See for example Martin O. Heisler, "Institutionalizing Societal Cleavages in a Cooptive Polity: The Growing Importance of the Output Side in Belgium," in *Politics in Europe* (New York: McKay, 1973), pp. 178–220; Cynthia Enloe, *Ethnic Conflict and Political Development: An Analytic Study* (Boston: Little, Brown, 1973).

Nixon. Although his efforts to elevate G. Harrold Carswell and Clement Haynsworth failed to win Senate approval, his four other appointees have contributed to a somewhat more conservative Court attitude on some civil liberties issues. On racial issues it has not actually moved backward but has demonstrated some reluctance to move forward in resolving remaining forms of racial discrimination.

A similar tenuousness exists with respect to the statutory and administrative actions that now protect crucial rights of blacks in the society. An example of this is the swiftness with which the House of Representatives seized on the alleged energy crisis to vote in favor of legislation prohibiting the busing of school children outside their neighborhood for purposes of racial integration. Another example was the action of the House of Representatives on October 1, 1974 approving by a 220 to 169 vote an amendment to a supplemental appropriations bill, which would prohibit the federal government from cutting off financial aid to schools that disobey desegregation orders as required by Title VI of the 1964 Civil Rights Act. The Senate later rejected both moves but they are illustrative of how quickly public policy can be reversed by a political system that has no real commitment to a multiracial

**"WE JUST WANT TO TAKE YOUR CLOTHES SO THAT WE CAN WEAVE YOU A WONDERFUL NEW OUTFIT."**
7/8/69

from *Herblock's State of the Union* (Simon & Schuster, 1972)

society based on the full equality of the races. Even more ominous is the fact that so vital a right as the franchise for Southern blacks is protected by legislation that must be extended periodically because it was passed for a five-year period only.[4] In 1969 the Nixon Administration narrowly lost in its bid to have Congress modify the Act in such a manner as to substantially weaken it. The Congress must again decide on whether to extend the Act in 1975, and again the franchise of Southern blacks will be at stake.

Governmental casualness toward the racial issue over time is matched by an equally disturbing pattern of equivocation in responding to specific demands by blacks for policy changes. As is demonstrated in the passage of the 1964 Civil Rights Act, government has moved to remedy grave racial injustices only when severely pressured and prodded, not voluntarily because it perceives a need for action. It responds by granting only the concessions that are virtually unavoidable, not in terms of carefully calculated remedies to solve a problem. Although the cumulative effect of several small steps taken in response to persistent pressure has been far-reaching, the impact is thus limited by their lack of coherence and their makeshift character. This pattern in governmental responses to blacks may be attributed in part to the attitudes of individual legislators and to the characteristics of decision-making structures. Nevertheless to a larger extent it is a reflection of the attitudes and will of the white society.

The many consequences of this pattern of governmental responses to the racial issue and to specific policy demands by blacks have profound significance. With depressing consistency, empirical research findings document a sharp decline in trust in the political system among blacks and demonstrate that blacks feel substantially less efficacious than do whites. Equally significant in this regard is the rapidly growing belief among blacks that a dignified future for black America can be realized only in a separate society. Among those who have not yet completely despaired of pursuing an existence as part of a single American society there is an almost frantic search for feasible approaches to remedying the continuing, serious disparities between the needs and aspirations of blacks in the society and the character and extent of governmental responses to them. In short, for these people who still comprise the majority of black America, the challenge of the hour is finding ways of influencing the policy process to ensure substantially greater attentiveness to blacks.

In politics "influence," like "power," defies precise, concrete definition but in this context we mean by political influence the opportunity and capacity to contribute visibly and tangibly to the formulation and implementation of public policy, ensuring thereby an equitable allocation of goods, services, and prestige to the black community. That blacks do not now enjoy

---

[4] The 1965 Voting Rights Act as initially passed was to run for five years. It was extended in 1970 for a second five years after attempts by the Nixon Administration to weaken the Act.

substantial influence on the policy process is apparent. At both state and national levels they are only peripherally and intermittently involved, if at all, in the formulation or implementation of policies which directly and vitally affect them. Thus they occupy the untenable position of being almost entirely dependent on the beneficence of a political system that has been so clearly unsympathetic over time.

Concern with this untenable position has prompted several proposals concerning ways by which blacks may acquire greater influence in the policy process at least at the national level. The major proposals fall into three broad though not exclusive categories. In the first category are those that recommend major structural changes in the political system including (1) alteration of the present basis for representation in Congress to ensure for blacks a proportion of representation consistent with their proportion in the population; (2) creation of states out of the major urban centers which, with their large black population, would increase the impact of blacks on Presidential elections and provide a broad range of new political opportunities for blacks; (3) provision of a substantial measure of autonomy for larger black communities to facilitate their control over institutions which directly affect their daily lives.[5] In the second category are those proposals that look toward a basic change in the attitudes of whites—especially the white ethnics of the urban areas—toward blacks to such an extent that cooperative political activities can be routinely undertaken and race ceases to be relevant in the allocation of resources or in the filling of political roles. The third category of proposed changes emphasizes several modifications in the character and level of black political activities.

Persuasive arguments can be advanced in favor of all of these approaches to increasing the political influence of blacks. In fact, it is highly unlikely that the disabilities experienced by blacks will be entirely eradicated without all three types of change. Clearly, however, they are not all equally likely. Changes in the first category would require major constitutional amendments, and attitude change among whites is an extremely long-range prospect at best. Thus the likelihood of major structural or attitudinal changes is remote, and such changes are probably unachievable.

Our concern here will be to identify some essential first steps which blacks can take in changing the pattern of their political activities in order to substantially enhance their influence on the policy process. It is naive to expect that such adjustments will entirely solve the problems blacks face in the political system, but it is a vital and logical first step for several reasons. (1) It is the approach over which blacks possess the greatest immediate control since it is not dependent on the acquiescence of whites. (2) Events of the past decade have substantially altered the specific policy interests of

[5]See for example Matthew Holden, *The White Man's Burden* (San Francisco: Chandler, 1973), 244–253. See also Joe Feagan and Harlan Hahn, *Ghetto Revolts* (New York: Macmillan, 1973).

blacks, rendering much of the traditional pattern of politics inappropriate and ineffective. (3) Eradication of most of the formal barriers to political activity by blacks permits and indeed requires exploration of new approaches to the political arena. (4) In the present context of American politics it is neither feasible nor morally defensible for blacks to expect that their interests will be pursued and protected by whites.

Earlier in this study we asserted that the character of black political life is a function of the subordinate status that the group occupies in the society. Status subordination shapes the internal organization and style of black politics by the psychological strains and other severe constraints it imposes, by determining the kinds of issues to which blacks are attentive, and by limiting the extent of their access to vital policy-making roles in the society. Therefore, when viewed against the pattern of politics within the society as a whole, black politics is to an extent "pathological." Maximization of black influence in the policy process requires that every effort be made to modify in some major respects these severe constraints on black political activity. Minimally, this modification should include a massive mobilization of the black community for sustained political action, considerable broadening of the issues and policy arenas to which blacks are attentive, and renewed efforts to penetrate vital, even if unspectacular, decision-making arenas. Focus on changing the pattern of black political activity does not suggest satisfaction with present structural arrangements, but such changes will considerably increase the prospects for inducing structural change.

## The Problem of Influence—Steps Toward a Solution

To a considerable extent the black power concept promulgated during the 1960s reflected a concern with the problem of influence on the American policy process. In their very thoughtful exposition on the concept, Stokely Carmichael and Charles V. Hamilton suggest that the goal of black power is "an effective share in the total power of the society," or more explicitly, "full participation in the decision-making processes affecting the lives of black people. . . ."[6] It rests on the basic premise that before blacks can effectively operate in the political system they must achieve group solidarity and internal organization. The advocacy of black power has lost the stridency of the 1960s but the conviction about the primacy of effective political involvement not only has not subsided but has been strengthened. In an address at the Annual Congressional Black Caucus dinner, Senator Brooke struck this note, asserting that

> Political power and public office have been the keys which
> opened the doors of opportunity for various groups in America since

---

[6] Stokely Carmichael and Charles V. Hamilton, *Black Power: The Politics of Liberation in America* (New York: Vintage, 1967), p. 47.

the founding of our country. Americans respect and respond to political power. Political power influences public policy at all levels. This is the nature of politics. And others have mastered the ground rules, and so must we.[7]

Today, blacks look with satisfaction at recent electoral successes that have substantially increased the number of blacks elected to public office. Many regard this as impressive evidence of major strides forward in the political arena. In fact, however, most of the new electoral gains are more symbolic than potential sources of influence. When viewed in terms of the needs of the group and their potential in the political arena, these new gains are extremely modest.

It is undeniable that white racism continues to be a formidable obstacle to black political advancement. The great debate initiated by Edmund Muskie during the Presidential primaries of 1972 about whether the country "was ready for a black Vice-President" is one example of the society's racism as an obstacle. The traditional patterns of leadership recruitment by the political parties, though modified somewhat in the Democratic party in 1972, also have operated to preclude the recruitment of blacks to influential leadership roles with only rare exceptions. However, an equally significant handicap is the failure of blacks to strive with sufficient vigor to secure a larger role for themselves in the political system. Notably, an effective consolidation of the resources of the black community in the manner envisioned by Carmichael and Hamilton has not been seriously attempted. In the face of broadening opportunities for political involvement, relatively little has been done to explore new methods of exploiting these new opportunities. Of the many steps which can and should be taken three seem particularly urgent: (1) the development of new leadership mechanisms to effectively mobilize the black community for sustained political action; (2) a broadening of the range of interest and attention to the policy process; and (3) greater efforts to participate more extensively in the policy process.

### Institution Building for New Leadership

The first vital step toward the goal of greater influence in the policy process is mobilization of the black population for more extensive participation in politics. Although we concluded in Chapter 8 that, all things considered, the level of black political participation is somewhat higher than that expected of individuals of their socioeconomic standing, the group's overall level of participation is still much lower than it can afford. The evidence is overwhelming that blacks have considerably more at stake in the political process than do whites and so cannot be satisfied with a comparable, or even slightly higher level of participation. In spite of this fact the group's most

[7] Quoted in *Focus* 1, 12 (October 1973), p. 2.

basic resource—its electoral strength enhanced by its strategic concentration in urban areas—is not being mobilized for maximum impact. This is evidenced by the fact that well over one-third of the eligible black voters fail to vote for any of a variety of reasons. While there has been a sharp increase in black voting in the South, there has been an equally sharp decline in voting outside the South, thereby canceling much of the impact of the 1965 Voting Rights Act.

Several investigators attribute the present level of participation, especially the decline among Northern urban voters, to rapidly declining trust in the political system. A second potent contributor to this level of participation is the tendency among blacks to ignore the electoral process when civil rights or other salient race issues are not directly involved. In both instances, however, nonparticipation is self-defeating. In the first place, it helps to further reduce the responsiveness of the political system to blacks and thus deepen the distrust. In the second place, because issues vital to their well-being are constantly being decided upon even when they do not emerge as salient issues in elections, there is a clear and urgent need for extensive, persistent participation by blacks.

Participation on the scale required in the face of the historical, psychological, and socioeconomic constraints on blacks requires a massive, continuing mobilizational effort by effective and alert community leadership. This mobilizational effort requires more than "get out the vote campaigns" financed by the major parties at election times. It requires a consistent program of increasing the political consciousness of the group, identifying and articulating specific goals, and identifying strategies for achieving these goals. This kind of need among blacks is not new, but at times it has loomed larger than at others. In his study of Negro leadership in Chicago, James Q. Wilson identified a number of long-standing weaknesses in community institutions and leaders which undermine the political effectiveness of the black community. He pointed out, for example, that the church and the press occupy especially strategic places in black communities, yet almost without exception they have failed to provide strong, stable bases for vigorous and sustained political activity. Wilson also found that conflicting styles and limited political resources have severely curtailed the effectiveness of black community leaders.[8] Although his findings are confined primarily to Chicago, indications are that these conditions are widespread.

Leadership among blacks, especially at the community level, has been extensively studied by social scientists. They have attempted to identify the social backgrounds of these "leaders," how they acquire leadership status, the styles or approaches they have taken in the pursuit of interests of their communities, and, in a few cases, the effectiveness of these leaders.[9] National

[8] James Q. Wilson, *Negro Politics, The Search for Leadership* (New York: Free Press, 1960), pp. 111–122, 169–213.

[9] See for example C. B. Johnson, "Negro Racial Movements and Leadership in the United States," *American Journal of Sociology* 42 (July 1937), 56–72; Everett C. Ladd,

studies have been more superficial and confined to measuring the level of support among blacks for nationally prominent and politically active blacks.[10] In fact, the emergence during the last decade of a number of highly visible political activists has resulted in a tendency to equate black politics with the activities of these "leaders."

This large volume of leadership studies reflects no clear, widely accepted criteria for determining who are black "leaders." Thus Matthews and Prothro identify as leaders "those people most frequently thought of as leaders by Negro citizens,"[11] while Holden suggests that black leaders usually are "those who seek (or claim to seek) the interest of the whole black population and who purport to do so by defining for blacks how they should relate to whites."[12] As these and several other similar definitions indicate, black "leaders" traditionally have been prominent blacks who came to be recognized by blacks and whites in any of a variety of ways as spokesmen for, and on behalf of, the race. On the national level, especially during the last decade, the heads of major nationwide black organizations—Roy Wilkins, Martin Luther King, James Farmer, Stokely Carmichael, Elijah Muhammed, Malcolm X—all have been designated as "leaders" and have behaved as leaders.

In the mid-1970s these prominent (and in some cases even charismatic) leaders have all but disappeared or now maintain a considerably lower profile than the era of protest politics permitted. The size and complexity of the black community as well as the changed issues and circumstances that now shape black political life now make untenable the emergence of other traditional "race leaders." This does not remove the need for effective leadership; on the contrary, it requires that blacks urgently seek to create new, effective leadership mechanisms to serve the black community in at least the following ways: (1) to identify and communicate to blacks the broad range of public issues with which they need to be concerned, especially those having a direct bearing on their daily lives; (2) to articulate in the various policy arenas the interests and aspirations of the black community to the extent that they can be identified; (3) to develop and maintain among blacks a high level of interest in, attentiveness to, and contacts with all areas of the policy arena.

These leadership tasks require effective, thoughtfully conceived leadership structures within the black community. What is contemplated therefore is a serious attempt at institution-building within black America as a basis for mobilizing the resources of the community for a more effective role in the policy processes of the society. I cannot provide here a blueprint for this effort, which must be the product of extensive consultation and unselfish

Jr., *Negro Political Leadership in the South* (Ithaca, N.Y.: Cornell University Press, 1966); Donald Matthews and James Prothro, *Negroes and the New Southern Politics* (New York: Harcourt Brace Jovanovich, 1966), pp. 175–202.

  [10] William Brink and Louis Harris, *Black and White: A Study of U.S. Racial Attitudes Today* (New York: Simon & Schuster, 1966), pp. 48–69.

  [11] Matthews and Prothro, *op. cit.,* p. 178.

  [12] Holden, *op. cit.,* p. 4.

cooperation among the various segments of black America. Clearly, however, any such institution must embrace all the major black population centers of the nation although it need not include every ideological orientation or point of view at the outset. It should have visible, efficient organizational structure and draw fully upon the experience and expertise of black Americans. It should be provided with a strong financial foundation from within the black community, and it should not presume or seek a monolithic black community but should approach the community's needs in a pragmatic, nonideological manner. Such an institution is not unrealistic and should not even be improbable because it is desperately needed and the resources for its creation—both technical and financial—are available to blacks.

Institution-building of the kind proposed here will not only contribute to the overall level and quality of black political activity but will serve as an essential part of the changing character of black political life. With a few exceptions the institutions that have been prominent in the political activities of blacks thus far were the joint creation of blacks and whites and were geared to relatively limited types of political activity designed to secure basic rights and privileges. In the substantially changing circumstances surrounding black political activity the contribution of these organizations can at best be extremely limited. New political institutions thus provide one opportunity for self-reliance while meeting the distinct needs of blacks today.

Recognition of the limited utility of existing organizations and the need for new efforts at institution-building of the kind suggested have already resulted in some tentative first steps in this direction. One such step was creation of the Congressional Black Caucus in 1969 by the black members of the House of Representatives. In communicating a list of policy proposals to the President in March 1971, the Caucus characterized itself as a new kind of leadership, noting that "it is petitioned daily by citizens living hundreds of miles from our districts who look on us as Congressmen-at-large for black people and poor people in the United States."[13]

Efforts by the Caucus to provide a "new kind of leadership" were vigorous but not entirely effective. It managed to articulate forcefully a number of important concerns, but even though it assembled a small staff and obtained considerable national exposure, the Caucus simply lacked the capacity to serve as an effective instrument of leadership for blacks. The members of the Caucus are, after all, legislators—and that role is an extremely demanding one requiring first the pursuit of constituency interests. Furthermore, although the Caucus gives a desirable focus to the activities of these legislators, it has the potential for undermining their effectiveness as legislators. Not surprisingly, therefore, one of its subcommittees recently recommended that "instead of being all things to all people, the Caucus should focus on the

---

[13] "Congressional Black Caucus' Recommendations to President Nixon," *Congressional Record,* 92nd Cong., 1st Sess., March 30, 1971.

legislative process, the one specific area where it possesses the greatest expertise. . . . The Caucus should provide a black perspective for any legislation that comes through the House, especially through its committees."[14]

Although it has not been able to fill the leadership role as initially envisioned, the Caucus initiated a separate, promising move toward major institution-building. It issued the initial call to a National Black Political Convention held at Gary, Indiana, in March 1972. The Convention was not a resounding success and the Black Agenda it eventually drafted failed to win the support of the Caucus, yet it created a continuing body, the National Black Political Assembly, composed of 427 delegates. Its mission has been identified thus:

> . . . to conduct the business of the convention, to endorse and support candidates for elective office, to conduct national voter education and registration programs, to lobby for black interests, to assess black programs and to make recommendations to the convention and the black community at large. It was also to be the primary power broker in dealing with white political institutions and establishing relationships with black people around the world.[15]

A smaller body selected from the Assembly—the National Black Political Council—has major operating responsibilities.

At present, this fledgling organization is still in its infancy and has yet to become actively involved in political matters either at the national or local level. In fact, one commentator observes that the organization has been unable to develop a strategy for community organization or to establish a grass-roots base. Contributing to this very slow start is the fact that the organization has not had the support of most elected black officials or the leaders of the major civil rights organizations.[16] These failings of the Council were starkly reflected in its second convention held at Little Rock, Arkansas, in March 1974. Not only did it fail to attract more than a few black elected officials or other nationally prominent personalities, but it apparently failed to achieve any significant results. At best then, these are tentative first steps, reflecting a recognition of the need for immediate, effective institution-building.

### Taking a New Approach to the Policy Process

Nowhere are the constraints imposed on black political life by their subordinate status more apparent than in their orientation to the policy

---

[14] Quoted in Alvin Poinsett, "The Black Caucus: Five Years Later," *Ebony* (June 1973), p. 72.
[15] John Dean, "Black Political Assembly; Birth of a New Force," *Focus* 2, 1 (November 1972), 4–5.
[16] *Ibid.*

process. By "policy process" we mean all the structures and processes by which public policies are formulated and implemented.[17] Status subordination prompted development of a very narrow focus on this policy process, encouraged attentiveness to a relatively limited set of issues (mostly those directly related to the struggle for racial equality), and reduced the opportunities and the inclination to actively seek some vital roles in the process. A second vital step toward increased influence in the policy process, therefore, is the correction of this feature of black politics by developing greater attentiveness to a much broader range of policy issues.

A factor contributing to these limitations on black orientations to the policy process is the essentially defensive character of black politics over time. The group has been compelled to concentrate all its efforts on struggling *against* a wide range of injustices and disabilities which together define its subordinate status. This defensive political posture means that by expending energies and resources in efforts to eradicate discriminatory policies and practices blacks have not been able to develop positive, programmatic approaches to politics. In this regard Wolman and Thomas observe that "the policy goals blacks have pursued have been short-run, direct and highly visible: primarily to attack overt racial discrimination and promote integration."[18] Thus while blacks have been able to secure substantial reduction in discriminatory policies and practices in areas such as education and housing, they have not been able to propose specific new programs in these areas. This defensive orientation continues to inhibit major contributions by blacks to the policy process because the principal politically active black organizations are still geared almost entirely to this antidiscrimination kind of activity. Furthermore, blacks have not fully recognized or adjusted to the fundamentally different circumstances surrounding their political activities today. Instead of expanding or developing the capacity to influence policy-making there has been a tendency to maintain the traditional organizations and styles of politics.

It should be noted that this defensive political posture is not peculiar to black Americans. On the contrary, it is typical of communities which have been victims of oppression and which have had to engage in protracted struggle to eradicate the oppression. One finds for example that in most colonial societies effective political movements among the indigenous people centered around the struggle against colonial rule. The common enemy provided the focal point for political activity, shaped political styles, and served as a powerful unifying force. With the eradication of colonial rule, the new societies face the crisis of readjusting to the new and more complicated

---

[17] John A. Straayer and Robert D. Wrinkle, *American Government, Policy, and Non-Decisions* (Columbus, Ohio: Merrill, 1972), pp. 6–7.

[18] Harold Wolman and Norman Thomas, "Black Interests, Black Groups and Black Influence in the Federal Policy Process: The Cases of Housing and Education," *Journal of Politics* 32 (November 1970), 94.

task of governing, and of formulating and pursuing national goals. In addition, the cohesiveness developed in the face of a common, highly visible enemy often disintegrates under the strain of readjustment. Black America is not an entirely "liberated" community, but most of the more visible symbols of their subordination have been eliminated creating a somewhat analogous situation.

Closely related to the politically defensive posture of blacks has been the tendency to focus attention almost exclusively on explicitly race-related policy issues. This limited focus is understandable, since it has been necessary for blacks to remain almost entirely preoccupied with self-improvement through removal of the enormous burden of racism. In their nationwide study in 1966, Brink and Harris demonstrated the extent of black preoccupation with racial matters, reporting that at the polls blacks were almost always preoccupied with the single issue, "Would the candidate help or hurt the cause of civil rights;"[19] A similar finding was reported in a study of the 1968 Presidential elections. The authors concluded that although blacks were more opposed to the Vietnam War than any other group in the society, in selecting their candidate for President, "Vietnam attitudes paled into insignificance by contrast with attitudes toward programs on civil rights within the country."[20]

Although this narrow focus is understandable, it has severe disadvantages. The policy process is extremely complex and issues are interrelated, especially when we move from broad, basic "civil rights" issues to specific ones involving economic and social well-being over which there is considerable competition. Influence by blacks requires extensive familiarity with the total process. The policy changes forged over years of intense struggle now permit, and in fact require, that blacks concern themselves with the entire range of policy issues in the political arena because few if any are unimportant to them. After all, the decisions made in the areas of defense, foreign affairs, or international commerce affect the level of resources available for domestic programs vital to blacks. In addition, through active involvement with issues not of direct concern to them, black groups may eventually be in a position to trade their support of such issues with other groups whose interests are more directly involved for support of those issues vital to blacks. Thus greater maneuverability can be achieved from broad familiarity with and involvement in the policy process.

In areas such as foreign affairs blacks continue to be almost entirely uninvolved, even when their interests are clearly at stake. Although they have demonstrated considerable interest in Africa and have attempted to emphasize their African roots, they have exhibited little apparent concern with U.S.

[19] Brink and Harris, *op. cit.,* p. 77.
[20] Philip Converse et al., "Continuity and Change in American Politics: Parties and Issues in the 1968 Election," *American Political Science Review* 63 (December 1969), 1085.

policies on that continent even when these policies are blatantly detrimental to the interests and aspirations of Africans.[21] Thus the United States has flagrantly and unconscionably supported, with massive financial and military assistance, a brutal Portugese colonial war aginst the Africans of Angola, Mozambique, and Guinea-Bissau while almost all of black America remains either unaware or unconcerned. In fact, the area of foreign affairs demonstrates clearly the difference between an attentive and influential minority group and an inattentive and uninfluential one. A recently enacted Foreign Trade Act prohibits the United States from extending to the Soviet Union routine trade concessions or credits for purchasing goods on the American market until it agrees to permit the free emigration of Soviet Jews. This was accomplished in the total absence of any precedent for such action and with no strong evidence of discrimination or mistreatment of Soviet Jews. On the other hand, the atrocities inflicted by the South African government on blacks in that country are common knowledge, as are the severe restrictions on their travel. Nevertheless, similar economic sanctions against South Africa have not even been contemplated. The fact is that while American Jews are actively involved in such foreign affairs issues, few black Americans are even aware of them. Furthermore legislators are so sensitive to the political influence of America's approximately six million Jews that support for the issue is virtually automatic.

A defensive and extremely limited range of policy interests by blacks has been accompanied by a limited view of the policy arena. The traditional battlegrounds have been the Courts and the Congress in efforts to obtain major policy changes on civil rights issues. In these arenas blacks have managed to develop visible expertise. However, these are not the only points in the policy process at which attention must be directed in order to influence policy decisions. For example, before proposals reach the legislature for action, considerable work is done in the appropriate departments or agencies of government and policy alternatives are formulated which form the basis of legislative action. In addition, after policies are decided upon, they must be interpreted and implemented. One group of scholars observe in this regard that:

> The records are full of stories of public programs which, although authorized, were rendered ineffective by the lack of funds or a lack of vigor by those charged with program implementation. Thus, individuals and groups who are interested in seeing some problem solved publicly will pay as much attention to the implementation of the program as to the actual passage of the legislation which created the program in the first place.[22]

[21] See Milton D. Morris, "Black Americans and the Foreign Policy Process: The Case of Africa," *Western Political Quarterly* **25**, 3 (September 1972), 451–463.

[22] Straayer and Wrinkle, *op. cit.*, p. 9.

By concentrating on the principal arenas only, blacks as a rule have entered the policy arena too late and left too early to have considerable influence on even those policies which affect them directly.

This very limited involvement in the policy process is not now merely a matter of choice—it reflects a genuine weakness in black political life. Wolman and Thomas report that at least in that portion of the bureaucracy dealing with education and housing policies, blacks lack the skills necessary to contribute to the development or implementation of policies. They suggest that in most cases blacks have had to rely on indirect representation of their interests by other groups such as organized labor because (1) civil rights organizations are generally uninformed about the policy process or, as one of their interviewees put it, "by and large most civil rights leaders and staffs are really babes in the woods so far as policy is concerned;" (2) black organizations lack effective and knowledgeable lobbyists—Clarence Mitchell, III is still the only expert lobbyist in Washington, D.C., on the behalf of blacks; (3) the styles of most black activists and organizations do not lend themselves to the lobbying necessary to influence policies because "lobbying emphasizes compromise, accommodation, patience," and most black groups take a highly moral and emotional approach more suited to the public rather than to the policy-making elite.[23] To be fully effective in the policy process, then, there is clearly a need for rapid development and application of new political skills and new orientations to the policy process.

### Helping Slice the Pie

In an intensely competitive society such as ours, how the "national pie" (goods and services of the society) is shared is largely a function of who participates in the slicing. Clearly, therefore, influence on the policy process for blacks requires extensive black involvement in this slicing process. We stated above that blacks have not been sufficiently attentive to the various policy arenas in which this process takes place and that they presently lack the structure and expertise to adequately articulate black interests in these arenas. Of even greater consequence than the inability to participate in the highly specialized and consistent manner characteristic of many interest groups, is the fact that very few blacks occupy strategic roles in the political system from which they can contribute directly and continually to the shaping of public policy or slicing the "national pie." The third major step in seeking increased influence on the policy process therefore is a calculated, massive effort at penetrating policy-relevant institutions at every level of government and even in potentially influential nongovernmental organizations.

[23] Wolman and Thomas, *op. cit.,* p. 893.

In examining decision making in the area of foreign affairs, Gabriel Almond observed that "policy influencers" generally come from four elite groups: (1) political elites—persons elected to national public office, appointees to high office, or prominent party leaders; (2) bureaucratic elites—those serving in the executive branch and who enjoy special privileges as a result of their expertise and contact with particular policy problems; (3) communications elites—those persons who are owners or controllers of important sectors of the media—radio, television, print media; and (4) interest elites—those representing the many powerful, private, policy-oriented groups. In fact, the entire policy process is influenced by members of these four elite categories and for several reasons blacks are sparsely represented among them.

Although the last decade has witnessed substantial increases in the overall presence of blacks among the political elites, their presence is still low in view of the total size of the black population. Of the 535 members of Congress, the very top of the political elite, only 16 are black. Because most of these are newcomers, they rank low in seniority—and in Congress low seniority means very limited influence. In the House, Charles Diggs is now the most senior black member. His seniority has given him chairmanship of the House Committee on the District of Columbia and Chairmanship of the Foreign Affairs Committee's subcommittee on Africa. No other black representative occupies key chairmanships in the House. In the absence of early, drastic Congressional reforms, blacks are thus very far from occupying a genuinely influential role in Congress.

The picture for elected officials at the state and local levels has improved considerably during the last eight years, but blacks are still severely underrepresented here. They still occupy less than one percent of the total elective offices in the United States, and a large percentage of the black elected officials hold relatively uninfluential positions. In the South, for example, 90 percent of the black mayors hold office in small communities of 4500 or fewer residents, and most of these communities have extremely limited resources.[24] Studies done in major urban centers outside the South also demonstrate a very sparse representation of blacks among political influentials.[25] Senator Brooke noted in this regard that there are only three blacks in the nation who hold statewide elective office, yet this kind of office is what provides a strong power base.

The black presence among the appointed political elite is now greater than it was ten years ago but nevertheless remains a major disappointment. These appointees, cabinet and subcabinet personnel, members of the several federal agencies, bureaus, and the like are in almost all cases "major power

[24] Charles S. Bullock, III, "Southern Elected Black Officials," paper prepared for delivery at the Southern Political Science Association, Atlanta, Ga., November 1973, p. 11.
[25] For example see Karl H. Fleming et al., "Black Powerlessness in Policymaking Positions," *Sociological Quarterly* 3 (Winter 1972), 126–133.

holders." At this level black appointees would provide vital symbolic assurance of black involvement in the policy process as well as opportunities for input in the total policy process. Thurgood Marshall's appointment as Solicitor General and his subsequent elevation to the Supreme Court, Robert Weaver's appointment as Secretary of Housing and Urban Development, and Andrew Brimmer's appointment as a member of the Federal Reserve Board are examples of black appointees at this level. Unfortunately, however, not only have these been too few but such top-level appointments have been declining, especially since 1969. Both Weaver and Brimmer have now left these positions.

The absence of blacks at this level illustrates the frustrating dilemma faced by blacks in their efforts to penetrate the policy process. Studies of the pattern of recruitment to these top political roles indicate that presidents and their advisers usually rely on two basic considerations in making recruitment decisions: "recognition of those who deserved appointment on the basis of service to the party; and recognition of the need to obtain the 'best talent' to serve in these demanding positions."[26] Because most presidents in recent times have been Democrats, and because blacks are the most loyal of Democrats, at least the first criteria should aid black appointees. Most presidents, however, are creating a "governing team" and do not perceive blacks as potential "team members." Therefore, when blacks are rewarded with positions, they are usually low level and safely noninfluential.

Examination of the backgrounds of the individuals appointed at this level further indicates why blacks are so few. A study of these appointees from Roosevelt to Kennedy reveal that they are overwhelmingly drawn from three career fields in which blacks are scarce—business executives, lawyers, and career civil servants. Although almost 80 percent had previous government service experience, most of the newcomers were drawn from the ranks of a few prominent Eastern educational institutions.[27] Thus the top political appointees are drawn disproportionately from a privileged elite. Before blacks are considered they must achieve national prominence against extreme odds in order to come to the attention of recruiters. Furthermore, most of these appointments must be confirmed by the Senate, and in the past race has been a serious obstacle to confirmation. How serious an obstacle is demonstrated in the case of Robert Weaver who was to be appointed Secretary of the proposed new Department of Housing and Urban Development by President Kennedy. Because several Senators strongly objected to this they blocked creation of the new department for some time.

Among the bureaucratic elites there are also important limitations on the black presence, although here, too, definite improvements have occurred

---

[26] Dean E. Mann,"The Selection of Federal Political Executives." *American Political Science Review* 58 (1964), 86.

[27] *Ibid.*, pp. 92–99.

in recent years. Blacks have been part of the bureaucracy at least since 1883 when the Pendleton Act introduced the merit system as a basis for most recruitment (there were 620 blacks in the bureaucracy in that year), but they have been victims of intense discrimination. Since 1940 when Franklin Roosevelt issued an Executive Order banning racial discrimination in some recruitment policies, every president has taken steps to eliminate it by Executive Orders and administrative decrees. The most recent Executive Order (11478) issued by President Nixon in August 1969 required each agency and department to develop plans for implementing equal employment opportunity. In the bureaucracy at present, the problem that blacks face is not one of underrepresentation in general—it is their concentration in the very low ranks. Thus in 1972 15.3 percent of all federal jobs (389,762) were held by blacks but less than half (157,600) were in the General Schedule category and only 6.2 percent of these were in grades 12–18. (the middle and upper levels of the bureaucracy).[28]

In some segments of the bureaucracy resistance to the recruitment of blacks continues to be formidable. The Department of State is one prominent example where the upper ranks have yielded to blacks only slightly and with considerable reluctance. Although almost one-third of the sovereign states in the international community today have mostly black populations, the United States Diplomatic Corps and Foreign Service Officer Corps remain almost entirely white. As of 1970, blacks constituted approximately 1.2 percent of this personnel,[29] this in spite of years of vigorous efforts by the NAACP to prod the Department into recruiting more blacks to top level jobs. Commenting on the situation, Clarence Mitchell has complained that "no matter who is Secretary of State there is an iron ring of prejudice in that Department which makes it impossible for blacks to make headway in the State Department."[30]

In urging that blacks make renewed efforts to secure positions at all levels of the bureaucracy, we do not overlook the many obstacles to such an effort. Blacks are handicapped in seeking such positions by (1) the more limited pool of highly educated or expert blacks available for such roles; (2) the established patterns of recruitment to some segments of the bureaucracy which favor a small, privileged segment of the population; and (3) the intrinsic institutional racism that makes upward mobility difficult and the general work atmosphere unattractive. In addition, even where these obstacles are being lowered, there is considerable doubt among some blacks about the utility, or even the morality, of becoming part of an insensitive and historical-

---

[28] *Minority Group Employment in the Federal Government* (Washington, D.C.: United States Civil Service Commission, 1972), pp. iv–vii.

[29] "Negro Officer Employment in the Foreign Service," in *Policy Toward Africa for the Seventies–Hearings Before the Sub-Committee on Africa* (Washington, D.C.: Government Printing Office, 1970), p. 269.

[30] "Statement by Clarence Mitchell Before the House Sub-Committee on Africa," in *Policy Toward Africa for the Seventies–Hearings Before the Sub-Committee on Africa, op. cit.*, p. 265.

ly racist institution. In spite of these considerations there are compelling reasons for extensive black involvement in this segment of government at the national level and below. The most obvious is that although bureaucratic roles are often tedious and unspectacular, they are vital sources of influence on the policy process. Bureaucrats, especially those at the upper level, gather and interpret data which form the basis for policy proposals, they interpret the often broad and vague policies formulated by the legislature, and they undertake the day-to-day implementation of policies. Substantial participation by blacks in the various policy-related activities, therefore, constitutes one important way in which blacks may help to slice the national pie.

It should be emphasized that in advocating increased black presence in the bureaucracy I am not encouraging merely the presence of more black faces as an end, nor do I propose that blacks be installed as agents for or representatives of "black interests" and "black programs." Matthew Holden, in warning against such a goal, notes that "no executive appointee, no senior bureaucrat, automatically represents the 'interest' with which he has, in the past, been most identified merely because of that past identification. The bureaucratic enterprise contains its own incentives which impose directions and constraints upon the functionary. Thus, it is fatuous to expect that a black functionary will automatically 'represent black interests' or that if he attempts to do this he will automatically be effective, without some external relationships."[31]

There are in fact three basic ways in which an increased black presence will be directly beneficial to blacks. The first, as already noted, is its symbolic impact. Black involvement has the effect of indicating to blacks that they are part of the total process, and this may encourage other blacks to approach the bureaucracy more readily to pursue their interests. Second, experience in bureaucratic roles adds to the pool of expertise vitally needed by blacks. Third, and most important, blacks bring to these roles values, perceptions, and styles that reflect their backgrounds, experiences, and aspirations. These are important determinants of the perception of problems as well as of the specific policy choices or recommendations that bureaucrats make.[32]

Thus far, our attention has been directed toward the policy process at the national level but similar involvement at state and local levels is also vital. Historically blacks have concentrated most of their efforts and attention on the national level of government because of the greater capacity at this level to meet pressing needs and because of the hostility or indifference of many state and local governments. However, important changes have been taking place in the overall pattern of governance in the society. Two aspects of these changes involving state and local level government are particularly note-

---

[31] Holden, *op. cit.*, p. 206.
[32] Herbert C. Kelman, "The Role of the Individual in International Affairs: Some Conceptual and Methodological Considerations," *Journal of International Affairs* **24** (1970), 10–14.

worthy. One involves the sharp increase in funds available to governments at this level to be used at their discretion, and the other involves the growing trend toward regional governments and regional or areawide development planning.

By the time Richard Nixon left office in August 1974 he had achieved substantial success toward his proposed "New Federalism." The most notable of these achievements are the general revenue sharing program inaugurated in 1972 which provided for distribution of large amounts of federal funds in direct grants to state and local governments to be used at their discretion; and the Housing and Community Development Act of 1974 which replaced a federally supervised categorical grant program for community development with a single bloc-grant program largely at the discretion of local governments. Although routine nondiscrimination provisions are written into the legislation authorizing these programs, it is becoming increasingly apparent that utilization of these funds in an equitable and nondiscriminatory manner will require vigorous and persistent participation by blacks in all phases of local policy-making.

The development of regional or areawide governmental planning institutions and processes is also a major new challenge to blacks. Although efforts in this direction have been underway for a long time (at least since 1951), such institutions and processes are now increasing rapidly in prominence and in numbers. Regionalism should be beneficial to blacks by facilitating more effective resource utilization and more equitable allocation of resources but these results are not automatic. Indeed, at present this development is as much a threat to blacks as it is a potential boon. There is the fear—not unfounded—that the white majority in large metropolitan regions will utilize regional governmental bodies to dilute the growing political influence of blacks in central cities and thus undo recent political gains. Furthermore, there is concern that these bodies do not now permit adequate black involvement and are not sensitive to the issues and concerns vital to blacks. It is essential, therefore, that blacks become familiar with these regional institutions and processes and penetrate them to the greatest extent possible in order to protect their interests. In short, the trend toward a reduced federal role in meeting many vital human needs and an increased role for state and local governments demands a major readjustment in black political activity to help shape decisions at the local levels.

## Coalitions and the Future of Black Politics

The basic reorientation of black political activities that is suggested here will not come swiftly or easily. In addition to the obviously tedious problems involved in institution-building for effective community leadership which must be resolved, the effort will require the surrender of personal ambitions for leadership and the abandonment of empty polemicism and ideological posturing that have become formidable obstacles to unified activities among blacks. Even granting the complete and reasonably speedy success of this effort, however, the realities of American political life are such that blacks will still be unable to achieve independently most of their primary policy objectives. As a relatively small minority in the society, even when fully mobilized, they will have acquired the capacity only to operate more effectively in a highly competitive, "pluralist" polity. Inevitably therefore, the future of black politics must include a search for potential allies in the political arena. This in turn raises the question of whether, and to what extent, race must continue to be the salient issue in politics.

The question of interracial coalitions long has been a topic of vigorous debate among concerned blacks. Willingly or otherwise blacks have been participants with whites in a variety of coalitions, but they have been deeply suspicious of such arrangements since in almost all instances they seem to have yielded much more than they gained. This was the case in their informal alliance with Southern whites in the Populist Movement of the 1890s and in their participation in the political machines which once dominated many urban areas. In his study of three distinct types of coalitions practiced in three Southern cities, Harry Holloway identified some of the disadvantages blacks encounter in coalition arrangements. He concludes that in all cases whites seemed to dominate because of their advantages. "They are the majority in most places. They have great economic resources at their disposal, including the wealth and prestige of top businessmen. They have the skills and established organization and they dominate all the organs of government."[33]

Most discussions of black-white coalition politics have focused on the electoral level at which the principal commodity that blacks bring to the coalition is the vote. This is clearly the crucial and in many cases the most important level for coalition politics. Nevertheless the thrust of these remarks is toward the use of coalitions in the national policy arena. Here, where national policy involving the allocation of goods and services for the entire society is made and implemented, expanded familiarity with and involvement in the policy process by an effectively organized black community will provide new capabilities and new resources for mutually beneficial coalitions with other groups.

Coalitions focusing on the national policy arena are not new to blacks and have been beneficial to them in several instances. In our discussion of the 1964 Civil Rights Act, we observed that a critical element in its passage was the informal alliance of blacks with "liberal" whites at one level and a more structured alliance of mostly white pressure groups with black organizations at another level. Similar coalitions were also vital in the passage of other civil

[33] Harry Holloway, "Negro Political Strategy: Coalition or Independent Power Politics," *Social Science Quarterly* 49 (December 1968), 545–546.

rights legislation starting in 1957 and became even more valuable when blacks attempted to block confirmation of President Nixon's nominees to the Supreme Court whose past record reflected insensitivity and even hostility to the rights of blacks. These coalitions were distinct in that they developed around primarily broad, moral issues to which whites felt persuaded to respond; nevertheless they demonstrate that under certain circumstances coalitions with whites have been valuable.

Most thoughtful students of the black experience are generally agreed about the necessity of interracial coalitions as long as suitable conditions for such coalitions exist. Carmichael and Hamilton provide one articulate and well-reasoned appraisal of the conditions necessary for coalitions. Rejecting the view that viable coalitions can occur between the politically and economically secure and the politically and economically insecure, or that coalitions can be sustained by a reliance on moral, friendly, or sentimental bases, they identify four preconditions for viable black-white coalitions:

> (a) recognition by the parties involved of their respective self-interests; (b) the mutual belief that each party stands to benefit in terms of that self-interest from allying with the other or others; (c) the acceptance of the fact that each party has its own independent base of power and does not depend for ultimate decision-making on a force outside itself; and (d) the realization that the coalition deals with specific and identifiable—as opposed to general and vague—goals.[34]

In an address to a recent gathering sponsored by the Black Caucus, Senator Edward W. Brooke emphasized the importance of coalitions in the future of black political activity. He observed that blacks in the past have taken too narrow a view of coalitions, regarding them as permanent and as a threat to black identity. Rejecting this view, he urged that blacks form "free-floating coalitions across racial lines. And these coalitions must be based on specific and pragmatic issues of common interest."[35] Similarly Sterling Tucker, a veteran black political activist, argues in favor of bold steps by blacks to form coalitions with whites on specific issues.[36]

Implicit in these assertions of the necessity for coalitions across racial lines is the recognition that the primary political objectives of blacks are no longer race specific. Civil rights laws were enacted in response to specifically black needs; however, today and in the foreseeable future, the primary goals of political action will be social and economic policies which are of equal concern to large segments of the society—black, white, Chicano, and Indian. In this regard, Senator Brooke observed that "our economic interests are clearly aligned with those of the majority of Americans. Inflation, unemployment, inequitable taxation, inadequate health care and housing are not black

---

[34] Carmichael and Hamilton, *op. cit.,* pp. 79–80.
[35] Quoted in *Focus* 1, 12 (October 1973), p. 2.
[36] Sterling Tucker, *For Blacks Only: Black Strategies for Change in America* (Grand Rapids, Mich.: Eerdmans, 1971).

issues, but issues affecting millions of Americans who suffer the agonies of our economy without ever sharing its abundance."[37]

Thus far, blacks have pursued several of these goals largely by themselves, making the effort part of the civil rights movement. It is noteworthy that Dr. King's last public act was not in support of a march to desegregate public facilities or to ensure voting rights for blacks, but an attempt to help striking garbage workers in Memphis, Tennessee. One of the last major "demonstrations" by the SCLC—the creation of Resurrection City in Washington, D.C.—was undertaken in an effort to relieve the plight of the poor. Furthermore, in its March 1971 policy recommendations to President Nixon, the Congressional Black Caucus focused primarily on such social and economic issues as manpower and employment practices, welfare reform, federal assistance to state and local governments, poverty programming, education, housing and urban development and the drug crisis rather than on explicitly racial issues. This linkage between civil rights interests and socioeconomic reforms is understandable, because while most of the poor are not black, most blacks have been poor and their poverty is a direct consequence of their systematic subordination. These efforts to secure adoption of policies to alleviate poverty and break the vicious cycle that keeps generation after generation its helpless victims have had relatively little success. Not only does the society refuse to concede the right of each of its members to a measure of social well-being, but increasingly poverty and related social problems are perceived as *black* problems.

In their efforts to secure social and economic policies which will improve the quality of life, blacks will need to cultivate new alliances involving all of those sectors of the society whose interests are directly involved. The precise composition of such coalitions will necessarily change with the issues at hand. Thus a coalition that would work for national programs to reconstruct and revitalize the dying cities in which most blacks live might be different from a coalition that would work for new and more effective educational or medical programs. Clearly blacks cannot be the sole determinants of the shape or extent of these coalitions, since some affected groups may be deterred from participating by their own racism. The important point here is that this is a promising path that should be fully explored.

In the long run, pursuit of a pragmatic coalition politics will require that blacks undertake a calculated deemphasis on racial politics in the policy arena. There is no apparent intrinsic value to the invocation of race in the policy arena except in pursuit of objectives that are race-specific. The policies that have been identified as now salient for blacks can and should be formulated in terms of "national interests" instead of the interest of blacks. Such a "deracialization" is essential to effective coalition building, and is consistent with the approach adopted by most successful special-interest

[37]*Focus* 1, (October 1973), p. 2.

groups. For example, the small group of oil producers who enjoy massive benefits through oil depletion allowances lobby to secure and protect their benefits under the guise of protecting the "national interest."

The suggestion that blacks move toward a deemphasis on race in the policy arena by no means contemplates abandonment of group identity or conscious concern with the problems and disabilities faced by blacks. It is possible to preserve these while reducing the saliency of race in the policy arena. Even without regard to the needs of formal coalitions, this approach will become increasingly necessary as the number of blacks elected or appointed to policy-making or administrative roles increases. Their effectiveness in these roles will be enhanced by the development of expertise—and by the insight and imagination they bring to the policy arena—rather than by their emphasis on race or their concern with entirely racial questions. In addition, an important element in the growth of an effective black presence in the policy process is the ability of blacks to secure support from whites in winning statewide office or office in constituencies with a majority of white voters. In these situations a deemphasis of race and explicitly racial issues is vital to success and to effective performance. Furthermore, over the long run such a deemphasis will make it more difficult for policymakers to cater to racial and other ethnic identities by making limited and symbolic gestures to each distinct group.

In suggesting a deemphasis on race in the policy arena we are not slighting the need to be vigilant about the impact of public policies on blacks, nor are we unaware that on occasions it will be necessary for blacks to "go it alone" in pursuing black objectives. On the contrary, the capacity for vigilance in the cause of black progress is vital and must remain unhindered by such deemphasis. The point is that the inclination to perceive all political conflicts in racial terms or preoccupation with "blackness" in the political arena are inconsistent with pragmatic coalition building and will be increasingly dysfunctional for a larger and more influential role for blacks in the political arena.

This study has traced in broad outlines the efforts of blacks in the United States to shed their subordinate status through political activity. A vital part of this process has been a struggle for access to the political arena as full participants. Elimination of virtually all formal obstacles to full participation now poses for blacks the challenge of maximizing their influence on the policy process in order to remove the last frustrating vestiges of subordination. Thus the study presents a view of black politics as focused on, and inseparable from, the larger political community, and assumes that many of the problems which blacks face in the society can be solved by vigorous and imaginative political action.

This perception of black politics is not universally shared. Some concerned blacks question the utility of continued efforts to operate within a political system which they view as inherently racist and insensitive to human needs.    Instead they view black politics as oriented toward the creation of a separate black nation or some still unspecified form of local self-government. Nevertheless, the evidence appears unassailable that blacks are inextricably involved in the total society and that this involvement will continue for the foreseeable future. Involvement in the political life of the society is therefore not merely a question of choice, it is an inevitable fact of life.

Assessments of what has been accomplished over the centuries of protracted political struggle by blacks in American society inevitably vary. It is not comforting to the victims of subordination to suggest that they are less unequal today than they were 50 years ago because inequality in any form is intolerable to a proud people. Because blacks still occupy a subordinate place in the society, it remains difficult to speak of progress, and because this subordination has been of such long standing it is equally difficult to suggest optimism about the future. Nevertheless, there are bases for reference to progress and optimism, and even a degree of pride in looking at the black political experience over time.

We observed at the outset of our study that racial or ethnic conflicts are global problems, the American experience being one of the most prominent. In assessing what has been accomplished in this society and the prospects for the future, it is useful to keep this larger picture in mind. Profound social cleavages are among the most formidable obstacles to social peace regardless of where they exist. The religio-political cleavage in Northern Ireland, cultural cleavages in the Soviet Union and Eastern Europe, tribal cleavages in Burundi and Nigeria, and racial cleavages in Southern Africa, Britain, the United States, and Malaysia all seem to resist resolution in spite of the widely different types of political, economic, and social systems within which they exist. In almost all of these cases there are few if any evidences of significant progress toward narrowing the cleavages; where there is evidence of progress it has been painfully slow.

Easily the most resistant cleavages are those based on race. The South African situation demonstrates resistance to change at its extreme. In fact, although we suggested that the basic political objective of blacks in societies like the United States and South Africa is transformation of subordinate-superordinate relations into a situation where race no longer defines one's status, nowhere has this goal actually been achieved. Despite the continuing problems that black Americans face in this regard, no other group of blacks has made as much progress toward that goal. This achievement of black Americans is significant in several respects and should not be overlooked or discounted. Viewed in its totality, it should be a source of considerable pride to black Americans and a basis for optimism to groups similarly situated in other societies.

Precisely how much progress has been achieved in transforming the pattern of American race relations is debatable, but the progress itself is a fact. A wide gap still exists in the quality of life between blacks and whites, but blacks can no longer be regarded as excluded from the political community. It is true that large segments of the white society still perceive blacks as inferiors, entitled only to a subordinate place in society, but as the political influence of blacks increases these perceptions will diminish in actual importance.

Just as important as the strides toward inclusion are the changes that have taken place within and among blacks. The pride and self-assurance that was once confined primarily to a very small black elite is now a mass phenomenon. Although divisions and disagreements among blacks continue, they have a solidarity and sense of common purpose today that are unprecedented. These healthy developments provide the basis for a profound faith in the inevitability of further progress toward a genuinely humane society in which color ceases to determine status or opportunity.

## SELECTED BIBLIOGRAPHY

**Abrahams, Henry.** *Freedom and the Court: Civil Rights and Liberties in the United States.* New York: Oxford University Press, 1967.

**Abrams, Charles.** "The Housing Problem and the Negro." *Daedalus* **115** (Winter 1966), 64–76.

**Balbus, Isaac.** *The Dialectics of Legal Repression: Black Rebels Before the American Criminal Courts.* New York: Basic Books, 1973.

**Bell, Derrick A.** "Racism in American Courts: Cause for Black Disruption or Despair?" *California Law Review* **61** (January 1973), 165–204.

**Berger, Monroe.** *Equality by Statute.* New York: Anchor, 1968.

**Blumenthal, Henry.** "Woodrow Wilson and the Race Question." *Journal of Negro History* **48** (January 1963), 1–21.

**Blumrosen, Alfred W.** "Administrative Creativity: The First Year of the Equal Employment Opportunity Commission." *George Washington Law Review* **38** (May 1970).

**Blumrosen, Alfred W.** "Strangers in Paradise: *Griggs vs. Duke Power Co.* and the Concept of Employment Discrimination." *Michigan Law Review* **71** (November 1972), 59–110.

**Blumrosen, Alfred W.** "The Duty of Fair Recruitment Under the Civil Rights Act of 1964." *Rutgers Law Review* **22**, 3 (Spring 1968), 465–536.

**Brest, Paul A.** "The Federal Government's Power to Protect Negroes and Civil Rights Workers Against Privately Inflicted Harm." *Harvard Civil Rights–Civil Liberties Law Review* **1**, 1 (Spring 1966), 2–59. Part II in **1**, 2 (Fall 1966), 1–51.

**Brimmer, Andrew F.** "Economic Developments in the Black Community." *The Public Interest* **35** (Winter 1974), 146–163.

**Bullock, Charles S., III,** and **Mary Victoria Braxton.** "The Coming of School Desegregation: A Before and After Study of Black and White Student Perceptions." *Social Science Quarterly* **54** (June 1973), 132–139.

**Carrington, Paul D.** "Financing the American Dream: Equality and School Taxes." *Columbia Law Review* **73** (October 1973), 1227–1261.

**Clark, Kenneth.** *Dark Ghetto.* New York: Harper & Row, 1967.

Claude, Richard. "Constitutional Voting Rights and Early United States Supreme Court Doctrine." *Journal of Negro History* 51, 2 (April 1966), 114–124.

Clayton, Edward T. *The Negro Politician: His Success and Failures.* Chicago: Johnson, 1964.

Cooper, Martin S. "The H.E.W. School Desegregation Guidelines." *Harvard Civil Rights–Civil Liberties Law Review* 2, 1 (Fall 1966), 86–114.

Coulter, E. Morton. *Negro Legislators in Georgia During the Reconstruction Period.* Athens, Ga.: *Georgia Historical Quarterly,* 1968.

Crain, Robert L., *et al. The Politics of School Desegregation—Comparative Case Studies of Community Structure and Policy-Making.* Chicago: Aldine, 1968.

Crockett, George, Jr. "Racism in the Law." *Science and Society* 33, 2 (Spring 1969), 223–230.

Davis, John A. "Black Americans and United States Policy Toward Africa." *Journal of International Affairs* 23, 2 (1969), 236–249.

Davis, John A., and Cornelius L. Golightly. "Negro Employment in the Federal Government." *Phylon* 6 (1945), 337–346.

Denton, John H. "The Effectiveness of State Anti-Discrimination Laws in the United States." *Race* 9, 1 (July 1967), 85–93.

Dimond, Paul R. "School Segregation in the North: There Is but One Constitution." *Harvard Civil Rights–Civil Liberties Law Review* 7, 1 (January 1972), 1–55.

Downes, Bryan T., and Kenneth R. Greene. "The Politics of Open Housing in Three Cities: Decision Maker Responses to Black Demands for Policy Change." *American Politics Quarterly* 1 (April 1973), 215–243.

Dulles, Foster R., *The Civil Rights Commission: 1957–1965.* East Lansing: Michigan State University Press, 1968.

Dye, Thomas R. "Inequality and Civil Rights Policy in the States." *Journal of Politics* 31, 4 (November 1969), 1080–1097.

Fleming, Harold C. "The Federal Executive and Civil Rights, 1961–1965," *in* Talcott Parsons and Kenneth B. Clark, eds., *The Negro American.* Boston: Houghton Mifflin, 1966. Pp. 371–400.

Forkosch, Morris D. "The Desegregation Opinion Revisited: Legal or Sociological." *Vanderbilt Law Review* 21, 1 (December 1967), 47–76.

Fryer, William Byrd. "Employment Discrimination: Statistics and Preferences Under Title VII." *Virginia Law Review* 59 (March 1973), 463–491.

Gamer, Peter. "Proposition 14 and the U.S. Supreme Court's Protection of Racial Groups." *Harvard Civil Rights–Civil Liberties Law Review* 1, 1 (Spring 1966), 60–128.

Gill, Robert L. "Civil Rights Legislation, 1865–1965: The Beacon of Ordered Liberty." *Quarterly Review of Higher Education Among Negroes* 33 (April 1965), 79–93.

Goldberg, Arthur J. "The Administration's Anti-Busing Proposals—Politics Makes Bad Law." *Northwestern University Law Review* 67 (July–August 1972), 319–368.

Golden, Harry. *Mr. Kennedy and the Negroes.* Cleveland: World, 1964.

Goodman, James. "FDR New Deal: A Political Disaster for Blacks." *Black Politician* 1 (October 1969), 33–36.

Greenberg, Jack. "The Supreme Court, Civil Rights and Civil Dissonance." *Yale Law Journal* 77, 8 (July 1968), 1520–1544.

Hamilton, Charles V. "Racial, Ethnic and Social Class Politics and Administration." *Public Administration Review* 32 (October 1972), 638–648.

Hamilton, James. *Negro Suffrage and Congressional Representation.* New York: Winthrop Press, 1910.

Harris, Charles W. "Blacks and Regionalism: Councils of Governments." *National Civic Review* 62 (May 1973), 254–258.

Hassan, Kirke M. *"MacGuire vs. Amos:* Application of Section 5 of the Voting Rights Act to Political Parties." *Harvard Civil Rights–Civil Liberties Law Review* 8, 1 (January 1973), 199–210.

Hatcher, Richard G. "The Black Role in Urban Politics." *Current History* 57 (November 1969), 287–289.

Hatchett, John F. "The Negro Revolution: A Quest for Justice." *Journal of Human Relations* 14, 3 (1966), 406–421.

Hellriegel, Don, and Larry Short. "Equal Employment Opportunity in the Federal Government: A Comparative Analysis." *Public Administration Review* 32 (November–December 1972), 851–858.

Hermalin, Albert and Reynolds Farley. "The Potential for Residential Integration in Cities and Suburbs: Implications for the Busing Controversy." *American Sociological Review* 38, 5 (October 1973), 595–610.

Hero, Alfred Q., Jr. "American Negroes and United States Foreign Policy: 1937–1967." *Journal of Conflict Resolution* 13, 2 (June 1969), 220–251.

Hope, John, II, and Edward E. Shelton. "The Negro in the Federal Government." *Journal of Negro Education* 32 (Fall 1963), 367–374.

Hornbeck, J. A. "On Fair Employment Practice." *Public Administration Review* 33 (September–October 1973), 460–461.

Horowitz, Harold W., and Kenneth Karst. *Law, Lawyers and Social Change.* Indianapolis: Bobbs-Merrill, 1969.

Jones, David M. *"Hayes vs. United States* Private Interference with School Desegregation." *Harvard Civil Rights–Civil Liberties Law Review* 8, 3 (May 1973), 643–657.

Kalvern, Harry. *The Negro and the First Amendment.* Chicago: University of Chicago Press, 1965.

Kinroy, Arthur. "The Constitutional Right of Negro Freedom." *Rutgers Law Review* 21, 3 (Spring 1967), 387–441.

Knowles, Louis, and Kenneth Prewitt, eds. *Institutional Racism in America.* Englewood Cliffs, N.J.: Prentice-Hall, 1969.

Kohl, Robert L. "The Civil Rights Act of 1866, Its Hour Come Round at Last: Jones vs. Alfred M. Mayer Co." *Virginia Law Review* 55, 2 (March 1969), 272–300.

Larson, Arthur. "The New Law of Race Relations." *Wisconsin Law Review* 2 (1969), 470–524.

Larson, Richard E. "The Development of Section 1981 as a Remedy for

Racial Discrimination in Private Employment." *Harvard Civil Rights–Civil Liberties Law Review* 7, 1 (January 1972), 56–102.

Lasok, Dominik. "Some Legal Aspects of Race Relations in the United Kingdom and the United States." *Journal of Public Law* 16, 2 (1967), 326–344.

Levy, Burton. "Effects of 'Racism' on the Racial Bureaucracy." *Public Administration Review* 32, 5 (1972), 479–486.

Lockard, Duane. *Toward Equal Opportunity.* London: Macmillan, 1968.

Lockard, Duane. "The Politics of Anti-discrimination Legislation." *Harvard Journal on Legislation* 3, 1 (December 1965), 3–62.

Lozin, Frederick A. "The Failure of Federal Enforcement of Civil Rights Regulations in Public Housing, 1963–1971: The Cooptation of a Federal Agency by Its Local Constituency." *Policy Sciences* 4 (September 1973), 263–274.

Lyttle, Clifford. "The History of the Civil Rights Bill of 1964." *Journal of Negro History* 41, 4 (October 1966), 275–296.

McCloskey, Robert G. "Reflections on the Warren Court." *Virginia Law Review* 51, 7 (November 1965), 1229–1270.

Marshall, Ray. *The Negro and Organized Labor.* New York: Wiley, 1965.

Miller, Judy Ann. "The Representative Is a Lady." *Black Politician* (Fall 1969), 17–18.

Morgan, Ruth P. *The President and Civil Rights: Policymaking by Executive Order.* New York: St. Martin, 1970.

Motley, Constance Baker. "The Legal Status of the Negro in the United States," in John P. Davis, ed., *The American Negro Reference Book.* Englewood Cliffs, N.J.: Prentice Hall, 1966. Pp. 484–521.

Moynihan, Daniel P. "The Schism in Black America." *Public Interest* 27 (Spring 1972), 3–24.

Murphy, L. E. "The Civil Rights Law of 1875." *Journal of Negro History* 12 (April 1927), 110–127.

Murray, Paul. "The Negro Woman's Stake in the Equal Rights Amendment." *Harvard Civil Rights–Civil Liberties Law Review* 6, 2 (March 1971), 253–259.

Nash, A. E. Keir. "A More Equitable Past? Southern Supreme Courts and the Protection of the Antebellum Negro." *North Carolina Law Review* 48, 2 (February 1970), 197–242.

Nash, A. E. Keir. "Fairness and Formalism in the Trials of Blacks in the State Supreme Courts of the Old South." *Virginia Law Review* 56, 1 (February 1970), 64–100.

Olson, Robert H., Jr. "Employment Discrimination Litigations: New Priorities in the Struggle for Black Equality." *Harvard Civil Rights–Civil Liberties Law Review* 6, 1 (December 1970), 20–60.

Orfield, Gary. *The Reconstruction of Southern Education: The Schools and the 1964 Civil Rights Act.* New York: Wiley, 1969.

Patterson, Orlando. "The Moral Crisis of Black America." *Public Interest,* 32 (Summer 1973), 43–69.

Patterson, Orlando. "Toward a Future That Has No Past—Reflections on the

Fate of Blacks in the Americas." *Public Interest* **27** (Spring 1972), 25–62.

Piven, Francis, and Richard A. Cloward. "Black Control of Cities," in Albert Shank, ed., *Political Power and the Urban Crisis.* Boston: Holbrook Press, 1969. Pp. 315–328.

Reeves, Earl J. "Making Equality of Employment Opportunity a Reality in the Federal Service." *Public Administration Review* **30**, 1 (1970), 43–49.

Rosenbloom, David H. "A Note on Interminority Group Competition for Federal Positions." *Public Personnel Management* **2** (January–February 1973), 43–48.

Rossell, Idrio. "Equal Employment Opportunity—Too Much or Not Enough." *Foreign Service Journal* (January 1969), 12–15.

Salamon, Lester M. "Leadership and Modernization: The Emerging Black Political Elite in the American South." *Journal of Politics* **35**, 3 (August 1973), 615–644.

Scheiner, Seth M. "President Theodore Roosevelt and the Negro, 1901–1908." *Journal of Negro History* **47** (July 1962), 169–182.

Schuwerk, Robert P. "The Philadelphia Plan: A Study in the Dynamics of Executive Power." *University of Chicago Law Review* **39** (Summer 1972), 723–760.

Sherman, Richard B. "The Harding Administration and the Negro: An Opportunity Lost." *Journal of Negro History* **49** (July 1964), 151–168.

Short, Larry C. "Equal Employment Opportunity as Perceived by Government Officials." *Public Personnel Management* **2** (March–April 1973), 118–124.

Smith, Samuel D. *The Negro in Congress, 1870–1901.* New York: Kennikat Press, 1966.

Straus, Peter. "Is the State Department Color Blind?" *Saturday Review* (January 1971).

Taylor, Alrutheus A. "Negro Congressmen a Generation After." *Journal of Negro History* **7** (April 1922), 127–171.

Taylor, Joseph H. "The Fourteenth Amendment, The Negro, and the Spirit of the Times." *Journal of Negro History* **45** (January 1960), 21–37.

Ten Broek, Jacobus. *Equal Under Law.* New York: Collier, 1965.

"The Internal Revenue Code and Racial Discrimination." *Columbia Law Review* **72** (November 1972), 1215–1248.

Trent, W. J., Jr. "Federal Sanctions Directed Against Racial Discrimination." *Phylon* **3** (1942), 171–182.

Tucker, Sterling. *For Blacks Only—Black Strategies for Change in America.* Grand Rapids, Mich.: Eerdmans, 1971.

Tussman, Joseph, ed. *The Supreme Court on Racial Discrimination.* New York: Oxford University Press, 1963.

Ulmer, Sidney S. "Earl Warren and the Brown Decision." *Journal of Politics* **33**, 3 (August 1971), 689–702.

Vines, Kenneth. "Federal District Judges and Race Relations Cases in the South." *Journal of Politics* **26**, 2 (May 1964), 337–357.

Vines, Kenneth. "Southern State Supreme Courts and Race Relations." *Western Political Quarterly* **18**, 1 (March 1965), 5–18.

Ware, Gilbert. "Civil Rights and Contempt of Federal Courts." *Phylon* **25**, 2 (Summer 1964), 146–154.

Warren, Roland W., ed. *Politics and the Ghetto.* New York: Atherton, 1969.

Wattenberg, Ben J., and Richard M. Scammon. "Black Progress and Liberal Rhetoric." *Commentary* **55** (April 1973), 35–44.

Weinberg, Kenneth G. *Black Victory: Carl Stokes and the Winning of Cleveland.* New York: Quadrangle, 1968.

Wildavsky, Aaron. "The Empty-hand Blues: Black Rebellion and White Reaction." *Public Interest* **11** (Spring 1968), 3–16.

Wilson, James. "The Flamboyant Mr. Powell." *Commentary* **41** (January 1966), 31–35.

Work, Monroe N. "Some Negro Members of Reconstruction Conventions and Legislatures of Congress." *Journal of Negro History* **5** (January 1920), 63–125.

Wyatt-Brown, Bertram. "The Civil Rights Act of 1875." *Western Political Quarterly* **18**, 4 (December 1965), 763–775.

# INDEX